WHAT IN THE WORLD IS GOD DOING?

The Essentials of Global Missions:
An Introductory Guide

C. GORDON OLSON

**Fourth Edition
Updated and Expanded**

GLOBAL GOSPEL PUBLISHERS

WHAT IN THE WORLD IS GOD DOING?
THE ESSENTIALS OF GLOBAL MISSIONS

GLOBAL GOSPEL PUBLISHERS
PO Box 138
Cedar Knolls, NJ 07927-0138
Telephone: (973) 267-2511

All Scripture quotations, unless otherwise noted are taken from the New American Standard Bible © 1960,1962,1963,1971,1972,1973,1975,1977 by the Lockman Foundation. Used by permission.

Cartoons on pp. 8 & 83 by Wayne Stayskal are reprinted from *Wherever* magazine, copyright 1981 and used by permission of TEAM, Wheaton, IL.

Cartoons by Joyce Thimsen on pp. 195, 197, & 202 are reprinted from *So What's the Difference?* edited by Fritz Ridenour, copyright 1967, Regal Books, Ventura, CA 93006 and used by permission.

The map on p. 56 was adapted from maps of Irving L. Jensen, *Acts: An Inductive Study* copyright 1968, by Moody Bible Institute of Chicago, Moody Press, and used by permission.

The study questions in Part I have been adapted from *Therefore Go: The Biblical Basis of Missions* copyright 1949 by InterVarsity Christian Fellowship of the USA and used by permission of InterVarsity Press, PO Box 1040, Downers Grove, IL 60515.

The diagrams on p. 88 are reprinted from Garry Friesen with Robin Maxson, *Decision Making and the Will of God* copyright 1980 by Multnomah Press, Portland, OR 97266, and used by permission.

Graphics on pp. 220 & 253, courtesy of Dr. Patrick Cate and Byron Barnshaw of International Missions, Inc., Reading, PA (modified slightly).

Olson graphics, pp. 56, 94, 129, 189, 190, 254, 268, & 288 computerized by courtesy of Dr. Eugene Priddy and Gerry Pruden of Bible Basics, International, Odessa, FL. Olson graphics on pp. 167, 172, 311, & 344 by Mark Mull.

The author is also greatly indebted to Patrick Johnstone of WEC, Int. for supplying prepublication data from his 5th edition of *Operation World* for the second edition.

Cover design by Bob Heimall, Inc., Sussex, NJ 07461.

First edition, December, 1989.
Second printing, June, 1991
Second, updated edition, July 1993
Third, revised edition, July 1994
Fifth Printing, September 1996
Fourth edition, updated and expanded, August 1998

2002   2001   2000   1999   1998

TABLE OF CONTENTS

PART III. THE CONTEXTUAL DIMENSION

PART IV. THE REGIONAL DIMENSION

LIST OF ILLUSTRATIONS

MAPS:

FIGURES (Tables, Diagrams, and Charts):

PREFACE

In over a score of years of teaching an undergraduate survey of world missions the author has been frustrated by the lack of a comprehensive survey text which does not presume too much of the student by way of a knowledge of geography, theology, or world religions. Writing a doctoral project provided both the stimulus and opportunity to write one myself. I trust it will meet a need for other missions teachers desiring to give an overview to Christian students who need to be "world Christians," whether they become missionaries themselves or not.

My debt to others will be obvious to the reader. Dr. J. Herbert Kane was my mentor for the beginning of this doctoral project until he was hospitalized in the summer of 1988 prior to his homegoing. His books have been the standard texts in the field for a decade and a half. The number of references to his works in this book is proof of my indebtedness to him. My dedication of this book is to him and to Dr. Timothy M. Warner of Trinity Evangelical Divinity School, who encouraged me greatly along the way.

Many others have made their contributions in different ways. Harold Cook's books were an advance in the field for two decades. Ruth Tucker's popular history of missions has shown the value of vignettes of key personalities to personalize the thrilling story and the use of graphics to help visualize it. Dr. Kane himself provided much data easily convertible into graphics. I have sought to maximize the impact of graphics to aid the student. Our debt to Ralph Winter relates to many details beyond the "hidden frontiers" concept. His beginning of a second era of missions history with Hudson Taylor's China Inland Mission was a great advance in organizing the historical material more coherently.

This is not to say that this book is merely a rehash of others' works. I trust that I have made a significant contribution of my own. After teaching Biblical Theology for a score of years, I came to the biblical section with the strong conviction that an inductive, diachronic approach would be of more value than an often overly deductive systematics approach. Study questions for the student, which played a major part in my own commitment to missions, are included. For maximum impact **these should be assigned before the reading of the relevant chapter.**

The issue of the lostness of the heathen demands a separate chapter since it is being widely questioned today more than ever. The discussion of the causes of the "Great Protestant Omission" deserves more than passing notice. In investigating these causes it became clear that the major impetus for missions has come from the "radical" branch of the reformation. Donald McGavran's focus on people movements is noteworthy, and my own missionary service among one such group in the Punjab motivated its inclusion.Since a major factor of Protestantism in the last hundred years has been the devastating impact of liberalism, its effect upon missions and the ecumenical movement required clarification.

Undergraduates come to college with a poor background in geography and even less concept of the world religions so essential to the study of missions. This present effort attempts to compensate for this. As an erstwhile independent missionary (but with extensive board experience), I have struggled with the biblical basis for boards and feel that I have advanced the discussion by highlighting the dimensions of Paul's missionary team.

I am thankful to many who had input into this book, but I take full responsibility for its content. Dick Bailey and Dr. Don Rickards critiqued the section on Islam. David Noden and Dr. Robert Foster were especially helpful in preparing the Africa map. Elaine Imber, Rosamond McCarthy, and Bob Bergstresser have proofread the text. My dear wife, Miriam, and family have been most supportive.

Ultimately the dedication of this book is to the Lord Jesus Christ, for He is what it is all about. He is the meaning of life, providing both the content for the gospel we proclaim and the motivation for world evangelism. May He get all the glory to Himself!

October 1989   C. Gordon Olson

PREFACE TO THE FOURTH EDITION

Continued response to this book by colleges and seminaries has been most gratifying. It is being used enthusiastically by many teachers. But the changing world situation demands continued updating. I had originally projected the chapter on the secular context of missions, which has now been included. I got convicted by my own preaching of Acts 1:8 to include the North America chapter. Far too little is being written on the needs of our Samaria. I am greatly indebted to Dr. Earl Parvin for use of his materials. Most of the statistics are from *Operation World*. Patrick Johnstone was kind enough to send me copy for my second edition even before his fifth edition went to press. I am always grateful for feedback from teachers over the years. Mark Davis, Dr. David Hesselgrave and Dr. Pat Cate have been of great help in critiquing sections. However, I take full credit for all the errors that may have slipped in.

July 1998   C. Gordon Olson

INTRODUCTION:
WHAT GOD IS DOING
IN THE WORLD!

What is the most earthshaking news item in the world today? Is it crime? Is it financial collapse? Is it AIDS? You won't hear about it on the TV news or read about it in *TIME* magazine or the *New York Times*. The media are almost totally ignoring the most important world news event that you can imagine. Of course, I am referring to the incredible global progress of the gospel of the Lord Jesus Christ in the last two centuries, in your lifetime, and even in the last decade. But it all had a small beginning.

Two hundred years have passed since a British cobbler named William Carey began a thrust which brought about a tremendous acceleration of the initially feeble Protestant missionary enterprise. In these two centuries since 1792 we have seen an incredible impact of the gospel of Christ upon the non-Christian world. Although Carey was ridiculed by most as a dreamer and a fool, the whole course of history has been radically changed by his willingness to go counter to the majority wisdom of his day and pioneer the modern missionary movement. Consider these major facts.

In 1886 Pastor Arthur T. Pierson surveyed the fruit of less than a century of modern missions. He wrote that in one century Bible translations had multiplied from 50 to 250 in number; mission boards from 7 to 100; male missionaries from 170 to 3000; contributions from $250,000 to $10 million; and converts from 50,000 to 2.5 million.[1]

In the century since then we have seen an even greater multiplication take place. The number of languages having some portion of the Bible translated has grown to 2200 today, the number of mission boards to about 2500, the number of Protestant missionaries to over 120,000, the total number of evangelical Christians to about 350 million, and the giving to $2½ billion from North America alone.[2]

1

Despite this most encouraging growth, many Christians today have a pessimistic attitude toward world missions because they really don't know what God is doing worldwide. Ted Engstrom, who has traveled to about a hundred nations and talked to thousands of national Christian leaders and missionaries over thirty years has written:

> It is easy to be pessimistic as we view the world scene. . . . It would seem that many Christians have given up. . . . However, I, for one, believe that we are living in the greatest day for Christian missions since the first century! Darkness abounds, but more and more lights around the world are being turned on for God. In every generation he has his faithful witnesses--and there are quantifiably more today than ever! I simply cannot accept the "hang dog" conviction what we do for Christ matters little or what anyone does makes no impact in our day.[3]

THE INCREDIBLE GROWTH OF MODERN MISSIONS

	AD 1690	AD 1792	AD 1886	AD 1998
Bible Translations	?	50	250	2200+
Mission Boards	1 ?	7	100	2500+
Protestant Missionaries	Few	170	3000 men	120,000
Finances	?	$250,000	$10 million	$2.5 billion
Converts	Few	50,000	2.5 million	200 million

What if William Carey had had that 'hang-dog' attitude? One man did make a vast difference! His motto was, "Expect great things from God; attempt great things for God." Today with a vastly improved outlook for world evangelization we need to venture out with the same kind of faith. Church historian Kenneth Latourette wrote, "The church has never been so widely planted or so deeply rooted as it is today."[4] Not only do the general statistics strongly support this, but the specifics are also most encouraging. Let us highlight some of the most encouraging facts about world missions today:

1. Church growth in Africa is so rapid that it seems that a majority of Africans have become professing Christians. Although not all of these are Evangelicals, there are over eighty million now who are. Considering

how difficult the early years of missions in Africa were, and how many of the pioneer missionaries died of disease in the 'white man's grave', it is thrilling to hear of the tremendous response to the gospel today.

2. In Latin America over 55 million are Evangelicals (11 percent) and church growth is very rapid in most countries. Considering that in 1900 there were only 50,000 Protestants in Latin America and the persecution the early converts endured, progress can only be termed phenomenal. Some estimate that there will be one hundred million Protestants by the end of the century. Despite guerilla warfare in some Central American countries, churches have tripled in a decade. **In most countries more Evangelicals now attend church than do Roman Catholics!**

3. The response by animistic tribes has been incredible. In the Pacific islands over sixteen percent are Evangelicals—converts from cannibalistic, stone-age peoples. Similar fruit has been gathered among similar animistic peoples in the northeast of India, the tropical jungles of Latin America, and many other areas. The ten million Quechua Indians of the Andes have been very unresponsive until recently, but now have turned to Christ by the tens of thousands.

4. Although response to the gospel has been somewhat spotty in Asia, church growth in the Philippines and Korea has been most encouraging. About twenty percent of the people in South Korea are Evangelicals, and some of the largest churches in the world are found there. There are 3¾ million Evangelicals in the Philippines, with rapid church growth being especially seen in the last decade. Indonesia has seen a number of revivals in recent decades, with about nine million Evangelicals at present. Some areas of India, especially in the south and northeast have a substantial number of Evangelicals, but in other areas there are very few Christians and little church growth as the number of missionaries declines. Encouragingly national missionaries from the south are starting churches in the needy areas of the north. Although foreign missionaries were expelled from Burma in 1966, there are reports of hundreds of home missionaries going into needy areas.

5. The incredible church growth among the over one billion people of mainland China arises out of a unique situation. When the missionaries were forced out in 1950, there were less than one million Protestant church members, who had to suffer over thirty-five years of persecution under the Communist government. As a result of the disillusionment with communism and Mao TseTung (Mao Zedong) that set in after his death, the spiritual vacuum is being filled with the gospel. Recent estimates range from 50 to 70 million Christians, mostly in house churches. Even if we take the lower figure, "it represents the largest influx of new believers into the Christian church, by confession of faith, anytime, anywhere, in two thousand years of church history."[5]

6. Even in the former Soviet Union there are over 2.5 million Evangelicals, despite the government's determination to stamp out Christianity. Under *glasnost* and the breakup of the union there are now astonishing new opportunities to help the Christians in Russia in their witness. A great harvest is beginning to be reaped in Russia and Ukraine, and other republics are opening to missionaries.

7. A number of formerly 'closed' countries like Nepal, Turkey, Mongolia, Albania, and other eastern European countries have been penetrated with the gospel, and churches are growing. Refugees from Afghanistan, Iran and Iraq are responding to the gospel as never before.

8. The number of two-thirds world (non-western) missionaries·is grow-- ing very rapidly. The most recent study indicates that the total has escalated to 36,000 by 1988 and is growing more rapidly than the number of western missionaries.[6] Missions conferences in two-thirds-world countries are stirring up great interest. In addition, international students in America are showing a new interest in world missions. This trend of international students converted here who make a great impact back home (like Bakht Singh of India) is being continued. Herbert Kane felt that Chinese Christians have the highest potential and are manifesting the greatest interest in world evangelization of any ethnic group. However, in actuality the Koreans are in the lead with over 2000 missionaries in other lands.

9. Many new mission organizations continue to be formed to meet spe-- cial needs. Although the total number of North American career missionaries has plateaued, there continues to be an explosion of the number of short-term missionaries. Although it was felt that this was undercutting the number of career missionaries, recent figures show that the short-termers are the 'icing on the cake'. Although there had been a decline in the number of missionaries from Europe, the thousands of graduates of Greater Europe Mission's dozen Bible colleges and seminaries are a new resource for world missions. Nine thousand participants attended an Urbana-like triennial mission conference sponsored by the European Missionary Association.

10. The percentage of Protestant missionaries who are evangelical continues to rise, so that the total number of evangelical missionaries is growing quite substantially.

11. Many formerly closed countries have now become 'creative-access' countries, as tentmaker (bi-professional) missionaries find creative ways to enter and carry on effective witness.

12. The new tools available for world evangelization in the last few decades have multiplied our efforts. Radio, TV, audio-visuals, missionary aviation, computers, satellite transmissions, scientific linguistics, literature, Theological Education by Extension, and Bible correspondence courses are a few of these new tools.

13. The study of the science of missions (missiology) is relatively new and growing rapidly. A number of seminaries have added graduate programs in missiology recently. The U. S. Center for World Mission in Pasadena, CA has also been a great stimulus to research and new methodology, as have a host of other research organizations. This has been accompanied by a new interest in the major unreached people groups among the Muslims, Hindus, Buddhists, and others.
14. Student interest in missions continues to grow. Not only have the number of students attending InterVarsity's Urbana Missionary Conferences continued to grow, but their attitude toward evangelistic missions has turned more positive.
15. The national churches are increasingly on their own and independent of western churches.
16. Thousands of national church leaders have been able to interact at a number of evangelical conferences on evangelism and missions in recent decades.[7]

This is not to say that everything is 'peaches and cream' in world Christianity. There are many problems, and we continue to face crises. We are told that the Chinese character for the word 'crisis' is made up of two smaller characters meaning 'danger' and 'opportunity'. The Apostle Paul put it so well, "for a wide door for effective service has opened to me, and there are many adversaries" (1 Cor. 16:9). We must not be blinded by the problems and crises and fail to see the tremendous opportunities opened before us in these days.

The purpose of this book is to provide sound information by which every Christian can become a 'world Christian'. The truth can free us from the myths and misconceptions regarding missions which have sidetracked so many Christians from God's will in this regard. Not every Christian can be a missionary, but every believer can be a missions-minded Christian—and should be!

It is my conviction that the five dimensions of world missions discussed in this book will give Christians a broadened perspective for understanding what God is doing in the world today. Certainly we must start with the biblical dimension—the foundation. We will try to look at the Bible inductively—that is, drawing out the truth that lies within. Then every Christian should understand the historical dimension—what God has been doing since the day of Pentecost. We shall try to survey the history of missions critically from an evangelical/fundamentalist perspective. Thirdly, Christians must understand the world into which the missionary goes—the contextual dimension. Indeed, today every Christian worker needs to understand world religions, since increasingly their adherents are flooding in among us here in the West. Fourthly, in our day of geographic ignorance, Christians need to get specific information about what missions has accomplished in each area of the world and what yet needs to be done—the geographic dimension. Lastly, every Christian should have a working knowledge of the way that 'missions' functions today—the functional dimension.

Missions is not optional for the Christian. It is even less optional for those who are training for Christian leadership. If the church is to accomplish God's will in the world for its day, every Christian must be a world Christian. Peter Wagner explains the consequences of rejecting or neglecting missions:

> 1. You will find yourself sitting on the bench while you could be in there playing the game. As I hope to convince you in this book, missions are on the cutting edge of excitement in the Christian life. Being left out means a dull existence as a child of God. It is less than God's best for you.
>
> 2. You will lose authenticity as a Christian. You say that Jesus is your Lord, but yet you will be failing to obey Him at a crucial point. Another word for that is *hypocrisy.*
>
> 3. You will be poorly prepared for the judgment day when what we have done here on earth will be tested by fire and only the gold, silver and the precious stones will survive (1 Cor. 3:12-15). Whatever else this means, Jesus will not be able to say to you, "Well done, good and faithful servant" (Matt. 25:23).[8]

1. Arthur T. Pierson, *The Crisis of Missions* (1886), p. 190.
2. See pp. 309-11 for the 1996 missionary statistics. Patrick Johnstone, *Operation World.* 4th ed. (1986), pp. 34-35; 5th ed. (1993), p. 643; *Missionary News Service,* 34 (June 5, 1987):4; *Mission Handbook,* 13th ed. (1986), pp. 39, 578-80; 14th ed. (1989), p. 51, 66; 15th ed. (1993), pp. 59, 68; 17th ed. (1998); Larry D. Pate, *From Every People* (1989) showed 36,000 third-world missionaries, an incredible increase. This would indicate that by 1988 the total number of Protestant missionaries had reached over 113,000. We do not have more recent worldwide statistics at present.
3. Ted W. Engstrom, *What in the World is God Doing?* (1978), p. 13.
4. Kenneth Scott Latourette, undocumented quote in ibid.
5. J. Herbert Kane, *Wanted: World Christians* (Baker, 1986), p. 22.
6. Larry D. Pate, *From Every People,* p. 12.
7. Statements in this summary are drawn from a number of sources documented above. Excellent summaries are found in C. Peter Wagner, *On the Crest of the Wave* (Ventura, CA: Regal, 1983), pp. 9-34, and Kane, pp. 17-38.
8. Wagner, p. 6.

PART I

HIS WORD:

THE BIBLICAL DIMENSION

"YOU KNOW, I HAVE A DEEP PEACE WITHIN ME... PROBABLY BECAUSE I WON'T HAVE TO FIGURE OUT WHO TO ANSWER TO FOR ALL THIS!"

"How shall they call upon Him in whom they have not believed? And how shall they believe in Him whom they have not heard? And how shall they hear without a preacher? And how shall they preach unless they are sent?"

—Romans 10:14-15a

DISPELLING THE FOG

Before we can talk intelligently about missions and missionaries, we must dispel the fog that surrounds even the basic definitions of these two terms. Normally we would look in the Bible to find how these terms are used there. However, neither term occurs in the Bible, per se.

Perhaps that helps to explain why there is so much confusion about what a missionary really is. Is a missionary a man with a pith helmet and shorts who is frequently in danger of being eaten by cannibals? This is the stereotype which is found in secular humor. Is it a person who goes from a civilized country to an uncivilized country to bring the blessings of civilization to the 'natives'? Or is it somebody who can't make it in the business world, and tries to find himself by 'seeing the world' or losing himself in another culture?

Let's not blame God that the common notions of missions are so confused. Just because the word 'missionary' is not in the Bible should not be a problem; the idea is very clearly there. Similarly, although the word 'Trinity' is not found in the Bible, the idea permeates the whole of Scripture. So it is with missions. The whole Bible is permeated with the idea of missions from Genesis to Revelation.

ISN'T EVERY CHRISTIAN TO BE A MISSIONARY?

Frequently one hears it said that every Christian is a missionary—that is, that every Christian ought to be a missionary. The little chorus puts it, "Be a missionary every day!" It sounds good, but this kind of fuzzy thinking only clouds the issue. Every Christian cannot be a missionary, nor should be. But what is wrong in saying that every Christian is to be a missionary?

First of all it is just like saying that every Christian ought to be a pastor, or that every Christian ought to be an evangelist. These statements are so obviously wrong that few Christians would make that mistake. But as pastors and evangelists are specially called by God for a ministry of the word of God, just so with the missionary! A missionary is specially called of God for a distinct ministry. But let us see what the Biblical data indicates before we go any farther.

The root of the words 'mission' and 'missionary' is the Latin verb *mitto* (I send). But since the Bible wasn't written in Latin, but in Greek and Hebrew, we need to find the same concept in the Greek New Testament. The verb *apostellō* has the idea of being sent, and from it comes the word for 'apostle' (*apostolos*), which means 'sent one'.

The apostles: the first missionaries

The Lord Jesus set apart twelve of His disciples as 'apostles' and sent them out to their own people Israel (Mk. 4:12; Matt. 10:1-6). They were sent to announce that Jews should repent since the Messiah-King had come and his kingdom was impending. Later God set apart others like Paul and Barnabas as apostles to the Gentiles as well (Acts 9:15; 13:3; 22:21; Gal. 2:7-9). The idea of 'being sent' is central in both cases. So the apostles were the first 'missionaries'—home and foreign.

But what were they sent to do that ordinary Christians were not commissioned to do? First we find that the twelve apostles had left their secular occupations and devoted themselves full time as disciples of Christ. Some had left their fishnets and boats long after they became believers in Christ. Matthew left his tax-collecting occupation. Now they devoted themselves full time to ministry, as Peter said, "But we will devote ourselves to prayer, and to the ministry of the word" (Acts 6:4). We find that Paul and Barnabas and the other apostles normally did the same when they had financial support from churches. Although when his money ran out in Corinth, Paul worked at tentmaking, when Silas and Timothy brought gifts from the Macedonian churches, he devoted himself again completely to the ministry of the word (Acts 18:1-5 NAS).

What else distinguished these missionaries to the Gentiles? The witness of Jews to the Gentiles involved crossing a cultural barrier. Not only did the Christians in Antioch begin to cross that barrier (Acts 11:19-20), but Barnabas and Paul seemed especially gifted in cross-cultural witnessing and were sent out as the first missionaries (Acts 13:3). So they were being sent to cross both geographical and cultural boundaries to win Gentiles to Christ (Acts 22:21). Paul traveled extensively in four Roman provinces during his three missionary journeys. Apparently he crossed other geographic and cultural boundaries in his ministry after Acts was written (as we infer from his letters). Although the oft-repeated saying is true that "crossing the ocean never made a missionary," crossing boundaries **is** an important part of what makes a missionary distinct.

There is another aspect which especially distinguished Paul's missionary career, which is worth noting. Paul's ambition was to preach Christ where He was unknown so that he might not build upon another man's foundation. "And thus I aspired to preach the gospel, not where

Christ was already named, that I might not build upon another man's foundation; but as it is written, 'They who had no news of Him shall see, and they who have not heard shall understand'" (Rom. 15:20-21).

A definition

Herbert Kane has suggested that although it is not possible to give a flawless, scientific definition of a missionary, the following one should suffice:

> In the traditional sense the term *missionary* has been reserved for those who have been called by God to a full-time ministry of the Word and prayer (Acts 6:4), and who have crossed geographical and/or cultural boundaries (Acts 22:21) to preach the gospel in those areas of the world where Jesus Christ is largely, if not entirely, unknown (Ro 15:20).[1]

It is difficult to improve upon this definition.

Retaining valid distinctions

Kane goes on to raise the problem of the notion many Christians have that, since we are all full-time Christians, there is no such thing as a distinct group of people who are in 'full-time Christian service.' This arises from a valid idea which has been carried to an extreme, illogical conclusion.

> There is abroad in evangelical circles a move to do away with all "artificial distinctions." Today's Christians are challenged to rethink their position and give up their narrow view of the Christian life with its rigid categories of black and white and right and wrong, and to embrace a more sophisticated view of the wholeness of life. Gone are the former dichotomies between the secular and the sacred, work and prayer, and service and witness. As for any special missionary call—forget it. All Christians are missionaries.
>
> The above point of view is not entirely wrong. It contains an element of truth that needs to be acknowledged and emphasized. On the other hand, if pushed too far it can become dangerous.[2]

The element of truth is that, in one sense, all of life is sacred. The obvious error is that God does separate some Christians for vocational Christian ministry and expects Christians to support such people financially, whether they are pastors, evangelists, teachers, or missionaries (1 Cor. 9:3-14; 12:28-29; Eph. 4:11-12).

Charles Ryrie has pointed out that we must distinguish between a general practice in the church and a special gift which God gives to some in that area. For example, all Christians are to give financially; only some have the gift of giving. All are to be witnesses; only some have the gift of evangelism and/or apostleship. Many other examples could be given.[3] The point then is that all Christians are to witness for Christ, but not all Christians are called for a full-time, specially gifted ministry of evangelism. All Christians are to be missionary-minded in obedience to the Great Commission, but not all Christians can be missionaries in the proper biblical sense of the word. We cannot all pack up and go! Some must stay behind and stand behind those who do go. Since a missionary is sent by God, it follows that a missionary must go somewhere. This is well illustrated from the events of World War II. All Americans were mobilized for the war effort. Housewives collected frying-pan oil; metals were collected from cellars and garages; everybody grew 'victory gardens'; housewives went to work in factories for the first time. Everybody was mobilized to win the war against the Axis powers. But not everybody could go into the Armed Services, and not even all of them could go to the front and personally be in the fight.

The same kind of distinction should be made in the spiritual warfare in which we are engaged. The total resources of the Christian church should be thrown into the battle for the souls of men on a global scale, and every member of that church should regard himself as being involved in the total mobilization required by such an operation. But not every church member is a missionary.[4]

The devastating consequences

What difference does it make after all? Are we merely nitpicking in our definition of a missionary? Look at it this way. If every Christian is already considered a missionary, then all can stay put where they are, and nobody needs to get up and go anywhere to preach the gospel. But if our only concern is to witness where we are, how will people in unevangelized areas ever hear the gospel? The present uneven distribution of Christians and opportunities to hear the gospel of Christ will continue on unchanged. It has been said that ninety percent of the Christian workers are ministering to ten percent of the world's population, and ten percent are working among ninety percent of the people of the world. Many Christian leaders have picked up Ralph Winter's analysis of world need which states that beyond the one-fourth of the world's population which is nominally Christian, only one-fourth of the world's people are being somewhat effectively evangelized by close cultural contact with Christians. The other half of the world's people are not being reached effectively because they are isolated from any real contact with Christians. This is hardly fair to those who have never heard! So in reality the idea that every Christian is a missionary is a 'cop out'. It avoids responsibility for the about three billion people who are not being effectively evangelized today. It means direct disobedience to the 'Go' of the Great

Commission!

WHAT DO WE MEAN BY 'MISSIONS'?

Now that we have gotten a working definition of a missionary we can try to define 'missions'. There is a lot of confusion as to what is meant by 'missions' and 'mission'. Some speak of the "mission of the church," by which they refer to just about anything that Christians do.

But over the years the term 'missions' came to be used in relation to the activity of that specially called and gifted group of people termed missionaries and those missionary-sending organizations which we call mission boards. It is an abstract noun referring to this kind of activity. That is the subject of this book.

Since we have already defined the missionary as a 'sent one,' our definition of missions should follow closely from this. Few writers have ventured a definition. We shall try: **Missions is the whole task, endeavor, and program of the Church of Jesus Christ to reach out across geographical and/or cultural boundaries by sending missionaries to evangelize people who have never heard or who have little opportunity to hear the saving gospel.**

George Peters has given a more detailed definition:

> *Missions* is a specialized term. By it I mean the sending forth of authorized persons beyond the borders of the New Testament church and her immediate gospel influence to proclaim the gospel of Jesus Christ in gospel-destitute areas, to win converts from other faiths or non-faiths to Jesus Christ, and to establish functioning, multiplying local congregations who will bear the fruit of Christianity in that community and to that country.[5]

Several decades ago ecumenical writers began to substitute the term 'mission' for 'missions' with the evident intention of broadening the focus to include things which had not previously been included, such as social-action programs and the 'social gospel.' In the intervening years many evangelicals have been undiscriminating in following this terminology. I will not do so since I am convinced that there is an essential difference between the terms. Peters clarifies:

> Much is being said today of *mission* and *missions*. The reader will find both words used in these pages. They are not synonyms. *Mission*, in my usage, refers to the total biblical assignment of the church of Jesus Christ. It is a comprehensive term including the upward, inward and outward ministries of the church.[6]

We will follow Peters in limiting our consideration of missions to the narrower sense. We will seek to spell out in more detail later just what is to be included in missions, but certainly cross-cultural evangelization is at the heart of our subject. The heart of the Great Commission is to "Go therefore and make disciples of all peoples" (Matt. 28:19).

WHAT DO WE MEAN BY 'CHRISTIAN'?

Before we can progress in dispelling the fog about missions, there is a far more basic and vital issue that must imperatively be clarified. This is the definition of a Christian. Almost one-third of the world's population can be called 'Christian' in some sense, which means about 1.8 billion people. This we might call 'World-Christian-Handbook Christians'. But how does this compare with 'Lamb's Book of Life Christians'? Almost all would agree that not all professing Christians are in the Lamb's book of life (Rev. 17:8; 20:15; 21:27). Are most included, or relatively few? How many are true Christians and not in name only? The problem of nominal Christianity is a most serious one, growing not receding with time. The issue is becoming fuzzier and more difficult to answer easily because of the growing confusion and fragmentation within Christian denominations. In most cases the truth cuts across denominational lines. Being a Baptist, or a Presbyterian, or a Pentecostal is no guarantee of salvation, but then again it never was. So who are the true Christians?

The Lord Jesus made it very clear that not all who profess His name really belong to Him. In Matthew 7:13-14 He spoke of the narrow gate to life and the broad road to destruction. Then He explained: "Many will say to Me on that day, 'Lord, Lord, did we not prophesy in Your name, and in Your name cast out demons, and in Your name perform many miracles?' And then I will declare to them, 'I never knew you: *Depart from Me, you who practice lawlessness*'" (Mt. 7:22-23). He also said, "Do not be afraid, little flock, for your father has chosen gladly to give you the kingdom" (Lk.2:32). There are other indications that the majority who profess His name do not genuinely belong to Him.

I see this as a most crucial issue because all through my growing-up years I was actively involved in an 'evangelical' church, but did not have a clue about salvation or eternal life until I was in college. Seven years later when I arrived in Pakistan as a missionary, I was shocked to find that only a small minority of the half-million professing Christians in that country (in 1956) had a personal relationship with Jesus Christ or could claim to have been born again. I found that before the 'Christians' of Pakistan could be mobilized to win the Muslims, they needed to be re-evangelized.

Defining an Evangelical

As Evangelicals we believe that true Christians must be essentially evangelical in faith, regardless of their denominational affiliation. Johnstone gives this working definition of an Evangelical in *Operation World*:

1. Commitment to a personal faith and emphasis on personal conversion or new birth. 2. Recognition of the inspired Word of God as the only basis for faith and Christian living. 3. Biblical preaching and evangelism.

. . . .

Evangelicals are here defined as: 1. All affiliated Christians . . . of denominations that are evangelical in theology as defined above. 2. The proportion of the affiliated Christians in other Protestant denominations and Anglican dioceses (that are not wholly evangelical in theology) who would hold evangelical views. 3. The proportion of affiliated Christians in denominations in non-Western nations . . . that would be regarded as Evangelical by those in the above categories.

. . . .

This is a theological and not experiential definition. It does *not* mean: 1. That all Evangelicals as defined above are actually born-again. In many nations only 10-40% of Evangelicals so defined may have had a valid conversion and also regularly attend church services.[7]

This is basic to *Operation World*, and although we could wish we had a better definition, it will have to serve us as well.

What is the gospel?

Actually the answer to the above question goes back to the even more basic one: what is the gospel of the Lord Jesus Christ? One important fog-dispelling perspective is seen in **the distinction between the objective, historic aspect of the gospel and the present, subjective, internal, and experiential aspect.** Both must be a reality for the Evangelical Christian. One or both is missing for the nominal Christian. The objective aspect is what Christ accomplished for the salvation of the world by His death, burial, and resurrection. The Apostle Paul insisted that this is foundational to the gospel (1 Cor. 15:1-3).

The second aspect of the gospel has to do with its application in the individual's life. This was emphasized by the Lord Jesus when He told Nicodemus that he needed to be born again (Jn. 3:1-16). All through John's Gospel there is an emphasis upon a personal appropriation of Christ. In John 1:12-13 the imperative of receiving Him is equated with believing on His Name in order to be born again; in 4:13-4 the Lord told the Samaritan woman that she must drink the water of eternal life; in 6:35 He symbolized faith as eating and drinking, as He also did in 7:37-8. So faith is a personal appropriation of Christ. So when Evangelicals emphasize "accepting Christ as your personal Savior," they are simply stressing what Christ stressed.

Confusion about the gospel

Some 'Christians' like those of liberal or neo-orthodox theology undermine the historical, objective dimension of the gospel message. They don't believe Paul's affirmation that the death and resurrection of Christ are essential to the Christian message. On the other hand, there are millions in Christendom who may intellectually assent to the historical propositions of the Christian faith, but who have never appropriated Christ personally. This was my condition before I was saved. They may be quite orthodox in their 'beliefs.' But that is not the same as saying that they have a personal faith and have been born again.

Another major area of confusion among those who accept the Bible to be the inspired word of God relates to the legalistic additional requirements that men add to the biblical requirement of simple faith as the only condition of salvation. The Protestant reformers were absolutely right in insisting on *sola fide*, faith alone uncomplicated by law works. This is based, of course, upon Paul's strong emphasis in Romans and Galatians upon justification by grace through faith alone and reinforced by Ephesians 2:8-9, Titus 3:5-6 and a host of other passages. Paul was opposed to adding circumcision or law works to faith as the condition of being saved. We believe that Paul told it like it is when he told the Philippian jailor, "Believe in the Lord Jesus, and you shall be saved, you and your household" (Acts 16:31). He didn't leave anything out!

The problem comes when people add other separate conditions to faith. Today instead of circumcision and law-works, they add a host of other things. I once saw a tract entitled, "13 Steps to Salvation," which listed confession of sins, repentance, baptism by their church, church membership (in their church), a life of good works, and many other things in addition to faith. This is hardly the simple gospel which Paul preached.

Most pernicious of all is the sacramentalism which sees baptism as efficacious in saving people. This view is know as baptismal regeneration, and is held by the Roman Catholic Church, many Anglicans (Episcopalians), many Lutherans, some other legalistic denominations, and some cults. It is probably the major doctrinal error in Christendom throughout the ages, and it still is today. Whether the christening of infants or the baptism of adults is viewed as making someone a Christian, the absurdity of it all in the light of Scripture is astounding. If ritual circumcision could not do it for Jews before Christ, what makes people think baptism could do it after Christ?[a]

---

[a] Baptismal regeneration is based in part upon mistranslation of key passages, such as, Acts 2:38, 22:16, 1 Pet. 3:19ff., as well as a magical, sacramental concept of the ordinances.

The cruciality of the message

The relevance of this to missions should be obvious. The content of the message which we are to proclaim to all the peoples of the world is a matter of life and death, heaven or hell! What is a valid mission field? Was it legitimate for Evangelicals to view Latin America as a mission field even though it was nominally Christian? Is Europe a legitimate mission field, even though it has been 'Christian' for a millennium?

Most importantly, the Lord Jesus Christ emphasized to His apostles at Caesarea Philippi the imperative of 'telling it like it is.' After He warned them to "beware of leaven of the Pharisees and Sadducees" (Matt. 16:11), which was a reference to their evil doctrines (16:12), He gave specific instruction as to how to build His church (16:18): "I will give you the keys of the kingdom of heaven; and whatever you shall bind on earth shall have been bound in heaven, and whatever you shall loose on earth shall have been loosed in heaven" (16:19 NAS 1st ed.).[b] The main point is that Peter and the apostles were charged to make sure that they proclaimed the message of forgiveness on heaven's terms. They were not to err like the Pharisees in binding on earth what God had not already bound in heaven, thus making salvation too hard (cf. Mt. 23:13). This is a legalistic corruption of the salvation message. They were not to err like the Sadducees in loosing on earth what God had not already loosed in heaven, thus making salvation too easy. They were to tell it on earth like it really is in heaven, since God's word has been settled forever in heaven (Ps. 119:89), and man must not tamper with it. Paul warned the Galatians Christians that those who preach another gospel are accursed (Gal. 1:6-9). So in fulfilling the Great Commission we must be extremely diligent to proclaim the message of salvation accurately and simply as given to us.

WHY IN THE WORLD
DO WE NEED MISSIONARIES?

Before we examine the abundant and unambiguous biblical evidence for missions, let us try to understand why some professing Christians are unenthusiastic about missions, or may actually be opposed. We would

---

[b] This translation of the perfect tense in Greek is confirmed by the Charles B. Williams, *The New Testament in the Language of the People* (1963), the *Amplified Bible,* and the Alfred Marshall *Interlinear Greek-English New Testament* (1958) renderings. Unfortunately, the NAS committee went back in later editions to a more traditional, but erroneous rendering, thus obscuring the main point of the passage. The rule in Greek grammar is that the action of a perfect participle must precede the action of the main verb. See Dana and Mantey, *A Manual Grammar of the Greek New Testament* (1927), p. 230, and Daniel B. Wallace, *Greek Grammar Beyond the Basics* (1996), p. 581.

expect non-Christians to be negative, but it is obvious that most church people in western countries couldn't care less about missions. The per capita giving to missions on the part of American Protestants is an abysmal 0.25 of one percent of disposable personal income, which amount to 25 cents per person per week — half enough to buy a can of soda. Evangelicals do a lot better than average Protestants, but still not enough for a can of soda. (The potential for more is incredible!)[8]

Why hostility to missions?

Many people will say, "Why in the world do we need missionaries?" Frequently we hear the platitude "Charity begins at home" used as an excuse. "There are just as many heathen here at home" is another favorite. And there are others. Why do professing Christians make such excuses and even oppose missions? Harold Cook has suggested four basic reasons:

1. **"The lack of a personal and vital experience of Christ"** — Many members of the old-line denominations simply have not been born again. No other explanation is needed since the Bible says, "a natural man does not accept the things of the Spirit of God; for they are foolishness to him and he cannot understand them, because they are spiritually appraised" (1 Cor. 2:14).

2. **"Preoccupation with self"** — Even born-again Christians may be unspiritual and wrapped up in themselves. Their selfish lifestyle is threatened by talk about missions; so they react.

3. **"Ignorance of actual conditions in other parts of the world"** — Many people ignorantly minimize the effects of sin upon mankind by thinking that the "native leads a carefree, happy-go-lucky life until the missionary comes to change his way of living and spoil his Garden of Eden." Others magnify the value of other religions. Still others minimize the power of the gospel to transform heathen people and see them as hopeless. It is amazing how the impact of travel abroad helps relieve people of these misconceptions by helping them see reality with their own eyes.

4. **Theological confusion and rationalization.** Cook points up the impact of hyper-Calvinism in undermining the Christian's responsibility.[9] This was the source of the first opposition that William Carey got and continues to be a contrary force. Liberal (modernistic) theology also cuts the nerve of missionary concern because it denies the uniqueness of Christ, His gospel, and the reality of eternal punishment.Cook also points up the impact of substituting 'mission' for 'missions' as noted before, since it substantially redefines what missions is and dissipates true missionary effort.[10] To these we add the rationalizations that the heathen might not really be lost. We will deal with some of these in chapter 5.

Developing a biblical basis for missions

Our first task then is to develop a more biblical basis of missions. Before we can sketch out the history of missions, look at the context into which missionaries go, survey the contemporary situation on the major fields, and see the contemporary function of missions, it is important to start with the biblical data. As Robert Hall Glover wrote in his classic text:

> A good deal of missionary interest and effort falls short of being satisfactory, because it rests upon an altogether inadequate conception of what the missionary enterprise really is. Mere pity for people of mission lands, called forth by some heart-moving tale of dire need or some instance of cruel suffering, is not enough, commendable though this may be. Something deeper and broader is needed to constitute a solid foundation for worthy and enduring missionary effort.
>
> The missionary enterprise is no human conception or undertaking, no modern scheme or invention, no mere philanthropy even of the finest kind. It did not originate in the brain or heart of any man, not even of William Carey, or the apostle Paul. Its source was the heart of God Himself. And Jesus Christ, God's great Missionary to a lost world, was the supreme revelation of His heart and expression of His love.[11]

1. J. Herbert Kane, *Understanding Christian Missions* (1974), p. 28.
2. Ibid., pp. 28-29.
3. Charles C. Ryrie, *Basic Theology* (1986), p. 371.
4. Kane, *Understanding*, p. 30.
5. George W. Peters, *A Biblical Theology of Missions* (Moody, 1972), p. 11.
6. Ibid.
7. Patrick Johnstone, *Operation World*, 4th ed., p. 496.
8. John Holzmann, "Financial Resources and the Kingdom of God," *Mission Frontiers* 9 (May 1987): 12.
9. Hyper-Calvinism describes a fatalistic and deterministic viewpoint adopted by some followers of John Calvin, which undoubtedly goes far beyond his own doctrine of predestination.
10. Harold R. Cook, *Introduction to Christian Missions* (1964), pp. 12-17.
11. Robert Hall Glover, *The Bible Basis of Missions*, (1946), p. 13.

KEY OLD TESTAMENT PERSONS/EVENTS

Enoch	Prophet	Prophesied coming judgment
Noah	Prophet/Missionary	Preacher of righteousness
Tower of Babel	Beginnings of Idolatry	Ziggurat for idolatrous worship
Abraham	Prophet/Missionary	Abrahamic Covenant: "In you all the families of the earth shall be blessed."
Isaac, Jacob, Joseph	Prophets/Missionaries	Covenant reconfirmed
Moses	Prophet/Missionary/ Deliverer	Mosaic Covenant: Israel was to be a nation of priests.
Caleb, Rahab, Ruth	Early Proselytes (converts)	Saw God's greatness revealed through Israel.
King David	Prophet/King	Missionary Psalms: "Thy salvation among all nations"
King Solomon	Sage/King	Dedicates temple for Israel and for foreigners.
Isaiah	Prophet	Temple: "House of prayer for all nations"; Messiah: "light of the nations", etc.
Widow of Zarephath, Naaman the Syrian	Early Gentiles blessed through Israel.	"Now I know that there is no God in all the earth, but in Israel."
Jonah	Prophet/Missionary	To Ninevah of Assyrians
Exile to Assyria/Babylonia	Israel forced out into the Gentile world	Out of isolation & compromise
Daniel	Prophet/Gov't Official	Revelation to 2 world empires
Synagogue Formation	After Ezra & Diaspora	"Moses read in synagogues every sabbath"
Septagint Greek OT translation	Beginning of Bible translation	*Lingua Franca* of the ancient world for centuries
Pharisees	Christ's description of Jewish sect	Traveled about on sea & land to make proselytes.

"The greatest scandal in the Old Testament is that Israel tried to be blessed without trying very hard to be a blessing."
—Ralph Winter

IS MISSIONS REALLY IN THE OLD TESTAMENT?

The missionary impact of the Old Testament has been obscured for many readers by the overwhelming focus upon one nation—the Jews. And yet for the alert student who has eyes to see, interwoven with God's dealings with Israel from the very beginning there is the clear theme of God's purpose for all the nations of the world. This is strongly supported by the fact that the revelation of God in the Old Testament is of a God whose very character implies missions in that He is the God of all men, not just of the Jews (Rom. 3:29).

It is obvious that missionary activity such as we see in the New Testament is not prominent in the Old. Yet the issue is clarified when we understand the distinctive nature of that activity. These are two distinct dispensations, and we would expect the mode of missionary activity to be quite different. We must also be careful to distinguish Israel as God intended and the Jewish people and their religion as they actually developed. It is clear that Israel fell far short of God's plan for them as a nation. To be honest we would have to admit that the same is true of the New Testament church, but to a lesser extent. But the gap between God's purpose for Israel and their performance is very real and substantial.

Harold Cook has very aptly raised three important questions about missions in the Old Testament: 1) Does the Old Testament have a missionary message? 2) Does the Old Testament show a missionary purpose? 3) Does the Old Testament reveal any missionary activity? Let us try to answer these three important questions.

DOES THE OLD TESTAMENT HAVE A MISSIONARY MESSAGE?

The Bible is the inspired record of the revelation of God about Himself

21

and His relationship to His creation. The character of the God who revealed Himself and this relationship in the Old Testament necessarily
implies a missionary message. If God is who He is revealed to be and
man is what the Bible says he is, then of necessity that message should
be shared with all men. Since the fall of Adam, mankind has always
been slow to catch on, to realize the implications of these central truths
about ultimate reality. Men before the flood didn't get the point; the
Jews were slow to grasp the implications of Yahweh (Jehovah), the God
who created man and revealed Himself to them; Christians over the
centuries have been slow to understand the implications of the gospel of
Christ as it relates to evangelism and missions. "What is a missionary
message? Very simply, **it is a message that one has and another needs.**
It is a message that by its very nature ought to be propagated, ought to
be spread abroad."[1]

The self-revelation of God

One God as Creator of the universe. The first verse of the Bible
stands as a marvelous refutation of most of the errors of mankind's confused religions. It denies atheism, agnosticism, evolution, polytheism,
materialism, and pantheism in one fell swoop. This is the basic truth of
ultimate reality that mankind as a whole strives to repress. The Animist
has some remembrance of God as Creator but thinks that He is not
concerned with man. The Hindu and the Buddhist have an eternal universe with no creator. The Shinto legends have evolving gods. So the
oneness of a personal, Creator God has been corrupted by the imag-
inations of man. The sophisticated modern evolutionist goes to great
lengths to deny the Creator and especially His direct role in the creation
of man. But if God has directly created the whole universe and mankind
(as He has), then it is of highest importance that mankind be reminded
of this truth and live in the light of it! But someone might ask, "What
difference does it make?"

It makes all the difference in the world for man to acknowledge his
Creator. Since God created us for fellowship with Him, it is an insult for
men to ignore God and repress knowledge of Him. But let us also think
about the ethical and moral demands of creation. If we owe our very
existence to God--the air we breathe, the water we drink, the food we
eat--then what a debt of gratitude we owe Him. He has the right to tell
us how to live, doesn't He? So He has given us the laws which are to
govern human existence. The All-Wise God has structured them for our
good, both individually and corporately. But we want to be independent
of God and "do our own thing." God didn't just create individuals; He
created man and woman, male and female. So He structured family life
and gave laws governing sexual behavior. As the human race grew by
sexual procreation, he gave other laws as to how men were to relate to
Him and to each other. But the day came when most of mankind could-

n't care less about God and His laws; in fact only eight believers were left. And this brings us to the story of the first missionary, Noah.

A righteous God of judgment. When God revealed to Noah that judgment would come upon a godless and lawless humanity by a deluge of water, Noah preached for 120 years that men must repent and turn to God (Gen. 6:3, 5-8). Noah is called a "preacher of righteousness" (2 Pet. 2:5). Indeed his ancestor Enoch had prophesied of the coming judgment on unrepentant sinners (Jude 14-15). The message of Noah was that God is righteous and holy and will judge sin.[a] The core error of heathen religion is the repression of this very truth. The gods of the ancient Greeks and Romans were not particularly moral; neither are the gods of the Hindus. Not that heathen religions don't have moral standards—they do. The problem is that the standards are not God's standards; they are man-made. But the main point is that Noah realized that since God is a righteous God of judgment, it was important to reach his fellow humans before God's judgment fell. They didn't believe that God's judgment was coming. The Lord Jesus made a big point of this: "For as in those days which were before the flood they were eating and drinking, they were marrying and giving in marriage, until the day that Noah entered the ark, and they did not understand until the flood came and took them all away" (Matt. 24:38-39).

A gracious God who provides salvation. The strongest missionary implication arises out of God's initiative in providing salvation for lost mankind. God is the One who provided a covering for Adam and Eve's nakedness and shame after their disobedience, which required the shedding of blood. It was God who stipulated the shedding of the blood of an animal sacrifice to atone for the sins of Cain and Abel.[b] It was God who revealed Himself to Abraham, Isaac, and Jacob. It was God who initiated the redemption of Israel out of Egyptian bondage. And it was God who gave promise after promise, prophecy after prophecy, of the coming Messiah and His salvation. It is this salvation that alienated mankind needs. They need to know that God is a God of love, who has initiated salvation for lost humanity. But this is exactly what man in his self-made heathen religions does not know. None of them has a con-

---

[a] Someone might quibble about whether Noah was a cross-cultural missionary. However, in Noah's day all men still spoke one language, and it is doubtful whether distinct cultures had yet developed, so the point is moot. Some might question whether Noah made an appeal for repentance, but there would be little point in preaching unless he did. In the Gospels we find examples of such an implicit appeal not made explicit. Compare Matt. 10:7 with Mark 6:12.

[b] Although some interpreters denigrate the importance of the blood of Abel's animal sacrifice, New Testament writers confirm the significance of the sacrifice itself (Gen. 4:3-7; Heb. 11:4; 12:24; 1 Jn. 3:12). This is adequate basis to imply that God had stipulated the kind of offering they should bring.

cept of a loving God initiating salvation for us. But we will examine the world religions in section III.

The revelation of man's nobility and depravity

Uniquely created in the image of God. The gap between man and the animals is clearly stated in Genesis 1:26-27. Because man was created in the moral, intellectual, and volitional likeness of God, he is noble enough to rule over the animals and responsible to obey His laws. God makes no moral demands of lower animals since they were not created in His image. The image of God in man makes us responsible moral beings.

The human race a unity. Evolutionists have difficulty proving the essential unity of the human race since they don't acknowledge the gap between man and the lower animals. Man is a "naked ape" according to Desmond. The Bible-believer holds to the unity of the whole human species. This means that the words of the children's chorus are both biblical and important: "Red, brown, yellow, black, and white; they are precious in His sight." If we share the same human blood, then we are responsible for all men, not just those of our nation, race, and color. Racial pride and discrimination thus becomes a violation of His creative order and the enemy of His redemptive plan. The Apostle Peter learned this truth with great difficulty: "I most certainly understand **now** that God is not one to show partiality, but in every nation the man who fears Him and does what is right, is welcome to Him" (Acts 10:34-35). Tragically, hundreds of millions of people are bound by ethnic religions which make no claim to universality: Shinto for Japanese, Hinduism for Indians, etc.

Sin and depravity universal. When Adam and Eve disobeyed God, they died spiritually (Gen. 2:16-17; Eph. 2:1-5) and plunged the whole human race into hereditary sin and depravity (Psa. 51:5; Rom. 5:12). No one has escaped this pollution, except for the Lord Jesus (Rom. 3:23). Universal depravity does not mean that all men manifest all the symptoms of the sin nature to an equal extent. But it does mean that all mankind have the same potential for evil and are equally unable to do anything pleasing to God in themselves (Rom. 8:6-7). This means that all men are equally in need of salvation, no matter how religious or moral they might be. The logic of this then is that no one has any more right to the message of salvation than anybody else; it is not to be hoarded. But we will look into this line of truth in the next chapter.

In conclusion, we can say that since God is our Creator, a righteous God who judges sin, and a gracious God who provides salvation, and since all men are equally alienated from God and under His judgment, therefore it is abundantly clear that the Old Testament has a missionary message!

DOES THE OLD TESTAMENT SHOW A MISSIONARY PURPOSE?

The nation Israel and many other interpreters have misread the Old Testament as being a basis for self-centered racial favoritism. Israel was God's chosen people — chosen from among all the peoples of the earth. But the purpose of that choice got lost in the shuffle. Israel failed to keep that purpose before them, and we also frequently fail to recognize it adequately as we read the Old Testament. In-depth study, however, shows that God's purpose was ever the salvation of the whole human race, not just the Jews. That purpose shines through clearly if we have eyes to see.

God's covenant with Noah and his sons

We have already noted Noah's missionary activity (cf. endnote #2). But God's purpose for the whole of humanity is seen in the covenant that God made with Noah and with his sons after the deluge. All human beings are descended from Noah and his seven family members, who alone survived the flood. It is obvious that Noah wasn't Jewish. Actually we don't know what color he was. But we do know for sure that all the diverse races of mankind — "red, brown, yellow, black, and white" — descended from those eight people. So all the genetic material of diverse humanity was present in those eight people. The simplest explanation would be that both Ham's wife and Noah's wife were racially diverse from their husbands. It is clear that Noah's three sons, Ham, Shem, and Japheth, were racially quite diverse, and there is archaeological evidence that Ham's four sons were racially very diverse.[2]

Admittedly, white people visualize those eight people as being white; black people as black; but that is impossible. We all are descended from those eight survivors. So the point is that God made a covenant with the whole human race: "Then God spoke to Noah and to his sons with him, saying, 'Now behold, I Myself do establish My covenant with you, and with your descendants after you'" (Gen. 9:8-9). Clearly God's concern was for the whole human race, not just the Jews or white people or any favored race.

God's covenant with Abraham, Isaac, and Jacob

After Noah's day the descendants of his sons degenerated into godlessness and idolatry fairly quickly. Although the details are obscure, we are told that at Babel God judged the rebellion of man with confusion of languages, which undoubtedly developed into diversity of cultures as well

(Gen. 11:1-9). The problem at Babel seems clearly to have been the beginnings of idolatry.   The tower was what archaeologists call a 'ziggurat', upon the top of which idolatrous worship was to be carried out. There is an obvious link with Nimrod, who founded Babel and was a key man in events of that time (Gen. 10:8-12).[3] It is probable that the Apostle Paul later described this degeneration of humanity before and after Babel in Romans 1:18-32, where he specifically mentions idolatry:

> For even though they knew God, they did not honor Him as God, or give thanks; but they became futile in their speculations, and their foolish heart was darkened, professing to be wise, they became fools, and exchanged the glory of the incorruptible God for an image in the form of corruptible man and of birds and four-footed animals and crawling creatures (Romans 1:21-23).

So this is the background out of which God called Abraham (Joshua 24:2; Isaiah 51:1-2). Abraham was not the only believer of his day, but God called him out of idolatrous Ur for a special purpose.

Before Moses recorded Abram's call out of Ur of the Chaldees, he left a vivid reminder of God's continuing interest in the other peoples of the earth. This is the genealogical record of the seventy nations descended from Noah's three sons (Gen. 10:1-32). It isn't that God turned His back upon the Gentiles (non-Jews) in separating out the nation Israel. No, his special purpose for Israel related directly to these peoples. Let us turn to the record in Genesis 12:1-3:

> Now the Lord said to Abram, "Go forth from your country, and from your relatives and from your father's house, to the land which I will show you; and I will make you a great nation. And I will bless you, and make your name great; and so you shall be a blessing; and I will bless those who bless you, and the one who curses you I will curse. And in you all the families of the earth shall be blessed."

Over the years most interpreters have tended to assume that since the ultimate fulfillment of the words about blessing to all the families of the earth was to be in the coming of the Messiah, therefore we should not look for much fulfillment before then. Ralph Winter calls this assumption, "The Theory of the Hibernating Mandate." He goes on to state:

> A more recent and exciting interpretation observes that Israel, as far back as Abraham, was accountable to share that blessing with other nations. In the same way, since the time of the Apostle Paul, every nation which has contained any significant number of "children of Abraham's faith" has been similarly accountable (but both Israel and the other nations have mainly failed to carry out this mandate).

The greatest scandal in the Old Testament is that Israel tried to be blessed without trying very hard to be a blessing.[4]

The mandate was given to Abram to be God's missionary to a new generation of corrupted humanity.[e] He was to relocate his center of operations to a relatively unpopulated country on the land bridge between Europe, Africa, and Asia, where he could establish a new civilization free from the idolatry of Babylon and Ur, as a witness and blessing to all nations. And God confirmed that covenant and mandate with Isaac and Jacob as well. Just because Abraham, Isaac, and Jacob failed in the main to obey that commission does not mean that the responsibility was not clearly theirs.

Abraham failed to a great extent because of sin problems that arose from following his godless cultural background (like lying twice about Sarah's identity and fathering Ishmael in a culturally acceptable way). But he did leave a tremendous example of faith in the God of the supernatural when he believed that God could give two old people a miracle child (Isaac), and when as he was about to offer up Isaac as a sacrifice, "he considered that God is able to raise men even from the dead" (Heb. 11:19).

God confirmed the covenant with Isaac (Gen. 26:1-4) and with Jacob (28:10-14), specifically reminding Jacob that "in you and your descendants shall all the families of the earth be blessed." Jacob himself was to be a missionary. But the story of Isaac and Jacob is similar to that of Abraham. Jacob was slow to develop spiritually and his witness constantly suffered. It wasn't until great-grandson Joseph that we see a powerful witness to the nations, especially Egypt (but more of that later).

In his waning years, there were two high points in Jacob's career: he blessed the Pharaoh of Egypt, and he gave prophecies about his twelve sons. Even though Jacob doesn't seem to have perceived his missionary responsibility very well, the Holy Spirit allowed him to see how blessing would come to the world through the tribe of Judah: "The scepter shall not depart from Judah, nor the ruler's staff from between his feet, until Shiloh comes (until He comes to whom it belongs, NIV), and to him shall be the obedience of the **peoples**" (49:10). However it is translated, this is clearly Messianic. But the key word is obscured in the Authorized (KJV) Version. The word 'people' is in the plural in the Hebrew. The coming Messiah is for all "peoples," not just Jacob's descendants.

God's covenant with Israel through Moses

It was sin and failure that got Israel into bondage in Egypt. They badly

---

[e] Walter C. Kaiser, Jr. defends the passive rendering of the *niphal* form in Gen. 12:3 in the evangelical translations (KJV, NAS, NIV), as opposed to the reflexive rendering in others: "bless themselves." *Toward an Old Testament Theology* (1978), p. 13.

backslid there into the idolatry of the Egyptians. The ten plagues on the Egyptians were specifically God's judgments upon the very idols the Egyptians worshipped.   Their idolatry was closely tied in to animals, insects, and the forces of nature, like the Nile River and the sun. God's judgment on these things they worshipped was a telling judgment on their idolatry and a witness to all the nations. This was God's word to Pharaoh, "for this cause have I allowed you to remain, in order to show you My power, and in order to proclaim My name through all the earth" (Exod. 9:16).

Then when God brought them out of Egypt by miracle after miracle and brought them to Sinai to give them His Law, He prefixed that important covenant with a clear statement of His purpose in molding Israel into a theocratic nation. The Law was not just for individual morality, but it was also to give the fledgling nation judicial and religious statutes upon which they could be a testimony to the surrounding nations. Here are the words of this preamble to the Law:

> Thus you shall say to the house of Jacob and tell the sons of Israel: "You yourselves have seen what I did to the Egyptians, and how I bore you on eagles' wings, and brought you to Myself. Now then, if you will indeed obey My voice and keep My covenant, then you shall be My own possession among all the peoples, for all the earth is Mine; and you shall be to Me a kingdom of priests and a holy nation" (Exod. 19:3-6).

After reminding them that He is Lord of all the earth, He clearly states His purpose that Israel should be a kingdom of priests. This phrase is loaded with meaning. To understand it, we must understand the function of a priest. A priest is to function as a mediator between God and man. So Israel was to be a whole nation of priests — intermediaries between the God who had revealed Himself to them and the pagan nations around them. They were to be a missionary nation. But to fulfill this they must be obedient to his word, keeping His Law and covenant as a holy nation. And there's the rub! Israel failed to be God's missionary nation because they failed to be a holy nation.

Israel's most critical failure, however, was a failure of faith when God brought them to the edge of the promised land at Kadesh-Barnea (Num. 14:1-10). Because of the bad report of the ten spies, Israel refused to enter the land. Moses interceded for them, and God pardoned the nation. But His words at this point are most important:

> So the LORD said, "I have pardoned them according to your word; but indeed, as I live, all the earth will be filled with the glory of the LORD. Surely all the men who have seen my glory and My signs, which I performed in Egypt and in the wilderness, yet have put Me to the test these ten times and have not listened to My

voice, shall by no means see the land which I swore to their fathers, nor shall any of those who spurned Me see it. But my servant Caleb, because he has had a different spirit and has followed me fully, I will bring into the land which he entered, and his descendants shall take possession of it" (Num. 14:20-24).

Note that despite forgiveness there were temporal consequences of their sin, and that even in judgment God's glory would fill the earth. That is the purpose of it all—that the whole earth should know the glory of God.

The place of Gentile converts in Israel

But there is a subtle irony in God's words in Num. 14:24. It comes out by identifying Caleb, Joshua's companion. Comparing Joshua 14:14, where he is identified as a Kenizzite, with Genesis 15:19, where the Kenizzites are identified as a Canaanite tribe, makes it clear that Caleb was a Gentile, not a Jew. Caleb is one of the first proselytes or converts mentioned in the Bible. So God is saying that His chosen nation had failed to obey Him, but this Gentile Caleb had followed God fully. See how God's purpose for the Gentiles shines through the record, if we study it carefully![d]

But Caleb wasn't the only Gentile convert. God had made provision in the Law for Gentile aliens to share in the observation of the Passover (Num. 9:14), for the offering up of animal sacrifices at the tabernacle (Lev. 17:8), and for just treatment at the hands of the Israelites (Exod. 22:21). Not only do we find reference to many other Gentile proselytes in the Old Testament, but Matthew goes out of his way to highlight the fact that four of them were women who figured in the genealogy of Christ (Matt. 1:3-6). They were Tamar, Rahab, Ruth, and Bathsheba. So God did clearly make provision for Gentiles to show their faith in the God of Israel by identifying themselves with His chosen people. Many did so over the centuries, as Kane points out.

> The book of Ruth is a beautiful example of the way in which these strangers were assimilated into the congregation. Ruth, a Moabite widow, was so impressed with her mother-in-law, Naomi, that she refused to leave her on her return to the land of Judah. In vain did Naomi try to dissuade her. In words as precious as they are poetic Ruth clinched the matter by saying to Naomi: "Entreat me not to leave you or go to return from following you; where you go I will go, and where you lodge I will lodge; your people shall be

---

[d]I am indebted to Sam Nadler for this insight. Many commentators do not admit the possibility that Caleb was a Gentile because they confuse him with another Jewish Caleb. However, because he was a Gentile, he had no inheritance in Israel, and Joshua had to make a special provision to give him one: Hebron (Josh. 14:13-15).

my people, and your God my God . . ." (Ruth 1:16-17).[5]

God's worldwide purpose
in the united kingdom

About half of the Psalms are attributed to King David. George Peters points out that there are about 175 references in the Psalms of a universal note referring to the Gentile nations of the world. Many of these references are to the ultimate reign of God and His Messiah over all the nations in the kingdom. They all show God's concern and purpose for all the Gentiles. Many speak of Israel as God's channel of blessing to the nations and of God's purpose to bring salvation to the nations.

> All the ends of the earth will remember and turn to the LORD, and all the families of the nations will worship before Thee (Psa. 22:27).
> Cease striving and know that I am God;   I will be exalted among the nations . . .(46:10).
> All the earth will worship Thee, and will sing praises to Thee . . .(66:4). That Thy way may be known on the earth, Thy salvation among all nations. . . . Let all the peoples praise Thee. . . .God blesses us, that all the ends of the earth may fear Him (67:2,3,7).
> And Thy godly ones shall bless Thee. They shall speak of the glory of Thy kingdom, and talk of Thy power; to make known to the sons of men Thy mighty acts, and the glory of the majesty of Thy kingdom (145:10-12).

Not only does the Psalmist speak of believers making known God's mighty acts, but there are at least three passages which command Israel to witness to the nations:

> Declare among the peoples His deeds (9:11).
> Sing to the LORD, all the earth. . . .Proclaim good tidings of His salvation from day to day. Tell of His glory among the nations, His wonderful deeds among all the peoples. . . .Tremble before Him, all the earth.   Say among the nations, "The LORD reigns" (96:1-3,9,10).
> Oh give thanks to the LORD, call upon His name; make known His deeds among the peoples (105:1).

Although King David was not permitted to build a temple for the Lord, his son Solomon was. Like his father, Solomon understood the global implications of the temple worship, which is expressed in his prayer of dedication:

> Also concerning the foreigner who is not of Thy people Israel, when he comes from a far country for Thy name's sake (for they will hear of thy great name and thy mighty hand, and of thine

outstretched arm); when he comes and prays toward this house, hear Thou in heaven Thy dwelling place, and do according to all for which the foreigner calls to Thee, in order that all the peoples of the earth may know Thy name, to fear Thee, as do Thy people Israel, and that they may know that this house which I have built is called by Thy name (1 Kgs. 8:41-43).

We usually think of the temple as a 'Jewish temple', but it is clear from the above prayer, as well as from Isaiah's statement centuries later, that it was dedicated for a worldwide outreach: "Also the foreigners who join themselves to the LORD, to minister to Him, and to love the name of the LORD, . . . For My house will be called a house of prayer for all the peoples" (Isa. 56:6-7). If that was true of the Old Testament 'Jewish temple', how much more should it be true of the New Testament church?

God's global purpose revealed through His prophets

Although many of the prophets of Israel, both before and after the exile, expressed the global purpose of God's dealings with Israel, it was Isaiah who most clearly describes the universality of God's salvation. Especially in the 'Servant' section of the book (ch. 42-53) the worldwide commission of God's two servants is seen. The prophet intermingles prophecies about Israel as God's servant with those about Messiah as His Servant. "Thus Israel as the servant of Jehovah and the Messiah as the ideal Servant both have universal significance and find their full meaning only in world service."[6] First we see the Messiah as the Messiah of all the nations:

Behold, My Servant, whom I uphold; my chosen one in whom My soul delights. I have put My Spirit upon Him; He will bring forth justice to the nations. . . . He will not be disheartened or crushed, until He has established justice in the earth; and the coastlands will wait expectantly for His law (Isa. 42:1,4).
He says, "It is too small a thing that You should be My Servant to raise up the tribes of Jacob, and to restore the preserved ones of Israel; I will also make You a light of the nations so that My salvation may reach to the end of the earth" (Isa. 49:6).
The LORD has bared His holy arm in the sight of all the nations, that all the ends of the earth may see the salvation of our God. . . Thus He will sprinkle many nations (Isa. 52:10,15).

Then we see Israel commissioned as witnesses to the nations:

"You are My witnesses," declares the LORD, "and my servant whom I have chosen. . ." (43:10).
"And you are my witnesses. Is there any God besides Me, or is

there any other Rock? I know of none" (Isa. 44:8).

The climax of the passage is where God turns and appeals directly to the heathen nations in the foolishness of their idolatry and denial of Him: "Turn to Me, and be saved, all the ends of the earth; for I am God, and there is no other" (Isa. 45:22). Many other quotations from others of the prophets could be given. The reader should check Jer. 3:17; Joel 2:28; Micah 4:1-4; Hab. 2:14; Hag. 2:7; Zech. 2:11; 9:10; and Mal. 1:11 for examples of a universality of thought that goes far beyond Israel.

WAS THERE REALLY MISSIONARY ACTIVITY BEFORE THE APOSTLES?

We have already referred to Enoch as the first prophet and Noah as the first missionary. We have noted that God's purpose was for Abram to become a missionary, but the witness did not develop until Joseph's godly testimony in Egypt, and that developed because of his brothers' sin. But we would have to acknowledge that there was not a lot of overt missionary activity in the early history of Israel, at least by New Testament standards.

A different mode of operation

However, this is the heart of the problem. There is a shift of emphasis between the testaments, but the essential of cross-cultural witness is found in both. We must not look for missions in the New Testament sense in the Old Testament. The difference is significant. Before Pentecost the major missionary method was for the nations to see God's dealings with Israel and to **come** to Israel to hear and be saved. After the day of Pentecost the church was to **go** out

Fig. 1   The Transition in Missions Emphasis

among the nations and witness among them. George Peters has suggested a helpful diagram (see fig. 1).[7] Once we recognize that the mode of operation for Israel is different from that for the church, it is easier to see indications of cross-cultural witness by the nation Israel. For Israel, casual cross-cultural witness was the norm and overt sending activity more the exception. On the other hand, for the New Testament church overt sending activity is to be the norm. We can see examples of God's care for Gentiles in Elijah's encounter with the widow of Zarephath (in Phoenicia) and in Elisha's witness to Naaman the Syrian army commander (1 Kgs. 17:9ff.; 2 Kgs. 5:1ff.). Notice how it involved the witness of a young servant girl at first.

Jonah

The book of Jonah is a striking example of sending missionary activity, anticipatory of the New Testament method. His is the story of a reluctant missionary who tried to go in the opposite direction because of his racial and ethnic pride. He reasoned that it would be better for Israel if their cruel Assyrian enemies in Ninevah perished. So he refused to go. But God had a 'plan B' for Jonah, and it wasn't for somebody else; it was for Jonah by way of the fish's belly. The impact upon Ninevah was astounding, especially in view of Jonah's failure to offer hope to Ninevah by preaching repentance (Jonah 3:9). He just preached Ninevah's destruction in forty days and got angry when the Ninevites repented and God relented from the judgment. The root of Jonah's problem was that he didn't have compassion for lost Assyrians as God did. He had rationalized the outcome, based upon his misunderstanding of the justice of God (4:2). He had reasoned that since God is compassionate and would not destroy Ninevah, he didn't need to preach repentance to them. In the same way today Christians rationalize that God won't judge the heathen, and so we don't need to send missionaries to them (but more of that next chapter).

The impact of exile and dispersion

In the main Israel failed to be that "kingdom of priests," the channel through which "all the families of the earth" would be blessed. They failed to be the true 'Jehovah's witnesses' because of compromise with the idolatrous religion and immorality of the very people they were to reach. So God judged Israel and Judah with exile in Assyria and Babylon, the fountainhead of idolatry and immorality. This began a dispersion of the Jews which seemed to have had a number of positive effects: 1) It cured them of idolatry. 2) It forced them to establish synagogues for the study and exposition of God's word. 3) It forced them into situations where the godly remnant did bear powerful witness to the true God.

The book of Daniel is an excellent example of the last of these. In chapter 1 we see young Daniel's and his companions' uncompromising stand for God in resisting attempts of the Babylonians to paganize them. Then in subsequent chapters their stand is vindicated by God's revelations and supernatural interventions on their behalf before the successive rulers of world empires — Nebuchadnezzar, Belshazzar, Darius, and Cyrus. As a government official in those empires, Daniel's testimony for the LORD must have been widely known. The book of Daniel probably became part of the official archives of the Persian empire, because centuries later the Magian wise men came from the eastern empire looking for the "King of the Jews." They probably had been studying the prophecy of Daniel 9:24-27 which gives the time of the Messiah's advent. So Daniel's testimony seems to have carried down the centuries. The book of Esther also is a story of the testimony by life of a young Jewish woman in the pagan Persian empire of a later period which eventuated in the preservation of the Jewish people from extinction.

After the return from captivity of a remnant of Jews, a majority remained in dispersion, increasingly scattered in many diverse Gentile nations. Out of this came the Septuagint Greek translation of the Old Testament in the third century before Christ and the establishment of synagogues in major cities of the ancient world. It is clear that many Gentiles attended synagogue services and came under the reading and teaching of the word of God. The statement of the Apostle James at the Jerusalem Council (about A.D. 50) confirms this fact: "For Moses from ancient generations has in every city those who preach him, since he is read in the synagogues every Sabbath" (Acts 15:21). We find numerous references in the book of Acts to the "God-fearing Gentiles" who attended synagogue services but had not yet converted to Judaism. They were inquirers after the Jewish faith. (They were also very responsive to Paul's preaching.) Apparently the Pharisees of Christ's time were very missionary minded because Christ accused them thus: "You travel about on sea and land to make one proselyte; and when he becomes one, you make him twice as much a son of hell as yourselves" (Matt. 23:15). Apparently their zeal was good even though their message was corrupted with legalism and hypocrisy. All of this does give clear indication that after the Babylonian captivity the Jews did engage in much more overt missionary activity than we might suspect from reading the Old Testament alone.

CONCLUSION

Does the Old Testament give evidence of a missionary message, a global purpose, and missionary activity? We believe the answer is a resounding "yes." The God of Abraham, Isaac, and Jacob was not a Jewish God in any sense. The universality of his concerns and purpose in calling Israel shines through very clearly. Even if the Jews didn't usually remember this, the essential fact is not at all negated. The God of the Old Testament was the Creator of all mankind, Who chose Israel to be His missionary nation for the salvation of all nations. Israel's ultimate failure, however, was in crucifying the Lord of glory. Following that, the missionary commission was transferred to the New Testament church.

STUDY SHEET #1
THE DOMINANT THEME OF THE OLD TESTAMENT

The nation Israel and many Christians have misread the OT as a basis for a self-centered racial favoritism. But as we trace through the theme of the OT we find that God's purpose for the salvation of the whole human race shines through clearly. These study questions seek to focus on that central purpose.

1. The first reference to God making a covenant with man in the OT is found in Gen. 9:8,9. What is significant about the identity of Noah? Was he Jewish?

2. When God chose Abram, did He turn His back on the other nations of mankind? Gen. 10:1-20.
    What was God's purpose in choosing Abram (Gen.12:1-3; 22:15-18) and through him a race? Gen. 26:1-4; 28:10-14

3. What prophetic insight was dying Jacob given regarding the purpose of God in sending His Messiah? Gen. 49:10 (Notice the plural usage in modern translations.)

4. Trace God's purpose through every stage of His dealings with Israel:
    a. in redeeming them out of Egypt? Exod. 9:16
    b. in making a covenant with them at Sinai? Exod. 19:5-6
    What would be the point of having a whole kingdom of priests?
    c. in their failure at Kadesh? Num. 14:20-24
    Was Caleb a Jew? Josh. 14:14; Gen. 15:19

5. What was the place of Gentiles in Israel? Num. 9:14; Lev. 17:8; Ex. 22:21
    What significance might there be in the fact that 4 Gentiles from early Israelite history are included in the genealogy of Christ? (Tamar, Rahab, Ruth, & Bathsheba) Mt. 1:3-6

6. Many Psalms spoke of God's concern for the whole world, of Israel as the channel of God's blessing to the nations, and of the ultimate conversion of the nations. Distinguish which of the following passages speak of God's rule over the nations and which emphasize salvation for the nations of the world. Ps. 2; 22:27; 67; 86:9-10; 96:1-13; 98

7. What did Solomon understand the purpose of the temple to be?
    1 Kings 8:41-43.
    What significance can be seen in the way Isaiah designates the temple?
    Isa. 56:6-8.
    What did Solomon understand would be a means by which Gentiles would receive blessing? 2 Chron. 6:32-3

8. Give examples of God's care for others outside of Israel.
    I Kings 17:9ff; 2 Kings 5:1ff

9. What was Isaiah's understanding of Israel's function in regard to bringing salvation to the nations? Isa. 42:1,6,7; 43:10, 45.22; 49:6; 52:10

10. Why did God so forcefully send Jonah to Ninevah? Jonah 4:11

11. The Babylonian captivity is an indication of Israel's failure. How did God work in this to give witness to Gentiles? Dan. 2:27-8,47 What personal characteristics can you see in Daniel which qualified him to be God's instrument? Dan. 1

12. How does one predictive theme of the prophets reveal God's concern for the nations? Isa. 2:2-3; Micah 4:1-4; Mal. 1:11

13. After the return from captivity a majority of Jews remained in the dispersion, translating the Scriptures into Greek and establishing synagogues all over the world. To what extent would it seem that they gave a witness to the true God? Acts 15:21; 17:4,17; Mt. 23:15

14. From your study thus far, summarize the dominant theme of the Old Testament.

---

1. Cook, *Introduction*, p. 51. The sequence of topics here is taken from this most perceptive treatment by Cook.

2. Benjamin Mazar, Michael Avi-Yonah, and Abraham Malamat, eds. *Illustrated Family Encyclopedia of the Living Bible* (Chicago: San Francisco Productions, 1967) 1:38-39.

3. Alexander Hislop has traced the archaeological and documentary evidence for this in his book, *The Two Babylons* (1943), pp. 21-40.

4. Winter, "The Long Look: Eras of Missions History" in *Perspectives*, (1981), p. 168.

5. J. Herbert Kane, *Christian Missions in Biblical Perspective* (1976), p. 27.

6. Peters, *Biblical Theology*, p. 116; p. 128.

7. Ibid., p. 22 (Peters' diagram modified somewhat).

"I have other sheep which are not of this fold,
I must bring them also, . . . and they shall
become one flock with one shepherd."

John 10:16

THE JEWISH MESSIAH'S
GLOBAL PLANS DISCLOSED

What part does global evangelism play in the ministry and teaching of
the Lord Jesus Christ? Some might have the impression that it is only
found in the 'Great Commission', which seems to them like an afterthought to His ministry since it is mentioned only after His resurrection.
Don Richardson put it directly: "Millions of us deep down in our hearts
secretly believe, if our deeds are an accurate barometer of our beliefs
(and Scripture says they are), that Jesus really uttered that awesome
command without giving the disciples ample warning."[1]

To further complicate matters, Christ's ministry and teaching, especially in the three Synoptic Gospels, seem to be very Jewish and limited
to God's chosen people Israel. He never traveled far from the borders of
Israel. In a sense we have the same problem that we discussed in the
Old Testament chapter, and in a sense the answer is similar too. That is,
how can there be a world-wide program when God has chosen to deal
primarily with one nation for two thousand years? Simply put the answer
is that Israel was to be God's channel to bring salvation to the nations.
And the Gospel records show us that Christ first had to give opportunity
to Israel to fulfill their mission, and only then could He turn to the
Gentiles upon their rejection of Him.

So as we look at the Gospel records, our task is threefold: 1) to observe the intimations in the preparation for His ministry that He was
indeed "Savior of the world," 2) to seek to understand the universality of
His earthly ministry as it relates to His own Jewish people, and 3) to
examine the various forms of the 'Great Commission' to focus our
thinking about them.

GLOBAL PURPOSE IN THE
PREPARATION FOR THE MESSIAH

Matthew and Luke both record many revelations from God relating to

Messiah's birth and preparation Most relate to Israel; a few hint at the universality of Messiah's ministry. Simeon was a godly Jew, who based upon Old Testament promises, was looking for the Messiah's coming The Holy Spirit not only assured him that he personally would see the Messiah, but also gave him a prophetic revelation about Him: "For my eyes have seen Thy salvation, which Thou hast prepared in the presence of **all peoples, a light of revelation to the gentiles,** and the glory of Thy people Israel" (Luke 2:30-32). Simeon was simply referring to (in the boldface words) one of the many Old Testament prophecies which highlight Messiah's relation to the Gentiles.

Thirty years later when John 'the Baptizer' began his ministry as herald of the Messiah-King, he identified himself as the "voice of one crying in the wilderness" of Isaiah 40:3, and the Gospel writers quote that prophecy to the effect that **"all flesh shall see the salvation of God"** (Luke 3:4-6). Some months later when the Lord Jesus actually began His ministry by being baptized by John, John twice referred to the Lord Jesus as "the Lamb of God who takes away the sin of the world!" (John 1:29,36) Although neither of these statements is explained, they are among the earliest intimations of the global dimension of Messiah's ministry.

CHRIST'S OWN INDICATIONS
OF A GLOBAL PURPOSE

In ministry to Gentiles

In the beginning of Christ's ministry, He visited Jerusalem and asserted His Messianic authority by cleansing the temple of the moneychangers who had infested the outer 'Court of the Gentiles' (John 2:13-22). Mark records (11:17) how a second time at the end of His ministry Christ again cleansed the temple, quoting Isaiah 56:7 as an explanation of His actions: "'Is it not written, **my house shall be called a house of prayer for all nations'?** But you have made it a **robbers' den.'"** The global purpose of the temple had been buried under the crooked commercialization of the outer court. George Peters states: "The indifference and callousness of Israel in relation to the religious plight of the nations, and her utter neglect and abandonment of any mission toward the nations of the world become consuming motives in the seeming violent reaction of Christ to religious ceremonialism and performances devoid of compassion for the spiritual well-being of others."[2]

Although most of Christ's ministry for almost three years was devoted to His own people Israel, there are a number of significant incidents in His early ministry in which He showed compassion upon Gentiles. The fourth chapter of John describes his extraordinary trip through Samaria, the conversion of the woman at the well, and through her witness the conversion of many other Samaritans also. When we remember that the Samaritans were despised half-breed Jews whose religion was also 'half-breed', we can understand how radical this ministry was.

We also read about the Roman Centurion who sent prominent Jews to Christ to ask Him to heal his servant. The Lord's comment is devastating:

> Truly I say to you, I have not found such great faith with anyone in Israel. And I say to you, that many shall come from east and west and recline at the table with Abraham, and Isaac, and Jacob, in the kingdom of heaven, but the sons of the kingdom shall be cast out into the outer darkness; in that place there shall be weeping and gnashing of teeth (Matt. 8:10-11).

Not only did Christ meet this Gentile's need, but He contrasted his great faith with the unbelief of Israel in most dramatic language.
On a number of occasions Christ's ministry brought Him to the borders of Israel, where He ministered to Gentiles. Across the Sea of Galilee were the ten Greek cities called Decapolis. Christ exorcised a legion of demons from a man in the Gerasene area, who was probably a Gentile (Mark 5:1-20). He healed a deaf man in Decapolis, and He fed the multitude of 4000 men plus women and children in Decapolis. In the region of Tyre and Sidon in Phoenicia, He cast out a demon from a Gentile woman's daughter (Mark 7:24-37). There were probably many other similar unrecorded incidents.

In His teaching

Although we have noted that the focus of the first part of Christ's ministry was to the Jews, there are strong intimations of a universal thrust to His teaching. One hint comes in the favorite title that the Lord Jesus used of Himself. More than forty times in the Gospels Christ used the title, 'son of man'.[3] Although it is a special Messianic title drawn from Daniel 7:13-14, it also clearly indicates His identification with all humanity, not just the Jews. He could have used the title, 'son of David', and others used it of Him, but He preferred 'son of man'.

At the beginning of His ministry, Christ went back to His hometown of Nazareth and after reading from Isaiah 61 in the synagogue, He claimed to be the fulfillment of this Messianic prophecy (Luke 4:16-30). When they struggled to understand how this local carpenter's son could make such a claim, He rebuked them by stressing how Elijah went to the Gentile widow of Zarephath and how the only leper that Elisha healed was Namaan the Syrian. This 'put down' of the Jews and reference to God's blessing on two Gentiles so infuriated the local people that they tried to kill the Lord. Their problem was that they were too Jewish. Because of their prejudice, they had no use for Gentile 'dogs.' The Lord Jesus made His point almost too well, didn't He?

In the Sermon on the Mount, He reminded Israel that they were to be
the "salt of the earth" and the "light of the world." He then proceeded to
show the Rabbinic misinterpretations and distortions of the Law which
kept them from being such. In Mark 14:9 He made reference to the
gospel being preached throughout the whole world. His parable of the
good Samaritan praises the conduct of a non-Jew and put the Jewish
religious leaders in a bad light (Luke 10:29-37). In Luke 13:28-29 He
repeats similar words to that commendation of Gentiles he had uttered
in connection with the Centurion's servant. In the parable of the great
feast in Luke 14:10-24 He spoke about a universal invitation to be
extended. In the parable of the wheat and the tares (Matt. 13:36-43) the
field in which the sowing takes place is neither Israel nor the church, but
He clearly declares it to be "the world."

In the Gospels' descriptions of Him

The Gospel according to the Apostle John contains the most universal
descriptions of Christ. In the Prologue he describes Him as "the true light
which, coming into the world, enlightens all mankind" (John 1:9, own
trans.).[a] John also records the words of the Samaritan converts in John
4:42 that He is indeed "the Savior of the world." In the bread of life discourse Christ claimed to be the "bread of God which . . . gives life to the
world" (6:33). He also claimed to be the "light of the world" (John 8:12),
come to "save the world" (12:47). He promised that the Holy Spirit
would come and "convict the world of sin, of righteousness, and of
judgment" (16:8). In His high priestly prayer He prays that "the world
may believe that Thou didst send Me" (17:21).

The transition from Israel to the Church

It should be noted that the most universal language of Christ comes
after His rejection by Israel as He begins speaking consistently in more
universal terms only in the last few months of His ministry. There is not
a precise turning point, but rather a fairly gradual shift of focus from
presenting Himself to Israel as their King in the first years of His ministry,
to predicting his passion at Jerusalem and speaking of the church in this
connection.   We must note several new things as Donald Grey
Barnhouse pointed out long ago:[4]

1) Matt. 11:20 - "Then He **began** to reproach the cities in which most
of His miracles were done, because they did not repent." He especially

---

[a] It is surprising that none of the common translations have recognized that
panta anthropon can easily be translated 'all mankind' in the generic sense, thus
resolving theological difficulties very simply. Obviously Christ's light has not
reached every individual human being.

excoriated Capernaum, Chorazin, and Bethsaida, because the greatest abundance of miracles occurred there.

2) Matt. 11:28 - "Come unto Me, all who are weary and heavy-laden, and I will give you rest." This is His first universal invitation extended to all.

3) Matt. 13:10-17, 34-35 - Christ **began** using parables, which He explained as "mysteries of the kingdom,"--new things "hidden since the foundation of the world." This includes an age of the sowing of the word of God in the field of the world, preceding the judgment of saved and lost.

4) Matt. 16:19 - ". . . upon this rock I will build my church." The first reference to the church in the Gospels.

5) Matt. 16:21 - "From that time Jesus Christ **began** to show His disciples that He must go to Jerusalem, and suffer many things from the elders and chief priests and scribes, and be killed, and be raised up on the third day." This is the first of a dozen prophecies of His passion given in just the last six to nine months of His ministry. The astounding truth is that for almost three years of His ministry, Christ never explicitly mentioned His impending death until Caesarea Philippi.[b]

6) Matt. 20:28 - "just as the Son of Man did not come to be served, but to serve, and to give His life a ransom for many." This is the first explanation of the meaning of His impending death: a ransom for many.

Problem Passages. So we should not be surprised if the universality of Christ's ministry does not shine through clearly until the last few months. This helps us to explain some of the difficult statements Christ made before the transition, which seem so narrowly Jewish.

One difficult statement was given on the occasion when He sent out His twelve apostles as ambassadors to His own nation Israel. "'Do not go in the way of the Gentiles, and do not enter any city of the Samaritans; but rather go to the lost sheep of the house of Israel. And as you go, preach, saying, 'The kingdom of heaven is at hand'" (Matt. 10:5-6). It was because He had a responsibility to Israel first, that He so limited the ministry of the Twelve. Israel was to be the channel of God's message to the world, but they had to be won first. He couldn't turn to the Gentiles until He had first given them opportunity to respond to the kingdom message.

The second difficult passage explained by this transition is the story of the Syrophoenician woman recorded in Matt. 15:21-28. His answer to pleas for the healing of her daughter seems very narrow: "I was sent only to the lost sheep of the house of Israel." We all recognize that He was testing her faith, and she passed with flying colors. However, His words

---

[b] This is not because it was an afterthought, but clearly God's eternal plan. It would have been inappropriate to speak of it earlier, before His rejection by Israel was crystal clear.

were intrinsically true at that point in time. He was not free to devote Himself to the Gentiles until He had fulfilled His responsibility to Israel. And of course, He did heal her daughter.

Intimations after the transition

In those last few months of His ministry after the Lord Jesus began to predict His death and resurrection and the church based upon it, His language turns more consistently universal and His global plans are more explicit. In the Good Shepherd discourse of John ten, for example, He makes reference to "other sheep, which are not of this fold." He goes on to state: "I must bring them also, and they shall hear My voice; and they shall become one flock with one shepherd" (John 10:16). The interpretation is straightforward. His Jewish disciples comprised "this fold." The other sheep which were not of "this fold" must be Samaritan and Gentile believers. Christ's plan was to unify both Jewish and Gentile sheep into one sheepfold. This was fulfilled potentially on the Day of Pentecost, when the Holy Spirit was given to baptize all believers into one body, the church (1 Cor. 12:13). The full historical fulfillment came a few years later with the incorporation of Samaritans (Acts 8) and Gentiles (Acts 10-11).

The apostle John also records an incident which took place at the beginning of passion week. Some Gentiles (Greeks), who had already become inquirers into Judaism to the extent that they had come to Jerusalem to worship at Passover, wanted to see the Lord. When Andrew and Philip told Him about it, the Lord made extensive comments which are best understood in the light of this Gentile inquiry. In John 12:23-24 He spoke about His glorification by reference to a grain of wheat having to die to bear much fruit. Indeed, that fruit, over the centuries, has been predominantly Gentile. Then He went on to say: "And I, if I be lifted up from the earth, will draw all men to Myself" (12:32). The phrase "all men" in the original Greek language can mean 'all kinds of men' or 'all mankind.' It also is an obvious reference to salvation going out to the Gentiles after His death since the context is the key to interpretation.

About that same time during passion week, the Lord had a heated discussion with the leaders of Israel. He gave them the parable of the landowner who leased a vineyard to some vinegrowers who mistreated and killed his slaves and finally killed his son (Matt. 21:33-46). As He applied this to His own situation, He said: "Therefore I say to you, the kingdom of God will be taken away from you, and be given to a nation producing the fruit of it" (21:43). Here the Lord is very explicit about this transition from Israel to the Gentiles in the plan of God. It was clearly caused by the rejection of the "chief cornerstone" by the leaders of Israel, which was a part of God's eternal plan.

A few days later the disciples' awe at the beauty of the temple building occasioned the extended prophetic sermon called the Olivet Discourse. As Christ described the end-time events related to His second coming He stated: "And this gospel of the kingdom shall be preached in the whole world for a witness to all the nations, and then the end shall come" (Matt. 24:14). Quite apart from the issue as to the exact time frame of this prediction in reference to the rapture of the church, it is clear that Christ predicted global evangelism of all the nations (*ethnē* = ethnic peoples). He could not have been more explicit. In that same discourse He describes Himself as the King, who after His return to earth, will judge the living nations (*ethne*) by separating the sheep from the goats (Matt. 25:31-46). This scene presupposes the evangelization of the nations just mentioned in the previous chapter.

Thus it should be abundantly clear that the Lord Jesus did not drop the 'Great Commission' on the apostles like a bolt out of the blue. He gave them ample warning. Nevertheless, they did not understand or obey immediately. But let us go on to examine the five forms of the commission itself.

THE AGE-LONG IMPERATIVE OF
THE GREATEST COMMISSION

It was appropriate that the Lord Jesus should reserve His direct command to the church to evangelize the world to the brief space of forty days between His resurrection and His ascension into heaven. It is clear that if He had given it to His apostles before the cross, they would not have understood it in the least. He made that clear in John 16:12 when He said, "I have many more things to say to you, but you cannot bear them now." It was only after He was crucified and risen from the dead that they might to a small extent understand this commission. This was the greatest burden upon His heart which He had to share with the apostles during those forty days of post-resurrection ministry. Thus about half of all the recorded words of Christ in this period comprise some form of the 'Great Commission.' It is found in different forms in all four Gospel records and in Acts one, just before His ascension.

The evening of resurrection day

The first time that Christ revealed Himself to His assembled apostles was in a locked room on the evening after His resurrection, as recorded in Luke 24:36-43, John 20:19-23, and possibly Mark 16:14-20b. After He showed them the wounds in His hands and feet, he ate some food in their midst, and said, "Peace be with you; as the Father has sent Me, I also send you" (John 20:21). Here Christ constituted them as missionaries. Just as He left heaven's "ivory palaces" to come into the foreign culture of sinful human existence, now He sends them out into foreign cultures as missionaries (sent ones). Christ then mentions the provision of the Holy Spirit, which was the necessary empowerment for the task.

Mark's account

It is possible that the account of Mark 16:14-15 refers to the same occasion just referred to in John 20. In any case, Christ's words here would be a further clarification: "Go into all the world and preach the gospel to all creation." Now it is more than a statement of God's purpose, it is a direct command in no uncertain language. The two imperatives are to 'go' and to 'preach' or 'proclaim' the gospel. There has been some question raised about the text of these last verses of Mark, but we will not belabor our study with that issue. Suffice it to say that the reality of the Great Commission is not dependent upon Mark's account alone. This reference does provide additional color to the account. Some also might wonder about Christ's use of the word 'creation' ("creature" -KJV). This term normally refers to all created beings, but is also used in the limited sense of 'mankind.'

On a mountain in Galilee

Matthew's record gives the most familiar form of the 'Great Commission.' It also is a direct imperative command: "All authority has been given to Me in heaven and on earth. Go therefore and make disciples of all the nations, baptizing them in the name of the Father and the Son and the Holy Spirit, teaching them to observe all that I commanded you; and lo, I am with you always, even to the end of the age" (Matt. 28:18-20). Note that first the Lord referred to the authority which makes this command binding upon us—the Father gave Him all authority. When we consider who He is—the Creator and Lord of the universe—it should make a vast difference in our response! His command is to be obeyed. Secondly, we should note that there is one verb in the imperative in the original language (make disciples); the others are participles which modify the action of the main verb. The essential thing, therefore, is to make disciples. In order to make disciples of all nations, it will be necessary first to 'go' to them. In connection with making disciples, we are also to baptize them and teach them obedience to all of Christ's word. Thus it seems clear that making disciples involves more than evangelism, although this is the first step. Thirdly, we note that He backed up His command with the promise of His presence (through the Holy Spirit). We noted that same promise in John 20:21-22 and will see it again in Luke 24:47-48 and Acts 1:8.

At this point it would be helpful to mention a most important misinterpretation of the Great Commission, which became current in the years after the Protestant Reformation. This misinterpretation (which we will put in historical context in ch. 8) was that the Great Commission was only given to the Apostles, who fulfilled it in the first generation of the church. Therefore, if the heathen are lost, it is their own fault, and we have no responsibility for their lostness. This apparently became the majority Protestant view for over two hundred years after Luther and Calvin, even though this was not necessarily the view of Luther and Calvin themselves, but rather of their successors.

How do we know that this is a misinterpretation? The answer is very obvious in Christ's words. Since we are to make disciples of all the nations and He promises His presence to the end of the age (lit. 'all the days'), it seems clear that this command must be operative and valid through the whole church age. There are nations (*ethnē* = ethnic peoples) which were not in existence when the apostles evangelized. They could not have reached all the ethnic and linguistic groups now spread throughout the world, and in point of fact they did not. It is a gross historical error to say that the apostles evangelized the whole world in the first generation. In any case, it is clear that Christians of each generation have to reach the people of their own generation. Nobody else can reach them. They are our responsibility.

His parting words to the apostles

Luke's record of Christ's last words to His apostles before ascending on high are not in the form of a direct command:

> Thus it is written, that the Christ should suffer and rise again from the dead the third day; and that repentance for forgiveness of sins should be proclaimed in His name to all the nations, beginning from Jerusalem. You are witnesses of these things. And behold, I am sending forth the promise of My Father upon you; but you are to stay in the city until you are clothed with power from on high (Luke 24:46-48).

He had been speaking about the things of Old Testament prophecy which must necessarily be fulfilled. The proclamation of repentance for the forgiveness of sins is just as necessary as His death and resurrection, if people are to be saved. That is the logic of His statement. Then He simply tells them that they are witnesses of these things. There was no other option for them. Since here also He referred to the proclamation to all nations, this responsibility devolves to us also in our own generation. In this context also He promised the Spirit's power to fulfill this otherwise 'mission impossible'. This promise was, of course, fulfilled on the day of Pentecost.

Luke's second book, the Acts of the Apostles, fills in the words of the Lord on this occasion which Luke had not included in his Gospel. The words of Acts 1:8 amplify the geographical dimensions of this commission. He left no doubt that God's plan went beyond Jerusalem and Judea, and even Samaria, to the "remotest part of the earth." Thus the command of the Lord does involve geography: being sent out to the remotest parts of the earth. Although "crossing an ocean never made a missionary," it surely is an essential part of God's global plan.

Even though all forms of the commission are not imperative commands, it makes little difference. Luke and John record predictive statements of Christ, not commands. But the difference is a mere technicality. We noted in Luke 24 that Christ mentions the necessary things in God's plan to fulfill prophecy. But since it is God who expresses His desire, to use the old phrase, "His wish is our command." Remember how one of King David's soldiers risked his life to fulfill David's wish for water from the spring under Saul's control. So because Christ is a divine person with divine authority, His wish should be our command. Thus the central importance of the commission is confirmed by the central place given to it. And yet as George Peters says, "While it does not create new duties for Christianity, it sharply focuses the missionary thrust and responsibility of Christianity beyond reasonable doubt and disputing."[5]

CONCLUSION

There is, therefore, no ambiguity about the global nature of Christ's purposes, plans, and ministry. It shines clearly through the whole of the Gospel accounts. We only fail to see it because of the attention Christ had to give to His own nation Israel in the first part of His ministry. Attempts to rationalize away the force and present applicability of the Great Commission do violence to the whole thrust of our Savior's ministry. Let us move on to see the way in which the church that He founded on the day of Pentecost was able to fulfill His worldwide program.

STUDY SHEET #2:
CHRIST'S WORLDWIDE PURPOSE

The New Testament is the outgrowth, fulfillment, and expansion of the Old as to God's redemptive purpose on a world-wide scale. Although Christ first focused His attention upon His own people Israel before His apostles could ultimately turn to the whole world of gentiles, there are strong indications, from the very beginning, of God's purpose for the salvation of all peoples and nations, not just Israel. This study traces the expanding development of the outworking of God's worldwide program.

1. What expectation of God's purpose for His newborn Messiah did godly Jews such as Simeon have? Luke 2:30-32.
    From where did he get this expectation?

2.   In introducing Christ to the nation Israel, what hint did John the Baptist give as to the scope of His ministry? John 1:29

3. Although Christ came first to His own nation Israel, He repeatedly declared the ultimate purpose of His coming. How does He express that purpose in His

dealings with the Centurion? Matt. 8:5-13
(What was a Centurion? Who were the "sons of the kingdom?")

4. In Mt. 12:17-21 Matthew quotes Isa. 42:1-4 in reference to Christ's ministry. What was his purpose(s) in doing so?

5. How is God's purpose expressed in Christ's description of the two sheepfolds in John 10:16? (What do they represent?)

6. How does the occasion on which Christ's words in Jn. 12:32 were spoken help to clarify their full significance? (Note Amplified Version: "attract all men [Gentile as well as Jew] to Myself.") See 12:20 for the context.

The explicit command for world evangelization had to await Christ's rejection by His own nation and His turning to the Gentiles at the end of His ministry. Thus it is at the close of each of the four Gospels and in the beginning of the book of Acts that we find the five records of the Great Commission. Compare these passages to get the common element in all. Mt. 28:18-20; Mk. 16:15; Lk. 24:45-48; Jn. 20:21; Acts 1:8. Put them together to get a combined commission.

7. Of the five occurrences of this Great Commission, which are commands? Which are prophecies? What connection is there between a command and a prophecy?

8. At what point in the ministry of Christ were these statements given? What significance does this give to the importance of the Great Commission?

9. Some have excused themselves from carrying out the Great Commission by saying that Christ's command was limited to the eleven apostles, although they do accept other commands of Christ as binding upon us today (Mt. 26:26; Jn. 15:12). What is there in Christ's words in Mt. 28:19-20 which makes it clear that Christ was not limiting His command to the immediate hearers?

10. What provision did Christ make for carrying out God's plan throughout the world? Acts 1:8

Perspectives reading enrichment: chapters A-10 & A-11.

---

1. Don Richardson, "A Man for All Peoples," in *Perspectives*, p. 83.

2. Peters, *Biblical Theology*, p. 49.

3. H. Cornell Goerner, "Jesus and the Gentiles," in *Perspectives*, p. 78.

4. Donald Grey Barnhouse, *His Own Received Him Not, But . . . : The Turning Point in the Ministry of Christ* (Revell, 1933), pp. 77-185. (A little known but germinal work by this renowned expositor.)

5. Peters, *Biblical Theology*, p. 174.

TEN SPIRIT-DIRECTED STEPS TO GLOBAL EVANGELISM

	Further MISSIONARY TOURS	GREECE: Cultural Center	EPHESUS: Religious Center	ROME: Political Center
TEN Acts 16 - 28	Further MISSION-ARY TOURS			
NINE Acts 15:1-31	JERUSALEM COUNCIL	JERUSALEM	OFFICIAL Confirmation of Direct Gentile Salvation	
EIGHT Acts 14:1-23	Idolatrous PAGANS Converted	S. Galatia: Iconium, Lystra, Derbe	Door of Faith Fully Opened (14:27)	Gentile Churches Planted.
SEVEN Acts 13:14-43	Devout GENTILES Converted	Synagogue of Pisidian Antioch	Bridgehead into the GENTILE World	A Responsive People
SIX Acts 13:1-3	PAUL and BARNABAS SENT	ANTIOCH of Syria	First Cross-Cultural MISSIONARIES	First Missionary Journey Begun
FIVE Act 11:19-26;13:1-3	ANTIOCH CHURCH	GENTILES Integrated into the Church	First Missionary-Sending Church	
FOUR Acts 10:1—11:18	CORNELIUS and Household	CAESAREA	Door of Faith Opened to GENTILES	Third Use of Keys by Apostle Peter
THREE Acts 8:26-40	ETHIOPIAN EUNUCH	PROSELYTE Converted	Physically GENTILE; religiously JEWISH	Probably founded church in Ethiopia
TWO Acts 8:1-25	SAMARITANS	HALF-JEWISH Converted	Follow-up of John 4	Confirmed by Peter's use of keys
ONE Acts 2	PENTECOST at Jerusalem	Diaspora JEWS Converted	CHURCH Founded & Converts dispersed	GENTILE Languages Spoken

"And He said to me, Go! For I will send you far away to the Gentiles."

-Acts 22:21

". . . the Gentiles, to whom I am sending you, to open their eyes so that they may turn from darkness to light and from the dominion of Satan to God, in order that they may receive forgiveness of sins and an inheritance among those who have been sanctified by faith in Me."

-Acts 26:17b-18

HIS CHURCH BRIDGES THE CHASM

Following the ascension of the Lord Jesus to heaven and His last charge to them just before His departure, His apostles struggled with a genuine "Mission Impossible." Their leader had been crucified like a common criminal; their treasurer had betrayed Him and committed suicide; their chief spokesman had denied that he had even known Him; and the rest were a sorry lot of scattered cowards. The task of witnessing to their own Jewish nation was itself formidable. After all, the powerful leaders had conspired to foment Christ's incredibly unjust execution, and now they were probably searching for His followers as well. But Christ had commissioned them to be witnesses to all the nations, not just Israel. As 'kosher' Palestinian Jews it must have seemed out of the question to them.

Since the Lord had alerted them to a momentous event about to happen in a week, and since Jews from all over the world were even now arriving in Jerusalem to celebrate the ancient feast of Pentecost at that time, the Apostles and over a hundred other disciples continually devoted themselves to prayer. God's sovereign plan to establish Christ's church and His apostles' obedience to Him met together in the momentous events of the day of Pentecost.

Pentecost was the first and foundational event in a sequence of ten Spirit-directed steps which were necessary to fully bridge the incredible gap between twelve Palestinian Jewish apostles and the raw pagan Gentile world they were to reach. These were: 1) opening the door of faith to Israel on the day of Pentecost; 2) opening the door of faith to the Samaritans (Acts 8); 3) the winning of Jewish proselytes like the Ethiopian official; 4) the winning of Gentile Cornelius (Acts 10); 5) the founding of the integrated Antioch church (Acts 11); 6) the sending out of the first cross-cultural missionaries (Acts 13); 7) the winning of many devout Gentiles (Acts 13); 8) the winning of idolatrous pagans (Acts 14); 9) the

Jerusalem Council decision regarding Gentile salvation (Acts 15); and 10) additional missionary tours into the cultural, religious, and political centers of the Roman Empire.[1] As we survey the book of Acts, these ten steps should stand out in our thinking. (All Scripture references are to the book of Acts, unless designated otherwise.)

THE POWER OF PENTECOST: A NEW MISSIONARY INSTRUMENT IS BORN

The events recorded in the second chapter of the book of Acts are in many ways just as significant and earthshaking as the events surrounding Christ's birth at Bethlehem. Yes, God had come to dwell among men in the person of the Lord Jesus. But before His departure Christ promised that the Father would send another Encourager, the Holy Spirit (John 14:17). As the Third Person of the Trinity, the Spirit's descent meant as real an advent of God among men as was the incarnation of Christ at Bethlehem. Therefore, it is imperative for us to seek to understand the full meaning of this climactic event, especially in its implication for missions.

Not only did the Holy Spirit come to indwell that new humanity, the church, which began on that eventful day, but the essential missionary nature of that church was signalled right from the beginning by the supernatural gift of languages given to the Apostles. God began to do a number of radically new things on that day, and among them was the foundation of this age-long cross-cultural witness to all the peoples of the earth.

The Holy Spirit's new ministries

Spirit baptism constituted the church. Many interpreters rightly link the references to Spirit baptism occurring for the first time on Pentecost with the important teaching that Pentecost was also the birthday of the church, which was intended to unite Jew and Gentile (Matt. 16:18; Acts 1:4-5; 1 Cor. 12:13). Baptism communicates identification, and by Spirit baptism the disciples were identified with the Lord as members of His body, the church. Christ had said, "I will build my church" (Matt. 16:18).

The Spirit-filled disciples' bold witness of His resurrection. In addition to Spirit-baptism, the disciples are also said to have been filled with the Spirit on the day of Pentecost and many times after that (Acts 2:4; 4:8, 31, 33; 5:32; 6:5; 8:55). In these early chapter of Acts, Luke connects the fullness of the Spirit and the boldness of their witness to Christ's resurrection. The resurrection was the unique aspect of the gospel message, and the Spirit-filled disciples were enabled to proclaim it with great boldness. Since the Spirit's ministry of conviction (Jn. 16:8-11) and regeneration (Jn. 3:3-5) are the keys to evangelism, it was essential that these witnesses be Spirit-filled (Eph. 5:18).

The missionary purpose of the church reaffirmed by the sign of diverse ethnic languages. The so-called gift of 'tongues' has been widely misunderstood and abused. Cutting through all the controversy surrounding it, it seems clear that the diaspora or overseas Jews heard the gospel in their own vernacular and dialect from the lips of the Apostles as a supernatural sign that God was now doing a wholly new work. Because Israel had rejected their Messiah, God had set Israel aside and has instituted the church to reach out to people of every tongue, tribe, and nation. Although the hearers were Jews from many lands (sixteen are mentioned in 2:9-11), God spoke to them through the languages of the Gentiles. This was a reversal of the confounding of the languages at the tower of Babel thousands of years before. The worldwide purpose revealed to Israel and then enunciated clearly by the Lord Jesus, was now being prefigured in this important sign. Peter, in quoting Joel 2 in his sermon, intimates the global dimension of Pentecost: ". . .that I will pour forth of My Spirit upon all mankind" (2:17). Later the Apostle Paul confirmed that tongues (languages) were a sign to unbelieving Israel (1 Cor. 14:20-22).

HOW GOD'S 'KEY MAN' OPENED
THE DOORS OF FAITH

The Apostle Peter's part in the events of Pentecost does not merely reflect his role as the natural spokesman for the group; Christ specifically commissioned him to open the door of faith to the nation Israel. At Caesarea Philippi some months earlier, when speaking of building His church, Christ had given Peter the keys of the kingdom of heaven, not of heaven itself (Matt. 16:19). Peter used those keys on three occasions, the first of which was on the day of Pentecost. Three thousand Jews entered the church because Peter opened the door of faith to Jewish people. And for a number of years only Jewish people were hearing and responding to the gospel of Christ.

Don Richardson has gotten to the root of the problem: "Hundreds of millions of Christians think that Luke's Acts of the Apostles records the twelve apostles' obedience to the Great Commission. Actually it records their reluctance to obey it."[2] Christ could not have made it clearer in the Great Commission; He had furnished abundant examples by showing compassion to Gentile individuals like the Roman centurion, the Syrophoenician mother, the Samaritan leper, and a Gadarene demoniac. Why did the Apostles not catch on for a dozen or more years? To understand this we have to understand how Pharisaic prejudice against Gentiles dominated Jewish thinking. They had been brainwashed!

The Samaritan breakthrough

Two incidents recorded in Acts chapter eight began the breakthrough toward the Gentiles. It was Philip, the Greek-speaking Jewish deacon, who started preaching the gospel to the Samaritans. The Jews were especially contemptuous of the Samaritans, since they were half-breeds both ethnically and religiously. Even though Christ had witnessed to the Samaritan woman at the well and through her to the people of Sychar, the Apostles' prejudice was difficult to overcome. Peter's failure to follow through in witness to the Samaritans really complicated things. Peter had the keys, but it was Philip who began to push the door open! Samaritans were beginning to profess Christ and be baptized, and yet the door had not been officially opened!

This helps us to understand why Peter and John had to come down from Jerusalem: Peter had to officially open the door of faith to the Samaritans. This he did when he and John laid their hands upon them thus identifying them with the church, and Jewish Christians with Samaritan Christians. This was revolutionary! And God confirmed this with some external sign of the giving of the Holy Spirit (possibly the sign of languages). God was now demonstrably in the business of saving Samaritans as well as Jews! How radical it must have seemed to them!

A proselyte converted

Philip was also the instrument for another breakthrough, as Luke records in the last half of the eighth chapter. Philip led an Ethiopian court official to the Lord under most unusual circumstances. But here is a Gentile who wasn't a Gentile. He was a black Jew! Apparently a convert or proselyte to Judaism, he had gone up to Jerusalem to worship at the temple.[3] So here we have another step toward the Gentile world, but still not fully there. Presumably though he started the witness in Ethiopia.

The breakthrough to the Gentiles

Since Peter 'blew it' as far as the Samaritans were concerned, God made sure that he got to the right place at the right time for the third use of the keys. Acts ten is the pivotal chapter in Luke's development of the progressively growing outreach of the gospel culturally. God gave Peter a vision to prepare him for witness to Gentiles, and Cornelius' vision made sure that Peter got there. When Cornelius' messengers arrived Peter was already pondering the meaning of the vision of unclean animals he had seen. By the time he arrived at Cornelius' house he perceived that the vision had to do with his Jewish prejudice against Gentiles as unclean people (Acts 10:28-29). So he preached salvation to Cornelius and his Gentile friends, and they were immediately saved. Again the Spirit confirmed this reality by supernatural signs accompanying their conversion (diverse Gentile languages again) to indicate to these

Jewish Christians that God was really in this matter.

But the church leaders up in Jerusalem were not as easy to convince. They really gave Peter a hard time until he told them how the Holy Spirit confirmed his actions with supernatural signs (11:15-17). Only then did they swallow their prejudice and acknowledge that God really is in the business of saving Gentiles (11:18). They might also have realized that Peter had been given that authority of using the keys to open the door of faith to the Gentiles.

Even though the door was now wide open (since the word Gentile means all non-Jews), the bridge over the chasm was not yet complete for two reasons. First, Cornelius was a special kind of Gentile. He had been impressed with Judaism and prayed to the God of Israel. He was what Luke later referred to as a 'devout Greek' (Gentile). He had not yet taken the step of conversion to Judaism, but had abandoned idolatry by looking into the faith of Israel. So this breakthrough had not yet reached a raw pagan idolater. Secondly, we don't read anything about Cornelius' incorporation into the Jewish church there in Caesarea. Luke doesn't tell us. Possibly the Jewish Christians there just couldn't accept a Gentile. We don't know. But we do know what happened at Antioch.

THE CROSS-CULTURAL TRANSITION OF ACTS

Palestinian » Jews	Hellenic » Jews	Samaritans »	Proselytes »	"Devout" Gentiles	» Gentile Idolaters
Apostles	Pentecost	Samaria	Ethiopian	Cornelius	Lystra
Acts 1	2	8	8	10	14

"Devout" Gentiles were inquirers into Judaism who had already abandoned their idolatry.

THE UNIQUE CHURCH AT ANTIOCH

The first multi-ethnic church

Luke immediately tells about the founding of the unique Antioch church. It seems clear that neither the Jerusalem church nor the Caesarea church followed through on Cornelius' conversion with a program of Gentile evangelism. About a decade had passed since the church had begun, and it was still solidly Jewish! But some unnamed Hebrew Christians from Cyprus and Cyrene started evangelizing Gentiles when they came to Antioch of Syria (11:19-21).[4] The remarkable thing is that these Jews of the dispersion, now converted to Christ, were able to bridge the cultural gap to the Gentile world. They not only preached to the Gentiles but embraced them as fellow Christians and fellow members of the body of Christ. And wonder of wonders, they even ate with them!

This may have seemed somewhat threatening to the kosher Christians up in Jerusalem, so they sent down to Antioch a converted Levite named Joseph Barnabas to make sure that things did not get out of hand. But Barnabas could see that God was in this brand new venture and encouraged them in it. As a result many Gentiles were getting saved. So for the first time since the day of Pentecost the reality of the one body was being realized—Jew and Gentile alike baptized by the Spirit into the body of Christ (1 Cor. 12:13; Eph. 3:2-6). In this connection Luke mentions that the disciples were first called Christians at Antioch. The people could see that this was not just some splinter sect of Judaism; it was a whole new entity.

The first missionary-sending church

It was not the Jerusalem church which sent out the first cross-cultural missionaries to the Gentiles; it was Antioch. It seems clear that their multi-ethnic, cosmopolitan character helped the Antioch church become the first to obey the Great Commission by sending out the first missionary team. Not only had they proved that Gentiles could be incorporated into the church; they had also proved that Gentiles could be won to Christ in substantial numbers. Indeed, this may have been a serious obstacle in the minds of many Jewish Christians in Judea: Is it really possible that more than a token number of these raw pagans could be converted? Is it really worth the while? What kind of Christians will these converted heathen become?[a] But these doubts were soon resolved for the Antioch church. Many of these converted pagans had become exemplary Christians, and some had even become leaders in the church (13:1).

These Gentile Christians had relatives scattered all over the empire who needed to have a chance to hear the Gospel.[5] So it was only a natural outgrowth of the Antioch church's multi-ethnic nature that they should pray for their lost relatives. And God intervened in their prayer meeting as the Holy Spirit explicitly told them whom to send out as missionaries (13:2-3). It was the two men whom God had used the most in their midst. They sent out the best that they had! Just as we saw in the beginning of the church, so now again; God's sovereign plan for world evangelism was worked out as God's people sought Him in prayer.

Remember that Paul had been called as a missionary to Gentiles at his conversion. Now over a decade later the Antioch church by the Holy Spirit confirmed that calling. Even though this was a radically new ven-

---

[a] William Carey struggled with similar questions from skeptical English Christians almost eighteen centuries later. Not only were there theological misconceptions, but most did not believe that heathen could be won because they thought them too depraved!

ture, the apostles were well prepared for the task. Even though they had been in Christian ministry for many years, now as they are **sent** out to other countries, the true nature of the missionary (apostle=sent one) is seen. But before we continue our consideration of the ten Spirit-directed steps, let us think for a while about the unique place of Saul of Tarsus.

THE UNIQUE MINISTRY OF THE APOSTLE PAUL

Why was the Apostle Paul so important to the early church? Luke records the story of his conversion in three different contexts (chapters 9, 22, 26). The answer comes through very clearly, not only in the three conversion accounts, but also in the nature of Paul's three missionary journeys and trip to Rome recorded in such detail.

The conversion of the principal enemy of Christianity has long been recognized as a powerful testimony to the truth of the gospel and the power of God. However, adequate attention has not been paid to one thing which is emphasized in all three accounts of the conversion of Saul of Tarsus: that God had chosen him as a unique means for the winning of the Gentiles to faith in Christ.

> "He is a chosen instrument of Mine, to bear My name before the Gentiles and kings and the sons of Israel" (Acts 9:15). And He said to me, "Go! For I will send you far away to the Gentiles" (22:21). "For this purpose I have appeared to you, to appoint you a minister and a witness not only of the things which you have seen, but also to the things in which I will appear to you; delivering you from the Jewish people and from the Gentiles, to whom I am sending you, to open their eyes so that they may turn from darkness to light and from the dominion of Satan to God" (26:16-18).

The Bible does not tell us why God 'leapfrogged' the twelve apostles to choose the Apostle Paul. A decade had gone by without the apostles following through on the commission to evangelize the Gentiles. Perhaps the cultural gap was too great for these Palestinian Jews to bridge. Later there was a perception that the Twelve should go to the Jews, and that Paul and Barnabas should go to the Gentiles (Gal. 2:7-9). However, there are indications outside of the Bible that John Mark did go to Egypt, the Apostle John to Asia Minor, and Thomas to Persia and India.

There may be a number of factors, natural and spiritual, which account for Paul's tremendous effectiveness as the first cross-cultural missionary of the gospel. Saul was raised as a bicultural person. He referred to himself as a "Hebrew of the Hebrews," which he was. But Saul was also raised in the Gentile city of Tarsus, and his sermons show considerable familiarity with Greek literature and culture. Barnabas also was raised in the Gentile culture of Cyprus (4:36). We know that Saul became the hard-driving leader of the opposition to Christianity in the Jewish community. He had sparked the persecution! And God used that same drive in his missionary ministry. Another important qualification Paul had was Roman citizenship. This put him among an elite group who could claim the protection of Roman law. As far as the spiritual factors are concerned, we know that Paul emphasized the grace of God and the importance of spiritual gifts in serving God.

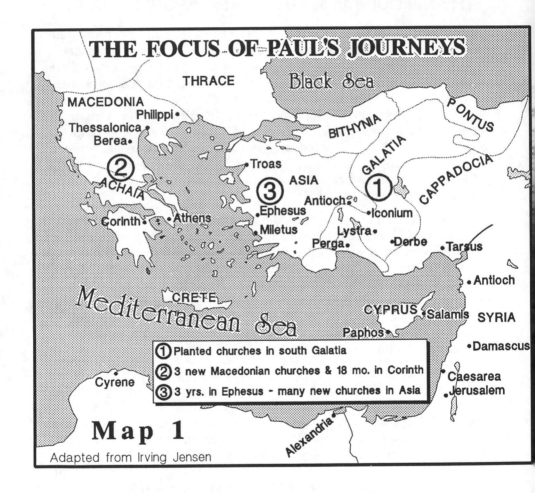

THE FOCUS OF PAUL'S JOURNEYS

THRACE — Black Sea

MACEDONIA
Philippi
Thessalonica
Berea
② ACHAIA
Corinth · Athens
Troas
③ ASIA
Ephesus
Miletus
Perga
Lystra · Derbe · Tarsus

BITHYNIA — PONTUS
GALATIA — CAPPADOCIA
Antioch · Iconium

CRETE
Mediterranean Sea
CYPRUS · Salamis SYRIA
Paphos
· Antioch
· Damascus

Cyrene
Caesarea
Jerusalem

① Planted churches in south Galatia
② 3 new Macedonian churches & 18 mo. in Corinth
③ 3 yrs. in Ephesus - many new churches in Asia

Map 1
Adapted from Irving Jensen

Alexandria

THE FIRST MISSIONARY TEAMS
PENETRATE THE GENTILE WORLD

Luke devotes half of the book of Acts to Paul's missionary journeys, so they are obviously of prime importance in our understanding of the out-working of God's plan. Now that a model of integration of Jew and Gentile existed in the Antioch church, the missionaries could seek to reproduce such churches around the empire. The first journey was

somewhat exploratory — the apostles never got very far from home territory. But it laid the foundation for more extensive and venturesome trips
and confirmed that God had indeed "opened a door of faith to the Gentiles" (14:27). This raised a crucial theological problem in the church
which was settled in the Jerusalem council: whether Gentiles shouldn't
first convert to Judaism before they could properly be part of the church.

The door of faith opened

Barnabas and Saul had no missionary experience. They had proved
themselves in evangelism, exhortation, and teaching. But no one could
tell them what to do on this first missionary tour. There were no
handbooks on missions to consult. So we should not be surprised that
this first trip was somewhat exploratory and tentative. The fact is that the
apostles never did get very far from home territory on that first attempt.
Cyprus was Barnabas's original home, and the South Galatian area of
Asia Minor they evangelized after that wasn't that far from Paul's home
town of Tarsus. As we noted before, there may have been some motivation to reach relatives in these areas. The cultural gap, however, did
become very great by the time they got to Lystra, as we shall see.

To the Jew first. The apostles first stop was Salamis on the island of
Cyprus. Quite understandably they headed for the easiest place which
could serve as a bridgehead—the Jewish synagogue. This became their
practice in every town where there were Jews. Indeed, some have
suggested that they headed especially for towns where there was a
synagogue. Even though commissioned as the apostle to the Gentiles,
Paul keenly sensed his responsibility to his own people Israel (Rom.
9-11). The apostles practiced "to the Jew first" (Rom. 1:16). This proved
to be a wise strategy, as we shall see. It is probably not a coincidence
that in Reformation history we note that failure to evangelize Jews has
been linked with failure to reach the Gentiles. (For a fuller discussion
see chapter 8.)

Following an evangelistic tour of Cyprus the apostles sailed to Pamphylia on the coast of Asia Minor. Luke does not explain why John Mark
left the missionary team. He was a young man from Jerusalem, which
may help explain his dropping out. Is it possible that he was the first
missionary to experience culture shock? He probably was quite 'kosher'
and found the totally pagan idolatrous culture of Pamphylia too much to
take. We are happy to report that he was one missionary dropout who
overcame the setback, wrote our second Gospel, and was later com-
mended highly by Paul (2 Tim. 4:11).

Breakthrough among proselytes in Pisidian synagogue. When the
apostles got to Pisidian (not Syrian) Antioch, they followed the strategy
developed on Cyprus of going first into the synagogue. Since Paul was a
rabbi and Barnabas a Levite, they had good opportunity to speak. Not

only did many Jews believe but also many Gentile converts to Judaism ("Godfearing proselytes" 13:43). These people had been impressed with the monotheism of Judaism and heard the Old Testament read in the synagogue every Sabbath, but were not yet bound in the traditionalism of the Pharisees. Thus they were 'raw meat' for the gospel of Christ. This became a major bridge into the Gentile community in most of the cities where the apostles preached.

On subsequent missionary tours, Luke mentions another distinct category of people who responded to the gospel in great numbers. These were the "**Godfearing Greeks**" (Gentiles), multitudes of whom believed in Thessalonica (17:4). These were the Gentiles who, like Cornelius, had abandoned their idolatry and immorality and started attending synagogue services. They were inquirers after Judaism. In one way they were even more open to the gospel since they had not yet made a commitment to Judaism by submitting to circumcision and proselyte immersion.

Planting churches among Galatian idolaters. But it was there in Lystra of Asia Minor that the Gospel was put to the most rigorous test. Paul and Barnabas got caught in the middle of a mob of idolaters who thought them to be Greek gods come down among men, because they had healed a lame man. The apostles didn't understand the local Lycaonian language and only belatedly perceived that the mob was about to make animal sacrifice to them as gods. This was the most extreme cross-cultural situation the apostles had faced. But in each of the towns of that area, pagans turned to Christ and churches were founded, even where there were no synagogues. Timothy was a half- Jewish young man won during that tour. So the apostles proved that cross-cultural evangelism among the most extreme idolaters was not only possible but greatly successful. When they reported back to the Antioch church, they all rejoiced how "He had opened a door of faith to the Gentiles" (14:27).

The issue of Gentile salvation settled

The apostles' missionary success occasioned a potentially divisive dispute (15:1-31). Some legalistically minded Hebrew Christians from Judea insisted that Gentiles had to convert to Judaism first **before** they could become Christians. They argued that Gentile converts should be circumcised and keep the Jewish Mosaic Law in order to be saved. They apparently did not understand the implications of salvation by grace through faith. But when the apostles and elders met with the Jerusalem church to decide the matter, direct Gentile salvation was confirmed. Peter argued that Cornelius' household was saved by simple faith, and the yoke of the Law should not be put upon Gentile converts. This decision was of great importance for the success and soundness of future missionary efforts. It laid the doctrinal foundation for further missionary work and put a stamp of approval upon the work Barnabas and Paul had started.

Churches planted in the cultural centers of Greece

On his second missionary journey the Apostle Paul and his growing team of new missionaries launched out into a whole new area--right to the cultural heart of the Empire. At first they went back to Southern Galatia to confirm the churches founded on the first tour. But as they moved outward to Greece, Paul and Silas picked up some new missionary workers, namely Timothy and Luke, one half-Jewish and the other an educated Gentile.

Multiplication by disagreement. The disagreement between Barnabas and Paul over John Mark led to two missionary teams going in different directions (15:36-41). God sovereignly overruled human foibles to expand the fledgling missionary endeavor. (This continues to happen today in the multiplication of mission boards.) Paul's choice of Silas, a leader from the Jerusalem church and a prophet (15:22, 32), not only began a fruitful relationship, but also began a pattern of Paul's co-opting new members for his missionary team. At Lystra Paul recruited Timothy, a young convert from the first tour (16:1-3). Then at Troas he recruited Luke the physician (16:10). There is some likelihood that he was a brother of Titus, a Gentile whom Paul brought back to Jerusalem after the first tour (Gal. 2:1-3).[6] If that is so, it would support the possibility that Luke also came to Christ as the outcome of the first missionary tour. After a couple years' ministry in Greece, Paul brought a Jewish couple, Priscilla and Aquila, from Corinth and left them as a witness in the Asian city of Ephesus. In a real sense they also were part of his missionary team.

The Macedonian vision. One of the most striking and significant events of Paul's missionary journeys was the vision of a Macedonian man Paul received at Troas (16:6-10). The Holy Spirit had guided the team not to spend more time in the Phrygian part of Galatia, where churches had been planted on the first journey, nor to evangelize the provinces of Asia, Bithynia, or Mysia, but to move on to Troas. The vision confirmed that leading onward and brought them at first to Macedonia and ultimately to the Greek province of Achaia, where they had an extensive ministry of over a year and a half (18:11). But why did God move them westward? Luke does not tell us. However a number of things can be said.

Clearly God wanted them to move onward to new territory, rather than doubling back to Bithynia. Apparently God had other plans for the evangelization of Bithynia because we know that the church was planted there early. Since the dominant culture of the Roman empire was still strongly Greek, we might surmise that the Lord wanted the missionaries to attack the cultural centers of Greece more boldly with the gospel. After planting many churches in Macedonia and leaving a witness in Athens, Paul focused on Corinth, where his ministry involved the dramatic conversions of two successive synagogue rulers, Crispus and Sosthenes (18:8, 17).

It is even clearer that the vision was not a 'missionary call,' since Paul and his companions were already missionaries. It was, however, a clear example of the fact that although Paul had a strategy, he was sensitive to the ongoing leading of the Holy Spirit and ready to abandon his plans for God's. Some have drawn the unjustified inference that God wanted Europe evangelized before Asia. It is true that this event tilted Paul's ministry westward and eventually affected all of Europe. But we know that God does not discriminate according to race or on an ethnic basis (10:34-5). We also know from church history that the gospel did spread eastward quite early through the witness of other Christians (1 Pet. 1:1).[7] One further thing should be noted from the record of the ministry in Greece. Whenever they went into the synagogues or places of prayer to reach Jews, they continued to get a great response from the **Godfearing (devout) Greeks** like Lydia in Philippi (16:14). Luke mentions it again in Thessalonica (17:4), in Berea (17:12), and in Athens (17:17). This was an important bridge to the Gentile world.

An expanded team plants
a church in an idol center.

Amid all the details of the three missionary tours, it is easy to lose the overview perspective that just as they spent most of the time on the first tour in south Galatia, and on the second tour in Greece, just so the missionary band spent the most time on the third trip in Ephesus (see map no. 1), and thus evangelized the whole province of Asia effectively (19:10, 26). Ephesus was one of the great cities of the empire and proved to be a strategic city. It was also the center for worship of the fertility goddess Artemis, with its massive temple.

On this third tour we note a continuance of Paul's practice of enlarging his team. At one point Paul sent Timothy and Erastus to Macedonia, whom Luke describes as "two of those who ministered to him" (19:22). When the riot occurred over the silversmiths' agitation, they dragged Gaius and Aristarchus into the amphitheater, whom Luke describes as "Paul's traveling companions from Macedonia" (19:29). When Paul himself went onward to Macedonia and Greece, we are told that "he was accompanied by Sopater of Berea, the son of Pyrrhus; and by Aristarchus and Secundus of the Thessalonians; and Gaius of Derbe, and Timothy; and Tychicus and Trophimus of Asia" (20:4). It is obvious by now that Paul was not a freelance individualist, but rather the leader of an effective team, two dozen of whom can be identified. Other names can be gleaned from the epistles (see ch. 21).

A prisoner evangelizes the imperial capital

Even the story of Paul's return to Jerusalem, his arrest and defenses, and his trip as a prisoner to Rome, all have a vital missionary interest at the core. Paul's principal motive for going back to Jerusalem oblivious to the warnings was the overriding concern to bind together the integrated churches from Gentile lands with the Jewish churches of Judea. The offering from the Gentile churches to the Jewish churches was intended to reinforce the unity of the body of Christ.

Paul's arrest occasioned many opportunities both to witness for Christ and to testify as to the supernatural nature of his missionary mandate (22:21; 26:16-18). Most striking are the key government officials to whom Paul was privileged to witness: not only the Jewish mob outside the temple, but before the very Sanhedrin itself; Governor Felix, his successor Portius Festus, King Agrippa, and ultimately before Caesar himself. Although Paul did not get to Rome as part of a missionary journey as he intended, his witness there in Rome was most effective. While his case was pending, he lived in his own rented quarters under house arrest, "and was welcoming all who came to him, preaching the kingdom of God and teaching concerning the Lord Jesus Christ with all openness, unhindered" (28:30-31). Even some of the Praetorian Guard, to whom he was chained, came to faith in Christ (Phil. 1:12-14). It seems probable that when his accusers did not arrive to press charges that Paul was released for additional missionary tours as indicated by his first letter to Timothy and that to Titus. We believe he fulfilled his ambition to evangelize Spain (Rom. 15:23). He did plant churches on the island of Crete (Titus 1:5) and probably elsewhere before his second arrest, trial, and execution at the command of Nero.

Communicating Christ's commission to his converts

The Apostle Paul not only was a model missionary for the church, but he also sought to communicate his burden for world evangelism to his converts both by word and by his letters. When he met with the Ephesian elders on his way to Jerusalem, he shared his great burden for cross-cultural evangelism: ". . . how I did not shrink from declaring to you anything that was profitable, and teaching you publically and from house to house, solemnly testifying to both Jews and Greeks of repentance toward God and faith in our Lord Jesus Christ" (Acts 20:18-35, esp. 20-21). Writing to the church in Corinth, he also shared this burden:

> For if I preach the gospel, I have nothing to boast of, for I am un-
> der compulsion; for woe is me if I do not preach the gospel, for if
> I do this voluntarily, I have a reward; but if against my will, I have

> a stewardship entrusted to me. . . .And to the Jews I became as a
> Jew, that I might win Jews; . . . to those who are without law
> [Gentiles], as without law, though not being without the law of
> God but under the law of Christ, that I might win those who are
> without law. . . . I have become all things to **all men,** that I may by
> all means save some (1 Cor. 9:16-22).

Paul was culturally flexible in order to win all kinds of people, yet without bending on the absolutes of God's revealed eternal word.

Later when he wrote to the **Romans** from Corinth, he expressed that
burden for people of every ethnic group and status in at least three passages: "For I have a great sense of obligation to people in our culture
and to people in other cultures, to the educated and uneducated alike.
So I am eager to come to you in Rome, too, to preach God's Good News"
(Rom. 1:14-15 NLB). In 10:12-17 he gave the soteriological basis (the
doctrine of salvation) for his concern for the salvation of all mankind:

> For there is no distinction between Jew and Greek; for the same
> *Lord* is Lord of all, abounding in riches for all who call upon Him;
> for "Whoever will call upon the name of the Lord will be saved."
> How then shall they call upon Him in whom they have not be-
> lieved? And how shall they believe in Him whom they have not
> heard? And how shall they hear without a preacher? And how
> they they preach unless they are sent? . . . So faith comes from
> hearing and hearing by the word of Christ.

And then in 15:20, 23-4 he shared his compelling ambition: "And thus I
aspired to preach the gospel, not where Christ was already named, that
I might not build upon another man's foundation. . . but now, with no
further place for me in these regions, . . .whenever I go to Spain—."
Then in 1 Timothy 2:1-6, and in 2 Corinthians 5:17-21 he showed the
implications of Christ's substitutionary death—that we are Christ's substitutes here in this world, his ambassadors. Just as Paul shared this responsibility with his converts, missionaries of every generation must
share it with their converts.

John's vision. The Apostle John was given the privilege to see the
outcome of all of this, which he recorded in the book of the Revelation.
In chapter seven he describes a great multitude of martyred saints in
heaven in the end- time drama: "After these things I looked, and behold,
a great multitude, which no one could count, from every nation and all
tribes and peoples and tongues, standing before the throne and before
the Lamb, clothed in white robes, and palm branches were in their
hands; and they cry out with a loud voice, saying, 'Salvation to our God
who sits on the throne, and to the Lamb'" (Rev. 7:9-10). Yes, that is
God's ultimate purpose in this age: that people of every ethnic group
should have opportunity to hear the gospel, believe, and be saved.

STUDY SHEET #3
THE WORLDWIDE PURPOSE OF THE CHURCH

1. Consider the whole book of Acts as the outgrowth of Acts 1:8 and show the progressive outreach from beginning to the end of the book. Jerusalem: Ch. 1--7 (5:28); Judea and Samaria: 8--12 (8:1,4); to the uttermost parts of the earth: 13--28 (Asia Minor, 13--15; Greece, 16--18; western Asia Minor, 19--21; onward to Rome, 22--28). Compare 28:28.

2. How would you characterize the first drive following Pentecost to fulfill the Great Commission? Acts 2:32, 39, 41, 47; 4:4, 33; 5:14, 29-32, 42; 6:7.

3. What two new dimensions are represented by Philip's ministry in Acts 8? (Who were the Samaritans?
    What is significant about the Ethiopian Eunuch?)

4. How does the activity of the disciples when they were scattered abroad show the central purpose of their lives? Acts 8:4, 25,40. Why might they have ceased witnessing for Christ? Acts 8:1

5. What was God's purpose in giving a special calling to Saul of Tarsus (Paul)? Acts 9:15

6. When did Paul begin his witness for Christ? Acts 9:20 How far did his witness take him? Acts 26:19-23 & Romans 15:18-20

7. How did God reaffirm and clarify His purpose to the Apostle Peter? Acts 10:9-17,34-35 And through him to the church leaders? 11:1-18. What was the major barrier to their understanding of God's purpose?

8. In what sense did the apostolic church fail to fulfill God's purpose for a number of years after the birthday of the church on Pentecost? Acts 11:19

9. Who were the first to follow through on this most important purpose of God? Acts 11:20 (Note the correct rendering "Greeks".)

10. What was the result of the broadened vision of the church at Antioch? Acts 13:1-3

11. Although the book of Acts highlights the witness of the apostles (missionaries), show how Paul's instruction to new Christians spreads the responsibility for witness to them also. Rom. 10:13-15; 2 Cor. 5:18-20; Eph. 4:7, 11; Phil. 2:15-16.

12. What is the extent of God's invitation as expressed in Rom. 10:12-13?

13. How did Paul's ambition in Rom. 15:17-24 affect the spread of the Gospel?

14. How did Paul express the ultimate purpose of Christ's ransom?
    1 Tim. 2:5-6. Upon what is it based? 2:1-4.

15. What part of Paul's words to the Ephesian elders expresses his great burden to fulfill the Great Commission? Acts 20:18-35. Was Paul present when the Great Commission was given?

16. In what way did Paul express this great burden he felt?

1 Cor. 9:16-22; Rom. 1:14-16.

17. To what extent did Paul go to obey the Lord's command?
2 Cor. 11:23-28

18. How is the culmination (consummation) of God's purpose to be fulfilled in Rev. 7:9-10?

19. How does Rev. 21:3-7 fulfill God's purpose in creating man? (Compare Gen. 1:26-30.)

20. There is considerable confusion in Christendom today as to the place of evangelism in missions. Many have substituted political activism, a "social gospel," economic development, and many other things for evangelism. What did the Apostle Paul put central in his ministry? 1 Cor. 1:18, 23; 2:2.

21. In the Jerusalem Council the Apostle James summarized the primary objective of the church in this age as recorded in Acts 15:14. What is it to be?

22. How important is the content of the message? Gal. 1:6-9. Sum up the elements of the gospel as Paul gives them in 1 Cor. 15:1-4. (Acts 3:15; 4:10; 5:30-32; 16:31; Rom. 1:1-4; 10:9-10; 1 Thess. 4:14; 2 Tim. 1:8-10; 2:8)

"Shall I spend my life for the purpose of world evangelization? . . .

This is a decision we do not make, because it has already been made. Whether we spend our lives for the purpose of reaching all men with the Gospel is not optional. Christ has commanded every Christian to do just this. . . .Now there are many different ways of accomplishing this one purpose. . . But, regardless of the particular work God has for each of us to do, the one aim of us all in doing our particular job for the Lord must be the evangelization of the whole world."

(G. Allen Fleece)

Perspectives enrichment: chapters A-12 through A-15

1. Cook, *Introduction*, pp. 36ff. suggests five such steps. I have modified and expanded his concept.

2. Don Richardson, "The Hidden Message of 'Acts'" in *Perspectives,* p. 89.

3. As a eunuch he could not have been a fullfledged proselyte, but that is of minor significance here.

4. Although there are both translational and textual problems in 11:20, the context demands the rendering of most modern translations. It was not Greek -speaking Jews (Grecians) whom they began to evangelize; it was Gentiles!

5. Donald A. McGavran, *The Bridges of God* (1955), pp. 21-27. McGavran shows how the "bond of relationship was the bridge over which the faith passed" (p. 24).

6. C. Gordon Olson, "The Famine Visit and Pauline Chronology," a paper presented at the Evangelical Theological Society, Briarcliff Manor, NY, April 18, 1980. I follow Lightfoot's identification of Galatians 2 with the Jerusalem council of Acts 15 based upon strong chronological and other evidence.

7. J. Herbert Kane, *A Concise History of the Christian World Mission* (1978), pp. 11-12.

> "Behind the shameful apathy and lethargy of the church, that allows one thousand millions of human beings to go to their graves in ignorance of the Gospel, there lies a practical doubt, if not denial, of their lost condition."
> —A. T. Pierson

THE ONLY LIGHT IN THE DEADLY NIGHT

The central issue in understanding the biblical basis and motivation for Christian missions is the uniqueness of Christ and the gospel He gave to His apostles to proclaim throughout the world. If Christ is not uniquely the Savior of the world, then there is little point to Christian missions! If other religions have a true knowledge of God and salvation, then why bother to send missionaries to them? If there is salvation to be found apart from the sacrificial death of Christ, then missions is a tragic mistake —indeed, Christ's death itself was a tragic mistake! So the essential basis of world missions is the uniqueness of Christ and His gospel and the lostness of the unevangelized.

However, with the massive immigration of third-world peoples, our western culture is becoming increasingly pluralistic. In our society we must defer to the sensibilities of not only Roman Catholics, Jews, atheists, and agnostics, but now Muslims, Hindus and others as well. "In a pluralistic world it is becoming increasingly difficult to maintain the uniqueness of the Christian faith." Kane goes on to point up the problem:

> When we move into the non-Christian world, where the missionary has to operate, we find that the exclusive claims of Christianity are vigorously challenged by the non-Christian religions now undergoing an unprecedented resurgence. It is safe to say that the most offensive aspect of twentieth-century Christianity is its exclusiveness. Such a claim does not make sense to the Hindu, the Buddhist, or the Confucianist.[1]

The problem is not just outside the church. Even among evangelical Christians we find a serious erosion of biblical teaching in this regard. A number of surveys taken over the last twenty years indicate that a shockingly large percentage of Christians do not believe that Christ is the only way of salvation, and that the heathen are lost and will go to hell. A survey of Christian collegians attending the Urbana '67 missionary conference indicated that less than forty percent of the students, who were mostly from secular colleges, believed that a person not hearing the gospel is lost. Although in Christian colleges the picture is much better, there still is cause for concern. Richard Bailey's 1971 study showed that twenty-seven percent in Christian liberal arts colleges and nine percent in Bible colleges did **not** believe that the heathen are lost.[2] My own surveys of freshman Bible college students confirm that the situation has not improved in the intervening years, but has probably gotten worse.

How can Christians hold such views? Actually the problem has a long history. A third-century Alexandrian church father named Origen advocated universalism, which is the view that all men will ultimately return to God and be 'saved.' Over the centuries, however, this view never gained any popularity since his doctrine was deviant in other areas, and this so obviously goes counter to the Bible, the authority of which was not seriously questioned. In the last century or two, with the widespread attacks upon the authority of the Bible, universalism has been revived. Because of the connection between unitarianism (with its denial of Christ's deity) and universalism, the merged Universalist-Unitarian denomination is the major overt representative of this viewpoint. But there are many universalists in the old-line liberal denominations. Even among those who claim a more orthodox theology (Neo-orthodoxy) like Karl Barth, there has been a revival of universalism, which Robertson McQuilkin calls the "New Universalism." But it also is not based upon full acceptance of the authority of the Bible, as might be expected.

But even among those who more consistently acknowledge the authority of Scripture, there are those who, while admitting that not all will be saved, hold that the sincere seeker after truth who has not heard the gospel will not be condemned by God. Robertson McQuilkin calls this the "Wider Hope Theory." Even more recently some have adopted a variant of this, the "New Wider Hope Theory," which states that

> Those who live by the light they have will be saved on the merits of Christ's death. We recognize that this is a more conservative version of the New Universalism. It doesn't say that all will be saved on the merits of Christ, but that some may be saved on the merits of Christ through general revelation, apart from the special revelation of Scripture.[3]

A number of supposedly evangelical scholars have expressed such sentiments from time to time, but without any substantial defense of their viewpoint. It would seem to be fuzzy thinking arising from an emotional reaction rather than biblical fact. More recently Clark Pinnock and John Sanders have written and spoken extensively for this view, calling it "inclusivism."[4] It is very harmful in that it distorts Scripture and seriously undermines the missionary program of the church. Indeed a century ago a missions-minded pastor put it well: "Behind the shameful apathy and lethargy of the church, that allows one thousand millions of human beings to go to their graves in ignorance of the Gospel, there lies a practical doubt, if not denial, of their lost condition."[5] Since this was written a century ago the number has escalated to over three billion, but the root cause of the church's apathy has not changed. So it is imperative that we examine the uniqueness of the Christian faith, the lostness of non-Christian peoples, and the inclusivistic denials of these foundations.

THE UNIQUENESS OF CHRIST AND HIS GOSPEL

When we compare the Bible's statements with other religions, we find that Christ's claims are unique. Christ's person and work are also unique in backing up His unparalleled claims. The nature of the salvation He procured for us has no equal in the religions of the world—nothing even comes close!

The unique claims of Jesus
Christ and His apostles

The Lord Jesus claimed to be a unique person. He claimed to have come from eternal existence with God the Father in heaven. He claimed equality with God. He used titles of Himself which are appropriate only to God. He claimed to have the attributes, offices, and prerogatives of deity. He accepted worship as God. The apostles also referred to Him in the same unique ways. Most striking is the title used by the apostle John, which is translated in the Authorized Version as the "only begotten Son of God." The Greek word used here is *monogenes* which means "'in a class by himself,' 'the only one of his kind,' or in other words 'unique.'"[6] The NIV translates it as "His one and only Son."

In addition, Christ claimed to be the only Savior of the world. His most direct statement is in John 14:6, "Jesus said to him, 'I am the way, and the truth and the life; no one comes to the Father, but through Me.'" The apostle Peter confirmed this in his words to the Jewish leaders, "And there is salvation in no one else; for there is no other name under heaven that has been given among men, by which we must be saved" (Acts 4:12). Later the apostle Paul also added his testimony: "For there is one God, and one mediator also between God and men, the man Christ Jesus" (I Tim. 2:5). If people can be saved apart from Christ, then Christ and his apostles made false claims.[7]

Sometimes we overlook the obvious. The astounding fact is that no founder of any world religion even made claims that compare with the claims that Jesus Christ made. Thomas Schultz's statement stands out boldly:

Not one **recognized** religious leader, not Moses, Paul, Buddha, Mohammed, Confucius, etc., have [*sic*] ever claimed to be God; that is, with the exception of Jesus Christ. Christ is the only reli-

gious leader who has ever claimed to be deity and the only individual ever who has convinced a great portion of the world that He
is God.[8]

Although this statement is mind-boggling, it could have been made
even stronger. Some of the founders of world religions didn't even have
much to say about God at all. It seems that Gautama the Buddha, Confucius, and Lao Tse were essentially agnostics in the sense that they did
not claim to know God or concern themselves with Him. Some of the
religions, like Hinduism and Shinto, do not have identifiable founders.
The two who came closest to a biblical concept of God were Zoroaster
(Zarathustra) and Muhammad. Although Zoroaster may have gotten
some concepts of God correctly passed down from Noah's day, his
teachings were not written down until after Christ and those writings
were undoubtedly influenced by the Christian view. In any case Zoroastrianism is a dying religion today with few followers.[9] It is a well known
fact that Muhammad borrowed heavily from Jews and Christians and
modified the concept of God considerably, but we will go into that more
in chapter 13. In any case, none of them claimed sinlessness, deity, or
the ability to save mankind. Even if any had, none of them would have
been able to make their claims stick! Only Jesus the Messiah's claims
are substantiated by His person and work.

His life supports His claims.

When one makes a careful study of the religions of mankind, one
finds that there is no parallel to the person and work of the Lord Jesus.
There are over a hundred detailed prophecies of His first coming that
were fulfilled in His ministry.[10] Even though Isaac and John the Baptist
were miraculously born of aged parents to prepare humanity's minds for
the virgin birth, He was the only one in human history born of a virgin.
He alone lived a sinless life. He alone revealed a loving, personal and
holy Father-God with whom He had fellowship eternally. He confirmed
His claims to deity by His unique miracles of love and compassion. God
had confirmed the ministry of the Old Testament prophets by wonderful
miracles, but none of them compares with Christ's. He alone made predictive prophecies which are continuing to be fulfilled, including a dozen
of His own death and resurrection. And then He alone died as a sinless
sacrifice for sin, which was sealed by His bodily resurrection from the
tomb. His resurrection was not just a restoration of physical life, but His
post-resurrection appearances in a glorified body made it unique. He
alone ascended into heaven bodily with the promise to return in the
same way to establish His rule upon the earth. **Not one of these things
can be said for Zoroaster, Gautama the Buddha, Lao Tse, Confucius,
Guru Nanak, or Muhammad.**

His unique salvation

The uniqueness of the fall. Just as striking as the unparalleled person of Christ, so also is His plan of salvation. Careful study of other religions uncovers nothing like it in any of its major features. Indeed, we could say that none of the world religions have any plan of salvation at all from sin and the fall. This is understandable since none of them, including Judaism and Islam, have any concept of man as a fallen creature under the sway of sin. All religions view mankind as essentially good, imagining that salvation by God is not necessary. Hinduism's *moksha* (realization) has to do with release from the cycle of life. Gautama the Buddha's *nirvana* (oblivion) has to do with release from the sufferings of life. Zoroastrianism and Islam do have a concept of paradise after death, but it is attained by human merit, not by the work of God.

The uniqueness of grace. This brings us to the key difference between evangelical Christianity and all other religions—salvation by grace. All other religions are based upon human merit, not the grace of God. But grace means 'unmerited favor.' We cannot earn it! Only biblical Christianity teaches that God reaches down to save sinful man. All the other religions see man struggling upward to God. The Sikhs of India use the word for grace (*parshad*) a lot, but they, like adherents of other religions, are striving to please God by their own works. Even the cultic corruptions of Christianity depart from the truth in this essential point, whether it be Mormons, Jehovah's Witnesses, or whatever. Roman Catholics also overwork the word 'grace' but do not understand salvation by grace alone. The Catholic tries to merit God's grace by baptism, confirmation, confession, attendance at mass, good works, and last rites. But salvation is not by human merit: "For by grace you have been saved through faith; and that not of yourselves, it is the gift of God; not as a result of works, that no one should boast" (Eph. 2:8-9).

Forgiveness and assurance. All systems of meritorious salvation undermine two important things: the forgiveness of sin and the present assurance of eternal life. No one can know for sure about salvation as long as it is based upon human merit. Indeed, unless it is claimed by faith in Christ, any sense of forgiveness is a deception. Although various religions differ in details, they are alike in striving to merit God's favor. For example, a tradition of Islam states that when Muhammad was dying, his daughter Fatimah asked him to pray for her salvation. His reply was, "Daughter, my prayer will do you no good! Only your own works will save you!" Muslims deny the cross of Christ and His redemptive sacrifice as a basis for forgiveness. This is typical of all other religions. Erich Sauer has well summarized the confused diversity of man's religions:

> Heathenism as a whole rests not only on error and deceit, but at
> the same time also on a spiritistic foundation. . . Through all this

the heathen, under demon influence, became the "creator of his gods." . . .

The Grecian says   : Man, know thyself.
The Roman says   : Man, rule thyself.
The Chinese says   : Man, improve thyself.
The Buddhist says   : Man, annihilate thyself.
The Brahman says   : Man, merge thyself in the universal sum of all.
The Moslem says   : Man, submit thyself.
But Christ says   : "Without Me ye can do nothing,"
    and in HIM
the Christian says : "I can do all things through Christ
                        Who makes me mighty" (Phil. 4:13).

"In his religion the heathen expresses his **godlessness**. Religion is **the** sin, namely, the sin against the first command, the replacing of God by the gods;" "the most powerful expression of the opposition of man against God and contradiction within himself."[11]

An historical salvation. Christian salvation is also without equal in being based upon real, historical events that God wrought among men. Most of the oriental religions are filled with myths and legends about their many man-like gods. Shinto has its creation-myth. Hinduism has legends about Krishna and many other deities. We are not sure **whether** Lao Tse even existed. We really can't know **when** Zoroaster lived. But Christianity is a historical faith, based upon what God did in human history in the incarnation, ministry, and passion of Christ and the work of the Holy Spirit through the church. The human authors of the Bible frequently tied their narratives in with secular history. Archaeology can confirm the essential historicity of many events in the Bible. Islam makes the strongest claims of historicity among the religions. That doesn't matter much, however, since Muhammad claimed to be neither God nor Savior. He didn't claim to work any miracles or to have risen from the dead. It is even more astonishing to know that Muslims believe that Muhammad is buried in a tomb in Medina, whereas they believe that the 'prophet Jesus' is in heaven. Paradoxical, isn't it?

ARE THE HEATHEN REALLY LOST?

In order to answer this question intelligently we must first define the term, 'heathen'? The dictionary definition is, "an unconverted member of a people that does not acknowledge the God of the Bible; a pagan."[12] Actually the definition could be broadened to include any unchurched person in any country since there are pagans everywhere.

What do we mean by 'lost'?

People can be lost in many senses—geographically, intellectually, emotionally, etc. But what really counts is what God means by the word 'lost.' The Lord Jesus said that the basic purpose of His coming was "to seek and to save that which was **lost**" (Luke 19:10). The biblical picture is that man is lost in reference to God. The consequences of Adam's fall were devastating: all mankind became separated from God. Not only did Adam and Eve die spiritually when they sinned (Gen. 2:17), but they caused the whole human race to be born spiritually dead and under God's wrath, without hope and without God in the world, and alienated from the life of God (Eph. 2:1-3, 12; 4:18).

Eternally lost. Man is not only lost in that he is presently without God, but apart from Christ's salvation that separation becomes eternal death (Rom. 3:23; 6:23). It is the Lord Jesus Himself who had the most to say about eternal punishment. Herbert Kane well summarizes:

> The Bible clearly teaches that there are two destinies open to man. One involves everlasting happiness in the presence of God and the holy angels (Lk 15:10; Rev 22:3-5; 1 Thess 4:17), the other involves everlasting misery in the company of the devil and his angels (Mt 25:41). The New Testament speaks of two gates—one strait and the other wide; two ways—one broad and the other narrow; two destinies—one life and the other destruction (Mt 7:13-14). In the day of judgment the sheep will be separated from the goats (Mt 25:31-46), and the wheat from the tares (Mt 13:36-43), the good from the evil (Jn 5:29). And in the resurrection there will be a separation between the just and the unjust (Acts 24:15)[13]

Universal spiritual and physical death. The Bible is very clear about the universality of man's lost condition—none are exempted. Paul writes that God's law shuts every person's mouth, that all the world is guilty before God, and that "death spread to all men, **because all sinned**" (Rom. 3:19-20; 5:12). The aorist tense of the last verb is best understood as a reference to the fact that we all sinned in Adam, since the aorist tense looks at the action as a point in past time. The whole human race shared in the sin of Adam and shares spiritual and physical death because of that disobedience, not just because we sin. We sin because we are sinners. People are not becoming lost—they are already lost! "Whoever believes in Him is not condemned, but whoever does not believe stands condemned already because he has not believed in the name of God's one and only Son" (John 3:18 NIV). This is true both of people who reject the gospel and of those who have never heard the gospel. Unless people are saved through Christ, they will stay lost for eternity.

All mankind's need of salvation

The Lord Jesus made it abundantly clear that all men need to be saved. This was true of God's chosen people, the Jews. In commenting on people who had died suddenly and tragically, Christ said, "Unless you repent, you will all likewise perish" (Luke 13:5). Christ even told a very religious Jewish leader, Nicodemus, that he needed to be born again in order to enter the kingdom of God (John 3:5). If that was true of Nicodemus, it is certainly true of pagan peoples. The book of Acts records the conversion of the first pagan Gentiles, the Roman centurion Cornelius and his household (Acts 10:1—11:18). Even though Cornelius had already given up his Roman idolatry and prayed to the true God of Israel, yet the angel told Cornelius that when the Apostle Peter came he would speak words by which they would be saved (11:14). Even though this devout and sincere heathen's prayer was answered, he was not yet saved until he heard the message of salvation from Peter. The inclusivists would have us believe that Cornelius was a "pagan saint," already saved through general revelation. They ignore Cornelius' contact with the word of God through Judaism and Peter's explicit statement that they were to be saved through Peter's message.

On his second missionary journey the Apostle Paul had opportunity to preach the gospel to some very civilized and intellectual Greek philosophers in Athens. Note that universalists rationalize that Greek philosophy was as good a preparation for the gospel as the Old Testament and the inclusivists claim the Greeks had the truth of God through the Greek writers to which Paul alludes. However, Paul told them bluntly that, "God is now declaring to men that all everywhere should repent, because He has fixed a day in which He will judge the world in righteousness through a Man whom He has appointed, having furnished proof to all men by raising Him from the dead" (Acts 17:30-31). Later Paul explained that repentance in a limited Christian context when he described his ministry as "solemnly testifying to both Jews and Greeks of repentance toward God and faith in our Lord Jesus Christ" (Acts 20:21). He did not mean repentance within the context of any pagan religion, but only as it is linked with faith in Christ.

What about those who have never heard?

We have gone into considerable detail to show the clarity of Bible revelation about the universal and eternal nature of man's lostness apart from Christ because these are exactly the points that the various kinds of universalism and inclusivism deny. We have sought to show that God's condemnation comes to all men until they are saved by faith in Christ. It is clear that the universalists and inclusivists have to contradict the Bible to hold to salvation outside of personal faith in Christ. Indeed, they do not hold to inerrancy of Scripture. However, many would raise the valid question, "What about those who have never heard the gospel of Christ and had opportunity to believe and be saved? It isn't really fair of God to condemn them to hell, is it?"

The heathen have a revelation of God. It is not as if the heathen did not have any knowledge of God. The Apostle Paul mentions two kinds of revelation of God that all men have by nature, which we refer to as 'general revelation'. In Romans 1:18-25 he traces the reason for God's wrath falling upon the heathen. He points out that the heathen were not always heathen. They, like all of us, descended from Noah, who knew God. But they suppressed the truth in unrighteousness (1:18), didn't honor Him as God or thank Him, but in pride in their own wisdom indulged in foolish speculations (1:21-22). So generation after generation, they got farther away from the true knowledge of God and ultimately fell into idolatry and immorality (1:23-25) (probably at the Tower of Babel). Indeed, a number of pagan tribes have a tradition about once knowing God and His book, but having lost that knowledge.[14]

Paul also emphasized the fact that all men have been given a revelation of God in nature when he wrote:

Because that which is known about God is evident within them; for God made it evident to them. For since the creation of the world His invisible attributes, His eternal power and divine nature, have been clearly seen, being understood through what has been made, **so that they are without excuse** (Rom. 1:19-20).

There are a number of impressive arguments philosophers have used for thousands of years for the existence of God. The cosmological argument reasons from the fact that this universe clearly had a beginning and therefore a Creator (Aristotle's "Unmoved Mover"). The teleological argument reasons from design and order in creation to show that there must have been a 'Designer God'. God's hand in creation is obvious to the unprejudiced mind. The more we learn about nature through modern science, the more we see design and order. Most of the Moody Science film series is based upon the teleological argument. But we don't need modern science to see this. King David saw it three millenniums ago: "The heavens are telling of the glory of God; and their expanse is declaring the work of His hands. Day to day pours forth speech, and night to night reveals knowledge. . . . Their line has gone out through all the earth, and their utterance to the end of the world" (Ps. 19:1-4). The heathen "are without excuse," Paul concludes, because they repress the truth about God and don't worship Him.

A second type of revelation is the human conscience—the law of God written on the human heart. Paul argues that men do not have to possess the written law of God to come under condemnation:

For all who have sinned without the Law will also perish without the Law; and all who have sinned under the Law will be judged by the Law; . . . For when Gentiles who do not have the Law do instinctively the things of the Law, these, not having the Law, are a law to themselves, in that they show the work of the Law written in their hearts, their conscience bearing witness, and their thoughts alternately accusing or else defending them, on the day when, according to my gospel, God will judge the secrets of men through Christ Jesus (Rom. 2:12-16).

Although the human conscience is a marred and weak testimony to God and His Law, nevertheless man is responsible for its light. By it all men are condemned as sinners, since no one even lives up to his own conscience. Although God's general revelation in nature and human conscience is adequate to condemn men, there is no hint in the Bible that it is adequate for salvation. General revelation tells man nothing about God's plan of salvation. It is **our** responsibility to tell them. Inclusivists claim that general revelation is adequate for salvation without any explicit Scriptural proof of this notion.

God's holiness and judgment. Those who rationalize away God's judgment on heathen who have not heard usually appeal to God's love. "Could a God of love condemn the heathen?" they ask. But they forget God's holiness and wrath. Yes, God in His love gave His unique Son that whoever believes on Him should not perish (John 3:16). But the Bible has a lot to say about God's wrath and judgment upon sinners. Indeed it was Christ Himself who gave the fullest revelation about God's wrath and judgment (see the Kane quotation above). Remember that God's judgment is not based upon relative merit—as in the Muslim's concept of God's scales. One sin is enough to condemn us to hell. No man, heathen or nominal Christian, can be holy and righteous enough to escape condemnation (cf. Hab. 1:13). The inclusivists totally ignore the mass of Scripture which emphasize God's signal judgments upon mankind, such as the Noahic deluge which destroyed the whole human race, the judgment upon the idolatrous worship of the tower of Babel, the ten judgmental plagues upon the idolatrous worship of Egypt, the order to exterminate the idolatrous and immoral Canaanites, and the many prophecies in the prophets of God's coming judgments upon the pagan nations surrounding Israel.

However, it should also be pointed out that there are degrees of judgment in hell. The moral heathen will not be judged as severely as those who sin against greater light (Matt. 11:20-24). The parallel truth is that for believers there are degrees of reward for faithfulness (over and above salvation, which is by grace). God is fair and just!

Reductio ad absurdum. One useful way to examine the logic of a proposition is called *reductio ad absurdum,* which means reducing it to the absurd. If you start with the premise that only those who consciously reject the gospel will go to hell, you will see how absurd the conclusion comes out. If that were true (and it isn't), then missionaries would be bringing condemnation to most heathen who have not heard. The fact is that the majority of heathen who hear do not believe and get saved. Most reject the gospel. If that majority was not lost before the missionary came, then the missionary would have brought condemnation to more people than he brought salvation to. I was a missionary to a Muslim country. When I preached and witnessed to Muslims, very few accepted Christ to my knowledge. Thus I would have brought condemnation to most all I witnessed to. How absurd the whole missionary enterprise then becomes! Indeed, if many heathen were really seeking for the truth (as some maintain), why don't missionaries experience them believing upon the first hearing of the gospel. The fact is that most heathen (like most western 'Christians') have to hear time and again before they believe and are saved. This shows the effects of sin and depravity. The Apostle Paul spelled it out quite clearly, "And even if our gospel is veiled, it is veiled to those who are perishing, in whose case the god of this world has blinded the minds of the unbelieving, that they might not see the light of the gospel of the glory of Christ, who is the image of God" (2 Cor. 4:3-4).

This brings us to another dimension of the problem—Satanic and demonic involvement. Earlier in this chapter we showed that man's religions are not a help toward God. We must also note that religion is something Satan uses to keep men from knowing God. Paul expands on this: "But I say that the things which the Gentiles sacrifice, they sacrifice to demons, and not to God" (1 Cor. 10:20). Even apostate forms of Christianity are the Devil's tool to keep men from the true knowledge of God. In the Sermon on the Mount Christ put it bluntly:

> Beware of the false prophets, who come to you in sheep's clothing, but inwardly are ravenous wolves. . . . Not everyone who says to Me, "Lord, Lord," will enter the kingdom of heaven; but he who does the will of My Father who is in heaven. Many will say to Me on that day, "Lord, Lord, did we not prophesy in Your name, and in Your name cast out demons, and in Your name perform many miracles?" And then I will declare unto them, "I never knew you; *depart from me, you who practice lawlessness*" (Matt. 7:15, 21-23).

Objections answered

Isn't sincerity enough? It is granted that there are many sincere followers of other religions, and from the human point of view it might seem that God would honor that sincerity. The fact is that the Bible gives no hint that God is at all impressed with so-called sincerity. Our God is a God of truth. Other religions do not lead to the One God—they are all false (for further details see ch. 13). Both Cain and Abel were sincere in their worship, but God rejected Cain's offering because it wasn't according to truth. Cornelius, the Roman Centurion, was sincere, but he wasn't saved.

Illustrations of this from the medical world are frequently given. A patient may be given the wrong medicine very sincerely, but may die nevertheless. This is very personal to me because my brother died of polio because of the wrong advice of a doctor. He may have been well trained. I presume that he was sincere in telling my sister-in-law to keep him in bed at home, but he was sincerely wrong! The engineers who built those bridges which collapse in the wind or flood were probably very sincere. But people who die in such tragedies get no solace from their sincerity. If sincerity isn't enough in medicine or engineering, what indications do we have that it is enough in the far more important sphere of man's eternal destiny?

Is it really fair of God to condemn those who've never heard? Our problem so often is that we look at things from man's point of view and fail to see God's perspective—and that's the only one that counts! Remember that God would be fair and just in condemning all men to Hell. We are all by nature children of wrath. It is only of God's grace and mercy that any of us are saved. We with our limited perspective and knowledge may deign to criticize the justice of the omniscient God. But our questions arise from our ignorance of all the facts. But on what basis is man judged? The word of God is very clear: "Now we know that God's judgment against those who do such things is based on truth" (Rom. 2:2 NIV). When God's judgment came upon Sodom and Gomorrah, Abraham's words of intercession for Lot expressed the truth: "Shall not the judge of all the earth deal justly?" (Gen. 18:25)

Doesn't God apply the merits of Christ's death to pious heathen apart from hearing and believing the gospel? Inclusivist writers have suggested the possibility that the heathen might be considered like the Old Testament saints, who were saved apart hearing the gospel. First of all, we should note that the Old Testament saints did believe the promises of the revelation God had given them concerning the coming Messiah. Thus the parallel breaks down, since the heathen do not have such a special revelation. We should also note that not only is there no indication in Scripture that such is the case, but also this would contradict the direct statements of the Bible. Some have misunderstood Paul's statement in Romans 3:25: "because in the forbearance of God He passed over the sins previously committed." However, it is clear that Paul is talking about the sins of Old Testament saints being forgiven in anticipation of the cross (this is clear from Heb. 9:15).

There are many specific Scripture statements which exclude those who don't personally believe in Christ. We have already referred to many of them such as John 3:5,16-18, etc. Christ was even more explicit in John 8:24 when He said, "for unless you believe that I am He, you shall die in your sins." Paul also left no room for doubt in referring to the second coming of Christ: "dealing out retribution to those who do not know God and to those who do not obey the gospel of our Lord Jesus" (2 Thess. 1:8). This is not an easy doctrine. Indeed, it is very difficult! But we must never allow our feelings to dictate what we determine to be truth. Let us just believe what God has said and act upon it.

A Critique of Contemporary Inclusivism

It has been in the last decade that inclusivists like Lesslie Newbiggin, Clark Pinnock, and John Sanders, while claiming to be Evangelicals, have become increasingly vocal about their denial of the lostness of the un-evangelized. They are getting a following from many who have not examined their lack of evangelical credentials. My own research has shown, for example, that Newbiggin, while touted as an ecumenical Evangelical, was neither an Evangelical nor a friend of Evangelicalism.[a] There are a number of responses from evangelical writers, who give a more thorough refutation than possible here.[15]

It has been clear for a score of years that Clark Pinnock has moved away from verbal, plenary inspiration of Scripture, and Ramesh Richard has shown additionally that his Christology is very defective[16]. Pinnock says that Christ's uniqueness and finality belong to Jesus only derivatively and he rejects an incarnational Christology as the norm, despite his claim to have a high Christology.[17] Thus the foundation for his doctrine of salvation is exceedingly weak, even heretical.

Richard shows how one of the axioms of Pinnock's inclusivism is his optimistic view of the universal love of God based upon global cove-nants, like that with Noah, the so-called "pagan saints" outside of Israel before Christ, and God's continuing dialog with the nations. His second "particularity" axiom means that salvation is only through the cross of Christ, even though explicit faith in Jesus Christ is not a necessary condi-tion of salvation. Indeed, salvation is not to be so narrowly defined as merely individual, spiritual salvation from hell, but is to be understood holistically and more corporately. Sanders speaks about the "faith princi-ple" in the unevangelized world, which does not necessarily require explicit faith in the Lord Jesus. They see this exemplified in premes-sianic believers, like Enoch, Noah, Job, Melchizedek, and ultimately Cornelius, among others. They believe that these "pagan saints" had faith

---

[a] In 1980 I wrote "An Evaluative Review of *The Open Secret* by Lesslie Newbiggin" (1978), in which I showed his nonevangelical view of inspiration, Christology (many Christolo-gies in the NT), and his almost universalist soteriology. He takes offense at the idea that we can have assurance of ultimate salvation, and carries his concept of "surprise" in the teach-ings of Christ to lead to the possibility that God is working through athiests, humanists, and Marxists and that they will be "surprised" to be included, while those who presume to think they are in will be surprised to find themselves out (pp. 196-8).

in the general revelation found in nature. Sanders suggests that the restrictive view is not the only motive for missions, and that there are other legs upon which the table can stand: the great commission and the needs of those who have only "implicit faith" (not explicit) and therefore haven't experienced the fullness of salvation we can share with them. There are many other details, but I believe I have fairly summarized their views.

A critique. I have already dealt with many of the issues earlier in this chapter. Additionally, we should note that the inclusivists' weak view of Scripture allows them to be very selective in the passages they treat. Their overly optimistic read on the universal love of God manifest before Christ significantly omits the very obvious judgments of God already alluded to earlier in this chapter. They also fail to take into account the substantial special revelation given to the so-called "pagan saints" of earlier dispensations and the passing down of the knowledge of the true God to the descendants of Noah, such as Job and Melchizedek. They were not dependent upon natural revelation alone by any means. Their faith was in the true God, Yahweh, and in the messianic expectation of salvation yet to be provided. As a dispensationalist, I would be quick to grant that they did not all have a clear understanding of the person and work of the Messiah as predicted and promised. Indeed, the prophets themselves searched to understand this salvation (1 Pet. 1:10-11). Charles Ryrie's suggestion is helpful that the content of faith required for salvation necessarily grew with each successive revelation and dispensation. In any case the New Testament clearly testifies that in this present age faith has to be put in Jesus the Messiah **explicitly**. Sanders questions, "A single statement by our Lord Jesus could have settled the controversy before it began."[18] The fact is that He did, and it is in the best know verse in the Bible, John 3:16, as well as a legion of other passages which stipulate that our trust has to be "in Him" (His one and only Son) in order that we should not perish. They cannot separate the objective, historical reality of the person and work of Christ from our subjective appropriation of that salvation by repentant faith in that divine Messiah. To do so is to violate the whole tenor of the New Testament proclamation.

The inclusivists tend to deal with generalities. Let's get specific. What about sincere religious Muslims, undoubtedly millions out of the one billion nominal Muslims in the world today. Muslims believe that to call the 'prophet Jesus' God incarnate is the greatest of all sins, a blasphemy. Therefore, the doctrine of the Tri-Unity of God is also blasphemous. They believe that the 'prophet Jesus' was not crucified, and that to see His substitutionary sacrifice as the basis for forgiveness of sin is heresy. Now what kind of "implicit faith" can a sincere Muslim have which might save him? Or let us consider sincere Hindus, who worship 33 million idolatrous gods and as pantheists deny the personality of God. They worship cobras, monkeys, rats, elephants, and especially cows. Remember what God did in judgment upon the religion of Egypt, where it was frogs, ibises, crocodiles, cats, and especially bulls which were worshipped, which worship was judged in the ten plagues. Or consider the hundreds of millions of Buddhists. At the end of the Congress of World Religions, which convened in Chicago in 1993, as they drew up a joint ethical statement, they had to leave out the word 'God' lest they offend the Buddhists, who do not believe in a personal God. Just who are these "pagan saints" of the inclusivists? We will examine these religions in more detail in subsequent chapters.

STUDY SHEET #4
THE DEADLY NIGHT

1. How inclusive is Romans 3:23? Can any human beings be excluded? (cf. Rom. 3:9-20; 5:12; Ps. 53:3; Isa. 53:6)
2. Some who will agree that all men are sinners nevertheless feel that the heathen have some excuse because they have not had the full light of the Gospel. What revelation from God do the heathen have according to Romans 1:18-20? (cf. Ps. 19:1; 97:6; Acts 14:17)
3. What additional revelation do all men have according to Rom. 2:14-15?
4. What does Romans 1:21-22 say that men did with the light they had? Give a present-day illustration.
5. Again there are some who would grant that the heathen are sinners and have not lived up to the light they have, but are still not convinced that they are absolutely lost and hopeless without Christ. What is the verdict of Psalm 9:17? (cf. Ps. 37:38; Rom. 2:12)
6. Then there are those who feel that though there may be unworthy elements in the various religions of the world, yet there is enough revelation of God so that if a man sincerely follows his religion he will get to God. What did Christ say about this in John 14:6? Peter in Acts 4:12?
7. Thomas Shultz wrote, "Not one **recognized** religious leader, not Moses, Paul, Buddha, Mohammed, Confucius, etc., have ever claimed to be God; that is, with the exception of Jesus Christ." How does Paul clarify in 1 Timothy 2:5 as to why only one name will avail for salvation?
8. How does the basis of salvation in true Christianity differ from that in other religions? Eph. 2:8-9 (cf. Rom. 3:20; 9:16; 10:1-3; Gal. 2:16; Titus 3:4-5)
9. Many followers of other religions are very religious and moral by their own standards. If salvation could be obtained on the basis of works or holy living, how much holiness would be required for salvation? Hab. 1:13 (cf. 1 Sam. 6:20; Ps. 5:4; Heb. 12:14; Rev. 15:4) Could anyone produce such holiness?
10. Some who believe that those who consciously reject the gospel message are condemned, nevertheless, still insist that those who have never had a chance to hear are not condemned. What is the condition of men before they believe in Christ? John 3:18. If we grant their premise that the heathen are not already lost, what would missionaries be bringing to the majority who hear and reject?
11. What is the condition of the world according to 1 John 5:19?

12. Since man apart from Christ is lost, what is my responsibility? Ezek. 3:16-19; Mark 16:15-16; Romans 10:13-17
13. What is my responsibility to unreached peoples? In my country? In other countries?

---

1. Kane, *Understanding*, p. 105.
2. Richard Bailey, "Missions--Christian Collegians' Concepts," *Eastern Challenge*, 7 (July 1971), p. 3; MARC, *Christian Collegians and Foreign Missions* (1968).
3. J. Robertson McQuilkin, "The Narrow Way," in *Perspectives*, p. 128.
4. Clark H. Pinnock, *A Wideness in God's Mercy: The Finality of Jesus Christ in a World of Religions* (1992); "Toward an Evangelical Theology of Religions," JETS, 33 (1990):359-368; John Sanders, *No Other Name: An Investigation into the Destiny of the Unevangelized* (1992); Sanders, ed., *What About Those Who Have Never Heard? Three Views on the Destiny of the Unevangelized* (1995).
5. A. T. Pierson, *Evangelize to a Finish*, p. 12. Cf. also *The Crisis of Missions*, p. 291.
6. James Oliver Buswell, Jr., *A Systematic Theology of the Christian Religion*, 2 vols. (1962), 1:111.
7. For a good summary of these claims see Henry C. Thiessen, *Lectures in Systematic Theology*, revised by Vernon D. Doerksen (1979), pp. 92-96.
8. Josh McDowell, *Evidence That Demands a Verdict* (1972), p. 92, citing Thomas Schultz, "The Doctrine of the Person of Christ with an Emphasis upon the Hypostatic Union" (Dissertation, Dallas Theological Seminary, 1962), p. 209.
9. John B. Noss, *Man's Religions*, 4th ed. (1969), p. 344. Paul C. Haagen in his chapter on Zoroastrianism in Howard F. Vos, *Religions in a Changing World* (1959), pp. 207-12, naively shows parallels between Christ and Zoroaster, without clarification. He was apparently unaware that Zoroaster had a human father and that the *Zend Avesta* was not written down until centuries after Christ, thus allowing Zoroastrians to invent such comparisons..
10. McDowell, *Evidence*, pp. 147-84.
11. Erich Sauer, *The Dawn of World Redemption*, trans. by G. H. Lang (1951), p. 85 (quotations from unattributed German sources).
12. *Webster's Collegiate Dictionary*, 5th ed., s.v. "heathen."
13. Kane, *Understanding*, p. 130
14. Don Richardson, *Eternity in their Hearts* (1981), pp. 28-120.
15. Ramesh P. Richard, *The Population of Heaven* (1994); Millard J. Erickson, *How Shall They Be Saved? The Destiny of Those Who Do Not Hear of Jesus* (1996); Ronald H. Nash, "Restrictivism," in John Sanders, ed., *op. cit.* (1995); also, Ajith Fernando, *Crucial Questions about Hell* (1991); Larry Dixon, *The Other Side of the Good News: Confronting the Contemporary Challenges to Jesus' Teaching on Hell* (1992); William V. Crockett and James G. Sigountos, eds., *Through No Fault of Their Own? The Fate of Those Who Have Never Heard* (1991); Edward Rommen and Harold Netland, eds., *Christianity and the Religions: A Biblical Theology of World Religions* (1995).
16. Richard, pp. 47-55.
17. Pinnock, *Wideness*, p. 53-62.
18. John Sanders, *No Other Name: An Investigation into the Destiny of the Unevangelized* (1992), p. 19.

"The term *missionary call* should never have been coined. It is not Scriptural and therefore can be harmful. Thousands of youth desiring to serve the Lord have waited and waited for some mysterious missionary call that never came."

–J. Herbert Kane

WHY IN THE WORLD SHOULD I GO?

Our journey through the Bible to understand its missionary heartbeat has left one important question unanswered! Indeed, in one sense it is **the** most important question because it affects our personal involvement in missions radically. The question is: how can I know whether I should become a missionary or not? Related to that is another controversial question: what is a missionary 'call', and how can I know if I am 'called'?

THE MISSIONARY 'CALL'

It has been common in modern missionary circles to talk about a 'missionary call'. Although there was little agreement as to what that 'call' consisted of or how to define it, there was general agreement until a generation ago that such a 'call' was needed to become a missionary. Missionary leaders struggled to clarify the confusion related to a call and eliminate the many myths surrounding it. For example, Harold Cook wrote the following in 1954:

> *To sum up*: (1) a *special* divine call is not necessary to witness for Christ beyond the national border; (2) the striking vision that Paul received at Troas, the so-called "Macedonian call," was *not* his missionary call, nor is it typical of such a call; and (3) the call to missionary service is not *necessarily* associated with a definite field at home or abroad.
>
> It might seem from this that we have completely ruled out the idea of a call. But that is not so.

Later, however, he goes on to say, "Sometimes in order to see the matter in its proper relationships, we might do well to drop the word *call* and speak of this as a matter of guidance."[1] He goes on to give the testimonies of seven great missionaries and shows that there is no pattern or mold into which they can be forced, nor can we get a definition from their experiences.

Herbert Kane is more definite. "The term *missionary call* should never have been coined. It is not Scriptural and therefore can be harmful. Thousands of youth desiring to serve the Lord have waited and waited for some mysterious 'missionary call' that never came."[2]

The biblical doctrine of 'calling'

How can we find out the reality of the 'missionary call'? Do we take a cross section of missionary experience? Of course not! We must go back to our sufficient authority: the Bible. The major usage of the word 'call' in the New Testament is the call to salvation. It would seem that the Apostle Paul used the word as a comprehensive term to encompass all that pertains to our conversion to Christ: hearing the gospel, believing, and the immediate consequence of the new birth, etc. The Apostle Paul also used this word of his call to apostleship in Romans 1:1 and 1 Corinthians 1:1. But we do not find any clear reference to a 'missionary call'!

There are two passages which might be so interpreted. One is Acts 13:2: "Set apart for me Barnabas and Saul for the work to which I have called them." Note that Saul of Tarsus was called at his conversion to be an apostle to the Gentiles. Ananias informed him of that (Acts 9:16; 22:21; 26:16-18) and God later confirmed it long before the leaders of the Antioch church were commanded by the Spirit to set apart Barnabas and Saul. So apparently this was just a confirmation of the call to ministry that Barnabas and Saul had already received. But it was not a separate and distinct call to missionary service. In a sense both Saul and Barnabas were already missionaries, working among Gentiles. But the ultimate dimension to which the Spirit was moving them as cross-cultural missionaries yet needed to be fulfilled.

The other passage which has been taken superficially as basis for a missionary call is the account in Acts 16 of the vision of the man of Macedonia which the Spirit used to lead the missionaries to cross over to Macedonia. "And when he had seen the vision, immediately we sought to go into Macedonia, concluding that God had called us to preach the gospel to them" (Acts 16:10). One of our great missionary hymns refers to the "Macedonian call," but the fact is quite obvious that Paul and Silas were already missionaries, indeed Paul was on his **second** missionary journey. This event was just part of a process that God used to move the apostles on into virgin territory.

But the key issue then is whether there is a separate call necessary to cross "geographical and/or cultural boundaries to preach the gospel in those areas of the world where Jesus Christ is largely, if not entirely, unknown." This much is clear: that whatever is needed, it is not referred to as a "call." Cook felt we should refer to it as guidance. James Weber feels that we should refer to it as direction.[3] Other words like 'appointment', 'conviction' and 'burden' could be suggested as a basis for missionary service, but it is clear that some sort of a visionary experience is not needed.

"NOW, YOU SAY YOU FEEL THAT THE LORD CALLED YOU TO 12 DEGREES, 5 MINUTES, 41 SECONDS NORTH LATITUDE, 18 DEGREES, 14 MINUTES, 6 SECONDS EAST LONGITUDE?"

Another thing is increasingly clear: the appointment is not to a particular geographical area. There are many serious problems with relating a missionary 'call' to geography. First, we find that some of the greatest missionary pioneers did not end up in the country that first caught their attention. William Carey was interested in going to the South Seas but ended up in India. Adoniram Judson was expelled from India and ended up in Burma after trying to go elsewhere. David Livingstone was waiting to get into China but the Opium War hindered, and he went to Africa instead. Furthermore, some of the best missionaries are those who have spent extended time in pastoral ministry before going out as a missionary. On the other hand, there are legions who served a number of terms abroad and subsequently came home to a fruitful ministry at the home base. Too rigid an idea of a 'missionary call' would exclude these scenarios. I myself did get a very clear burden to become a missionary in Pakistan and served there for some years. But how do we account for a colleague who has served not only in Pakistan, but in India, Afghanistan, Iran, Lebanon, Bahrein, and Hong Kong as well? Was he confused about his missionary 'call'? No, someone has well said that choice of a mission board is far more important than choice of a country.

A mandate to the corporate church

In past chapters we have focused upon the command of Christ to the church in a corporate sense. This is explicit and permanent up to the present. It cannot be avoided. If individuals are not responding, it is up to the whole church ultimately to find a way. Paul and Barnabas did not go out as freelancers. The Holy Spirit guided the leadership of the Antioch church to set apart these two most useful men. Quite apart from the issue of the content of the message, was it really so wrong for the Jesuits and other Catholic orders to simply select the men and order them to go? It seems that Paul directed the movements of his missionaries, like Timothy or Silas.

John G. Paton, the great pioneer to the New Hebrides Islands, tells how the Reformed Presbyterian Church of Scotland tried for two years to get a volunteer to join John Inglis in the islands there but with no success. Finally they agreed to cast ballots for the pastor who should be relieved of his pastorate to go out as a missionary. When there was no unanimity, Paton himself volunteered.[4] But what would be so unbiblical about a corporate decision? This is what Holy Spirit did through the Antioch church. The least we can say is that the decision should not be wholly individual, but should have the agreement of the leadership of the local church.

The Lord Jesus made a statement that is still operative today, even though he uttered these words long before Pentecost: "The harvest truly is plentiful, but the workers are few. Therefore beseech the Lord of the harvest to send out workers into His harvest" (Matt. 9:37-8). The church has a corporate responsibility to find out why after nineteen centuries the workers are still so few. Certainly prayerlessness and apathy are major factors. Certainly confusion about the nature of the 'call' has contributed to the problem. Francis Steele (of North Africa Mission) has said that confusion produces complacency.[5] The church has a responsibility to dispel the confusion and see that workers are sent out. If the confusion is caused by an unbiblical 'fixed idea' of the necessity of a 'call' that we may have fastened upon, let us by all means get rid of that notion, no matter how entrenched it may be in our evangelical traditions. But the ultimate responsibility rests upon the corporate church.

The 'call' of James Thoburn, Methodist pioneer to India, also graphically illustrates the corporate principle. After a year in pastoral ministry he read about the church's need for six young men to go to India. Powerfully moved by the appeal and praying about it, he decided to ask his presiding elder for his advice. Upon meeting him, the elder related how he had met the Bishop who was looking for the six missionary candidates and went on to say, "James, how would you like to go?" That settled it for Thoburn. He went and became a missionary great. But God used the corporate leadership of the church to help him to understand God's will. We Westerners tend to be too individualistic and fail to appreciate how God wants to work through the corporate body of Christ. At the very least we should expect some confirmation of a missionary 'call' by the prospective missionary's local church.[6]

Relative spiritual need

The missionary speaker in the Bible college missions conference was very blunt: "The need constitutes the call." He went on to illustrate it by having ten students try to lift the piano by positioning nine at one end and one at the other. He made his point by saying that the fact that nine out of ten Christian workers are ministering to the one-tenth of the world which is most evangelized while only one out of ten workers are thinly spread through the nine-tenths of the world which has the greatest need; this is appalling. It is as ridiculous as nine men at one end of the piano ignoring the one poor guy trying to lift the other end all by himself. After the meeting the students were very perplexed because the day before another missionary had said, "If you don't have a clear-cut missionary call, don't become a missionary, whatever you do. You'll do more harm than good if you go." This missionary was just reflecting the view of many in the past like Robert Hall Glover, author of several classic missions textbooks: "Nothing could be more vital to anyone setting out for the mission field than to be clearly assured of the call and leading of the Lord in taking that step."[7] On the other hand Glover goes on to quote some missionary greats on the other side of the issue:

It has been truly said that "a need, knowledge of that need, and ability to meet that need constitute a call." It was this *logic of facts* that appealed to Keith Falconer, that heroic Scottish nobleman who blazed the Gospel trail into the "ignored peninsula" of Arabia. Said he: "While vast continents still lie shrouded in almost utter darkness, and hundreds of millions suffer the horrors of heathenism and Islam, the burden of proof rests upon you to show that the circumstances in which God has placed you were meant by Him to keep you out of the foreign mission field." James Gilmour, the brave pioneer among the nomads of Mongolia, spoke in words no less forceful and convicting: "To me the question was not 'Why go?' but 'Why not go?' Even on the low ground of common sense I seemed called to be a missionary. For is the kingdom not a harvest field? Then I thought it only reasonable to seek the work where the work was most abundant and the workers were fewest."[8]

Again we must come back to the Scripture. The Apostle Paul strongly supported the principle of need in Romans 15:20, 23: "And thus I aspired to preach the gospel, not where Christ was already named, that I might not build upon another man's foundation; . . . but now, with no further place for me in these regions, . . ." Certainly need must play a prominent part in our sense of guidance toward a place of ministry. If we have a choice and unless there are compelling reasons to the contrary, the Christian worker should choose the place of greatest need! Failure to give adequate consideration to this factor has caused the incredible inequity in the distribution of workers. As someone has said with a great measure of accuracy, "Why should anyone have a chance to hear the gospel twice until all have had a chance to hear it once?" This may be an overstatement, but it raises a valid question which must be answered. I suspect that most mission boards would far rather have a flood of candidates apply and have to screen out a large percentage of unqualified ones, than have the present shortage of candidates, which sometimes forces boards to accept too many marginally qualified people.

THE NEEDIEST CONTINENTS TODAY[9]

CONTIN.	POPU-LATION Million	EVAN-GELICAL Million	EVAN-GELICAL %	CROSS-CULTUR. MISSION.	NON-EVANG. Million	RATIO Miss. / Million
EUR-ASIA †	290	2.6	0.9	1073	288	3.7
MIDDLE EAST	378	1.5	0.4	2211	377	5.9
ASIA	3210	99.5	3.1	23,828	3110	7.7
EUROPE	515	14.4	2.8	9961	500	19.9
LATIN AMER.	456	50.6	11.1	15409	405	38.0
AFRICA	558	73.6	13.2	19,864	484	41.0
CARIB-BEAN	38	4.2	11.1	1988	34	58.5
PACIFIC	28	4.4	15.8	4348	24	181

Note: The righthand column represents the number of Prostestant cross-cultural missionaries per million of non-Evangelicals on each continent.

† Eurasia is Johnstone's term for the republics of the former U.S.S.R. and is the neediest part of the world spiritually. The neediest are at the top of the table.

Today in America we have the spectacle of modest churches receiving hundreds of resumes from prospective pastoral candidates. Something is 'out of whack'! Mission boards don't receive even two applications (resumes) for each opening on the mission field. They are happy to get even one. Bible colleges here in America receive many resumes from qualified applicants for each open teaching position. It is strange that Bible institutes and colleges abroad have a hard time filling faculty positions. The ministry is the same (albeit usually in a different language). Could it be that some mysterious 'calling' is lacking in one case and not in the other?

Perhaps our western notion of 'falling in love' contributes to the confusion. The Bible says nothing about 'falling in love' before getting married. Isaac's marriage was arranged by his father's servant with a girl he had never seen before. Our western romantic idea of 'falling in love' seems to be a dismal failure because far too many Americans seem to be 'falling out of love', and the divorce rate is a national scandal. There may be a parallel with the romantic notion of a 'missionary call'. Just as we expect to be struck with 'falling in love' before marriage, perhaps we also expect to be struck with a 'missionary call' before becoming a missionary. It is a false expectation, I strongly suspect. But what then replaces it?

The Spirit's guidance

Many have suggested that the term 'guidance' is more appropriate to describe what is involved in becoming a missionary. I myself have frequently used the term 'burden' used by Old Testament prophets. God has a love, concern, compassion, or burden for a lost, alienated world. He shares that burden with His church. As the Holy Spirit uses the word of God and the spiritual needs of a lost world in our lives, a burden develops for a portion of that lost world. Indeed it should start as a burden for the souls of lost people right around us. As God uses us in ministry at home, that ministry can be expanded to other areas. This was clearly the case with the Apostle Paul. After his conversion he began to witness in Damascus immediately. After a period of preparation, he went back to his hometown of Tarsus and possibly began to plant a church there (Acts 15:41). Barnabas recruited Paul for ministry in Antioch (Acts 11:25-6). After a year's teaching in Antioch, Paul and the leaders of the Antioch church developed a burden for the Gentiles in other areas without the gospel. In their case uniquely the Holy Spirit's guidance was very explicit. Paul had been called to ministry among the Gentiles right from his conversion, and now the Holy Spirit was confirming that calling.

But there is considerable discussion today as to how explicit we should expect the Spirit's guidance to be. Garry Friesen has written an important book, *Decision Making and the Will of God,* in which he argues that there is no biblical basis for the traditional view of seeking for a blueprint of the will of God for each individual. He argues that the 'will of God' is usually a reference to the revealed moral will of God for the Christian, and that we are to use divinely given wisdom in making our decisions in Christian freedom. He argues that there is no 'dot' in the very center of the circle of God's will for each individual, which we must strive to attain. Rather we must give priority to obeying God's moral will, which, of course, includes witnessing to the lost and obeying the Great Commission. Thus he takes an even more extreme position in rejecting the need for a 'missionary call'.

THE TRADITIONAL VIEW   FRIESEN'S VIEW

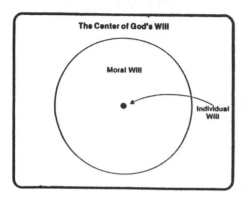

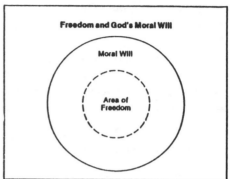

Friesen shows how the New Testament emphasizes the moral and spiritual qualification of Christian leaders, whether pastor-elders, deacons, or missionaries. When Paul co-opted Timothy as a member of his missionary team, it was because he was "well spoken of by the brethren" in his home town (Acts 16:1-2), not because he had a 'missionary call'. Friesen summarizes his view in regard to missions:

> Once missionary outreach was set in motion by the Holy Spirit in Acts 13, all subsequent decisions related to missions were made on the basis of applied wisdom. (The one exception to this process was the Macedonian Call in Acts 16:6-10, which we discussed earlier.) In the actual practice of the New Testament church, the decisions concerning timing, destinations, and personnel were all made by the appropriate people with a view to obeying God's moral will in the most effective manner possible. There is a remarkable absence of any reference to the call of God beyond Acts 16.[10]

Friesen is concerned about the overly subjective nature of the decision-making process in the traditional evangelical approach and the distress caused by trying to find the blueprint, when in reality God gives us considerable freedom within the biblically revealed moral will of God. I hasten to point out that the Great Commission is part of the revealed moral will of God for all Christians, and it is sin for us to be unconcerned about fulfilling it.

Spiritual gifts

Peter Wagner has written extensively to show that spiritual gift is the main consideration in becoming a missionary. "To come right to the point, there is essentially no difference between the call and the gift."[11] He suggests that a good way for a 'world Christian' to discover whether one has a 'missionary gift' is to undertake a short term as a missionary for a year or two. Many might not go as far as Wagner in identifying 'call' with 'gift', but his point is well taken that the spiritual qualifications are the most important thing. Most mission boards today emphasize spiritual and moral qualifications as the primary thing they look for in a missionary candidate, no matter whether they look for an explicit call or how they might define it.

MOTIVATING INCENTIVES

Motivation and incentive are important matters in everyday life. Parents must work hard to motivate their children to obey and to spend their time profitably. Children must be motivated to learn. This carries right on into college. Students must be motivated to study and learn. In the business world the study of incentives for employees to produce has almost become a science. As Christians we are God's children, and motivation for obedience and good works is of prime importance. God knows 'what makes us tick', and has provided strong incentive in His word for motivated Christian life and service. Let us investigate the motivation factor in God's plan of redemption.

It is very clear that God's motive for providing salvation for us was His self-giving love (John 3:16). God's love reached out to alienated, hostile sinners (Rom. 5:6-8). Christ was God's missionary (sent one) to a lost world, motivated by his love and the anticipation of the fruit that would be borne by His saving sacrifice (John 20:21; Heb. 12:2). The Apostle Paul was the greatest of the New Testament missionaries. When we examine Paul's life we find a number of different motivations. In 2 Corinthians 5:14-15 he states that it is the "love of Christ" which "controls" and "compels" him to serve Christ. This probably includes both Christ's love for us and our love for Him in response (1 John 4:10). Love is the highest motivation and is proved by our obedience to Him (1 John 5:3). Our hearts well up in gratitude for all that He has done for us. But love is not the only motive or incentive for godly living.

The Old Testament over and over again records God's compassion for His people. Clearly it was Christ's compassion for the multitudes of people straying like sheep without a shepherd which motivated the Lord Jesus (Matt. 14:14). When Paul was in Athens, his spirit was provoked when he saw the gross idolatry. This motivated him to seek to win the Athenians to Christ (Acts 17:16). In 2 Corinthians 5:10-11 Paul refers to another, lower motivation which caused ꟼꟼꟼꟼ ꟷꟷ seek to persuade the lost—the fear of the Lord. This can be understood best in the light of the preceding reference in verse 10 to the judgment seat of Christ at which every believer will have to give account of his service for Christ. That reverential fear of God should also be a powerful motivating force in our lives. There are many other motivations to obey and serve God which He gives us in His word. Certainly God rewards His faithful servants. There is also the personal satisfaction we get in this life from serving Him, as the hymn goes, "There is joy in serving Jesus." Many others could be mentioned.

HOW TO GET THERE FROM HERE

Friesen suggests seven steps to get to the mission field. No matter what view one takes, one cannot go wrong with these:

1. *Commitment.* The first issue, really, is availability. And that issue ought to be settled by grateful submission to the Lordship of Christ (Luke 9:23-26; 14:25-35). One reason there aren't more missionaries is not that God hasn't called more; it's because more people haven't responded to the clear commission already given. There might be many valid reasons for not becoming a missionary; but unwillingness is not one of them (Luke 9:59-62).

2. *Investigation.* An important means for gaining wisdom is the gathering of facts. Ask questions: What do missionaries do? What does it take to become a missionary? What does it cost? What does it require?

. . . .

3. *Involvement.* Every believer who reads this book can personally and actively participate in Christ's worldwide mission right now. The first means is effectively bearing witness in one's own "Jerusalem." [He lists ministry in the local church, giving to missions, intercessory prayer, ministering to the needs of missionaries, and promoting missions in churches.]

4. *Evaluation.* Each believer should take a personal inventory of himself, evaluating his potential by the standard of missionary qualities and qualifications. [He shows how such evaluation can help us determine whether we are missionary raw material or can better serve at home.]

5. *Consultation.* Personal evaluation should not be carried out in a vacuum. The New Testament carefully records the involvement of local churches in recognizing, choosing, and sending those best suited for international outreach. [He points out how both the individual and the church have mutual responsibilities in this regard.]

6. *Preparation.* . . . The most important of these steps, whether one becomes a missionary or not, is to enroll in the school of spiritual growth. The motto of that school is: "Discipline yourself for the purpose of godliness" (1 Timothy 4:7). [He lists many types of formal and informal training one can get to prepare for serving abroad.]

7. *Prayer.* Pray for wisdom, strength, and open doors of opportunity. And submit, in advance to the sovereign will of the Lord of the harvest (Luke 10:2). Then proceed, as you pray, to obey His moral will — with the confidence that He is at work in you "both to will and to work for His good pleasure" (Phil. 2:13).[12]

STUDY SHEET #5
THE IMPELLING PERSONAL MOTIVATION

In the previous study we saw the inescapable command of Christ to evangelize the whole world. Because many Christians are failing to obey Christ's command, the burning question is, "Why should we obey it?" This study examines the motivation and personalization of missions.

1. What was God's motivation in providing salvation for a rebellious world? John 3:16

2. As humans we find it difficult to love those who do not respond to our love. In what way does God's love go far beyond human love? Rom. 5:6-8

3. List several things that God's love cost Christ: Phil. 2:6-8; Isa. 52:13; 53:2-6; 1 Pet. 2:24.

4. Why did Christ voluntarily submit to these things? Heb. 12:2; Isa. 53:11

5. In what respects was Christ a missionary? John 20:21; Mt. 20:28; Lk. 19:10.

6. What was the compelling motive of Paul's ministry? 2 Cor. 5:14-15. Does "the love of Christ" mean Christ's love for us or our love for Him? (Either is possible in the Greek.) Compare with 1 John 4:10.

7. What is the proof of our love for Christ? 1 Jn. 5:3
    How then can we know what God expects of us personally in regard to world evangelization? Some say that the command of Christ and the needs of the foreign fields are the 'call'. Others say that one should never become a missionary without a 'special call'. Let us try to find out the element of truth in both statements.

8. What motive moved God to send a missionary to Egypt? Ex. 3:7-10. What motivated Christ's service in Mt. 14:14? Paul's in Acts 17:16?

9. Beyond the command of Christ, what principle determined Paul's sphere of ministry? Rom. 15:20-21; 2 Cor. 10:14-16

10. Statistics show that about 90% of Christian workers minister to the 10% of world population who speak English. There are many areas where there are no workers and where hundreds of millions have not heard the gospel clearly. Apparently many Christian workers are not considering need in determining their place of ministry. What part should it play?

11. How do Isaiah 6:8 (positively) and Jonah 1:3 ? (negatively) show what should be the attitude of every Christian in facing Christ's command and the fact of the world's desperate spiritual need?

12. There are many instances in the Bible of an individual call to specific service. How specific was God's call as to field of service and type of ministry in the following? Gen. 12:1-2; Ex. 3:10; Josh. 1:2; Isa. 6:9; Jer. 1:4-8; Amos 7:14-15; Mt. 4:18-22; Acts 13:2; 26:16-18.

13. Is God's calling and guidance only for 'spiritual ministries'? Ex. 31:1-5; Acts 6:3-6.

14. What was the attitude of the early church toward's Christ's command? Acts 8:4

15. God has promised definite guidance (Ps. 48:14; Isa. 30:21), but before we can expect or be sure of that conviction of His will, certain things are essential. What condition of guidance is given in Rom. 12:1-2?

16. What other essential is suggested by Mt. 9:36-38? (Jn. 4:35; Acts 16:9-10)

17. What third essential is described in Rom. 8:14; Acts 15:28 & 16:10?

18. What channel for knowing God's will is given in Ps. 119:105? (Dan. 9:2)

19. What circumstances were used to guide Paul in his ministry? Acts 11:29-30; 15:1-2; 20:3

20. What other means should be used in seeking God's will? Acts 13:1-3.
    (2 Chron. 20:1ff)

---

1. Cook, *Introduction,* p. 85, 88.

2. Kane, *Understanding Missions,* p. 41.

3. James M. Weber, *Let's Quit Kidding Ourselves about Missions* (1979), p. 48.

4. Cook, *Introduction,* p. 94.

5. Weber, *Quit Kidding,* p. 47.

6. Cook, *Introduction,* pp. 98-99.

7. Robert Hall Glover, *The Bible Basis of Missions,* p. 127.

8. Ibid., pp. 138-39.

9. Johnstone, *Operation World,* 5th ed., pp. 21, 643. (1995 population figures)

10. Garry Friesen, *Decision Making and the Will of God* (1980), p. 327.

11. Wagner, *Crest of the Wave,* p. 67.

12. Friesen, *Decision Making,* pp. 331-34.

PART II

HIS STORY: THE

HISTORICAL DIMENSION

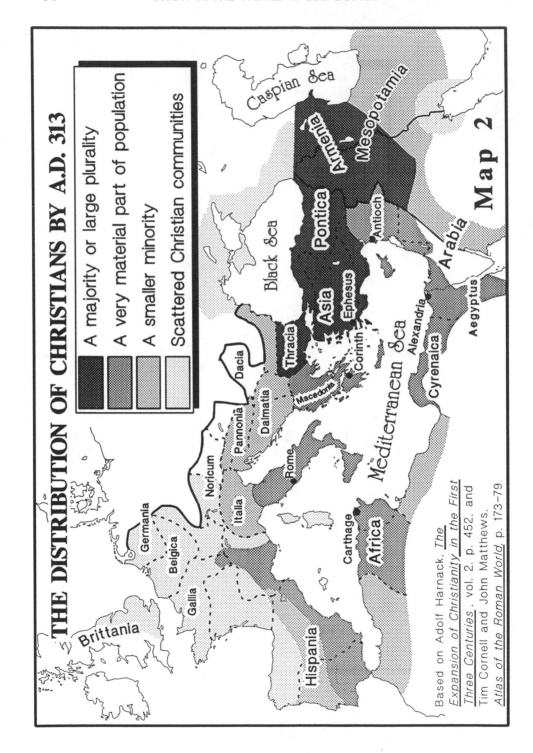

THE DISTRIBUTION OF CHRISTIANS BY A.D. 313

A majority or large plurality
A very material part of population
A smaller minority
Scattered Christian communities

Map 2

Based on Adolf Harnack, *The Expansion of Christianity in the First Three Centuries*, vol. 2, p. 452, and Tim Cornell and John Matthews, *Atlas of the Roman World*, p. 173–79.

"The kingdom of heaven is like a mustard seed, . . . which is the smallest seed you plant in the ground. Yet when planted, it grows and becomes the largest of all garden plants, with such big branches that the birds of the air can perch in its shade."
—Matthew 13:31; Mark 4:30-1

PREREFORMATION CHURCH EXPANSION AND MISSIONS (A.D. 33-1517)

Christianity and missions. The two are inseparably linked. It is thought provoking to speculate where Christianity might be today without the vibrant missionary outreach that sprang forth after Pentecost and continued for the next few centuries. Perhaps, as Zoroastrianism, it would be an obscure religion of the ancients, studied by scholars but known little beyond the borders of its homeland. But from its very inception Christianity was different from all other religions. The command to go forth with the good news was the very heart of the faith. (Ruth Tucker)[1]

THE ROMAN EMPIRE: EVANGELIZED OR CHRISTIANIZED? (A.D. 33-500)

The Roman Empire was the main, but not the only, arena of the spreading flame of Christianity for five centuries after the day of Pentecost. Not only was there extensive evangelization of the empire in the first three centuries until Emperor Constantine's day, but following his 'conversion' there was an increased pace of Christianization, stimulated by the declaration of Christianity as the official state religion. Before A.D. 313, when the Edict of Toleration ended the ten major periods of persecution of Christians, we may accurately use the term 'evangelization' to describe how it came about that ten percent of the population professed Christ. After Constantine's professed conversion a decade later, however, it became politically expedient to become a Christian, and we may question the genuineness of many of the converts, including Constantine himself. It took another half century before Christianity was declared the official state religion of the Roman Empire (A.D. 375). After that, masses were baptized with such dubious motives and understanding that we

95

believe the broader term 'Christianized' would be more appropriate. This is not to deny that many in this period were genuinely born-again.

The Apostolic Period of Church Growth (A.D. 33-95)

We have already studied the New Testament record of the expansion of the church during the apostolic period. The record highlights the ministry of the Apostle Paul and his missionary team in evangelizing the four Roman provinces of Galatia, Asia, Macedonia, and Achaia, and probably Spain and other areas before his martyrdom about A.D. 67. Clement of Rome wrote in the second century that Paul evangelized at the western edge of the empire, which is probably a reference to Spain. We know that the Diaspora Jews converted on the day of Pentecost must have returned to their homes to form the nucleus of new churches scattered around the empire. Traditions mentioned in the writings of early Christian leaders (church fathers) indicate that all the original apostles became missionaries except James, who was early martyred. We also know that converts were quite mobile within the empire and spread the gospel wherever they went. We see this from the Acts and the epistles of Paul. There are casual references to churches in Syria and Cilicia (Acts 15:23), Pontus, Cappadocia, and Bithynia (1 Pet. 1:1). There is a tradition in India that the apostle Thomas planted churches there. But as Herbert Kane well says, "One thing is certain; the Acts of the Apostles does not tell the whole story."[2]

Evidence is quite clear that the apostle John finished out his long ministry in Asia Minor (modern Turkey). After the destruction of Jerusalem in 70, multitudes of Jews migrated to Asia Minor and that included Jewish churches. It is encouraging to note that by the beginning of the fourth century the areas where Paul and his fellow missionaries evangelized were the areas where the church had experienced the greatest growth: in Asia Minor and in the area north of Philippi close to half the people professed Christ. In Cyprus, Syria, Greece, lower Italy, and parts of Spain (among other areas), Christians had become a very material part of the population by that time (see map no. 2).[3] Early in the second century the Christians multiplied rapidly in Asia Minor, especially in Bithynia and Pontus. So much was this the case that Pliny, Governor of Pontus, wrote to the Emperor Trajan for instruction in how to deal with the situation that threatened to get out of hand. During the third century a mass movement took place in Pontus under the leadership of **Gregory Thaumaturgus**. It was said that when he became overseer of the church in his native city about A.D. 240 there were only seventeen Christians, but when he died thirty years later there were only seventeen non-Christians. Since the Apostle Paul laid such a good foundation in his ministry, it is appropriate that missionaries follow his example, not only for zeal, but also for methodology and strategy. Significant books on Paul's missionary strategy have been written by John Nevius and Roland Allen.[4]

Post-Apostolic Expansion (A.D. 95-313)

Coming to the second and third centuries we find that information regarding the expansion of the Christian church is even more meager. We read of large and influential churches in Alexandria, Carthage and Edessa; but we do not know when or by whom they were established. Here again there are wide gaps in our knowledge. It would seem that Christianity continued to spread along the main roads and rivers of the empire: eastward by way of Damascus and Edessa into Mesopotamia; southward through Bosra and Petra into Arabia; westward through Alexandria and Carthage into North Africa; and northward through Antioch into Armenia, Pontus, and Bithynia. Later still it reached Spain, Gaul, and Britain before crossing the borders of the empire into more remote parts such as Ireland, Ethiopia, and China[5].

Thus Kane encapsulates two centuries. Latourette has also given us a good overview of progress during the second century: "it is clear that it [Christianity] continued to grow in numbers of adherents and that before A.D. 200 Christians were found not only in all of the provinces of the Empire but also outside the empire in Mesopotamia."[6]   Ruth Tucker comments that during this period "Christianity penetrated the Roman world through five main avenues: the preaching and teaching of evangelists, the personal witness of believers, acts of kindness and charity, the faith shown in persecution and death, and the intellectual reasoning of the early apologists."[7] Let us trace the church's expansion outward from the area of the evangelization by Paul's missionary team as mentioned in the book of Acts.

Westward across Europe

The church in Rome was already in existence when the apostle Paul wrote to it on his third missionary journey. The Christians in Rome seemed to have evangelized much of southern Italy and possibly even the Roman colony of Carthage in North Africa in the first three centuries. The Latin translation of the Bible was among the earliest translations made (today about eight thousand ancient Latin manuscripts survive). Who spread the gospel westward to the Roman province of Gaul (in modern France) is unknown. We do know that by A.D. 175-200 Irenaeus was Overseer (bishop) of the church in Lyon, and preached to both Celtic and Latin-speaking peoples with discouraging response.[8] In Romans 15 Paul stated his ambition to evangelize Spain, but he was arrested and tried at Rome before he could get there. We believe he was released and had opportunity to plant the church in Spain. There is further evidence of the church there by the beginning of the third century, but it was not a spiritually strong church.

Britain was conquered by the Romans in A.D. 43. We do not know how the gospel was introduced into Britain, but we do know that it came early. The Roman soldiers were unlikely bearers of Christianity. "It is much more likely that Christianity was carried to Britain by ordinary people — traders from Gaul and other parts, it may be. Or Britons who had occasion to visit other parts of the empire may have come in contact with the new faith and carried it home."[9] But we do have clear testimony that by the end of the second century the church was planted in Britain and within a century began to play a significant part in church history.

Eastward through the Tigris-Euphrates valley

Syriac-speaking people. Among the earliest significant expansion we know about was the spread among the Syriac-speaking people of Syria. The Syriac translation of the New Testament was among the earliest of the versions. There is also the possibility that the apostle Peter ministered among the Jews of Babylon (if we take 1 Pet. 5:13 literally, not as a code word for Rome). In any case we are sure that some of the Jews converted on the day of Pentecost were from the smaller kingdoms east of the borders of the Roman Empire: "Parthians and Medes and Elamites, and residents of Mesopotamia . . ." (Acts 2:9). There are traditions that associate the apostles Thomas and Bartholomew with 'India.' By A.D. 180 Pantaenus of Alexandria traveled to 'India' (Arabia?) and found a Christian community founded by Bartholomew. There is also substantial evidence that Christianity had reached the city of Arbela, the capital of Adiabene (north of the Tigris River in Mesopotamia) before the end of the first century. The Jewish historian Josephus tells about the conversion of Queen Helena to the Jewish religion about A.D. 45.[10] This could well have prepared the way for gospel preaching in this area. By the "middle of the second century the city of Edessa (modern Urfa), east of the upper Euphrates, emerges as the chief centre of Christianity in that area." By about 200 even the king, Abgar, was converted to Christ, although the Romans shortly conquered the area and overthrew him. The people of Mesopotamia spoke Syriac and contributed to the translation of the Bible. Indeed, Tatian's Syriac *Diatessaron* was an interweaving of the text of the four Gospels.[11]

Armenia. By the third century the kingdom of Armenia was a buffer state between the Roman Empire on the west and the new Sassanid Persian Empire on the east. Kane points out that:

> As a result of a mass movement led by the great missionary, **Gregory the Illuminator,** and sparked by the conversion of King Tiridates, Armenia became a Christian kingdom. The New Testament first appeared in the Armenian language in 410. The Armenian church has weathered many a storm and is today one of the

oldest churches in Christendom.[12]

Southward to Arabia

Arabic-speaking Jews were among those converted on the day of Pentecost (Acts 2:11). Some probably returned home. The apostle Paul makes mention of a visit to Arabia shortly after his conversion (Gal. 1:17), but it is unlikely that he founded a church there (although we would expect him to have given bold witness as in Damascus from the beginning). Latourette gives a good picture:

> Long before the end of the third century Christianity had gained adherents in Arabia. Some of them were in the parts of Arabia on the eastern borders of the Roman Empire and were presumably the fruits of commercial and cultural contacts. There were probably others in the South of Arabia, a region which had commercial intercourse with the Mediterranean world, especially through Alexandria, a city where. . . Christians were numerous.[13]

Westward across North Africa

We don't know much about the evangelization of Egypt "except that Christians were reported in Alexandria in the reign of Hadrian (c. 125) and that by the end of the century there was a strong church there."[14] Jewish Christians from Cyrene took the gospel to Antioch (Acts 11:19). We assume that they also took the good news to their homeland, just west of Egypt. We should note that the churches in Egypt have a strong tradition that John Mark was the founder of their churches. We don't know whether the gospel spread from there to Carthage, or whether it came across the Mediterranean Sea from Rome, since Carthage was a Roman colony. But we do know that there were strong churches there early, which produced an early Latin translation of the New Testament and outstanding Christian leaders, like polemicist **Tertullian** (160?-230?), teacher **Cyprian** of Carthage (200?-258), orator and apologist Lactantius (260?-340?), and dominant theologian **Augustine** of North Africa (354-430).

Ten periods of persecution

One of the significant factors in church expansion, as mentioned above, was the testimony of Christians who were willing to suffer persecution and even death for Christ. This was true of the Macedonian churches which Paul founded and it was true through the ten periods of persecution during the first three centuries. **Polycarp** (59?-156?) was one such church leader, overseer in the church of Smyrna in the second century. He was a disciple of the Apostle John and had a fruitful ministry in Asia Minor, which was ended in A.D. 156 at the age of eighty-six by his martyrdom at the stake. His strong refusal to deny Christ left an indelible impression upon the witnesses and encouraged others to openly declare their faith in Christ. Many other examples of martyrdom in this period could be given.[15]

After the Conversion of Emperor Constantine

The conversion of the Roman Emperor Constantine to Christianity was a major turning point in the history of the expansion of the church. First there was the Edict of Toleration of Christianity in A.D. 313 followed by his conversion ten years later. It is estimated that the Christian population in the empire at that time was about 10 to 15 percent. Constantine took certain Christian initiatives, like convening the Council of Nicea to decide the issue of Christ's full deity which was dividing the churches. He had to go slowly in order not to offend the non-Christians. Thus it was not until a generation later that Christianity was declared the state religion of the Roman Empire. These events opened up the doors of the churches to a flood of converts, many of whom came with ulterior motives. With the new prestige and political power gained by the church, it was quickly corrupted by compromise with Roman religion and by being politicized.

Was the conversion of Constantine a positive or a negative factor? What seemed to be a great victory for the Christians ended up in reality as a negative factor for the spiritual growth of the churches. To complicate things further, many sincere Christians reacted against the compromises and corruption of the church by turning toward asceticism, or withdrawal from the world, as the solution. Thus the church was diverted in two directions.

Not only within the empire, but also outside its borders the political victory of Christianity was a mixed blessing. Now that the empire was 'Christian' the attitude of people outside the boundaries of the empire became more hesitant about Christianity. They feared and opposed the political power of Rome, and naturally became more reluctant to accept the religion of the imperial government. To make matters worse, the spiritual fires so necessary to missionary concern were quenched by the politicizing of the church. Now that Christianity had become dominant within the Empire, it seemed less important to evangelize outside it. But there were notable instances of missionary activity in the centuries after the Edict of Toleration.

Ulfilas, missionary to Goths

One of the outstanding missionaries in the post-Constantine period was **Ulfilas** (310?-383), missionary to the barbarian Goths, who lived in the area of present-day Romania, across the Danube River outside the Roman Empire. Ulfilas was raised among the Goths and converted to Christ while in Constantinople on diplomatic service. After ten years he was sent back as bishop of the Goths (possibly some churches already existed). Forty years of evangelism proved to be very fruitful. He translated most of the Bible into the unwritten Gothic language, for which he had to devise an alphabet. In A.D. 348 opposition from the Gothic chieftain Athanaric forced Ulfilas to move his Gothic Christian community across the Danube River into the safety of the empire. But the evangelization of the Goths continued through many of his converts. The major negative aspect of Ulfilas' ministry was that he held "a mild form of Arianism," which was weak in its view of the full deity of Christ.[16] Nevertheless, Ulfilas' missionary career is still remarkable.

Patrick, missionary to Ireland

The fifth-century missionary **Patrick** (389?-461?) is grossly misrepresented today. He was an evangelical Celtic believer from Britain who owed nothing to the church in Rome (which was now becoming increasingly compromised). Although his father was a deacon in the Celtic church, Patrick did not have a personal faith in Christ until he was carried captive by an Irish raiding party and enslaved in Ireland. After six years he escaped back to Britain and went on to Gaul for study and ordination. In A.D. 432, past the age of forty, Patrick arrived in Ireland as a missionary. Although there were scattered Christian congregations, the vast majority of the people were Druid pagans, worshipping objects of nature and practicing magic and even human sacrifice. He encountered stiff opposition from the Druid priests but eventually persuaded King Loigaire to grant religious toleration to Christians. But that was only after surviving many perilous situations. In over thirty years his ministry resulted in about two hundred churches and an estimated one hundred thousand converts. Although there seemed to be some compromise with pagan practices, Patrick stressed spiritual growth through teaching of Scripture and encouragement to involvement in ministry and witness.[17]

Patrick's influence continued long after his own time and extended beyond the borders of his own country. The monasteries which became an integral part of Celtic Christianity were not only centers of Christian culture but also of missionary zeal. As such they played an important role in the evangelization of northern Europe in the following centuries.[18]

The conversion of the Franks

Not all of the spread of Christianity came through the work of missionaries directly. The conversion of rulers like the emperor Constan-tine helped in the extension of the church. Most significant was the conversion of Clovis, the king of the Franks in Gaul (modern France) along with three thousand of his warriors in 496. Although some of the Franks were already Christians, this accelerated the flow of converts substantially.

Since Clovis's own motives were clearly mixed with the issue of victory in battle, this mass movement undoubtedly increased the adulteration of the church with merely nominal Christians. As spiritual standards and emphasis upon a personal faith in Christ weakened, this sort of mass conversion became more common in the christianization of Europe.

MEDIEVAL MISSIONARY EXPANSION
(A.D. 500 TO 1200)

Nestorian expansion to the east

East of the Roman Empire Christians had spread into Mesopotamia and Persia, which were controlled by the Persian Empire. The churches there came under the influence of some exiled followers of Nestorius, the deposed former Bishop of Alexandria, and came to be known as Nestorian churches. They held a different view of the two natures of Christ than the Roman church. Although it possibly was weaker than the 'orthodox' view, their view helped to avoid the evil of Mariolatry, which was spreading in the Roman churches.

Not being bound up to the Roman Empire, the Nestorian churches proved to be very missionary-minded. Latourette affirms:

> In spite of prohibitory laws they won numbers of converts from Persian Zoroastrianism, more than they were later to gain from the Moslem Arabs. South and East of the Caspian, in Central Asia, they had many communities and missionaries. There were Nestorian churches and bishops and even metropolitans in some of the caravan cities of Central Asia, among them Merv, Herat, and Samarqand. Before the Arab conquests Christianity seems to have spread widely among the non-Christian peoples of this area, notably among the Turks and the Hephthalite Huns.[19]

It seems clear that the Syriac Nestorians spread into the southern tip of India and are today known there as the Mar Thoma churches (possibly founded by the Apostle Thomas himself). It was the Nestorians who first introduced Christianity into China in A.D. 635, where it only survived as a minority religion for about two centuries until an imperial decree against monasteries, aimed at the Buddhists, forced the Nestorians out. How tragic that this monastic aberration caused this failure.

The Christianization of Europe

Britain. There is clear evidence of churches in Britain by the time of the Emperor Constantine, as seen in the presence of three bishops from Britain in the Council of Arles in 314. However, the pagan Anglo Saxon invasions in the fifth century so devastated the churches that Britain had to be reevangelized in the sixth century, as missionaries were sent both from Ireland and from Rome.

Since Ireland was safe from the pagan invaders, it was the Irish Celtic church which was to be a major force in evangelizing Europe. **Columba** (521-597) was an Irishman who, with twelve companions, is renowned for forming a missionary center on the island of Iona, between Ireland and Scotland. From Iona they not only evangelized Scotland, but missionaries continued to go out from Iona for two centuries to evangelize Britain and continental Europe. In the seventh century **Aidan** evangelized the fierce Angles and Saxons of Northumbria. About the same time the Roman Bishop, Gregory the Great, sent forty Benedictine monks to England under Augustine (not the fifth century bishop of Hippo). King Ethelbert was ultimately converted, and the Roman form of Christianity won out in England.

Continental Europe. The names of the Celtic missionaries who evangelized (or re-evangelized) the Continent are many. **Columban** (543-615) and twelve companions re-evangelized Gaul and what is today Switzerland in the sixth century. **Willibrord** (657?-739) and eleven companions became the first missionaries to the Frisians of the Low Countries. Despite political tensions, they succeeded in establishing a strong church among the Frisians. In the eighth century an English noble turned Benedictine missionary named **Boniface** (680-754) spent forty years evangelizing the pagan tribespeople of Germany who worshipped the gods of nature. He won a great victory for Christianity by chopping down the sacred oak of Thor at Geismar in Hesse. Through this 'power encounter', thousands recognized the bankruptcy of paganism and came for baptism. Boniface also tried to reform the corrupted Frankish church (from the mass movement of Clovis) but was only partially successful.

Scandinavia. Kane's description here is most apt:

> The Vikings of Scandinavia were the scourge of England and the Continent during the ninth century. So devastating were their raids on the monasteries and churches that for a time they threatened to terminate the missionary outreach of the English Church. The tide was turned only when Alfred the Great won a decisive victory in 878 and forced some thirty leading Vikings to accept Christianity.[20]

It took several hundred years, however, before the missionaries to Scandinavia saw any great turning to Christ. The great missionary **Anskar** (801-865) first evangelized Sweden. Later he trained missionaries to reach Denmark. The conversion of Norway was accomplished more by the visits of some of their kings to England which brought about their conversion. It took several centuries of pressure from the throne, however, to bring about the complete conversion of the people by the eleventh century.

Eastern Europe. Just as in the west the Roman form of Christianity became dominant, so in the east the Greek form was dominant, with its headquarters in Constantinople (ancient Byzantium). This Byzantine form of Christianity of the Byzantine Empire was not as missionary-minded as the western form. However, two brothers named **Cyril** (827?-869) and **Methodius** were outstanding in the ninth century in evangelizing eastern Europe. They were first sent to the Slavic people of Moravia (in modern Czech Republic) and having reduced the language to writing began to translate the Bible. They aroused the opposition of the western churches by their use of the vernacular rather than Greek or Latin in worship. After their deaths the Moravian Christians were forced to flee to Bulgaria, where King Boris had been converted. By Boris's death in 907 Bulgaria had become a Christian center in the Slavic world. From there Russia and Poland were evangelized by the end of the twelfth century. Although there were two abortive attempts to convert the Ukrainians, it was not until Prince Vladimir was baptized in Kiev in 988 that Christianity took a permanent hold in Russia. It was during this same period that Christianity penetrated the royalty in Poland which was becoming the largest kingdom in Eastern Europe. After some centuries of struggle, missionary work there was successful in the conversion of the masses.

Thus it can be concluded that by 1200 all of Europe was Christianized. As has been noted, it was both through direct missionary effort and the conversion of kings that this was accomplished. As with the conversion of the Emperor Constantine, the conversion of these kings was not necessarily a spiritual matter and frequently introduced a carnal element into the conversion process. Sometimes it involved merely baptizing many people and things that were more pagan than Christian. But it did open up Europe to the more spiritual evangelism of those smaller bands of evangelical Christians who persisted in different parts of Europe over the centuries which we call the Dark Ages.

CONFRONTATION WITH ISLAM

The pagan Animism of the European tribal peoples was not the only obstacle Christianity had to fight to win Europe. In the seventh and eighth centuries and again in the fifteenth, Islam was to become a most formidable opponent to the spread of Christianity. In Europe, conquering Muslim armies were a continuing threat.

The first tide of conquest

When the 'Prophet' Muhammad died in A.D. 632, ten years after his migration from Medina to Mecca, his followers controlled the whole of the Arabian Peninsula. After his death they continued to expand their conquests, as Davil Johnson describes:

Muslim armies rapidly overran the nations of the Fertile Crescent, from Syria to the Persian Gulf, and then moved to conquer Egypt. Twenty-five years after Muhammad's death, the religion had reached east as far as Afghanistan and west into Tunisia, North Africa. By the early eighth century, the religion had reached Morocco and was moving through Spain into France. Islam was on its way to conquering Europe when Charles Martel defeated the Muslim Moors at Tours, France, in A.D. 732. At the same time it moved deep into Asia, north and east into what is now Pakistan. . . . Later, Spain and Portugal were retaken by Christian Europe; and the Crusades made their mark upon Palestine by leaving a population of Christian immigrants.[21]

Note that the Battle of Tours was exactly one century after Muhammad's death, and halted the first surge of the Muslim advance. For the next five or more centuries there was a stalemate in the conflict, which focused around the changing fortunes of the Crusades. Although from 1096 to 1244 a series of four major Crusades succeeded in holding Jerusalem for less than a century, they succeeded mainly in weakening the 'Christian' Byzantine Empire and in alienating the Muslims by the savagery of the warfare.

The second surge

Two centuries after the retaking of Jerusalem by the Muslims in 1244, Constantinople, the capital of Eastern Christendom, also fell to the Muslim Turks (1453), whose armies penetrated the Balkans to the walls of Vienna. About this time Mongols from central Asia, having been converted to Islam, invaded northern India and established the Moghul Empire, which ruled north India for centuries until the British ascendancy there.

From India Islam spread down the peninsula of Malaya and across the straits to the East Indies. From there it spread east and north to the Philippine Islands, where its march was stopped on the island of Mindanao by the Roman Catholics moving south.[22]

It should not be assumed that all this was accomplished directly with the sword. Although millions converted under threat of the sword, Christians and Jews were to have been tolerated as "people of the book." What then happened to the 'Christians' of North Africa? Apparently over generations, military, political, social, and religious pressures brought about their apostasy from Christianity and conversion to Islam. As we noted previously, Muslim traders and businessmen brought Islam to many areas that were not militarily conquered, like Africa south of the Sahara. So by the time of Christopher Columbus, Islam was the largest of the world's religions. That was changed by Roman Catholic advances and the Protestant missionary movement.

ROMAN CATHOLIC MISSIONS

As we have seen, the energies of the developing Roman Catholic church in Europe were dissipated in the confrontation with Islam and in the conflict between the western and eastern branches of the church. But by the end of the thirteenth century a number of Catholic orders began a missionary outreach outside of Europe which outflanked the Muslim expansion and ultimately regained for the Catholic Church more than she was to lose from the Protestant Reformation.

But first we should mention some early attempts to win Muslims to Christ during the medieval period. **John of Damascus** (675?-749), an Eastern Church theologian, debated the Muslim Caliph. **Francis of Assisi** (1182-1226) made three attempts to reach the Muslims, none of which were particularly successful. In 1219 he presented the gospel to the Sultan of Egypt, but language barriers made communication difficult. More fruitful were the efforts of **Raymond Lull** (1235-1315), a wealthy nobleman from the island of Majorca off the coast of Spain. Some years after his conversion in his early thirties from a life of debauchery, he began to aggressively promote missions to Muslims as far better than military crusades. In 1276 he opened a training center for Franciscan monks to reach out to Muslims and ultimately made three missionary trips to North Africa. The first two ended in prison and banishment, but returning in 1314, past the age of eighty, he was able to win a few converts and ultimately was stoned to death by the Muslims. It does not seem that any of the Franciscans followed his example. Thus Raymond Lull was a brief bright star in the dark ages.[23]

Another early Catholic missionary effort was the first of two to penetrate the great Chinese empire. It began with the ministry of Franciscan friar, **John of Monte Corvino**, from 1294 to 1330, during which one hundred thousand converts were won. By 1368 the Ming Chinese rulers came to power and expelled the missionaries, resulting in Catholicism dying out in China. Another more successful attempt was made two hundred years later by Jesuit **Matteo Ricci** (1552-1610) who became influential by adopting Chinese culture and opened up China to other Jesuit missionaries. By 1650 they had won a quarter million converts. Later Franciscan and Dominican missionaries opposed the compromises with Confucian religion which the Jesuits had made, and the ensuing controversy between the Pope and the Chinese emperor brought about a persecution of the Catholics and a major setback for the church.

The greatest development of Roman Catholic missions arose out of the exploration and development of the empires of Roman Catholic countries, especially Spain, Portugal, and France. Catholic missionaries accompanied all of the exploratory expeditions of the Portuguese down the west coast of Africa and on to India and the East Indies (Indonesia) in the fifteenth century. Then after the discovery of the New World, priests accompanied the Conquistadors on their colonization and subjugation expeditions (see ch. 18 for more detail).

The Roman Catholic Church was fortunate in having at its command scores of religious orders whose dedicated members were trained and ready for any kind of service. Their vows of obedience and celibacy provided the two most desirable qualities for pioneer missionary work, servility and mobility.

. . . .

Four orders in particular were called upon to share the burden and the glory of the missionary enterprise: the Franciscans, founded by Francis of Assisi (1182-1226); the Dominicans, founded by a Spanish priest, Dominic (1170-1221); the Augustinians, organized by Pope Alexander IV in 1256; and the Jesuits, founded in 1540 by a Spanish Nobleman, Ignatius Loyola.[24]

Most of the outstanding Catholic missionary efforts took place after the Protestant reformation, stimulated by the worldwide explorations of the period. **Francis Xavier** (1506-1552) was probably the greatest and most famous of the Jesuit pioneers. In 1542 he began a three-year ministry in the Portuguese colony of Goa in South India. Another three-year ministry on the Malay Peninsula was followed by two years in opening up Japan with two other Jesuits and a Japanese convert as interpreter.

Xavier and his companions arrived in Japan at an opportune time both politically and religiously. Converts "came from all classes: Buddhist monks, Shinto priests, scholars, samurai, and the common people. . . . By the turn of the century [1600] Christian [Catholic] converts numbered half a million." But the political situation changed radically with the assassination of the Mikado's chief minister, who had been favorable to the Catholics. Kane continues:

> Following the anti-Christian edicts of 1606 and 1614, all foreign missioners were expelled and the Japanese Christians were called upon to recant or face death. The persecutions which followed were as barbaric as any in the history of the Christian mission. . . . For 230 years Japan remained a hermit nation, effectively sealed off from contact with the rest of the world.[25]

The story of the Spanish colonization of the Philippine Islands and of the Catholic missionary endeavor there is much more positive. **Father Legaspi** began the Augustinian work in 1564, other orders followed, and within a century they had baptized two million converts. The Catholic missions built hospitals, schools, and colleges and gradually trained an indigenous clergy. Almost four centuries of Spanish rule and Catholic missions has made the Philippines the only nominally Christian country in Asia. Even though there has been much compromise with the pagan beliefs of the Filipinos, resulting in a generally superstitious type of Catholicism there, there are two positive factors. The Catholic Church stopped the spread of Islam from the south on the island of Mindanao, and the Catholic population has been much more open to the preaching of evangelical Christianity in this century.

It was the French Jesuit **Alexander de Rhodes** (1591-1660) who spearheaded the mission to French Indochina (Viet Nam). He met with immediate success in baptizing hundreds of thousands of converts. Today there are millions of Catholics in Viet Nam (which now is under communist rule). It is noteworthy that Jesuit Rudolf Acquaviva (1550-1583) was invited to represent the Catholic Church in the court of the Muslim Moghul emperor Akbar of North India. Although Acquaviva and his successors had tremendous entree into the court, Akbar remained a Muslim and few converts resulted. An Italian Jesuit named **Robert de Nobili** had considerably greater success in Madura in the south of India in 1605 by adopting the Indian food and dress. As a result today there are over ten million Roman Catholics in the south of India.

On the other hand, the story of early Catholic missions to Africa is one of essential failure. Promising starts in country after country proved to be abortive, with the result that "by the middle of the eighteenth century there was hardly a trace of Roman Catholic missions in Africa."[26] Modern Catholic missions to Africa have been more successful and Catholicism has become a force in Africa today (see chapter 17).

How can we evaluate the impact of Catholic missions? A number of observations are in order:

1) Roman Catholics, operating out of a strong power base, were able to do what Protestants had not yet ventured to do.
2) The value of the Catholic orders in missionary work was significant.
3) It is obvious that the priests baptized millions who had only a dim perception of what Catholicism was (and less of the true gospel).
4) Frequent compromises with animistic religion weakened the church.
5) The superficiality of the conversions was shown by a lack of perma nence in many places.

PREREFORMATION EVANGELICALS

In order to understand the currents of the work of God leading up to the Protestant Reformation and the restoration of evangelical missions, it is important to understand that there was a lot of evangelical activity going on outside the evolving Roman Catholic church. There were a host of persecuted Christian groups which operated independently of the dominant church. But because they were persecuted by the dominant church's use of civil power, the records of these Evangelicals have been destroyed, repressed, and misrepresented. Indeed the excuse for persecution was often that they were heretics, and there were heretical

groups. But there was a continuing succession of truly evangelical believers throughout the centuries who continued to worship and evangelized according to the Scriptures.

It was not long after the rule of the Emperor Constantine that the
previously persecuted church began to misuse civil power to persecute
true believers. **Priscillian** was a wealthy Spaniard who along with six of
his followers became the first victim of this abuse, being beheaded in
A.D. 385. The discovery a century ago of some of his writings makes it
clear that he was not a heretic, but rather a zealous evangelical Christian.[27] We know little about such groups in the next few centuries, but
we do know that a substantial evangelical movement called the
Paulicians arose in the last half of the seventh century and seemed to be
active for about three hundred years. The Paulicians saw the Roman,
Greek, and Armenian churches as apostate and opposed the common
magical view of the sacraments and other corruptions which had developed.[28]

The list of such believers and groups is long and beyond the purpose
of this book to examine. Writers like Broadbent, Orchard, Newman and
others have done so. But we should at least mention the **Bogomiles,**
Peter deBruys, Arnold of Brescia, Tanchelm, Henry of Lausanne, Eudo
deStella, **Peter Waldo and the Waldenses,** Marsilius of Padua, Peter
Chelcichy, the **Bohemian Brethren, the Albigenses, John Wycliffe and the
Lollards, John Hus,** the Taborites, the Brethren of the Common Life,
Menno Simon, the Anabaptists, and many others (see time-line chart). In
a real sense they were the forerunners of the Reformation. These evangelical believers were fully occupied with evangelism and survival amidst
ongoing persecution and did not have opportunity to think of missions.
But they did lay a spiritual foundation for the radical branches of the
reformation out of which the modern missionary movement arose.

Perspectives enrichment: Chapters B-1, 2, 4, 5

1. Ruth A. Tucker, *From Jerusalem to Irian Jaya*, (1983), p. 25.

2. J. Herbert Kane, *A Concise History of the Christian World Mission* (1987), p. 9.

3. Adolf Harnack, *The Expansion of Christianity: The First Three Centuries*, vol. 2, pp. 452-53, 456-68.

4. Roland Allen, *Missionary Methods: St. Paul's or Ours?* (1962); and John L. Nevius, *Planting and Development of Missionary Churches* (1958).

5. Kane, *Concise History*, pp. 9-10.

6. Kenneth Scott Latourette, *A History of Christianity* (1953), p.76.

7. Tucker, *Jerusalem to Irian Jaya*, p. 26.

8. Kane, *Concise History*, p. 11.

9. F. F. Bruce, *The Spreading Flame* (1958), p. 354.

10. Flavius Josephus, *The Works of Flavius Josephus*, trans. William Whiston (1911), p. 600.

11. Ibid, p. 284-86.

12. Kane, *Concise History*, p. 12.

13. Latourette, *History*, p. 80.

14. Kane, *Concise History*, p. 10.

15. Tucker, *Jerusalem to Irian Jaya,* pp. 31-35.

16. Latourette, *A History of the Expansion of Christianity: The First Five Centuries,* vol. 1 (1970), p. 213.

17. Tucker, *Jerusalem to Irian Jaya*, pp. 38-40.

18. Kane, *Concise History*, p. 13.

19. Latourette, *A History of Christianity*, p. 323.

20. Kane, *Concise History*, p. 43.

21. David L. Johnson, *A Reasoned Look at Asian Religions* (1985), p. 152.

22. Kane, *Understanding Missions*, p. 186.

23. Tucker, *Jerusalem to Irian Jaya*, pp. 52-57.

24. Kane, *Concise History*, pp. 58-59.

25. Ibid, p. 61-2.

26. Ibid, p. 71.

27. E. H. Broadbent, *The Pilgrim Church* (1931), pp. 36-40.

28. Albert Henry Newman, *A Manual of Church History* (1899), I: 379-86. Also see G. H. Orchard, *A Concise History of Baptists* (1956).

Fourteen Centuries of Advance Through Opposition

400 500 600 700 800 900 1000 1100 1200 1300 1400 1500 1600 1700

Roman Catholic Missions

Friar John/China •1294   Jesuits •1534
Xavier/India •1542
Xavier/Japan • 1548
Legaspi/Philippines • 1564
Ricci/China •1583
DeNobli/India • 1605
DeRhodes/Viet Nam •1650

Reformation Missions

Eliot/Algonquins 1644 •
Von Welz /Surinam 1664 •
Danish—Halle/India 1705•
Egede/Greenland 1722 •
Zinzendorf/Herrnhut 1722 •
Moravians/Caribbean 1732•
Moravians/Africa 1737•
Brainerd/N.A. indians 1743•

Early Pioneer Missions

•348 Ulfilas/Goths
432•Patrick/Ireland
496•Clovis/Franks
d.596•Columba/Scotland
595•Augustine & Benedictines/Britain
585• Columban/Gaul
635• Nestorians/China
692•Willibrord/Frisians
722 •Boniface/Germany
823• Anskar/Scandinavia
865•Boris/Bulgars
869•Cyril & Methodius/Slavs
878 •Viking kings conv.

Persecuted Evangelical Witnesses

385
•Priscillan beheaded
650•— Paulicians
870•——•970
Bogomiles——•1111
Peter deBruys• 1104
Tanchelm •1115
Henry of Lausanne • 1116
Arnold of Brescia • 1140
Eudo deStella• 1148
Peter Waldo/Waldensians • 1170
1312• Marsilius of Padua
1384• Wycliffe/Lollards
1415• Hus burned
1415• Taborites
1419•Chelcichy
1457•Bohemian Brethren

The Muslim World

620 • Islam founded
732•Battle of Tours
1096–1291 •Nine Crusades•
1212• Francis' mission/Syria
1276• Raymond Lull /Tunisia
Turk & Mongol conquests
Fall of Constantinople•1453
Budovetz/Constantinople • 1577

313
Edict of Toleration

TWO CENTURIES OF THE
GREAT PROTESTANT OMISSION

DATE:	PERSON/EVENT:	OUTCOME:
A.D. 1555	Huguenot chaplains to Brazil	Murdered by Catholics
1577-81	Verceslaus Budovetz to Istanbul	One Muslim convert
1590	Saravia's chapter on missions	Theodore Beza disputed
1595	Dutch East Indies chaplains' Malay Bible translation	Malay churches
1649	Society for the Propagation of the Gospel in New England	Missions to American Indians
1644-71	John Eliot's mission to Indians	Algonquin Bible and churches
1651	Count Truchsess' question to Lutheran leaders of Germany	Leaders rationalized missions to the heathen
1661	Quaker Founder George Fox sent 3 missionaries to China.	Disappeared
1664	Baron Justinian VonWelz went to Dutch Guiana as missionary	Johann Ursinius disputed; VonWelz died of disease.
1698	Society for the Propagation of the Gospel	First Anglican mission board for colonists
1701	Society for the Propagation of the Gospel in Foreign Parts	Mission to reach colonists and Amerindians
1705	Danish-Halle Mission: Ziegenbalg & Plutshau to Tranquebar in India	First Lutheran missionary churches and continuing missionary enterprise

"I know your deeds, that you have a name
that you are alive, but you are dead. Wake
up, and strengthen the things which remain,
which were about to die; for I have not
found your deeds completed in the sight of
my God."   Revelation 3:1-2

REFORMATION MISSIONS:
MISSION IMPOSSIBLE?
(A.D. 1517-1705)

The Protestant Reformation was an attempt to restore the church to
apostolic Christianity. One would imagine that shortly after the reformation the Protestants would seek to establish foreign mission efforts of
their own, especially in the light of the Roman Catholic efforts so recently
developed. Unfortunately, the opposite was true. It took the Protestants
almost two centuries to get around to any significant missionary enterprise, and all the while the Catholics were recouping their losses from
the Reformation by sending out priests from a number of orders to convert the heathen. Indeed, it is said that they gained more by missionary
effort than they lost to the Protestants.[1]

How can we account for this shocking fact—this great omission? If
we visualize the Reformation as a full-fledged restoration of apostolic
Christianity, then the facts are unexplainable. But if we realize that the
Protestant Reformation was a complex movement involving political,
economic, social, cultural, and spiritual factors, it then becomes more
comprehensible, though no less reprehensible. There is a vast literature
on the connection of the secular Renaissance to the religious Reformation. Certainly the invention of the printing press half a century earlier
paved the way for the Protestant movement, especially since it was
based upon a return to Scripture and the necessity to disseminate the
truth. But for the most part the Reformation did not go far enough in the
recovery of God's truth, with the result that a number of theological,
circumstantial, and spiritual obstacles remained to the restoration among
Protestants of God's program of worldwide evangelism.

MISSION HARBINGERS IN
TWO BARREN CENTURIES

The two centuries after the Reformation were not totally devoid of missionary activity. However, what few and feeble efforts can be traced did not come from the main stream of Protestants for the most part, but rather from the more radical part of that Reformation, as we shall see in the next chapter. First let us survey the indications of missionary interest in the two centuries before the Danish-Halle Mission of 1705.

The earliest indication is also the most controversial. In 1555 a group of a few hundred **French Calvinist Huguenots** went to Brazil to start a Protestant colony. They requested John Calvin to send some chaplains from Geneva to participate, and four did go. We are not sure how much of their concern was for the spiritual welfare of the colonists and how much to evangelize the heathen (the letters are lost). There were some attempts to preach to the Indians but without results, mostly because of the language barrier. The colony failed and most of the colonists were murdered by the Portuguese Catholics.[2]

Verceslaus Budovetz of Budapest was probably the first Protestant missionary to the Muslims. Raised in the Unitas Fratrum church, which sprang from the ministry of John Hus, he studied in the Protestant Universities of Western Europe and became a Calvinist. He lived in Constantinople (Istanbul) from 1577 to 1581 and witnessed to the Muslims, winning only one to Christ. Later he wrote a book against the Quran. He was greatly impressed with the hold that Islam had upon the people.[3]

In 1590 a Reformed pastor in Belgium named **Hadrian Saravia** included a chapter on missions in a book he published, seeking to show that the Great Commission is still binding on us today since the Apostles did not fulfill it completely. However, Calvin's successor in Geneva, Theodore Beza, disputed Saravia's interpretation of the Great Commission by claiming that it was binding only on the Apostles.

By 1595 the Dutch Calvinists were sending chaplains out with the Dutch colonialists to the East Indies (today Indonesia) and Ceylon. They translated the Bible into the Malay language and baptized many converts in both areas, many of whom probably converted with ulterior motives. Nevertheless, there is a substantial Reformed community in present-day Indonesia as a result.[4]

It took another half century before an actual mission board was formed. In 1649 the **Society for the Propagation of the Gospel in New England** was formed to reach the Indians of New England. In 1644 a nonconformist pastor in Roxbury, Massachusetts, named **John Eliot,** had become burdened for the nearby Algonquin Indians. After two years of difficult language study he began to preach to the Indians. By the second sermon the Indians began to ask questions, and within a few months Eliot had seen some genuine conversions. As the number of converts grew, Eliot got land set aside for Christian Indian villages, the first of which was Natick. By 1649, when he began translation work, he also was appointed as the first missionary of the S.P.G. in New England. By 1663 he completed the translation of the whole Bible into Algonquin, and by 1671 he had gathered more than eleven hundred Indians into fourteen "praying towns."[5]

The next few stirrings of missionary interest are not as positive to report. In 1651 **Count Truchsess** of Wetzhausen, Germany, a prominent Lutheran layman, challenged the theological faculty of Wittenberg as to why Lutherans were not sending out missionaries in obedience to the Great Commission. Their response is a sad testimony to the thinking common in Protestant circles in that day. They argued that the Great Commission was given only to the Apostles and was fulfilled by them. Then they said that if the heathen are lost, it is their own fault since they rejected God's word from Noah on down to the Apostles, who evangelized the whole human race. They also argued that it is the responsibility of the government, not the church, to provide for preaching to the heathen.[6] In contrast in 1661 **George Fox**, the founder of the Society of Friends (Quakers), sent three missionaries to China, but they never reached the field.

Three years later an Austrian Lutheran nobleman named **Justinian Von Welz** began to advocate the cause of foreign missions. When Baron Von Welz's sharp admonitions to Lutheran church authorities fell on deaf ears, he "proceeded to Holland, were he abandoned his baronial title. Following ordination as an 'apostle to the Gentiles,' he sailed for Dutch Guiana (Surinam), where he died an early death before he could reap a harvest."[7] An official refutation of Von Welz's views had been given by **Johann Ursinius**, a Lutheran theologian, citing the difficulty of the missionary task and of recruiting missionaries, the deep depravity of the heathen making conversion next to impossible, the great need at home, and the responsibility of Christians already living in heathen lands to make the gospel known. Gustav Warneck's comment on this viewpoint is apt: "Where there are Christians, missions are superfluous; and where there are no Christians, they are hopeless.[8]

Our survey of the feeble missionary efforts during the sixteenth and seventeenth centuries brings us to the founding of two Anglican (Church of England) missions. Although the Society for Promoting Christian Knowledge was organized in 1698 for the purpose of strengthening the religious life of the white settlers in the New World, it gradually became a missionary agency in reaching out to the non-Christians. Three years later the **Society for the Propagation of the Gospel in Foreign Parts** was also formed for the dual purpose of ministering to the settlers and also to evangelize the heathen. It is noteworthy that both of these missions represent the High Church, that is, the Anglo-Catholics in the Church of England. Thus ironically we see missionary interest in both edges of the reformation movement, but little in the mainstream.

So we see the resistance on the part of Protestant leaders to their responsibility for world evangelization, an attitude that almost totally squelched any missionary initiative for two centuries. How can we reckon with the fact that the Reformation restored the message of salvation, yet did not care to share that message with a lost world? Let us seek to understand the reasons.

REASONS FOR THE GREAT OMISSION

A number of explanations have been given by various writers to account for the lack of missionary interest and activity on the part of the Protestant reformers and their followers. We have already noted a few of the reasons given by Protestant leaders themselves during those centuries. We believe that there were many factors involved. Let us try to understand what the reality was.

The difficult circumstances of the Protestants

Although the Protestant movement grew very rapidly, it was always a minority in Europe and had to fight for its very existence for centuries. Although it flourished in parts of Germany, Scandinavia, the Low Countries, Switzerland, and ultimately England and Scotland, the struggle in France continued until 1685 when the **St. Bartholemew's Day Massacre** and the revocation of the **Edict of Nantes** devastated the Protestant Huguenots. Most survivors fled the country. The Roman Catholic Church did not take the Reformation lying down, but organized a Counter Reformation religiously, economically, politically, and organizationally. Europe was wracked with a series of religious wars in which the Protestants struggled for survival.

To make matters worse, the Protestants quibbled among themselves theologically and in no way presented a united front against the Catholics. Not only did the Lutherans and the Calvinists hurl anathemas against each other, but they joined in persecuting the Anabaptists because of their belief in the need of a more radical reformation of the church.

Arising out of the circumstances of the Reformation was the fact that the Protestant countries were geographically more isolated from Africa and Asia and got involved in colonial enterprises more belatedly. While this factor was clearly present, it does not excuse the Protestant slowness, for even after the Dutch, Scandinavians, and English had begun to establish colonies around the world, they still did little to evangelize the non-Christians there. Indeed, the trading companies which they set up hindered the spread of the gospel in most cases.

The lack of parachurch orders

A number of writers have pointed out how the Protestants, in reacting against the monastic orders of Roman Catholicism, seem to have 'thrown out the baby with the bath water.' The lack of an effective structure for missions hindered Protestant missions for two centuries. While the Roman Catholics were making full use of the **Franciscans, Dominicans, Augustinians, and Jesuits,** the Protestants had no such orders to function as mission boards. Indeed, Ralph Winter argues very forcefully that there are biblically and historically two structures for carrying out God's work: the church and the parachurch mission board.[9] It was not until parachurch mission boards were organized that the modern Protestant missionary movement really began to flourish.

Common rationalizations

It is also very clear that some of the same rationalization found among Christians today were in vogue at that time. How many have used the expression "Charity begins at home" to justify unconcern for missions? Over three centuries ago Johann Ursinius used the argument that the many Jews and heathen at home should be reached before going to pagans in far-off lands. It sounds very familiar. The truth is that we can never totally reach our own homeland, so the time will never come when we will send out missionaries on that basis. We have already noted Ursinius's argument of the responsibility of Christians already in pagan lands to do the work of evangelization. He saw no room for sending missionaries at all. The most serious rationalization was that the heathen are too depraved to respond to the gospel. Ursinius misinterpreted Matthew 7:6: "The holy things of God are not to be cast before such dogs and swine."[10] Christ here is not referring to the heathen but to the false prophets and religious teachers (cf. Matt. 7:15-23; 2 Pet. 2:22). Clearly Ursinius did not understand that the doctrine of depravity involves all men, not just the heathen. He seems not to have understood the power of the Holy Spirit to convict and convince men of the truth of the gospel. Of course, centuries of successful missions have put the lie to his pessimism.

The theology of the reformers

There is considerable controversy over the missionary perspective of the great sixteenth-century reformers, **Luther, Calvin, and Zwingli.** It is generally agreed that by the second generation of the reformation, leaders like Beza and Melancthon rationalized away Christian responsibility. But what about Luther and Calvin? A number of writers have sought to defend the essential harmony of their viewpoint with missions to the heathen.[11] But when all the argument is done, the embarrassing fact remains: for two centuries Protestant leaders did virtually nothing to advance the cause of world evangelization. And from where did the second generation reformers get the distorted perspective that they show? They surely didn't get it from the Bible! There are a number of distinct theological problems.

We have already noted the view that the missionary mandate was only given to the Apostles, that they fulfilled it in their generation, and that since there are no apostles today, the commission is not binding on us today. Although this view cannot be attributed directly to Luther or Calvin, Coates admits that:

> It cannot be gainsaid, however, that Luther's expositions of great missionary passages as Matt. 28:19-20 and Mark 16:15 are usually devoid of any missionary emphasis. Moreover, there is a good deal of validity to the contention that Luther's concept of "mission" dealt primarily with the correction of unchristian conditions prevailing within Christendom at his time.[12]

The idea that the Apostles evangelized the heathen world in their own generation is so absurd historically to us today that we are amazed that they could make such statements. It is true that most translations of Colossians 1:23 might give that impression. But the ingressive aorist participle should be translated **"the gospel that you have heard, which is beginning to be proclaimed in all creation under heaven."** So neither the Bible nor church history support this absurd notion. Most evangelicals today would agree with the reformers that technically the office of apostle is no longer operative. However, since the missionary takes up part of the responsibility of the apostles and since the same Holy Spirit who was given at Pentecost is working through the church today, we are not thereby excused from obedience to the missionary mandate.

Another weakness inherent in the Reformers' theology was in their concept of the relationship of church and government. The Anabaptists, like most evangelicals today, held to separation of church and state. Unfortunately the Reformers did not see a sharp separation. Indeed, the prevailing view was of a *Landeskirche*, a territorial church. This is still common in Europe. Since all citizens in a territory are baptized into the territorial church, whether Roman Catholic, Lutheran, Anglican, etc., a close relationship exists between the government and the dominant church. (Other churches were viewed as illegal.) Luther and many of the Reformers clearly believed that it was the responsibility of the government to send out the missionaries. Although there was some government involvement in missions, for the most part governments can't be expected to do the work of the church.

The Reformers also seem to have had a distorted understanding of the implications of God's sovereignty. Luther, for example, did have a concern for Jews and Turks: "I do hope that our Gospel, now shining forth with a light so great, will before Judgment Day make an attack also on that abominable prophet Mohammed. May our Lord Jesus Christ do this soon."[13] Note that Luther seems to leave the responsibility with God to break through to the Muslims. The same seems to be the case with Calvin. Although many defend the Calvinistic view of sovereignty as compatible with missions, the fact is that many Christians right on down to William Carey's associate Dr. John Ryland have either misused the doctrine of God's sovereignty or else they have a distorted view of His sovereignty. The responsibility to fulfill the Great Commission is ours, not God's.

Finally we note that the Reformers' view of prophetic truth affected their view of missions. Apparently, most of the Reformers believed that the end of the world was near. There was no time for world evangelization before the end. This despite the clear statement of Christ that no one could know the time of His coming (Matt. 24:36).

Their limited concept of missions

The Reformers did not seem to have developed a biblical concept of missions. Luther had the idea that missions involved the church merely growing at its boundaries with heathen lands, using the illustration of ever-broadening ripples caused by a stone tossed into the water.[14] It is clear that this concept would have been very unsatisfying to the Apostle Paul (and to the Holy Spirit), since he leapfrogged the area of Asia Minor on his second journey to be moved on by the Spirit to Greece. Another common misconception in that day (and ours) is that one needs a direct commission or call from God to become a missionary. We have already dealt with that issue in chapter 6. Suffice it to say that the notion of a direct missionary call is without adequate Scriptural support as to allow the lack of it keeping missionaries from reaching a lost world of billions.

The spiritual weakness of the Reformation

Although we have identified many different reasons for the Great Omission, ultimately there is only one reason, and it a spiritual one. The Protestant Reformation did not have deep enough spiritual roots. The Reformation was not a great revival in which tens of millions of people were born again. Probably there were only a minority of Protestants who really came to the saving knowledge of Jesus Christ. The rest were swept along with the tide. With the territorial church arrangement of Europe it was not hard to be a Protestant without being born again. It is important to understand that the Reformers did not spell out a clear doctrine of regeneration or new birth. Much reliance was placed upon baptism and communion, which were seen as 'sacraments'. Luther himself saw the problem:

> If one considers rightly how the people now act who wish to be Protestant (by profession), and who know how to talk much about

Christ, there is nothing behind it. Thus the more part deceive themselves. Tenfold more were they who made a beginning with us, and who had serious pleasure in our teaching, but now not a tenth part of them remain steadfast.

· ·

If I were now to begin to preach the gospel I would act differently. The great rude masses I would leave under the rule of the Pope. They do not advance the gospel, but only abuse its freedom.[15]

The more we learn about the spiritual state of the reformation churches, the more it seems like Christ's words to the Sardis church in Revelation 3:1 apply, "I know your deeds; you have a reputation of being alive, but you are dead."[16] Before there could be world evangelism, there had to be spiritual renewal. That was two centuries in coming.

---

1. Kane, *Concise History*, p. 73.

2. Gustav Warneck, *Outline of a History of Protestant Missions*, p. 23.

3. Samuel M. Zwemer, "Calvinism and the Missionary Enterprise," *Theology Today* 7:213.

4. Kenneth Scott Latourette, *A History of Christianity*, pp. 933-35.

5. Ruth A. Tucker, *From Jerusalem to Irian Jaya*, pp. 84-89.

6. Warneck, *Outline*, pp. 27-28.

7. Kane, *Concise History*, p. 76.

8. Warneck, *Outline*, p. 38.

9. Ralph D. Winter, "The Two Structures in Redemptive Mission," *Perspectives*(1992), pp. B-45ff. For further discussion of this issue see chapters 4 and 21 of this text.

10. Warneck, *Outline*, p. 38.

11. Thomas Coates, "Were the Reformers Mission-Minded?" *Concordia Theological Monthly*, 40:9, 600-11; Charles Chaney, "The Missionary Dynamic in the Theology of John Calvin," *The Reformed Review*, 17:64, 24-38; Samuel M. Zwemer, p. 206-16; Harry R. Boer, *Pentecost and Missions* (1961), p. 18. Boer faults all the Reformers but Bucer in this regard.

12. Coates, "Reformers," p. 604.

13. Martin Luther, *Sammtliche Schriften,* 2d ed., ed. Joh. Georg Walch (St. Louis: Concordia Publishing House, 1880-1910), vol. 14, p. 305.

14. Coates, "Reformers," p. 601.

15. Martin Luther, quoted by Johannes Warns, *Baptism: Studies in the Original Christian Baptism,* trans. G. H. Lang (1957), p. 248, 252.

16. There is a striking parallel between the 7 churches and 7 major epochs of church history. There may be a secondary application here.

"I know your deeds. Behold, I have put before you an open door which no one can shut, because you have a little power, and have kept My word, and have not denied My name." —Revelation 3:8

MISSIONS RESTORED: COASTLANDS PIONEERS (A.D. 1705-1865)

For almost two centuries the lone voices for missions in Protestantism were ridiculed and isolated. We have seen that the underlying cause was spiritual. "Before the Protestant churches could launch a continuing missionary endeavor they must be inwardly renewed."[1] That renewal first sprang from a movement within the Lutheran state churches called 'Pietism'. Then it was augmented by movement from within the more radical branches of the reformation. It was further advanced by the Great Awakenings in England and America. Then there was further reinforcement arising from the vitality of the more radical nature of American Protestantism.[2] Spiritual renewal brought about an honest facing up to the biblical mandate which resulted in thousands of missionary pioneers being sent out to every continent in the next century and a half. The cost was very great in lives and sacrifice. Results were not always immediate or great. But the degree of dedication springing from that spiritual renewal was sufficient to advance the cause of Christ to an incredible degree.

EIGHTEENTH-CENTURY PIONEERS

Pietism and the Danish-Halle Mission

As we have seen, Protestantism right after the Reformation for the most part lacked spiritual depth. The state churches were composed of far too many people who had never been born again and knew nothing of personal Bible reading and prayer. There was a dead orthodoxy which was more concerned with a correct view of the sacraments than with a life lived in obedience to Christ. Pietism was a movement started by a Lutheran pastor named **Philip Spener** (1635-1705), who sought to cultivate the spiritual life by small-group Bible study and prayer meetings. Pietists stressed the necessity of a personal conversion experience which was a matter of the heart, not just the head. Spener was grieved by the arid and bitter theological disputations and the low moral state of both laity and clergy in the Lutheran state church. Essentially he began to develop "little churches within the church." His principles were published in his book, *Pia Desideria* in 1675. His ministry in Frankfort and Berlin drew a wide following.

Prominent among his followers was **August Franke** (1663-1727). Franke was born again while a professor at the University of Leipzig. Although forced out of the university because of his pietistic meetings, he helped the Elector (ruler) of Brandenburg to found the University of Halle in 1694. Through him this university became a chief center of Pietism. "He was the dominant figure on the theological faculty and in the training of young men for the ministry. A faithful pastor in his own parish, he brought to the lecture room not only theory but practical experience."[3] Pietism spread throughout the Lutheran churches of northern Europe. Missionaries went out from Halle to reach Jews and ultimately to India.

It was Pietism's spread to the royal court of Denmark that gave the original impetus for the first significant Protestant mission--the **Danish-Halle Mission.** King Frederick IV had become an ardent Pietist and commissioned his chaplain to find missionary candidates to go out to Denmark's colonies in the Orient to evangelize the native population. Failing to find volunteers in Denmark, they got two candidates from the pietistic University of Halle: **Bartholomew Ziegenbalg** and **Heinrich Plutschau.** These two were ordained by the Danish Lutherans despite strong opposition and ridicule, and by 1705 sailed with the King's support to the small colony of Tranquebar on the southern tip of India. Little did they know that on the same ship secret instructions were being sent from the Danish East India Company to the Governor of the colony to hinder their work in every possible way. Although they had many other obstacles besides the Governor's opposition to contend with, they made remarkable progress in learning the languages and witnessing for Christ. Ziegenbalg became fluent in Tamil in less than a year and completed the New Testament translation in the third year, the first in any language of India. Their statement was, "If the Lord should be pleased to grant us the Conversion of but one soul among the Heathens, we should think our Voyage sufficiently rewarded."[4]

Within the first year, this was more than fulfilled as they began to baptize converts, both heathen slaves and Hindus. Ziegenbalg and a new recruit, John Grundler, finished the Old Testament translation. Plutschau's health did not allow him to continue beyond five years. When Ziegenbalg died young in 1719 there were about 350 converts. Grundler died the following year, but other German missionaries, like Christian Schwartz, expanded the work into the city of Madras and translated Bible portions into Telegu and Hindustani as well.

Hans Egede: pioneer to Greenland

Another early Pietistic missionary pioneer was a Norwegian Lutheran pastor named Hans Egede (1686-1758). From childhood Hans had heard of the spread of Christianity to Greenland in the days of explorer Leif (the Lucky) Eriksen. Although the church in Greenland had its own bishop by the twelfth century, he had heard that they had relapsed to heathenism by his time. Because of his pietistic background, Pastor Egede became burdened for the people of Greenland and petitioned King Frederick IV to authorize a mission effort. After discouraging delays and incredible problems, the Egede family arrived in Greenland in the summer of 1721. He found almost no remnants of the Viking colonies or Christianity and found a serious language and cultural barrier to the Eskimos. However, with the help of his sons, who picked up the language much more quickly (a common missionary experience), and by sheer determination he began to win converts. In 1733 Moravian missionary, **Christian David** and two colleagues arrived and worked with Egede until his return home after his wife's death in 1736. Egede's son Paul proved to be very effective in continuing and expanding his father's work, but in the main it was the Moravian missionaries who provided for the continuity of the work. But we will need to go back a step to see the important place of the Moravian Church.

The Moravian Church missions

For the rest of the eighteenth century, Moravian Church missionaries dominated the field. Until William Carey started a chain reaction toward the end of the century out of which many mission boards were formed, the Moravian Church provided the main follow-up of the start made by the Danish-Halle Mission. "Between 1732 and 1760, 226 Moravians entered ten foreign countries."[5]

Like the Pietists, the Moravian Church also was part of the more 'radical fringe' of the Reformation. Kane explains:

> The origin of the Moravian Church goes back to 1467, when the persecuted followers of John Hus, with certain Waldensians and Moravians, banded together to form the *Unitas Fratrum* (United Brethren). After being almost wiped out by the Counter Reformation, the remnant, under the leadership of Christian David, migrated in 1722 to Saxony, where they were given refuge by Count Zinzendorf on one of his estates near Dresden. Known as *Herrnhut* (The Lord's Watch), this colony became the source and center of a missionary movement destined to circle the globe.[6]

Count Nicholas von Zinzendorf (1700-1760). Nicholas was raised in a warm evangelical pietism, studied under August Franke at Halle, and went on to Wittenberg to study law with a view to a government career. At the age of 19 a spiritual crisis caused him to determine to give his life over to Christ for service. By 1722 Moravian Christian refugees began arriving on his estate and the next five years were spent in developing and nurturing this Christian community. Despite problems caused by their diverse backgrounds, the Holy Spirit wrought great revival in their midst in 1727. A few years afterward Count Nicholas represented his government at the coronation of the Danish king. There he met two Eskimo converts of Hans Egede and an African slave from the West Indies, who pled for more missionary help (especially since the new king was not going to continue Egede's work). Within a year the first two missionaries went out from Herrnhut to the Virgin Islands in the West Indies (1732), "and in the two decades that followed, the Moravians sent out more missionaries than all Protestants (and Anglicans) had sent out in the previous two centuries."[7] It was Zinzendorf who provided the leadership for the movement for the next thirty years. But the Moravian Church advance continued on around the world for centuries as a model of missionary zeal for other Christians. Let us get a glimpse of another leader in the movement.

Christian David (1690-1751). Christian David was raised in a religious Roman Catholic family in Moravia (now Czech Republic). Converted at age twenty-seven through reading a Bible given him some years earlier, he became a traveling lay preacher. After leading many of the persecuted, discouraged Christians to Count von Zinzendorf's estate, he traveled around Europe preaching and recruiting settlers. When the spiritual need of Greenland and news of Egede's intended departure was shared with the Moravian Church community, Christian David and two younger men were sent out. They found that Hans Egede had been able to stay on in Greenland, and so they sought to work together. This was not so easy, both because of differences of language and viewpoint. Egede was a more strictly doctrinaire Lutheran of harsher personality, but the Moravians had a more winsome emphasis on the love of God in Christ. The situation was complicated by an outbreak of smallpox, which ultimately caused many Eskimos to become more open to the gospel. It seems that the Moravians reaped the harvest from Egede's sowing of the seed and hundreds of Eskimos responded to their simple emotional gospel appeal.[8]

Other Moravian influence. By 1735 a party of Moravian missionaries to Georgia met the Anglican chaplain John Wesley and his brother Charles on the ship. Their witness ultimately led to the conversion of the Wesleys and the beginning of the mighty Methodist movement in England and America which contributed to the Great Awakening of that time. In addition to work among the Creek Indians of Georgia and settlements and Indian evangelism in Pennsylvania, the Moravians carried on extensive work in the West Indies, Surinam (where Von Welz had died a century earlier), among the blacks of the Carolinas, the Hottentots of South Africa, the Guinea coast, Ethiopia, Persia, Ceylon, Palestine, and in many European countries.[9] Thus this 'fringe' Protestant group, springing from the more radical branch of the Reformation, proved to be not at the fringe but at the heart of God's plan for world evangelization. They found the spiritual dynamic so necessary for effective missionary vision and service.

David Brainerd's short mission to Indians

David Brainerd (1718-1747) is important to missions, not only because of the success of his work among American Indians, but because of the impact that the story of his life had on others, especially William Carey and Henry Martyn. Although his ministry was five short years, his journal and biography were published after his death by Jonathan Edwards. Raised in a well-off family in the Connecticut Valley of Connecticut and saved at the age of twenty, he went to Yale College where the impact of the Evangelical Awakening was being felt among the students. College authorities were not too happy about the religious "enthusiasm" of the student prayer and Bible study meetings. During student days he heard Ebenezer Pemberton challenge the students about missionary opportunities among the Indians. Through an unfortunate incident he was expelled from Yale as a convenient scapegoat to discredit the spiritual revival on campus.

He immediately applied to Pemberton's mission board, the Society in Scotland for the Propagation of Christian Knowledge, and was appointed to work in Kaunaumeek, New York, under veteran missionary John Sergeant, serving in nearby Stockbridge, Massachusetts. In eight years Sergeant had baptized a hundred converts, and Brainerd would have done well to learn from his experience. However, he prematurely started work on his own, ignorant of the language or wilderness life. After a year of fruitless hardship in preaching to the Indians there, David was assigned to the forks of the Delaware River in Pennsylvania (in the northeast corner across from New York state). He was greatly discouraged by the drunken condition of his interpreter, Tattamy. A very difficult trip to preach to the Indians of the Susquehanna River also proved to be discouraging. After a year his only converts were Tattamy and his wife.

But his most fruitful ministry was to Indians at Crossweeksung (Crosswicks), New Jersey, eighty-five miles south. Within a few weeks there he had baptized twenty-five converts, and shortly thereafter revival broke out among the Indians. After moving the Indians to Cranbury, New Jersey, further revivals brought about a total of nearly 150 converts. But his strength was ebbing from tuberculosis, and after a final trip to the Susquehanna River valley in Pennsylvania, his missionary work was over. He spent his last months in the home of Pastor Jonathan Edwards, whose daughter Jerusha he had hoped to marry. She nursed him for nineteen weeks to no avail, for he died of the tuberculosis. But his witness lived on in his journals and biographies, which continue to have an impact for missions up to the present. He was not the most successful missionary to the native Americans, but his great significance lay in his diary published posthumously by Edwards.[10] It put the lie to the erroneous notion that the heathen were so depraved that they could not be saved.

BREAKTHROUGH AMONG THE BRITISH

William Carey: British pioneer

Carey's initiative. For ninety years the Danish-Halle Mission and the Moravians virtually had the field all to themselves. In the previous chapter we had noted the three British missions which targeted the New World colonies. The Great Evangelical Awakening of the middle of the eighteenth century was laying a spiritual foundation for a much more significant advance, the father of which was William Carey (1761-1834). Carey has been called the "father of modern missions" but it might be more accurate to describe him as the great popularizer of missions in the English-speaking world. He did not father the movement, since there were already seven mission boards, with 170 missionaries in his day.[11] But the initiative of his ministry in a spiritually prepared England caused missions to leap over the restricted boundaries of the German Pietists, the Moravians, and the Anglicans, to the now rapidly expanding nonconformist churches of the United Kingdom.

Carey was a Baptist pastor, having left the Church of England following his conversion at the age of eighteen. Thus he was in that stream of dissenters from the established Anglican state church to which the Wesleys had made such a significant contribution in the half century before Carey. His initiative caused a spate of about forty mission board foundings, which would be inexplicable apart from the spiritual preparation. Kane aptly summarizes:

> Even before Carey's time there were stirrings of missionary interest in England. In 1719 Isaac Watts wrote his great missionary hymn, "Jesus Shall Reign Where'er the Sun." Several of Charles Wesley's compositions also bear a missionary theme. In 1723 Robert Millar of Paisley wrote A *History of the Propagation of Christianity and the Overthrow of Paganism*, in which he advocated intercession as the primary means of converting the heathen. The idea soon caught on. Twenty years later prayer groups were to be found all over the British Isles. Their chief petition was for the conversion of the hea-

then world.

In 1746 a memorial was sent to Boston inviting the Christians of the New World to enter into a seven-year "Concert of Prayer" for missionary work. The memorial evoked a ready response from Jonathan Edwards, who the following year issued a call to all believers to engage in intercessory prayer for the spread of the gospel throughout the world.[12]

The irony is that Christians sang and wrote and prayed about missions, but it took several generations before an Englishman did anything about it! It seems clear that overemphasis on God's sovereignty and underemphasis upon man's responsibility, already alluded to in the last chapter, was the major factor in their inaction. The story of William Carey confirms this.[13]

Raised in poverty, Carey took up the shoemaker's vocation. After his conversion he became active in ministry in a Baptist church and was ordained to the ministry at twenty-six. Few Baptist churches could support their pastors so he taught school and cobbled for a living. One wonders how he was able to teach himself Latin, Greek, Hebrew, Italian, French, and Dutch in his spare time. But it was his fascination with the geography of the 'world out there' which got him interested in missions. We know he read David Brainerd's *Life and Diary* and every travelogue and geography he could get his hands on. Despite his intellectual prowess, Carey had at the age of twenty married the illiterate sister-in-law of his employer.

But the Scripture was his first love. By 1792 he published an eighty-seven page book, An *Inquiry into the Obligation of Christians to Use Means for the Conversion of the Heathens*.[14] In it he answered the prevailing misconceptions about missions (discussed in the previous chapter) and proposed that Christians should form mission societies (boards) to implement the missionary mandate. The reference to "means" in the title reflects the strong predestinarian views of his day which opposed use of human means to accomplish God's work. Although Carey himself was a Calvinist, he recognized that human means are clearly commanded and exemplified in the Bible. When he later presented the same challenge at the Baptist Ministers' Association at Northamptonshire, his mentor, John Ryland, squelched him with the words, "Young man, sit down. When God pleases to convert the heathen, He will do it without your aid or mine."[15] Carey proved Ryland to be wrong, and to his credit he also became a supporter of the missionary endeavor.

Another serious obstacle which Carey addressed was the view that it was impossible to convert the heathen. Here it seems clear that the key obstacle was lack of faith in the power of God. Carey simply showed that Eliot, Brainerd, and the Moravian missionaries had had success in winning the heathen and we must "Expect great things from God; attempt great things for God." By October 2, 1792, they formed the **Particular Baptist Society for Propagating the Gospel among the Heathen.** Although it was a small beginning with a dozen poor Baptist pastors, within a quarter century almost another dozen mission boards had been formed out of this impetus: four in Great Britain, three in America, and some others on continental Europe.

Carey the missionary. But Carey's problems only began when he got his reluctant Baptist colleagues to form a mission board. Kane put it well:

> It was one thing to pass a resolution to form a mission; it was another to get the mission under way. Difficulties abounded on all sides, pertaining to family, finance, and field. Carey's father considered him mad. His wife refused to accompany him. But one by one the problems were solved; and after some delay and not a little discouragement, William Carey sailed for India on June 13, 1793. He was accompanied by a reluctant wife, four children, and two companions. Five months later he arrived in India, the land to which he gave forty years of unbroken service.[16]

It would be an understatement to say that no warm welcome awaited the missionary party when they arrived in Calcutta. The British East India Company was in virtual control of the British-held areas of India and was opposed to missionary work. To avoid deportation and become self supporting, the Careys moved to an area near malarial swamps, which brought not only sickness but resentment from his wife. Moving three hundred miles north to Malda, Carey got a job as a foreman in an indigo factory, which greatly helped their financial distress. Despite the death of one son and the deteriorating emotional condition of his wife, he concentrated on translation work, preached, and established a Baptist church by 1795. Although many Bengali people attended the services, after seven years Carey did not yet have an Indian convert.

Upon the arrival of new missionaries from England, Carey moved the mission to the Danish-controlled territory of Serampore, where he continued on for thirty-four more years. Within a year there they rejoiced over their first convert. "By 1818, after twenty-five years of Baptist missions to India, there were some six hundred baptized converts and a few thousand more who attended classes and services."[17] Carey himself made three Bible translations: Bengali, Sanskrit, and Marathi; translated portions into many more languages, and helped his colleagues with many others. They set up a large printing operation and a number of schools. By 1819 he founded Serampore College to train national church workers. While at Serampore he became Professor of Oriental Languages at Fort William College in nearby Calcutta, which put him in better standing with the British East India Company and provided needed income for the mission.

The first fifteen years of his ministry at Serampore were blessed by relative harmony among the missionaries. His wife Dorothy, who never recovered emotionally from the death of their son in the early years, died after seven years at Serampore. Soon afterward he remarried, this time to a Danish lady of the nobility who was living at Serampore. With her gift for linguistics Charlotte became a real help in the Bible translation work. The last twenty years were disrupted by a revolt that had been brewing among the new generation of missionaries. The junior missionaries did not want to submit to the direction of their seniors and caused a split. The mission board in London (many of whom had never met Carey and the senior missionaries) sided with the younger missionaries (whom they had appointed). The matter was resolved by the senior missionaries' compliance, but the erroneous principle of control from London was introduced.

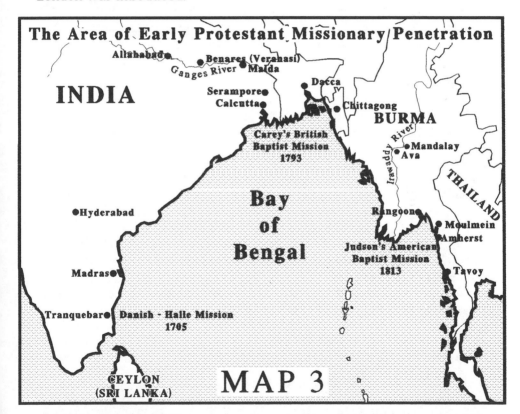

The Area of Early Protestant Missionary Penetration

INDIA

Allahabad
Benares (Veranasi)
Ganges River   Malda
Dacca
Serampore
Calcutta
Chittagong

BURMA

Carey's British
Baptist Mission
1793

Mandalay
Ava

Irawaddy River

THAILAND

Bay
of
Bengal

Hyderabad

Rangoon

Moulmein
Amherst

Judson's American
Baptist Mission
1813

Madras

Tavoy

Tranquebar   Danish - Halle Mission
1705

CEYLON
(SRI LANKA)   MAP 3

Carey's legacy. Carey died in 1834 without ever having returned to England and having left a tremendous legacy of accomplishments. In addition to the previously mentioned translation, printing, and the college, others should be mentioned: the opening of a dozen mission stations all over northern India, Burma, and Ceylon by his colleagues, the production of grammars and dictionaries in many languages, getting the Government to abolish some of the grosser social evils of Hinduism, the translation of some Hindu literature into English, and even pioneering horticultural research (for which he was honored by scientific societies). Carey was a model missionary in a number of things: his emphasis upon establishing churches on an indigenous basis, his attempts to understand the indigenous religions and cultures, his belief that the primary task of the missionary is training nationals to evangelize their own people, his modest lifestyle and sacrificial giving to support the other missionaries, and last but not least was seeing four of his sons become missionaries also.

Even though the Serampore missionaries were only partly supported by funds from London, Carey sent back detailed reports of their activities. These were published and had a tremendous impact upon British Christians in stimulating missionary activity. His advocacy of missions, his example of missionary sacrifice and activity, and the encouraging fruit of his initiative — all made an incredible impact upon the English speaking world.

Other early India missionaries. We can only mention a few of the host of early missionaries to the Indian subcontinent. Alexander Duff was a Church of Scotland (Presbyterian) missionary who arrived in Calcutta in 1830 to reach the high caste Hindus by means of Christian educational institutions. Reginald Heber was an early Anglican missionary and Bishop of Calcutta, who is famous for his great missionary hymns, such as, "From Greenland's Icy Mountains." John Scudder was the first medical missionary to India, serving under the Reformed Church of America. The London Missionary Society was founded as an outgrowth of Carey's initiative in 1795 and sent its first worker to India in 1798. The Scottish Missionary Society's workers reached Bombay in 1823. The Wesleyan Methodists started work in Madras in 1819 and subsequently in Bangalore and Negapatam. Some of the early 'Plymouth Brethren' began work in Madras in 1836, which has spread all over the subcontinent. Others will be mentioned subsequently.[18]

The London Missionary Society's thirty South Sea pioneers

In 1795 the **London Missionary Society** was the first other mission to be formed out of the stimulus of Carey's initiative, and that was just two years after his own board. At first it was a nondenominational mission, but in time it effectually became a Congregational board.[19] Their first burden (as had been Carey's) was for the South Sea Islands, the plight of which Captain Cook had so graphically described. Springing out of the growing momentum, they were able to send thirty male missionaries along with six wives and three children on their own mission ship, the

Duff, on a seven-month voyage to be dropped off on Tahiti, Tonga, and the Marquesas. These missionaries faced the two opposite problems that early missionaries to the South Seas faced: either a hostile response from chiefs who had no respect for human life, or a too warm welcome from native women who freely dispensed sexual favors.

On Tonga the missionaries were caught in between warring factions of natives, and three were killed. On Tahiti they had to contend with a brutal king named Pomare. Although at times he responded favorably to their attempts to win his friendship, at other times he treated them like enemies. After his death his son, Pomare II, came to power and made a profession of faith in Christ. Although his life did not show much evidence of conversion, ultimately the missionaries baptized him. He gave up his dozen idols, which the missionaries shipped back to England for display.

The missionaries were ill prepared for the opposite problem. Many of them were single men, and a few succumbed to the temptation and 'went native'. Later the mission had second thoughts about sending out single men. On Tahiti the progress was slow. Some missionaries got discouraged and left. Ruth Tucker tells the story:

> But for the perseverance of a stubborn, uneducated bricklayer, **Henry Nott** (who worked for sixteen years without any visible signs of success), the work would no doubt have been abandoned. . . But as dangers and problems multiplied, other missionaries gave up (eleven departing at one time), and Nott found himself left with three others, and even they spoke of going home.[20]

Even though Pomare's baptism was not followed by a consistent life, his baptism did make it possible for many of his subjects to openly confess Christ and in many cases there was every evidence of a Christ-transformed life. Infanticide, cannibalism, and war became things of the past. Although the early years on most of the South Sea islands were exceedingly difficult, as the work was increasingly turned over to national evangelists genuine 'people movements' developed, in which large families, villages, and even whole tribes turned to Christ. Today about seventeen percent of the population can be considered evangelical Christians.

Among the many other early missionaries in the South Seas was **John Williams** of the L.M.S., who was outstanding in procuring a ship for better transportation between the islands (despite the opposition of the Board back in London). His martyrdom at the hand of cannibals challenged Presbyterians John Geddie and later **John Paton** to enter the New Hebrides Islands. Paton became famous for his "play-by-play coverage of natives clubbing missionaries, published in his widely-read, tension filled autobiography. Paton, by his own account, tasted so many close calls at the hands of the natives that it was impossible to enumerate them all."[21] But God worked through these and a host of others in the evangelization of the south sea islands.

Robert Morrison, pioneer to China

Converted at the age of fifteen, Robert Morrison (1782-1834) soon became interested in the articles about the new missionary movement that were increasingly being published. After ministerial training in London he was accepted by the London Missionary Society to go to China. He sailed alone on an American ship by way of the United States in 1807. When the ship's owner sarcastically interrogated him, "And so, Mr. Morrison, you really expect to make an impression on the idolatry of the great Chinese Empire?" Morrison responded, "No, sir, but I expect God will."[22] Canton was one of only two ports open to foreigners. China at that time was very closed to foreigners, both because of the Chinese pride in their ancient civilization and their view of westerners as "foreign devils," and also tragically because of the British pressure upon them to open up to the opium trade. Although he had started studying Chinese in London, further study in Canton had to be done in secrecy since the officials of the British East India Company prohibited anything related to evangelizing the Chinese. He found two Roman Catholic converts who at great personal risk were willing to tutor him. He began compiling a dictionary and translating the Bible. Ultimately his dictionary so impressed officials of the East India Company that they hired him as a translator. He accepted reluctantly, knowing that he had to come to terms with the 'Company', which had such great political control.

His first convert came after seven years of undercover witnessing. When his New Testament was published, he was ordered dismissed by company officials, but he was so indispensable to them by then that the order was never carried out. By 1813 the British Parliament revised the company's charter to guarantee missionaries the freedom to carry on their work. After completing his translation of the whole Bible, in 1824 he returned to England for his first furlough (after seventeen years) and was surprised to find himself a celebrity in England. His last ten years in China involved a continuation of evangelism and translation of Christian literature. As an employee of the company, however, much time was taken in company business, and also family responsibilities increasingly burdened him. But as the pioneer Protestant missionary to China and the translator of the Chinese Bible he left a substantial legacy upon which other missionaries could build the church of Jesus Christ.

There were many other outstanding missionaries to China. However we may evaluate **Karl Gutzlaff** (1803-1851), an early German missionary to southeast Asia, we cannot ignore him. After a start with the Netherlands Missionary Society in Indonesia (Dutch East Indies), he became an independent missionary in Bangkok, Thailand, and adopted the native lifestyle. After Bible translation work in the Siamese (Thai), Cambodian, and Laotian languages, in 1831 he started evangelizing along the Chinese coast and even penetrated the interior. There was an abortive attempt to hire native evangelists, who apparently were deceiving the 'gullible white man'. Although Gutzlaff's reputation was tarnished by this, the Chinese Evangelization Society came out of his efforts, which later sent out J. Hudson Taylor (more of him in the next chapter).[23]

Robert Moffat: pioneer to Africa

Protestant missions to subsaharan Africa began in the Cape Colony with the Moravians in the eighteenth century. By the early nineteenth century missionaries were penetrating three major beachheads. They tackled the west coast beginning with Sierra Leone, the east coast starting with Ethiopia and Kenya, and from the south they established their mission base at Capetown.[24]

Robert Moffat was not the first missionary to the Cape Colony; that was **John Vanderkemp** (1747-1811), a Dutch physician, who was recognized as one of the great pioneers of the London Missionary Society, although his ministry was a short twelve years (1799-1811). Robert Moffat was not the most famous one either. That honor went to his son-in-law David Livingstone. But among the pioneers Robert Moffat stands out as an evangelist, a translator, an educator, a diplomat, and an explorer. Moffat was raised in Scotch Calvinism, but saved through the relatively new Methodist movement. Because of his limited education the London Missionary Society rejected him the first time until he studied theology privately with a director of the mission. Upon arrival at Capetown in 1816 Moffat was disturbed by the prejudice against missionaries among the European colonists and the serious problems among the missionaries themselves. Moffat was able to go into the interior of Namaqualand, where he met Afrikaner, a Hottentot chief, who had recently been converted through the ministry of a Dutch missionary. Moffat lived two years in Afrikaner's camp. Moffat gained a lot of credibility in Capetown for the missionary cause by bringing Afrikaner back with him to the coast when he went to meet his fiancee, Mary Smith.

After marriage, they traveled six hundred miles north to Kuruman, which was to be their home for most of their ministry. Moffat tried to combine Christianity and civilization by making Kuruman a model mission station. Although after much hardship he succeeded in making it a model, and gained much credibility among the Bechuana tribe because of his success in mediating tribal warfare, the Bechuanas were not turning to Christ. He had failed both to understand their religion or culture, and he had tried to use a trade language to reach them. When in 1827 he realized his shortsightedness, he concentrated on language study and began Bible translation. Since the European colonists would not print his Bible translation, he had to bring a printing press to Kuruman. Two years later he began to see his first conversions. Although the church at

Kuruman didn't grow beyond two hundred in his lifetime, Moffat's influence with tribal chiefs was very helpful in opening up other tribes for other missionaries. After fifty-three years in Africa with only one furlough, the Moffats returned to England where he became famous as a missionary statesman, advocating missions throughout the British Isles.[25]

David Livingstone (1810-1873) was another Scotch missionary under L.M.S. who became perhaps the most famous missionary to Africa. After marrying Moffat's daughter Mary, David carried on a semi-nomadic ministry of exploration and witness. His exploration opened up central Africa to both missionaries and colonialists with controversial results. Henry M. Stanley was an American newspaperman who was sent to Africa to find Livingstone. After his famous meeting with Livingstone in central Africa in 1871, Stanley was recruited as a missionary and explorer by Livingstone. But the more extensive evangelization of inland Africa took a couple more decades, which will be discussed subsequently.

THE AMERICANS JOIN IN

George Lisle: first American missionary?

We have already noted John Eliot and David Brainerd as early home missionaries in America, and there were many others who worked among the American Indians. Adoniram Judson is generally called the first American foreign missionary. Yet an unsung liberated black slave named George Lisle was really the first American to go abroad to plant a church. But because he only went to the island of Jamaica and was a black man reaching blacks, he hasn't been recognized for what he was: the first American foreign missionary. It is true that the cultural, linguistic, and racial gap that he crossed was not as great as that which Judson crossed some years later, but we must take note of this significant servant of God.[26]

George Lisle was a freed slave who was ordained in 1775 and then planted two Baptist churches in the South. After the Revolutionary War an attempt was made to re-enslave him. As he prayed for a solution, a Baptist officer, Colonel Kirkham, told him of the large black population in Jamaica which was in need of the gospel. Kirkham and a friend lent Lisle the passage money for his wife and himself to get to Kingston. Arriving in 1782 he got a job in the customs house, repaid the loan, and began preaching. He rented a house for a meeting-place and within seven years had baptized five hundred converts on profession of faith in Christ. In 1791 he built and dedicated the first Baptist church of Jamaica. One of his converts named Moses Baker founded the second church at Crooked Spring. Some years later they wrote to Carey's colleague, Dr. John Ryland, President of Bristol Baptist College in England, requesting that they send some missionaries, and in 1814 John Rowe arrived to help in the work. This was the same Dr. Ryland who had twenty years earlier told William Carey to sit down when he proposed missions.[27]

Adoniram Judson: pioneer to Burma

The haystack prayer meeting. There is a monument on the campus of Williams College in the northwest of Massachusetts to mark the spot where a monumental prayer meeting was held. Samuel Mills was a student at Williams College in 1806 who stirred up five of his classmates to join him in prayer for missions. One day they were caught in a sudden thunderstorm on the way to their place of prayer and found shelter in the lee of a large haystack and so prayed right there. After prayer there was a strong conviction that "we can do it if we will," and they resolved to become America's first foreign missionaries. Several of them went to Andover Seminary where they were joined by Adoniram Judson from Brown University and other likeminded students from other colleges. Judson had been strikingly converted from intellectual skepticism in 1808 and through a published sermon by a chaplain to the East India Company was convinced of the centrality of missions. After reading the book he exclaimed, "Why, how stupid, stupid I have been! Missions, why, the New Testament is all missions!"[28]

Two new mission boards. In June of 1810 four of them presented a proposal to the Congregational ministers of New England that a foreign mission board be formed, to which the ministers agreed. The **American Board of Commissioners for Foreign Missions** was constituted at Farmington, Connecticut in September 1810. They sent Adoniram Judson to London to get advice and help from the London Missionary Society, but his ship was captured by a French privateer, and Judson ended up in a filthy French prison. With the help of an American he escaped and got to England. After all that, the British mission leaders suggested that it was better for the Americans to launch out on their own. As a result eight missionaries were sent out to India early in 1812: Judson, Samuel Newell, Samuel Nott, Jr. with their wives, Gordon Hall, and Luther Rice. It might seem that 1812 was not a good year to start a new missionary venture since war with England broke out that year. But missions cannot wait for favorable seasons. To complicate matters further, en route to Calcutta the Judsons became convinced of the Baptist viewpoint on one ship, as was Luther Rice separately on another ship. They were immersed at Serampore by William Ward, one of Carey's colleagues. They sent letters resigning from the American Board and contacting the Baptists of New England about the possibility of the formation of a Baptist missionary society. Many tumultuous months later it was decided that Luther Rice would go back to America to encourage the Baptists to stand behind them. His mission was very successful, eventuating in the formation at Philadelphia in May of 1814 of the **American Baptist Foreign Mis-**

sion Society (to which the name was later changed).[29]

Harassed to Burma. Far more serious than the change of mission society, however, was the continued harassment from the British East India Company, aggravated by the beginning of the war of 1812 between England and the United States. The Newells were forced to depart for the island of Mauritius off the coast of Africa. After some months of trying to evade the officials' attempts to deport them, the Judsons sailed to Mauritius and found that Mrs. Newell had died. Sailing back to Madras, South India, they found that their only option left was a ship to Rangoon, Burma. Since Judson's original burden had been for Burma, they accepted this as the will of God. After an extremely difficult voyage, in July of 1813 they were welcomed there by William Carey's son, Felix, a pioneer to Burma, who had started translation of the Bible into Burmese.

Bridgehead in Rangoon. Burma proved to be as difficult a field as the Judsons had feared. It was the kingdom of a very cruel and despotic king; it was a stronghold of the most hard-core form of traditional (Theravada) Buddhism; it had no European community like India; tropical diseases were rampant, exacerbated by the relatively primitive conditions; and ultimately Great Britian's invasion of Burma made life impossible. Other missionaries had come and gone. Felix Carey accepted a government position and left soon after the Judsons arrived. But the Judsons plunged into language study and the beginnings of translation. Impressed with the Burmans' literary interest, within three years Judson published a pamphlet in Burmese, *A View of the Christian Religion.* Judson witnessed to small groups in public and put great emphasis upon translation work, finishing the Gospel of Matthew in another year.

Health was a continuing problem for the Judsons. First their seven-month old son died. Then Judson took a sea voyage to Chittagong, India, to restore his own health and to recruit some national Christians from the mission there. He never reached Chittagong. The destination of his ship was changed and the "crazy old craft" was unmanageable. It was eight months before he got back to Rangoon, his wife Ann having despaired of his life. Shortly after his return in 1818, reinforcements from America arrived. But it was seven years before they saw their first convert. One by one others turned to Christ. But when the local Viceroy obstructed Judson's work, he went up country to the capital city of Ava to appeal for the Emperor's permission to teach Christianity. The Emperor's refusal put the whole mission in jeopardy. But the handful of converts pled with the Judsons to stay, even if it meant martyrdom for them. Ann Judson's health necessitated return to America, which resulted in a two-year separation. After her return and a move to the capital city with their colleague, Dr. Price, things were beginning to look better. The Emperor had even invited them to Ava. But upon arrival things immediately turned bad.

Prisoner of war. In May of 1824 the British conquered Rangoon and war was declared. Judson and Price were thrown into "Death Prison" as presumed spies and tortured, awaiting execution. After one and a half years of suffering in prison, Judson was released to help as an interpreter in the peace negotiations with the British. Although the Judsons enjoyed two weeks together at the English military camp at Amhurst, they were separated during months of negotiations. Before he could return to Amhurst, Ann died, and a few months later baby Maria also died.

The next fourteen years were spent in translation and evangelism, completing the Burmese Bible in 1840. He had married Sarah Boardman, a thirty-year-old widow in 1834. She, like Ann, proved to be a good missionary companion, but in 1845 while they were returning to America for their first furlough (in thirty-three years for him), she died. Judson brought back a new bride from America, and they served three years together until he died in 1850. Judson's five surviving children with Sarah, despite long separations and loss of their mother, all grew up to distinguish themselves. But the greatest legacy Judson left was the Burmese Bible and a vibrant Burman church.

THE BIBLE SOCIETIES

In the main the first era of modern missions was carried out on a denominational basis. However, early on it was recognized that Bible publication should be a cooperative effort. In 1804 the British and Foreign Bible Society was formed, followed shortly by other national Bible societies. Now fifty-nine of them belong to the United Bible Societies with headquarters in London. Although the translation is done by missionaries from various societies, the UBS aids in expert linguistic advice and does the publication and initial distribution, usually at subsidized prices. But the main burden of distribution has been upon the missionaries, evangelists, and pastors. The American Bible Society was founded in 1816.

Perspectives enrichment: Chapters B-3, 6, 7, 9

---

1. Kane, *Concise History*, p. 76.

2. Latourette, *A History of Christianity*, pp. 951-64. Earl D. Radmacher, *What the Church Is All About* (1972). Groups like the Anabaptists, Mennonites, Moravians, Pietists, Baptists, and non-conformist Congregationalists are referred to as the "radical" reformation because they sought to reject everything not found in Scripture. Most of these fled to America for refuge.

3. Ibid, p. 896.

4. Bartholomew Ziegenbalg, "Letter of Sept. 1, 1706," in *Propagation of the Gospel in the East*, ed. Anton Boehme (London: Joseph Downing, 1718) Part I, p. 41, cited by V. Raymond Edman, *Light in Dark Ages* (1949), p. 353.

5. Kane, *Concise History*, p. 79.

6. Ibid.

7. Tucker, *Jerusalem to Irian Jaya*, p. 71.

8. Ibid, pp. 74-79.

9. Edman, *Light in Dark Ages*, p. 361.

10. Tucker, *Jerusalem to Irian Jaya*, pp. 90-93.

11. Pierson, *Crisis in Missions*, p. 190.

12. Kane, *Concise History*, pp. 83-84.

13. Walter Bruce Davis, *William Carey: Father of Modern Missions* (1963), p. 105; see the Appendix of this book in which I document the influence of Andrew Fuller's theology on Carey, from Samuel Fisk, *Calvinistic Paths Retraced* (1985), pp. 141-154.

14. Excerpts from this book are found in *Perspectives*, pp. B-94ff.

15. Kane, *Concise History*, p. 85.

16. Ibid, p. 86.

17. Tucker, *Jerusalem to Irian Jaya*, p. 118.

18. Glover, *The Progress of World-Wide Missions*, ed. J. Herbert Kane (1960), pp. 69-76.

19. Kane, *Concise History*, p. 94.

20. Tucker, *Jerusalem to Irian Jaya*, pp. 200-201.

21. Ibid., p. 214.

22. Sherwood Eddy, *Pathfinders of the World Missionary Crusade* (1945), p. 34.

23. Tucker, *Irian Jaya*, pp. 171-73.

24. Ibid, p. 141.

25. Ibid, pp. 141-47.

26. Today we would call him a M_1 missionary and Judson a M_3 missionary to indicate the degree of cultural gap bridged.

27. Inez Knibb Sibley, *The Baptists of Jamaica: 1793 to 1965* (Kingston: Jamaica Baptist Union, 1965), pp. 1-3.

28. J. Mervin Hull, *Judson the Pioneer* (1913), pp. 12-25.

29. Ibid, pp. 23-78.

"And thus I aspired to preach the gospel, not where Christ was already named, that I might not build upon another man's foundation; ... but now, with no further place for me in these regions, ... whenever I go to Spain. . ."

–Romans 15:20, 23, 24

MISSIONS EXPANDED: INTERIOR FRONTIER PENETRATION (A.D. 1865-1945)

It has been the common practice in missions histories to see William Carey as beginning the "great century" of Protestant missions. It is true that the nineteenth century was indeed a great century of missionary progress. But we are indebted to Ralph Winter for pointing out that a second era of Protestant missions really began around 1865 with the founding of the **China Inland Mission** by J. Hudson Taylor. Although the pioneers of the first era after Carey did penetrate inland to some degree, by and large most missionary work was being carried out on the coast or in a few big cities. Although in civilized countries like India the pioneers were able to penetrate to interior cities, in hostile cultures like China or uncivilized areas like Africa, mission work was slow to move into the interior. It was Hudson Taylor's burden for inland China and the founding of the CIM which triggered the founding of many other missions which had as their explicit goal the penetration of unreached inland or inaccessible areas. Winter points out:

> As a result, directly or indirectly, over 40 new agencies took shape to compose the faith missions that rightly should be called frontier missions as the names of many of them still indicate: China Inland Mission, Sudan Interior Mission, Africa Inland Mission, Heart of Africa Mission, Unevangelized Fields Mission, Regions Beyond Missionary Union.[1]

In addition, Kane points out that there were two other major factors in missions which actually began in the nineteenth but became potent in the twentieth century: **the Bible Institute Movement and the Student Volunteer Movement.** This period from 1865 to 1945 was also significant in the opening up of many new fields: South America, North Africa, Japan, Korea, and the Philippines. It was characterized as well by mass movements of tribes and ethnic groups (peoples) toward Christ (called "people movements" by Donald McGavran). This period was the heyday of colonialism, during which the former hostility of colonial officials toward missions mitigated substantially and a new period of cooperation began. It was during this era that liberal theology or modernism began to penetrate and undermine the missionary movement. It was toward the end of the period (the twentieth century) that the Ecumenical Movement arose out of the great worldwide missionary conferences. Therefore, we believe with Winter that it will be more helpful to divide the nineteenth century at about 1865. Winter goes on to point out, however, that the division is not sharp, and there is usually an overlap or transition of about 45 years (see figure). Indeed it took about twenty years for the greatest surge of new 'faith missions' to be founded.

THE PIONEER 'FAITH MISSIONS'

During the previous era most of the missionary work was carried out by denominational missions. Even though the earliest boards were interdenominational (strictly speaking, nondenominational) like the London Missionary Society and the American Board of Commissioners for Foreign Missions, ultimately they became in effect Congregational denominational boards. We have seen the early prominence of Lutheran, Moravian, Anglican, and Baptist boards. Each of the other denominations in America formed their own boards early in the nineteenth century: the Methodists in 1819, the Episcopalians in 1821, the Presbyterians in 1831, etc. By mid-century, a number of new interdenominational boards were founded. In the main they were formed to meet a need which the existing boards were not moving to meet. We have noted the frontiers emphasis of many of them. Others saw an unmet need and sought to fill it. The earliest of such were the needs of women in India. Missionary wives did not have adequate leisure to reach the oppressed women of India, and because of the Muslim *purdah* system, which isolates the women, it was improper for men to do so. The existing boards were not accepting single women. Thus in 1852 the **Zenana** (women) **and Medical Missionary Fellowship** was formed in England, sending out single women on an interdenominational basis. By 1860 the **Women's Union Missionary Society** (now merged with its British counterpart) was formed as the earliest 'faith mission' in America. Also that same year the British Syrian Mission was formed to reach an area of the neglected middle eastern Muslim world.

It was the great success of the China Inland Mission (1865) which stirred the imagination of other missionary leaders and stimulated a flood of other mission foundings: North Africa Mission (1881), Christian and Missionary Alliance (1887), CIM's American branch (1888), The Evangelical Alliance Mission (then the Scandinavian Alliance, 1890), Sudan Interior Mission (1893), and the Africa Inland Mission (1895) to name a few.[2] It should be noted that these have been called 'faith missions' because Hudson Taylor emphasized the faith principle of missionary support in order not to be in competition with existing agencies. Thus his principle of non-solicitation of funds was important to the CIM. Most of the 'faith missions' have not kept this policy as rigorously as Taylor proposed, but the name has stuck.

Hudson Taylor's China Inland Mission

As we have just noted, the movement was already developing when the CIM was founded. However Tucker highlights Hudson Taylor's significance:

> No other missionary in the nineteen centuries since the apostle Paul has had a wider vision and has carried out a more system-atized plan of evangelizing a broad geographical area than Hudson Taylor. His sights were set on reaching the whole of China, all four hundred million people, and it was to that end that he labored, though not single-handedly. He had a knack for organiza-tion, and he possessed a magnetic personality that drew men and women to him and to his point of view. The China Inland Mission was his creation and the pacesetter of future faith missions. In his own lifetime the missionary force under him totalled more than eight hundred, and in the decades following his death continued to grow.[3]

Although raised in a godly home, Taylor was not converted until age seventeen under the striking circumstance of his mother seventy-five miles away praying for his salvation just at the time he trusted Christ. Perhaps this is why Taylor came early to believe implicitly in the power of prayer. He immediately got involved in evangelism and missionary concerns and began taking medical training under the sponsorship of the Chinese Evangelization Society (CES). In addition, he adopted a rigorous program of self-discipline in preparation for the field. When word came that a professing Christian had become emperor of China, the mission encouraged him to leave for Shanghai immediately.

A term of preparation. Upon arrival in the international settlement in Shanghai in 1854, Taylor found himself in an awkward situation. "The CES was a small disorganized mission board, and there was no one in China to welcome or work with the young missionary recruit."[4] To make matters worse, promised funds did not arrive, a common failing of the CES. Taylor was not happy living among the many missionaries in the international settlement for he felt that they were lazy and living in luxury. After a year of language study, he made a tour up the Yangtze River, visiting fifty-one villages where Protestant missionaries had never gone.

Although in Shanghai he went unnoticed, in the interior his foreign appearance made him an object of great curiosity, so much so that people weren't paying attention to his message. He decided to follow the example of the Jesuit missionaries in adopting native dress. This involved shaving his head and wearing a black-dyed pigtail. Although most of the missionaries ridiculed him, his traveling companion, William Burns, followed his example. About this time God had opened the hearts of three or four young men to whom Taylor had been witnessing and they requested baptism. But it was his association with Burns, the Scotch evangelist that was especially blessed of God. Burns had been greatly used of God to bring revival in churches in Scotland, Ireland, and England. For about seven months as they went on evangelistic tours together, Burns' zeal to win people to Christ was a tremendous spiritual stimulant to Hudson. He had strong convictions about the imperative of using lay-evangelists in missionary work, which influenced Taylor.

But many problems continued to plague him: native doctors ran him out of town; his servant absconded with all his money and belongings; and support from England was erratic. Finally in 1857 he resigned from CES and became independent. Taylor's singleness was also a problem. Two girls in England had turned down his mail proposals. After some evangelistic trips into the interior he came to Ningpo on the coast and met Maria Dyer, who had been born in China, orphaned, educated in England, and now had returned to teach school. His proposal of marriage was rebuffed through the strong influence of Miss Aldersley, the head of the school, who said that he was "uneducated, unordained, unconnected (with a mission society), and uncouth." Ultimately they were able to get her uncle's permission to marry (1858).

> Maria was the very woman Taylor needed to polish the rough edges of his personality and to help focus his enthusiasm and ambitions, and from the start their marriage was a true partnership. They remained in Ningpo for three years, during which time Taylor was unexpectedly thrust into the supervision of the local hospital, a position that was clearly beyond his capability.[5]

But within a year at Ningpo, Taylor was able to establish a little church with eight members.

Founding a mission. The Taylors had struggled with severe health problems, so furlough to England in 1860 was necessary for recuperation. Hudson also took further medical studies, getting a Diploma from the Royal College. Taylor brought back a Chinese assistant to work on a revision of the Ningpo New Testament, which was completed with the help of another furloughing missionary. Furlough was to stretch out to over five years but they were far from wasted years. He contacted a number of mission societies to present the needs of inland China, especially since the interior was now more accessible. He also traveled around England sharing his burden for inland China with the churches. And more directly he prayed for and recruited five new missionaries, all of whom departed for China during their furlough. But of even broader impact was the publication of a small book entitled, *China's Spiritual Needs and Claims*.[6] Taylor kept a big map of China before him as he worked on the translation. As he compared the small districts he had touched during his ministry there with the vast un-reached regions, his heart became burdened in a new way. God was also speaking to him through the Bible text they were translating. As he brooded over the statistics he discovered that there were only 91 Protestant missionaries in China compared with 115 five years earlier. But it wasn't until 1865 that it became clear that a new mission agency was needed and he began to pray for 24 new workers. By 1866 he had founded the China Inland Mission, recruited the 24 new missionaries, and the Taylors with the new missionaries sailed for China, all on the same ship. This mission was to be run from China, not London.[7]

The struggles of a new team. It would be wonderful to report that the missionary party arrived in harmony and launched into the work at hand. But where God is at work, the devil redoubles his efforts, and in this case sowed dissension among the missionaries. Although the policy of wearing Chinese clothing had been fully agreed to in England, some of the party rebelled. It took the death of eight-year-old Gracie Taylor to bring about reconciliation, but even then four missionaries had to be dismissed to enable the mission to move ahead in harmony. Then there were external problems. The mission house in Yangchow was set on fire in 1868, and the missionaries barely escaped with their lives. Even though it caused an international controversy, the missionaries quietly went back in and saw a church established there. But personal tragedy awaited the Taylors in 1870 when five-year-old Sammy died. Five months later Maria died from complications of childbirth, and the baby also died. Taylor took Jennie Faulding, one of the original team, back to England to marry her and be reunited with his children, who had been sent home earlier.

After a year's furlough spent in setting up a mission council, they returned to China. Every two years or so Taylor had to go back to England to stir up interest in inland China, and each time he returned with new recruits. "By 1882 the CIM had entered every province, and in 1895, thirty years after its founding, the CIM had more than six hundred and forty missionaries investing their lives in China." In 1899 at the age of sixty-seven Taylor left China for the last time aware of disturbances which were to be catastrophic.[8] The end of the nineteenth century brought a holocaust to missionary work in China in the form of the Boxer Rebellion. Many foreign nations were trying to carve China up into their own colonies, either by force of arms or strong-armed paid leases, as the British did. Resentment against foreigners broke out in the imperial decree that all foreigners and Christians should be executed. One hundred thirty-five missionaries and thirty-five children were brutally slain, the majority of which were with CIM. Neither Taylor's retirement nor his subsequent death slowed the growth of CIM. By 1914 it had become the largest foreign mission organization in the world, and by 1934 it peaked at 1368 missionaries.

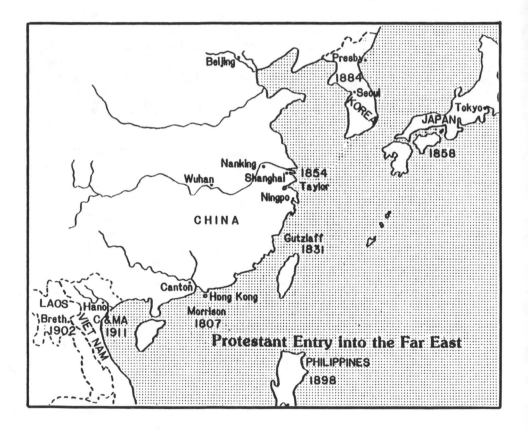

Mention has already been made of the current explosion of the church on mainland China. Although there were less than a million Protestants in 1950 when the missionaries were forced out by the communists, today it is believed that the number of Christians is between thirty to seventy million. Certainly the sacrifices of the CIM missionaries have not been in vain as they laid the major foundation for the wonderful church growth in mainland China today.

THREE ERAS OF MODERN MISSIONS

	Era of Pioneers	Era of Expansion	Era of Hidden Frontiers
	Coastlands Mostly Denominational	Interior Growing Interdenominational	Ethnic/Religious

Timeline columns: 1790 1800 10 20 30 40 50 60 70 80 90 1900 10 20 30 40 50 60 70 80 90

Southern Asia
- 1793 ● Carey in India
- 1803 ● Pfander in India
- 1806 ● Martyn in India
- 1812 ● Judson in Burma
- 1830 ● Duff in India
- 1836 ● Brethren in India
- 1851 ● Zenana & Medical Mission
- 1872 ● All-India Conference
- Chuhra People Movement in Punjab
- 1925 ● Ecumenical Church of S. India
- 1938 ● Madras World Miss. Conf.
- 1947 ● Independence & Partition of India
- 1961 ● New Delhi W.C.C. — I.M.C. Merger

Sub-Saharan Africa
- 1795 ● Baptist Miss. Sierra Leone
- 1799 ● Vanderkemp at Cape
- 1816 ● Moffat in S. Africa
- 1825 ● Kuruman
- 1842 ● Livingstone
- 1844 ● Krapf in Kenya
- 1871 ● Stanley/Livingstone
- 1871 ● Baptist Miss. Congo
- 1875 ● Scott in Kenya
- 1893 ● Sudan Interior Mission
- 1895 ● Africa Inland Mission
- 1910 ● Studd in Africa
- 1921 ● Kimbangu Church Congo
- 1960 ● "New Life for All" Nigeria
- 1960 ● Congo Independence
- 1964 ● Simba Rebellion

Far East
- 1807 ● Morrison in Canton
- 1814 ● First Convert
- 1831 ● Cong. Enter Thailand
- 1831 ● Gutzlaff/China
- 1844 ● Presby./Korea
- 1854 ● Taylor/Shanghai
- 1858 ● Japan open
- 1865 ● Thomas/Korea
- 1865 ● China Inland Mission
- 1888 ● Goforth/China
- 1900 ● Boxer Rebellion
- 1907 ● Manchuria Revival
- 1911 ● C &MA/Viet Nam
- 1932 ● 11 TEAM Martyrs
- 1934 ● Stams Martyred
- 1948 ● FEBC/Manila
- 1949 ● Mao/China Takeover
- 1965 ● Indonesia Upheaval

Latin America
- 1791 ● Lisle/Jamaica
- 1847 ● Ind. Mission/Chile
- 1855 ● Kalley/Brazil
- 1856 ● Presby./Colombia
- 1864 ● Baptists/Argentina
- 1890 ● Cent. Amer. Mission
- 1917 ● Townsend/Guatemala
- 1929 ● Cakchiquel NT
- 1931 ● HCJB/Quito
- 1943 ● 5 New Tribes Martyrs
- 1956 ● 5 Auca Martyrs
- 1963 ● TEE/Guatemala
- 1968 ● Liberation Theology

Pacific / Near East
- 1796 ● "Duff"/South Seas
- 1817 ● Williams/S. Seas
- 1819 ● Pomare Baptism
- 1820 ● Hawaiian Mission
- 1838 ● Tahitian Bible
- 1839 ● Williams Martyrdom
- 1848 ● Gedie/New Hebrides
- 1856 ● Paton/New Heb.
- 1881 ● Glenny/N. Africa Mission
- 1885 ● Keith-Falconer/Aden
- 1890 ● Zwemer/Arabia
- 1912 ● Zwemer & Borden/Cairo
- 1964 ● NAM Expelled Tunisia
- 1967 ● Morocco Closed

Europe
- 1793 ● British Baptist Mission
- 1795 ● London Missionary Society
- 1799 ● Anglican CMS
- 1804 ● British Bible Society
- 1856 ● Spurgeon's College
- 1858 ● End/British East India Comp.
- 1910 ● Bible Christ. Union/Germany
- 1910 ● Edinburgh Miss. Conf.
- 1913 ● Worldwide Evangelization Crusade
- 1949 ● Greater Europe Mission
- 1954 ● TransWorld Radio
- 1965 ● Vatican II Council
- 1974 ● Lausanne Congress

North America
- 1810 ● Amer. Board Com. For. Mis.
- 1814 ● American Baptist Mission
- 1816 ● American Bible Society
- 1819 ● Methodist Board
- 1831 ● Presbyterian Board
- 1845 ● Southern Baptist Mission
- 1882 ● Nyack Missionary Institute
- 1886 ● Moody Bible Institute
- 1886 ● Stud. Vol. Mov.
- 1887 ● C & M A
- 1890 ● T.E.A.M.
- 1890 ● 1900 ● New York Miss. Conf.
- 1910 ● I.F.M.A.
- 1920 ● Baptist Mid-Missions
- 1932 ● Laymen's Missionary Inquiry
- 1934 ● Summer Inst. Linguistics
- 1945 ● E.F.M.A.
- 1966 ● M.A.R.C.
- 1976 ● US Ctr for World Mission

Adapted from charts of Ralph Winter & Ruth Tucker

BELATED ENTRY INTO NEW FIELDS

Although the Second Era of Protestant missions was in general characterized by missions pressing on into the interior of the major fields like Africa, India, and China, it was also a period of initial entry into other significant areas of the world. The process of opening up new fields continued in a substantial way. While Hudson Taylor was beginning his initial term in China, Commodore Perry was opening up Japan to foreign commerce. A more liberal treaty negotiated with America in 1858 allowed missionaries to enter. Immediately several American denominational missions (Episcopalians, Presbyterians, Dutch Reformed, etc.) transferred personnel from other fields to Japan.

South America. Because South America was considered a 'Christian' continent, there was no early push to recruit missionaries for this part of the world. Indeed, many of the European mission leaders did not feel that it was a mission field. But it was a Scotch doctor, **Robert Kalley,** who began the first continuing work in Brazil in 1855, which became the nucleus of the Evangelical Union of South America (now Gospel Missionary Union). The United Presbyterians began work in Colombia in 1856; the American Baptists in 1864; the American Methodists began their Spanish work in Argentina in 1867; and in Chile an independent work dating back to 1847 was taken over by the United Presbyterians in 1873. Other countries were entered one-by-one, many not until the beginning of the twentieth century.

Muslim World. Sub-Saharan Africa was entered in the early part of the century, but North Africa was neglected until the end. With the opening of the Suez Canal in 1869, missionaries began to sail by North Africa on their way to other lands. Undoubtedly the strong Muslim entrenchment in North Africa deterred missionary initiative until 1881 when Edward Glenny arrived in Algeria with two co-workers. Out of this came the North Africa Mission (Now Arab World Ministries), which entered the other North African countries in succession.[9]

As the heartland of Islam, the Arabian peninsula has proved to be most formidable for missionary work. **Ion Keith-Falconer** from Scotland arrived in 1885 to establish work near Aden. He died within two years, but the Church of Scotland (Presbyterian) took over the work and started a hospital there. When news of Keith -Falconer's death was received at the Reformed Seminary at New Brunswick, New Jersey, several students volunteered for service in Arabia. One of them was **Samuel Zwemer,** who became the best-known missionary to Arabia and was called the "Apostle to Islam." Kane appraises his significance:

> Zwemer was a rare combination of the pious and the practical, the saint and the scholar. He was a world traveler, a prolific writer, a

dynamic speaker, a brilliant scholar, and a great personal worker. He knew more about Islam and the Christian approach thereto than any other man in the first half of the twentieth century. He founded and for many years edited *Muslim World*, a scholarly journal devoted to the Christian mission in the Muslim World.[10]

Central America.   In the 1880's it came to the attention of **C. L Scofield** (of Reference Bible fame) that there was only one Spanish-speaking gospel witness in all of Central America.   Convinced that we had neglected "our Samaria," he founded the Central America Mission in 1890.   Most of the Central American countries were entered in that decade.   Costa Rica was first in 1891 (although a few years earlier Baptists from Jamaica had begun work), El Salvador in 1894, Honduras in 1896, Guatemala in 1899, and Nicaragua in 1900.[11]

Asia.   The visits of Commodore Perry's ships to isolated Japan in 1853 began to open up three port cities to foreigners, and thus to missionaries. After very restricted beginnings, Presbyterian Dr. James C. Hepburn and Reformed missionary Guido Verbeck began to see significant fruit after 1872, with the founding of the first church.   By the next year the laws against Christianity were rescinded and more overt evangelism became possible, as Japan increasingly opened up to the outside world.

Early efforts to evangelize Korea were limited to Scripture distribution along the coast and up the rivers (1832-1884) with no settled missionary. In 1884 the American Presbyterians began to arrive and the next year the Southern Methodists.   The Presbyterian missionaries decided in 1890 to adopt the indigenous principles of missions (as advocated by **John Nevius**), which helps to account for their remarkable church growth in that land.

With the annexation of the Philippine Islands by the United States after the Spanish-American War (1898), missionaries began to arrive there in considerable numbers. Within three years the American Presbyterians, Methodists, Baptists, Disciples of Christ, the Congregationalists, the Episcopalians, and the Christian and Missionary Alliance had begun work. Although the only nominally Roman Catholic country in Asia, the Philippine Islands are the scene of rapid evangelical church growth today. Other Southeast Asian countries were also late in receiving Protestant missions: Swiss Brethren arrived in Laos in 1902; the Christian and Missionary Alliance in Vietnam in 1911 and in Cambodia in 1923. They were about the only Protestant work in these countries when the Communists completed their takeover in 1972.

TWO NEW MOVEMENTS AT HOME

Herbert Kane has highlighted three movements which began in the end of the nineteenth century and had a great impact on world missions on into the twentieth. We have looked at the faith mission movement. Let us take note of the other two.

The Bible Institute Movement

A. B. Simpson was a missionary leader who, although never becoming a missionary, had an incredible impact upon world evangelization. In the 1880's he launched the predecessor organizations to the Christian and Missionary Alliance, and in 1882 he established a missionary training school in New York City. That school, which was later moved to Nyack, became the forerunner for the Bible Institute Movement, which has become the Bible College Movement today. By 1886 D. L. Moody had founded the Moody Bible Institute, and a succession of other institutes and colleges has followed. Although denominational missions have drawn their personnel mostly from their denominational seminaries, the Faith Mission Movement has drawn the vast majority of its missionaries from the Bible Institute Movement. Hudson Taylor became convinced that China would never be evangelized if missionaries had to have both university and seminary training since few in England attended college in his day. He drew upon laymen with minimal formal education to penetrate inland China. Although faith mission boards gradually upgraded their educational requirements, a few years of Bible institute courses have generally been deemed acceptable. Simpson, Moody, and a host of other missions-minded leaders have provided hundreds of Bible schools to train those missionaries. There are about 30,000 students in North American Bible colleges, and a host of others are training in missionary programs in Christian liberal arts colleges and universities.

Although the Bible Institute Movement has been a distinctly North American phenomenon, the idea has been transplanted to Great Britain and the Continent. Actually Spurgeon's College in London (1856) is antecedent to Nyack. With about thirty schools in Great Britain it is clear that the movement never gained the same momentum there as here. Many of the forty institutes on the Continent today were planted by American missions in the post-World War II era, especially prominent among which is the Greater Europe Mission.

The Student Volunteer Movement

A number of the evangelical leaders of this period who had an incalculable impact upon missions, without themselves being missionaries, include D. L. Moody, Arthur T. Pierson, A. J. Gordon, Robert P. Wilder, and John R. Mott. The first three were participants at Moody's conference grounds at Northfield, Massachusetts in 1885, who issued a call for prayer for missions. The last two were among the three hundred university students who were present there the next year. At the end of that conference, one hundred consecrated themselves to the work of missions and began organizing a student movement which came into being in New York City two years later as the Student Volunteer Movement for Foreign Missions, with Mott as chairman and Wilder as traveling secretary. This movement mushroomed to impact thousands of college students in the next thirty years. Tens of thousands attended quadrennial missionary conventions held from 1891 to 1936, over twenty thousand of whom became foreign missionaries.

It is ironic that at the time of its founding one of its visionaries, Pastor Arthur T. Pierson, had issued a warning in his book *The Crisis of Missions* about liberal theology which would ultimately become the undoing of the movement.[12] At that very time modernistic rationalism was just getting a foothold in the seminaries and organizational structures of the major Protestant denominations of America. As the Spirit of God was working so mightily through Moody and his colleagues and in the student groups, Satan was sowing his destructive leaven of theological liberalism in the churches. Kenneth Kantzer has stated that in 1890 all of the major Protestant denominational seminaries in America except Harvard were evangelical, and that by 1920 they had all become liberal.[13] It is no accident that 1920 was the highwater mark of the Student Volunteer Movement, and that by 1936 during the heyday of liberalism it had virtually died. Liberal denial of the inspiration of the Scripture, the deity and resurrection of Christ cut the heart out of missions. Unfortunately Pierson's warnings were not heeded by the Movement's leaders, and they remained within the growing ecumenical movement (which we shall discuss shortly). Even though the SVM went out of existence, the Student Missions Fellowship of Inter-Varsity Christian Fellowship has taken up the burden. Its triennial Urbana missionary conferences have been tremendously successful in attracting up to seventeen thousand students, many of whom have made a commitment to missions.

THE HEYDAY OF COLONIALISM

One external factor which played an important part in this era of missions was colonialism, which was in its heyday from 1858 to 1914, according to Stephen Neill. He suggests a number of events around 1858-63 which advanced colonialism to its acme: the phasing out of the British East India Company which put India under the direct control of the British crown; the conclusion of a series of treaties between China and the colonial powers, giving foreigners and Christians far greater rights; the opening up of Japan; David Livingstone's book and speeches appealing for penetration into the heart of Africa by Christianity and civilization; and the spreading of the Second Evangelical Awakening from America to the British Isles.[14]

Time and again we have seen the serious opposition to the missionaries from the British East India Company. But after 1858 the British government officials who took control were more inclined to be favorable to the missionaries. Throughout this period there tended to be a close association of missions and colonialism. Indeed, in Africa David Livingstone actually encouraged penetration by colonial powers, so that the heinous slave trade and intertribal warfare could be put to an end. But what was the effect of colonialism? Was it good or evil?

Colonialism did have some good features. It gave an advantage to the missionaries as far as access to many countries was concerned and in protection by the colonial authorities. Some of the more enlightened forms of colonialism did significantly develop countries which otherwise would not likely have developed economically. Some colonial governments brought law and order to areas which had never had it. Colonialism did bring education and western civilization to parts of the world that did not have much of either.

In the main, however, colonialism was an evil. It started out with a commercial motive. This might have been justifiable if the commerce had not been backed by the gun. It was the unequal commerce which was necessarily exploitive of the national populations. The most notorious example of this would be the British East India Company's forcing China to buy the opium grown in India. Today we call drug trade criminal. Then it was viewed as just a part of colonialism. But from the point of view of the evangelist, the greatest evil of colonialism was the resentment against western 'Christians' which developed in the heart of the nationals. Colonialism was, after all, an oppression, and the oppressed always resent the oppressor. This close identification of the hated colonialists with Christianity did far more harm in the long run that the benefits it brought. The large number of missionaries killed in the Boxer Rebellion of 1900 in China were in a real sense the victims of colonialism.

How did the missionaries view colonialism? Undoubtedly many viewed colonialism as a positive good. Many missionaries of this period believed in postmillennialism, which emphasized progress in christianizing the world before Christ returns. Some postmillennialists did not distinguish clearly between evangelizing and civilizing. They saw it all as part of progress toward the ideal millennial state. Connected with this frequently was the concept of "Manifest Destiny" and the white man's burden. But Hudson Taylor rightly saw the importance of a premillennial understanding of Scripture in avoiding the confusion between evangelism and civilization.[15] Many other missionaries saw colo-nialism as the lesser of two evils. Some saw it as an evil instrument which God chose to use for his sovereign purpose. But by and large most missionaries were only too conscious of its evils.[16] Although the United States has had its own lapses into colonialism, since it is more repugnant to the American mindset, American missionaries in general felt more uncomfortable with colonialism than the Europeans did.

THE SWEEP OF GREAT PEOPLE MOVEMENTS

Missionaries have long wondered at the uneven response to the gospel by different tribes at different times. Why do two tribes respond so differently: in one fruit comes handpicked, while in another they come by the hundreds and thousands? Or within one tribe, for decades the gospel is preached and few respond; then strangely things change radically. They come by hundreds and even thousands. Why the difference? At first this phenomenon was referred to as a "mass movement." In 1955 Donald A. McGavran wrote his important book, *The Bridges of God*, in which he preferred to call them "people movements" and sought to analyze the factors that account for them (see the Glossary).[17]

Most of the pioneers of the first era of Protestant missions saw little of people-movement conversions. They ploughed the soil and scattered the seed. Many of them did not reap a great harvest, or if they did see a people movement it wasn't where they expected a response. But for the most part people movements began to be seen significantly in the second era. Here are two classic examples of a fairly common missionary experience.

The Karen of Burma

Adoniram Judson was one pioneer who did see a people movement. He had a servant named Ko Thah-Byu who was from an animistic tribe called the Karens. The Buddhist Burmans didn't think of them as Burmans at all. They despised the Karens as untamable. To make it worse Ko Thah-Byu had been a robber and a murderer. For months Judson worked with him to get him to understand the gospel, but with no success. It took a year or two before he was baptized by George Boardman, Judson's colleague. When Boardman was sent to Tavoy, Ko Thah-Byu begged to go with him to witness to the Karens in that area. He had wonderful success among his own people, and it was not long before they came to Christ by the thousands. Meanwhile the Burmans, upon whom Judson was focusing his attention, were responding very sparsely. One factor was the traditions which the Karens had of creation, the temptation, and fall of man. Even more striking was a tradition that their "younger white brother" would come across the sea with the "white book" which their ancestors had lost, through which they could be reconciled to the Creator.[18] In addition to the impact of these traditions, McGavran suggests that the gospel spread along chains of families among the Karen. He speaks of a web of family relationships so important in penetrating tribal cultures.[19] In any case this people movement did not stop with the Karen, but leaped the boundaries to the quarter-million Kachin people in the 1890's, the Lahu and the Wa in the beginning of this century, and the Lisu of China after that.

The Chuhras of India and Pakistan

Among the tens of millions of outcaste untouchables of Hinduism was a tribe of a million or more in the Punjab called Chuhras. Their livelihood consisted of that which caste Hindus could not do: skinning dead cattle, curing the skins, selling skin and bones, and carrying away the 'night soil' (excreta) from latrines. In 1873 a Hindu convert named Nattu won a Chuhra named Ditt to faith in Christ. They walked thirty miles to the town of Sialkot and approached Presbyterian missionary Samuel Martin with the request that he baptize him immediately. Ditt was not an impressive convert: a dark little man, illiterate, lame in one leg. Martin urged him to stay for instruction, as was the custom with converts before baptizing them. Ditt, however, insisted on going back to his village right away. With great misgivings Martin agreed to baptize him, never expecting to see him again. When Ditt returned to his village, he was ostracized. But instead of fleeing back to the missionary, he continued to live Christ before his relatives and witness to them. Two months later Ditt returned with his wife, two daughters, and two near neighbors whom he had won to Christ. Upon examining them Martin was astonished to find that they really had intelligent faith in Christ, and he baptized them. Over six months later Ditt returned with an uncle and three other men for baptism. In other districts a few other Chuhras were turning to Christ and although, like Ditt, they experienced initial opposition, many of their caste were responsive to the claims of Christ. By 1881 conversions accelerated to 100, and a people movement was underway. By 1882 there were over 200; for the next three years, 500 per year; and in 1886, almost 2000. Although the rate dropped off considerably by 1897, by 1905 conversions were on the increase again, peaking at about 3500 in 1909, and continuing at over a thousand a year into the 1920's. Many other thrilling examples like these could be given from around the world.[20]

THE SPAWNING OF ECUMENISM OUT OF GLOBAL MISSIONARY CONFERENCES

One of the striking developments of the second era of Protestant missions was the radical shift from an initial emphasis upon intermission cooperation and conferences in the early years to the Ecumenical Movement of modern times, with its goals far removed from those of the missionary movement. It could be said that this which started as an essentially missionary movement evolved into something which was essentially anti-missionary in the original sense of the word. It has forced a significant regrouping of evangelical missionary forces today.

Intermission cooperation, conferences, and councils

The early history of the modern Protestant missionary movement is full of examples of activity which transcended denominational bounds. Some of the earliest missions were nondenominational, and on the field there were many intermission conferences in the early days which questioned the transplanting of Western denominational differences abroad and fostered intermission cooperation. For example, a number of regional conferences in India were followed by the first All-India Conference held in 1872 in Allahabad with 136 missionaries attending.

Comity. The concept of 'comity' developed very early, which was the principle of agreement among the missions not to compete in the same geographical areas. In effect the various missions agreed to divide up the country as far as their church-planting efforts were concerned. Since the fields were vast and the laborers were few, it made sense to agree to divide up geographically. (Today, however, the value of comity is cast into serious doubt by the shift to Ecumenism which has brought many negative factors into the picture.)

Consultation and cooperation between the home organizations developed early. Mission administrators met regularly in England starting in 1819. The Evangelical Alliance, formed in 1848, sponsored the first of the general missionary conferences, the London Conference of 1854. A similar conference was held in New York that same year.

International Conferences. The London Conference of 1888 was more international in scope. Most significant about it was a paper by the great German missionary scholar, Gustav Warneck, proposing regular international conferences, more intermission cooperation, and attempts to "bring about gradually, by such fraternal alliances, a certain amount of unity in Protestant missionary labours." The next great international conference was the Ecumenical Missionary Conference held in Carnegie Hall, New York in 1900.

For sheer size it was the largest missionary conference ever held. No fewer than 162 mission boards were represented—64 from North America, 50 from Europe, 35 from the British Isles, and 13 others. A total of 175,000 persons attended the ten-day conference. Most of the missionary giants of that day were present— Bishop Thoburn, Hudson Taylor, Timothy Richard, John Paton, John R. Mott, Robert E. Speer, and others.[21]

The Ecumenical Movement

The word ecumenical strictly means 'worldwide'. That probably was the sense in which it was used in 1900. However, the word has taken on a new meaning in the intervening years. Arising out of these great international intermission conferences was the Ecumenical Movement, which incorporates two major branches which were not necessarily in view in 1900: the **World Council of Churches** with its aggressive organizational thrust toward a superchurch, and the Church Union Movement which involves actual church union of denominations on a regional or national basis. Let us trace the development of this movement.

The **Edinburgh Conference of 1910** began to manifest this new meaning of the term. Its Continuation Committee was reorganized in 1921 into the **International Missionary Council.** The IMC sponsored five world conferences: Jerusalem, 1928; Madras, 1938; Whitby, 1947; Willingen, 1952; and Ghana, 1957-58. Out of this activity the World Council of Churches was inaugurated in 1948 at Amsterdam. Since that time the **World Council of Churches** has had the organizational unity of Christendom as its major goal, and evangelical doctrine, evangelism, and missions have been minimized and repressed.[22] By 1961 at New Delhi the IMC was swallowed up by the WCC. Although there are still many evangelicals in the WCC, the vast majority of evangelical missionaries today are not a part of the WCC. Indeed, the total number of missionaries affiliated with the WCC has shrunk to a less than 6% of Protestant missionaries (cf. ch. 21). A major cause of this has been the infiltration of liberal theology within the denominations of the WCC. In order to understand how Satan has been able to sidetrack this great organizational effort, it is important to understand this infiltration of liberalism, to which we will now turn.

Liberal theology undercuts missions

Whenever we see God's people advance, we see Satan's counterattack, frequently on another front. Since he didn't succeed in repressing the great missionary movement in its first era, he began to cause it to be undermined in the second era. So just as Hudson Taylor was beginning the CIM, another Englishman, Charles Darwin, was promulgating evolutionary doctrines in his *Origin of the Species*. About this time also, destructive higher criticism of the Bible was developing upon this evolutionary basis. Graf, Wellhausen, and Kuenen were beginning to cut up the books of Moses to conform them to their evolutionary presuppositions. Not only were the accounts of creation and the fall of man in Genesis undercut, but the attacks expanded to the Gospel accounts of Christ's unique person and work. The Liberals no longer accepted the Gospels as historical and thus attacked the virgin birth, miracles, bodily resurrection, and deity of the Lord Jesus. Supernatural salvation springing from his saving death and resurrection was rejected. The 'social gospel' was put in its place. Now the goal of reaching lost sinners was replaced with programs of saving society from its problems of poverty, injustice, inequity, war, ignorance, and disease. The judgment of God was no longer a factor for these 'modern Christians', since hell was a myth and a superstition in their view. They humanized God, deified man, and rejected the supernatural gospel of Christ.

In the first era, the word 'missions' meant sending cross-cultural evangelists to win adherents of non-Christian religions to salvation from sin through new birth in Christ. Now among the Ecumenicists it became popular to drop the 's' and talk about the 'mission' of the church. Evangelism, if acknowledged at all, became a minor part of the ecumenical agenda.

Evangelicals/Fundamentalists regroup

In the light of the above facts we can say with certainty that the development of the 'faith mission' movement in this period was providential. Not only did it provide a vehicle to advance the cause of world evangelism by leaps and bounds, but it also provided a structure for the continuation of evangelical missions after the apostasy of the 'mainline' denominations became evident. At first the WCC denominations took an 'inclusivist' stance in which they accepted missionary candidates of diverse theological viewpoints, whether liberal or evangelical. By 1932 the **Laymen's Missionary Inquiry** advocated that only liberal missionaries should be sent. Evangelicals were being squeezed out of their denominations and had to regroup. In 1917 a number of North American 'faith' missions organized the **Interdenominational Foreign Mission Association (IFMA)**. In 1945 a number of evangelical denominations formed the **Evangelical Foreign Missions Association (now Evangelical Fellowship of Mission Agencies)**. In 1969 the more separatist **Fellowship of Missions** came into being. In addition, many independent missions, representing almost forty percent of North American missionaries, do not belong to any of the above associations of missions.

THE IMPACT OF TWO WORLD WARS AND THE DEPRESSION

The end of the second era of missions was marked by two world wars and the great worldwide economic depression of the 1930s. Although the beginnings of the third "new frontiers" era developed in the period between the wars, the distinctive features of this era came to the fore after World War II. The end of colonialism began with the first war, and the second war brought about its almost total demise. Not only did these three circumstantial factors reduce the size of the missionary task force, but the shift to the newer evangelical mission agencies began to take place at this time.

German missions were particularly hard hit by the two wars. German missionaries became isolated from their home country by war. Only the help of British and North American missions in this period kept the German missions alive. Since until recently most German Protestants lived in former communist East Germany, full recovery has been difficult.[23] The economic depression by itself might not have had such a great impact if it had not been accompanied by the heyday of Protestant liberalism in the thirties. But after World War II a whole new breed of missionaries surged out to the mission fields and implemented the ideas of men like Cameron Townsend, reacted to the colonial past, utilized the new technologies available to them, and created new approaches to world evangelism of their own. But this is the subject of our next chapter.

Perspectives enrichment: Chapters B-10, 11, 13.

1. Ralph D. Winter, "Four Men, Three Eras, Two Transitions: Modern Missions" in *Perspectives*, pp. B-33 ff.

2. Kane, *Concise History*, pp. 101-3; 88, 94-95.

3. Tucker, *Jerusalem to Irian Jaya*, p. 173; see Daniel W. Bacon, *From Faith to Faith* (Singapore: OMF, 1984).

4. Ibid., p. 175.

5. Ibid., p. 178-79.

6. A brief extract from the book is found in, *Perspectives*, pp. B-110 ff.

7. Basil Miller, *J. Hudson Taylor: For God and China* (1948), pp. 57-67.

8. Tucker, *Jerusalem to Irian Jaya*, p. 185.

9. Kane, *A Global View of Christian Missions* (1971), pp. 241-2; 315.

10. Kane, *Global View*, pp. 306-307.

11. Tucker, *Jerusalem to Irian Jaya*, pp. 304-307.

12. Pierson, *Crisis*, pp. 273-99.

13. Kenneth Kantzer, Staley Lecture given at Northeastern Bible College, Essex Fells, N.J., March 8, 1983.

14. Stephen Neill, *A History of Christian Missions*, pp. 322-25.

15. J. Hudson Taylor, "The Call to Service," in *Perspectives*, pp. B-103 ff. Premillennialism holds that Christ will return to earth to establish His reign for a 1000 yr. kingdom.

16. Kane, *Understanding Missions*, pp. 252-55.

17. McGavran, *Bridges*. I do not accept all of McGavran's concepts of people movements and have written an evaluation of valid and invalid forms of the phenomenon: C. Gordon Olson, "What About People-Movement Conversion?" *Evangelical Missions Quarterly* 15 (July 1979):133-142.

18. Don Richardson, *Eternity in their Hearts* (1981), pp. 73-102.

19. McGavran, *Bridges of God*, pp. 68-72.

20. Ibid., pp. 71-72.; Frederick and Margaret Stock, *People Movements in the Punjab* (1975), pp. 33-126; Andrew Gordon, *Our India Mission* (Philadelphia: Andrew Gordon, 1886), pp. 421-433.

21. Kane, *Understanding Missions*, pp. 175-76; cf. pp. 172-83. Cf. American Tract Society, *Ecumenical Missionary Conference: New York 1900*.

22. Arthur P. Johnston, *The Battle for World Evangelism* (1978), and *World Evangelism and the Word of God* (1974).

23. Kane, *Understanding Missions*, p. 162.

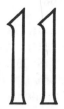

> ". . . for a wide door for effective service has opened for me, and there are many adversaries."
>
> –1 Corinthians 16:9

MISSIONS IN TRANSITION: THE CONTEMPORARY SCENE (1945--)

"The 25 unbelievable years" is what missions strategist Ralph Winter, in his book by that title, called the period following World War II. He suggested that this period was unbelievably transitional and traumatic in its impact upon world missions; and yet that the unbelievable progress made during this period is the basis of great optimism. Today that transition is not over, nor is the exciting progress of missions and worldwide church growth. Since Winter wrote his book, it has extended to over five decades, and its impact is still being felt around the world. Although the political situation in the world changed most radically in the decade after the war, the reverberations of those changes are still being felt. Although the changes in the home and foreign churches were also probably greatest in the immediate post-war years, things have by no means crystallized and remain extremely fluid. The same can be said for the mission boards and especially their relationship to the younger churches. This is seen not only in the indigenization of the churches and the shift of missionary personnel, but also in the continuing development of missions methodology. Although there was a plateau in the growth of missionary personnel in the 1970's, the growth seems to be accelerating, fueled by short-termers and non-Westerners. And most importantly, church growth has been most encouraging overall, especially taking into account the last decade's explosion of house churches in Red China.

THE RADICALLY CHANGING POLITICAL ENVIRONMENT

The retreat of the West

It is hard for young people to grasp the radically different world in

which we live and into which the gospel of Christ has gone since World
War II. Winter describes the "retreat of the West" by stating that prior to
1945, 99.5 percent of the non-western world was under western political
domination; by the end of 1969, 99.5 percent of the 'third-world' was
independent of western colonialism.[1] Although he undoubtedly overstat-
ed his case since China and Japan were hardly colonies before the war
(although China had suffered from Western colonialism for years), the
dramatic retreat of the West is nevertheless fact. We have already seen
how missions and colonialism related in the history of missions, and how
colonialism reached its peak in the nineteenth century. But as the colonial powers introduced western education (to varying degrees) into their
colonies, the nationals began to long for and agitate for independence.

An outstanding story was that of the struggle in British India which
reached its climax during World War II, when the Japanese armies were
advancing through Burma. The Indian leaders agreed to fight on the side
of the British only if independence was promised after the war. The
British made good on this promise in 1947, when India, Pakistan, and
Ceylon (Sri Lanka) received independence. The last to give up control
were the Portuguese both in India and Africa (Angola, Mozambique, &
Guinea). In a few countries independence came as a result of guerilla
warfare and terrorism (i.e. the MauMau in Kenya; rebels in Algeria), but
in most cases independence came through more peaceful, non-violent
agitation. Herbert Kane suggests that the missionaries sowed the seeds
of nationalism. This was especially true in Africa and to a lesser extent
in Asia.[2]

The rise of nationalism

Corresponding to the demise of colonialism and the retreat of the
West was the rise of nationalism. As nationalism reached its fruition with
the political independence of so many new nations, it had its impact
upon the national churches and the missionaries as well. The following
specifics should be mentioned:

1. It hastened the indigenization of those churches which had already
been founded on a nonindigenous basis. This means that churches
which were dependent upon the mission for financial help, direction
(control), and evangelistic initiative, now had to be turned over to national leadership. National Christians had increasingly to take up the
support and control of their own churches in the new environment of
national control in the secular areas. This was a positive factor.

2. It highlighted the imperative of starting new churches on an indigenous basis. A century ago John Nevius and then Roland Allen had written about the importance of the indigenous principle of missions.[3] Now
additional obvious evidence supported their recommendations, which
were beginning to be taken much more seriously.

3. It changed the status and role of the missionary. As was happening in the political and commercial sector, so now in the church the western missionary was no longer the *barda sahib* (great master) who could dictate to the national church. Increasingly the missionary became a 'coworker' or perhaps even a servant of the church. This was definitely for the good.

4. It exposed the tensions between church and mission—between national leader and missionary. Nationals had been repressing a natural resentment of the dominance of the western missionary. This now began to come out into the open. The missionary's tendency to dominate must be recognized as from the flesh, as was the national's resentment. The new role has hopefully resolved much of the tension.[4]

5. It tested the genuineness and soundness of the national church. In the most extreme case of Red China, the extreme nationalism of the government proved to be a fiery test of both the genuineness and soundness of the various national churches. In some African countries the newly independent governments' pressure for "authentic African culture" brought persecution to the church. Some stood the fire well; others were badly burned!

6. The image of Christianity was de-westernized. The dominance of westerners in both government and church had given the churches a bad, western image. With nationalization and indigenization, this image has greatly improved.

Communist expansion

Although Marxism gained its first victory in 1917 with the take-over of the Russian Government by the Bolsheviks, until World War II the Communists did not succeed in expanding their power base. With the Allies' victory over Hitler's Germany in 1945 a power vacuum developed which the Communists filled. Russia directly annexed Latvia, Lithuania, and Estonia. Under the intimidation of the Russian occupying armies and political intrigues and assassinations, they brought all of Eastern Europe under Communist control. (This included Poland, East Germany, Hungary, Czechoslovakia, Romania, Bulgaria, Albania, and Yugoslavia.) This was followed in 1949 by the victory of the Communist armies of Mao Tse Tung (Mao Zedong) in China over the Nationalist Government of General Chiang Kai-Shek. In the ensuing years Communist regimes have gained control in North Korea, North Viet Nam, South Viet Nam, Cambodia, and Laos in Asia; Angola, Mozambique, and Ethiopia in Africa; and Cuba and Nicaragua in Latin America. This has had a dramatic, unparalleled impact upon missions.

Since Marx was an atheist and argued that "religion is the opiate of the people," Communists have usually used force to try to destroy the church. Although their tactics have varied, the pressures upon the churches have been heavy. Pastors and Christians have been imprisoned and martyred, evangelism throttled, Bibles and Christian literature destroyed and repressed, seminaries closed, churches forced underground, and Christian young people denied education and jobs. Nevertheless, the churches have survived and grown despite the severe persecution. It seems clear that the church has done better under communist persecution in Eastern Europe than it has with government support in Western Europe.

In mainland China the picture has been even more dramatic. When the Communists took over in 1949 there were less than one million Protestants. Government pressure upon the Christians forced the withdrawal of all of the missionaries, the last ones leaving when they were released from prison. Christians were severely persecuted until the death of Mao in 1976, especially under the cultural revolution of the Red Guards in the late '60s. But the disillusionment of the people with communism and the more open attitude of the present government has allowed the church to bloom in the '80s, so that knowledgeable authorities estimate that there are thirty to seventy million Christians in mainland China today. This can be better understood by realizing that communism relieved the Chinese of the ancient bondage of ancestor worship, ultimately making them more responsive to the gospel message.

Have these political changes of the post-war world been for the good or bad of the church? We can answer this from two points of view. Although in the short term the changes frequently seem to have had a negative impact on the church, with the passage of time it becomes increasingly clear that they are for the good. China is undoubtedly the clearest example of the necessity of taking the long look at things. We should also emphasize God's sovereignty in human history. He is at work to overrule the program of the Devil in this world.

THE RESURGENCE OF ANCIENT RELIGIONS

At the end of the Second World War, some of the world religions seemed to be weak and dying. Shinto in Japan was severely damaged when the Emperor Hirohito was forced to announce to his people that he was not divine. Muslims were under the almost total domination of the western powers and had not had any Caliphate (religio-political leader) of their own since the demise of the Ottoman Empire after the First World War. But with the development of Shinto sects, Shintoism has become resurgent in Japan, and one sect is even making disciples in California. With the independence of most Muslim peoples, the establishment of dozens of Islamic Republics, and the windfall of oil money, Islam is resurgent and on the offensive again. For a while in Africa Muslim growth seemed to be greater than that of the Christians. That situation has now reversed. But Muslims are making a great thrust into the spiritual vacuum of Europe.

Although Buddhism, Taoism, and Confucianism have suffered serious reverses in Red China, some Buddhist and Hindu sects have been very active in recent years, not only in their historic areas, but also in proselytizing in the western world. So it is clear that Satan has not allowed the non-Christian religions to lie down and die. Just as we might expect from biblical prophecy, Satan's opposition to the gospel of Christ will continue on vigorously until Christ returns.

TRANSITION WITHIN CHRISTENDOM

A Protestantism gone astray

In the last chapter we mentioned the inroads of liberal theology in the old-line Protestant denominations and thus in the great missionary conferences in the first half of this century. This culminated in the formation of the World Council of Churches (WCC) in Amsterdam in 1948 as the ultimate ecumenical organization.

The original purpose of the Edinburgh Missionary Conference of 1910 was to gather missionary leaders from all over the world to chalk out a strategy for world evangelization. The founding of the **International Missionary Council (IMC)** at Lake Mohawk, NY in 1921 was to provide a continuing organization for that goal. But the growing impact of liberalism upon the churches was reflected in the Jerusalem Conference of 1928. No longer were non-Christians seen as lost and in need of salvation, but rather a broader approach was advocated.[5]

The liberal perspective was advocated more aggressively by the Laymen's Missionary Inquiry of 1932, which openly advocated the 'social gospel' and the removal of evangelism and Evangelicals from missionary work. Subsequent conferences in Madras, India (1938) and Whitby, Canada (1947) reflected the struggle between the older liberal viewpoint, evangelical or fundamentalist doctrine, and the newer neo-orthodox (Barthian) movement. Although the founding documents of the World Council of Churches in Amsterdam seemed evangelical on the surface, in the ensuing years the liberal and neo-orthodox viewpoint became dominant. The International Missionary Council merged with the World Council of Churches in Accra, Ghana, in 1958, and the evangelical concept of 'missions' was submerged by the ecumenical concept of the 'mission of the church'.[6] Evangelism in the historic sense was replaced by sociopolitical programs which eventually resulted in the WCC subsidizing Marxist guerillas in Rhodesia (now Zimbabwe).

What is the significance of this? A worldwide movement which began with a great missionary perspective has ended up in essential hostility to the biblical concept of missions! Glasser has characterized the Ecumenical movement as having an inclusivist message, uncertain missionary outreach, and an aggressive organizational outreach.[7] Since the

WCC professes to represent all Protestants and Eastern Orthodoxy with a constituency second only to the Roman Catholic Church, this worldwide organization has considerable power with governments and the media. A small group of liberal administrators and church leaders claims to represent hundreds of millions of Christians. Neither do they really reflect the viewpoints of all the churches they supposedly represent, but they also abuse the great political and economic power they hold in order to repress evangelical missions. But how is this possible?

Ecumenical leaders have leverage to repress evangelical witness in a number of ways. Certainly the evangelical segments in the old-line denominations do not get fair representation by these more liberal leaders. Evangelicals are kept out of prominent pulpits and influential administrative posts within their denomination and mission boards. Evangelicals who are not a part of the old-line denominational mission boards face problems in representation to their home and foreign governments since the WCC claims to represent all Protestantism. This affects getting visas, claims of comity violation, access to the public media, etc. Ecumenical leaders lure evangelical youth into liberal educational institutions with generous scholarships in order to get them to abandon their evangelical beliefs and become part of the ecumenical thrust. Despite that aggressive organizational thrust, the actual constituency of the ecumenical denominations has been shrinking here in the West, and their missionary force has shrunk even more rapidly. However, the damage was done in that they left national churches infected with liberalism. But we will give more details about that shortly.

A fragmented Roman Catholicism

Roman Catholicism has historically used its immense political power, money, and prestige to oppose Protestant missionary efforts, especially where it has had substantial political influence as in Latin America and southern Europe. This continued to be true after the Second World War when, for example, priests would continue to incite mobs against Protestants in Colombia, and Protestants were denied civil liberties in countries like Spain and Portugal.

However, with the Vatican Council II of 1962-65 the whole attitude of Romanism changed, and Protestants who had been vilified previously were now referred to as "separated brethren." Indeed the Roman Church itself began to change internally. Liberal, evolutionary theologies, which had been repressed previously, now were being taught in many Catholic seminaries. Out of this ultimately came Liberation Theology, which advocated the violent overthrow of oppressive governments. The Pope has been very slow to condemn such diversity, with the result that it is flourishing in many Catholic countries. To further complicate the situation, the Charismatic Movement, which started in Protestantism in the 50's, spilled over into Catholicism and has become quite powerful in some areas.

In addition, the political situation has changed in many Roman Catholic countries. Formerly Roman Catholic-inclined governments have been replaced by more neutral ones, thus giving greater freedom for evangelical evangelization. For example, in Spain after half a century of General Franco's Roman Catholic, Fascist dictatorship, a Socialist government took over in 1975. Although there had been slight liberalization of restrictions in Franco's latter years, the new government has given full civil rights to Protestants.

MISSIONARY PERSONNEL
AND RELATIONSHIPS

Every bit as dramatic as the radical changes in the political sphere, have been the changes in the number, kind, and relationships of missionary personnel since the Second World War. Not only was there a surge of new North American missionaries right after the war, but the ratio between evangelicals and ecumenical missionaries began to shift. The process of nationalizing and indigenizing the national churches brought about a change in role for the missionary. Nineteenth-century relationships between missionary and national left much to be desired and necessarily began to change. Then in more recent decades, two-thirds-world nationals began to form their own mission boards and send out their own missionaries.

The postwar surge of missionaries

We have already noted in the previous chapter the impact of liberal theology, the great economic depression, and two world wars upon the missionary task force. From a peak of around 31,000 Protestant missionaries in 1927 the numbers dwindled to about 21,000 by 1945.[8] Although Europe was ravaged by the Second War, and the number of European missionaries continued to decline after the war, the number of North American missionaries began to surge. Many Christians serving in the armed services during the war saw the desperate spiritual needs of Europe and Asia and determined to go back as missionaries. The 'GI Bill' of educational aid for veterans enabled them to devote full time to preparation for missionary service and get right back to the field. New mission organizations were formed to meet the needs they saw during the war. Although the Student Volunteer Movement had died in the 1920's because of liberal theology, Inter-Varsity Christian Fellowship's Triennial Missionary Conferences in Urbana have contributed substantially to missionary recruitment and attendance continues to grow encouragingly.

In this connection, we should note that Europe was not really viewed as a mission field until after World War II. Although there were a few

American missions in Europe before the war, after the war a number of new missions were formed, and existing missions opened new work in Europe. In the mid 1980's there are roughly four thousand North American missionaries working in Europe.

More recently another dimension has been added to the missionary personnel situation. Since the mid 70's the number of short-term missionaries has increased remarkably. By 1996 there were about 7000 one to four-year short termers and over 66,500 who stay from two months up to one year.[9] At first it was feared that short termers would replace career missionaries in the totals and be a less efficient use of resources. However, the latest statistics show that the number of career missionaries is stable, so that the short termers are 'icing on the cake'. Indeed, many short termers have been found to return as career missionaries.

Ecumenical/Evangelical ratio

In the period between the two world wars evangelical churches were regrouping as a consequence of the great modernist/fundamentalist controversy and its impact upon the older established denominations. Thus the number of evangelical missionaries began to grow rapidly, while the ecumenical missions began to shrink under the continuing impact of liberal theology. This was also influenced by the growth of the IVCF Urbana missionary conventions. That trend has continued unabated right up to the present. Ecumenical missionaries, as represented by the Department of Missions (DOM) of the National Council of Churches, "hovered around 10,000 for about 20 years following World War II. Then from about 1967, most DOM agencies began a precipitous decline." By 1992 this number had shrunk to under 2500 missionaries, and the DOM itself was dissolved. By 1996 NCC Protestant denominations reported only 2040 career missionaries. Over the same period the total number of North American Protestant career missionaries was increasing from 33,290 to peak at about 43,000, and evangelical mission agencies overall experienced substantial growth.[10] I hardly need to underline the fact that the ecumenical movement has been incredibly destructive of missions; the numbers speak for themselves! (See chapter 21 for full statistics.)

Missionary attitudes

With the growing nationalization of government and commerce after the war, it was only natural that the same transition should take place in the churches as well. The indigenous principles that John Nevius had implemented in Korea a century ago and Roland Allen had expounded at the beginning of the century, were finally being put into practice around the world. This required new attitudes toward nationals on the part of the missionaries. It demanded a greater trust in the Holy Spirit to work in the nationals what He works in western Christians. It was not always easy for the missionaries to let go of the reins.

Although Hudson Taylor had pioneered ideas of closer identification with nationals a century earlier, most missionaries had not come around to his viewpoint. The typical nineteenth-century (second era) missionary kept a distance between himself and the nationals he was working among. He was not particularly concerned to identify with the indigenous lifestyle, either in clothes, food, or social relationships. Many of the younger missionaries were more sensitized to the feelings of the national Christians in this regard and sought to break down the barriers. This sometimes caused friction between the senior missionaries and their juniors, but change was absolutely necessary.

Another area of tension among evangelical missionaries has been the charismatic issue. There has long been the problem of the relationship of Pentecostal missionaries to other evangelicals. They have tended to 'do their own thing'. The issue has been heightened with the spillover of charismatic practices into the old-line denominations. It is natural that missionaries, with their desire for spirituality, should be among the first affected. Subsequently some other evangelical missions were affected. In some cases the dispute brought division and even the shipwreck of whole teams of missionaries. As a result, there have been divided attitudes among evangelicals in regard to relationships with Pentecostal/charismatic missionaries. That tension continues today.

THE DEVELOPMENT OF METHODOLOGY AND THE SCIENCE OF MISSIOLOGY

The postwar period has seen a host of innovations in missionary methodology and the further development of pre-existing methods. Some are a product of the new technology available today, but some ideas have arisen out of careful research.

The Bible translation surge

Evangelicals had always believed in the importance of Bible translation, and this was a primary task of the great pioneers. However, **Cameron Townsend** was a missionary to Guatemala during the First World War who was impressed with the difficulty of reaching Indians through a Spanish language which they only poorly understood. He noted that his missionary colleagues were naively putting dependence upon a trade or literary language to reach the people, rather than through the language of the heart. He found that selling Spanish Bibles to the Indians was practically useless. The question from an Indian which really unsettled him was, "Why, if your God is so smart, hasn't he learned our language?" Townsend spent the next thirteen years learning the intricacies of the Cakchiquel language and translating the New Testament. When a professional advisor suggested that he quit trying to force Cakchiquel into the mold of Latin grammar and find out its own logical linguistic pattern, his study was revolutionized. Out of this experience came the founding of Camp Wycliffe in 1934 to train linguistic missionaries, which became the **Summer Institute of Linguistics/ Wycliffe Bible Translators.**[11] Wycliffe has now grown to become the largest mission board by far with over 5500 missionaries in 1985. But language reduction and Bible translation work has not by any means been limited to Wycliffe. Thousands of other missionaries have been trained in scientific linguistics and done language reduction and Bible translation under other missions. The result is that 2200 languages now have some part of the Bible in their own language, and over 350 have a complete Bible. Along with the basic literature work a growing literacy thrust has also been developed to teach people to read in their own mother tongue.

Bible correspondence courses

Another pre-existing approach which has come into its own in recent years is the Bible Correspondence School. It is an effective method for training Christians, and in the Muslim world it has also proved to be a useful evangelistic tool. Non-Christians who are interested in understanding the Bible have taken introductory courses in great numbers. Because Muslims are curious about the Bible and can study in the privacy of their homes, this approach has brought many to faith in Christ.

Literature ministries

Christian literature has always been important to missionary endeavor. However, with growing world literacy and education, the production and distribution of Christian literature has taken on increased significance. This involves not only Bibles, but also tracts, booklets, books, literacy materials, correspondence courses, Sunday School materials, newspapers, magazines, etc. A number of specialized organizations like Evangelical Literature Overseas focus especially upon this strategic ministry.

Modern media

The use of slide and filmstrip programs for evangelism goes back many generations, even when the projectors used kerosene lighting. However, now audio-visuals, radio and television are becoming even more important in evangelism and discipling. The pioneer missionary radio station was **HCJB** in Quito, Ecuador, founded by **Clarence W. Jones** in 1931. After the war **Far East Broadcasting Company** was started in Manila and **Trans World Radio** got established in Monte Carlo. Both have multiplied transmitters in many locations. Between them and other missionary radio stations most of the earth is covered at least once, if not many times. The major missionary radio organizations have over 50

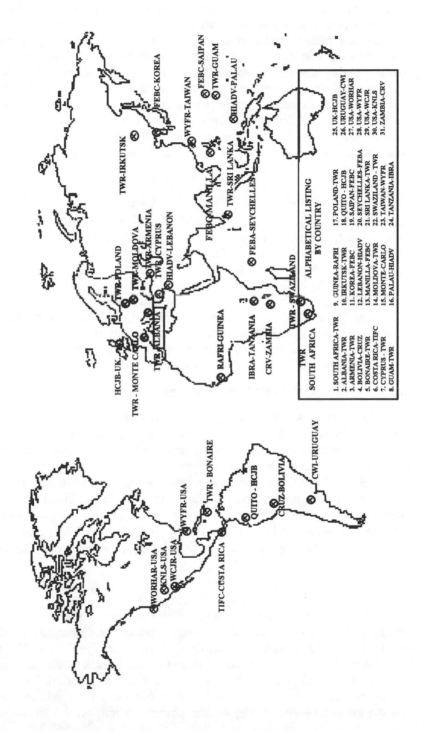

MISSIONARY INTERNATIONAL RADIO COVERAGE

ALPHABETICAL LISTING
BY COUNTRY

TWR
SOUTH AFRICA

1. SOUTH AFRICA-TWR
2. ALBANIA-TWR
3. ARMENIA-TWR
4. BOLIVIA-CRUZ
5. BONAIRE-TWR
6. COSTA RICA-TIFC
7. CYPRUS - TWR
8. GUAM-TWR

9. GUINEA-RAFRI
10. IRKUTSK-TWR
11. KOREA-FEBC
12. LEBANON-HIADV
13. MANILLA-FEBC
14. MOLDOVA-TWR
15. MONTE-CARLO
16. PALAU-HIADV

17. POLAND-TWR
18. QUITO - HCJB
19. SAIPAN-FEBC
20. SEYCHELLES-FEBA
21. SRI LANKA-TWR
22. SWAZILAND - TWR
23. TAIWAN-WYFR
24. TANZANIA-IBRA

25. UK-HCJB
26. URUGUAY-CWI
27. USA-WORHAR
28. USA-WYFR
29. USA-WCJR
30. USA-KNLS
31. ZAMBIA-CRV

transmitters broadcasting the gospel internationally from 31 locations in 242 languages. There are additionally many local missionary stations. With the multiplication of portable transistor radios, most people, even in remote places, can hear these stations as never before. Add to this the growing availability of television and Christian television programming and opportunities become unlimited. We should also mention the significance of the use of recordings in reaching isolated peoples. Joy Ritterhof was the founder of Gospel Recordings, Inc., which has put gospel messages in thousands of languages on disk. Now missionaries can easily use audio and video cassettes as well. The "Jesus" film is available in 270 languages and is widely used.

Modern technology

A most beneficial spinoff of World War II was the stimulus to use modern aviation and radio technology in missions, especially in pioneer work in less accessible areas. In 1945 **Mission Aviation Fellowship** was formed as a service mission to other missions. Following an accident on a commercial airplane in Latin America, Cameron Townsend, the founder of Wycliffe Bible Translators, realizing that missionaries needed their own properly-serviced and dependable planes, founded Jungle Aviation and Radio Service (JAARS). A number of other missions have also developed their own aviation and communications facilities. Additionally, computers have many functions for the missionary, including E-mail.

Church growth research movement

In 1955 Donald A. McGavran published his innovative book *The Bridges of God* in which he analyzed what he termed "people-movement conversion" and advocated research into how ethnic people groups turn to Christ.[12] Although his ideas, as expressed in his many other books, have been controversial, they have stimulated a lot of research and writing by other missionaries and scholars. This has also stirred up a lot of interest in using the insights of scientific anthropology and sociology in missionary strategy. There is no doubt that the whole discussion has given missionaries new insights into developing more effective approaches to the lost.

Saturation evangelism

About 1960 two missionary leaders were separately developing a new approach to evangelism on two different continents. Kenneth Strachan, the Director of Latin America Mission, started **Evangelism- in-Depth** in Central America. About the same time Gerald Swank of Sudan Interior Mission was developing a program called New **Life for All** in Nigeria. Both programs were based upon the idea of saturating a whole country with the gospel by mobilizing all the Christians and all the churches to simultaneously emphasize evangelism. The campaigns focused upon a certain limited area for a period of time, usually one year. The enthusiasm for saturation evangelism has faded somewhat when research showed that to some extent the results did not show up in church membership statistics commensurate with the effort expended. But there are some continuing efforts to use this from time to time in various parts of the world.[13]

Theological education by extension

In 1963 Ralph Winter and James Emery conceived a solution to the small enrollment problem at a seminary in Guatemala City. Indian pastors in the mountains needed more training but could not afford the money or the time to come into the capital to get it. So if the student couldn't come to the seminary, let the seminary go to the student! Programmed study materials were developed so that the students could study at home and then meet with the instructor periodically in a class situation at some central place to go over their work and get needed help. This put the teacher on a rigorous schedule of travel to meet with a number of groups on a regular basis. But this kind of in-service training proved to be so effective and efficient that it has spread all over the world since then. It is extremely popular in Latin America, but Africa and Asia are not too far behind in their use of this method.

Research in and teaching of missiology

In 1945 most seminaries and Bible institutes had only a minimal program of missions courses—usually a history of missions and a study of world religions. Frequently the teacher had not himself been a missionary. Now most evangelical Bible colleges and seminaries have a Missions Department with a host of courses on various phases of missiology: the science of missions. This instruction is supported by a number of organizations like the American Society of Missiology and the **Evangelical Missiological Society.** A growing number of institutions have graduate programs in missions, with several at the doctoral level. This has been a vast help in training missionaries who can use the best skills possible to reach a lost world in our generation.

Specialized mission boards

This century has also seen the formation of specialized mission organizations to meet special needs. We have already mentioned those for missionary radio and Bible translation. But a host of other needs presented themselves: literacy, literature, aviation, orphanage and relief work, leprosy patients, the Jews, the deaf, the blind, etc. Many of these are service missions which provide service to other missions as specialists.

Perspectives enrichment: Chapters B-12, 14, 15, 16, 17

THE NEEDIEST COUNTRIES/AREAS IN THE WORLD

COUNTRY	Non-Evangelical Million	Evangeli-cals %	Protestant Mission'ies	Ratio: Miss./Mill Non-Evang
Afghanistan	23.1	0.0	0?	0.0
Iran	64.5	0.03	0	0.0
N. Korea	25.4	0.4	0	0.0
Brunei	0.3	1.4	0	0.0
Vietnam	74.4	0.8	19	0.25
Croatia	4.8	0.2	2	0.4
Bangladesh	132.1	0.1	325	2.5
11 Pr. India*	570	<0.25	???	??
Lithuania	3.8	0.3	4	1.1
Georgia	5.6	0.3	8	1.4
L.R. China@	420	<1.9	???	<1.2
Poland	39.3	0.2	77	2.0
Armenia	3.4	0.6	10	2.9
Byelarus	10.4	1.0	6	0.6
Russia	150.0	0.6	509	3.4
Middle East	346.4	0.2	1572	4.5
Pakistan	141.3	0.2	743	5.3
Muslim CIS	55.4	0.26	458	8.2
Yugoslavia	10.3	0.2	66	6.4
Sri Lanka	18.2	0.4	125	6.7

*11 least-reached states of India with less than 1% Prot. State-by-state figures of Evangelicals not available, so % shown may include Catholics.

@13 least-reached provinces, 2 cities, and 6 ethnic minorities of China with less than 3% Professing Christians are included in estimate.

1. Ralph D. Winter, *The 25 Unbelievable Years: 1945-1969* (1970) pp. 11-13.
2. Kane, *Understanding Missions*, pp. 257-62.
3. John L. Nevius, *Planting and Development of Missionary Churches* (1958); Roland Allen, *Missionary Methods: St. Paul's or Ours?* (1962).
4. Kane, *Understanding Missions*, p. 264-65.
5. Eric S. Fife and Arthur F. Glasser, *Missions in Crisis* (1961), pp. 111-43.
6. Arthur P. Johnston, The Battle for World Evangelism, pp. 77-120.
7. Fife and Glasser, *Missions in Crisis*, pp. 128-34.
8. Winter, *Unbelievable Years*, p. 54.
9. MARC, *Mission Handbook*, 17th. ed. (1998), pp. 74, 84.
10. Ibid, 12th ed., pp.119-35; 13th, pp. 38-40; 17th ed.; *Pulse*, 24:19; & IFMA & EFMA 1996 reports. MARC no longer tabulates the missionary figures for the various associations, and the DOM no longer exists, so I had to make my own tabulation of NCC missionaries.
11. Tucker, *Jerusalem to Irian Jaya*, pp. 351-57.
12. Donald A. McGavran, *Bridges; Understanding Church Growth* (1970); and many others.
13. George W. Peters, *Saturation Evangelism* (1970).

PART III

HIS ALIENATED WORLD

THE CONTEXTUAL DIMENSION

WORLD POPULATION BY RELIGION

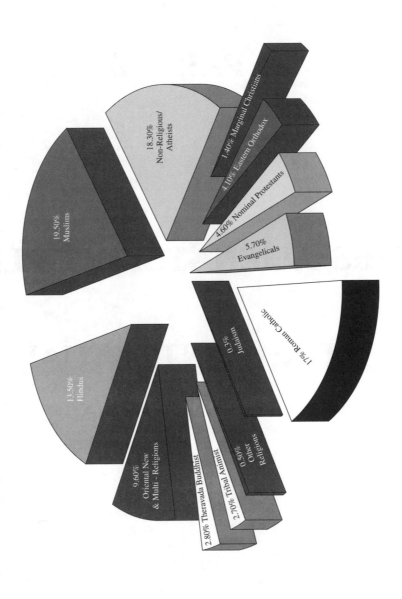

- 18.30% Non-Religious/Atheists
- 1.40% Marginal Christians
- 4.10% Eastern Orthodox
- 4.60% Nominal Protestants
- 5.70% Evangelicals
- 19.50% Muslims
- 17% Roman Catholic
- 0.3% Judaism
- 13.50% Hindus
- 9.60% Oriental New & Multi - Religions
- 2.80% Theravada Buddhist
- 2.70% Tribal Animist
- 0.50% Other Religions

12

NONTHEISTIC RELIGIOUS CONTEXTS:
WITHOUT THE TRUE GOD

ANIMISM: THE RELIGIONS OF
NONLITERATE TRIBAL PEOPLES

Introduction

Animism is a term used to describe tribal religions or the religions of
nonliterate societies. They are sometimes called traditional or aboriginal
religions. They are erroneously referred to as primitive religions although
they are really quite complex.

There are probably about 100 million such tribal people scattered
among thousands of different tribes on every major continent and the
islands of the sea. Some major examples would be the various American Indian tribes of both North and South America, the tribes of tropical
Africa, New Guinea, Oceania, and the primitive aboriginal tribes of Aus-
tralia, New Zealand, India, and Japan.

There are considerable differences between the diverse religions and
cultures of these groups, but there are many common themes that can
be identified through careful study of them. Missionaries and secular
anthropologists have provided data to seek to understand these groups.
There has been a lot of misinformation caused by failure to learn the
language and spend the years necessary to win their confidence and
discover the innermost secrets of their religions. Despite a century of
study there is still a lot of controversy and disagreement about certain
points. To further complicate the study many tribes are dying off or being
integrated into civilization. Nevertheless, there are many valid generalizations which we can make about animistic religions.

There is also much basic Animism to be found among the adherents
of the 'developed' religions, such as Muslims, Buddhists, and nominal
Christians. There is even a major substructure of our own western cul-

ture which derives from the Animistic religion of our ancestors. We call them superstitions, such as "bad luck when a black cat crosses one's path." Such taboos are common in animistic religion. Houghton's definition is helpful:

> Derived from the word 'anima' (breath), Animism can be more simply and popularly defined as 'Spirit Worship', as distinguished from the worship of God or gods.
>
> The extent of its ramifications in primitive religious thought shows how basic it is to natural, as opposed to revealed, religion. It includes Necrolatry, a term which conveniently describes the worship of the souls of men and animals, especially of the dead; Spirit Worship, involving the worship of spirits not particularly associated with bodies or objects; and Naturism, which sums up the worship of spiritual beings who direct the phenomena of nature. As such, it is not only the religion of wild and savage tribes before contact with civilization, but the background of the religious philosophy of the Hindu, the Buddhist, the Shintoist, the Confucianist, and the Muslim, and is at the bottom of the folklore of Christendom in Europe, as well as of the mythology of Egypt, Babylonia and Assyria, Greece, Rome, and Scandinavia.[1]

There is a host of practices and concepts which are common to many animistic religions. Most have some communal ritual acts, rites of passage (relating to birth, puberty, marriage, death, etc.), clan feasts, magic, myths and legends, fertility cults, fetishism, priests/ shamans/witch doctors, mana (impersonal supernatural power), spirits, divination and sacrifices, taboos, totemism, and veneration of the dead. We will try to simplify our consideration of these beliefs and practices under the three headings suggested by Houghton, but we must remember that these three categories overlap and are not mutually exclusive.

Necrolatry (worship of the dead)

Concern for the souls of the dead plays a prominent part in tribal religion. It may be reverence for a departed ancestor or it may be fear of the soul of some other dead person. Tribal people frequently think of departed ancestors as still part of the clan and feel concerned to keep them favorably inclined toward the living by appropriate rituals. The tendency is to fear the harm that the departed can do to the living. This is especially true in the case of those who die unnaturally. Such a soul will "come back to haunt" the living unless it is helped on its journey to the land of the dead by some appropriate ceremonies.

Spirit worship

Not only does tribal religion show concern for the souls of the dead, but also the existence of personal spirits or demons, as well as of impersonal spiritual forces in nature called *mana* by the Polynesians. Most tribal religions evidence belief in a host of evil spirits which inhabit the earth, air, fire, water, trees, mountains, and in animal life as well. The whole of life is governed by taboos and rituals designed to placate the spirits.

Shamanism. Very commonly a *shaman* or priest/witch doctor serves as the expert mediator, who knows the proper sacrifices and incantations. He is especially called in at times of sickness, but has many other functions also. It is also quite common in many tribes for other individuals to perform the rituals themselves.

Magic. In many cases, the spirit is not seen as a personal being, but rather some impersonal force of nature as mentioned above. Tribes have developed magical beliefs and practices to use these forces resident in nature for their own purposes. Imitative magic seeks to bring harm to an enemy by attacking a representation of him (e.g., a voodoo doll). Contagious magic describes those practices which depend upon the connection between a person and something associated with him, such as hair clippings, nail parings, or feces.

Magic can also be used for the good of the individual. The blood of a predatory animal may be drunk to gain the strength of the animal. This is carried a step further in cannibalism, where frequently the enemy is eaten to gain his power.

Fetishism. The concept of *mana* also helps us understand the use of charms, amulets, or fetishes. They are generally not thought of as inhabited by a personal spirit, but rather by some spiritual energy or force. Of course, such charms and amulets are not limited to animistic tribes. Many civilized westerners, as well as Muslims and other religionists, are superstitious about charms of various sorts. This takes the place of science in tribal cultures.

Naturism

Naturism is the personification and worship of the forces of nature, such as the sun, moon, and stars, fire, volcanoes, storms, or animals. This was common among the religions of the ancients, like the prominence of the sun in ancient Egyptian religion. Naturistic ideas also are evident in many of the 'higher' religions, such as the sacred cow of the Hindus of India or the sacred mountain of Japanese Shinto. It is also difficult to make a sharp division between the magical practices mentioned above and naturism. However, in many cases nature is actually worshiped. Quite commonly naturism develops into idolatry and polytheism (the worship of many gods).

Many naturistic practices relate to fertility, both in agriculture and in human reproduction. Worship, rituals, and sacrifices are intended to guarantee fertility. It seems that human sacrifices are an extreme form of this, as exemplified by the Mayan religion of precolonial Mexico or the formerly savage Nagas of northeast India and Burma.

Totemism. Perhaps totemism can be included here as an aspect of naturism. Totemism is a term derived from an American Indian word meaning 'brother-sister-kin', which emphasizes the unity of the clan with some sacred plant or animal. This is an aspect of the continuity the tribalist sees between human life and nature around him. The totem animal or plant is thus sacred to the tribe and must not be eaten except at special ceremonial feasts.

Conclusion

William Paton has suggested four characteristics of animistic religion and culture: 1) The whole of life is pervaded with fear. Fear governs most of the actions of tribal peoples. 2) The absence of love and consolation from his religion. The animist may have a concept of a creator God, but He is so aloof from human affairs that they do not concern themselves with Him. Thus there is no hope expressed in their religion. 3) There are no absolutes of morality. Sin is not seen as sin, but as the violation of culture, custom, and natural forces. 4) The lack of relationship with God causes a fatalistic attitude since all the events of life are predetermined and controlled by nature or demons.[2] The Christian appraisal of animistic religion would have to start with the Apostle Paul's explanation in Romans 1:21-25 of how Noah's descendants who once knew God degenerated into animistic practices. Houghton quotes an apt anonymous summary: "The common essence of heathenism is not a denying of God . . . but an ignoring of Him in worship of natural powers and mysterious demonic powers through magic and magical sacrifices and ceremonies."[3]

HINDUISM: INDIAN PANTHEISM/POLYTHEISM

Introduction

Hinduism is the term used to describe the pantheistic religion of a majority of more than 700 million (82%) of the almost 900 million people of India. It is not one unified religion but more like a congress of religions. It is the religion that grew out of the historical developments of the Indian subcontinent. Although most Hindus still live in India, there are more than 100,000 Hindus in each of twenty other countries, and Hindu ideas have spread to the western nations, especially in recent years. Hindu sects and teachers (gurus) have invaded the West, and terms like *yoga, karma,* transcendental meditation, 'the force', etc. are common now. But where did this all come from?

Its origins: the interaction of two civilizations

Hinduism is the outcome of the interaction of the religious beliefs of the indigenous **Dravidian** peoples of India with the Sanskrit-speaking **Aryan** invaders, who migrated into the subcontinent from the northwest about 1500 to 1200 B.C. and conquered the indigenous peoples. The caste system of India and most Hindu beliefs and practices can be best understood from this fusion of the two civilizations and religious beliefs and practices.

Apparently the dark-skinned Dravidian people had established an advanced civilization by 2500 B.C., ruins of which can be seen on the Indus River plains. The religion of the Dravidian civilization was polytheistic and idolatrous with a fertility-cultic worship of a mother goddess. They seem to have had some ideas about **reincarnation** and *karma,* the belief in the inevitable consequences of man's deeds affecting an individual's reincarnation. Like most idolatrous religion, it was closely tied into human sexuality with immoral practices.

The light-skinned Aryan invaders were related to the Greeks and the Persians ethnically, their Sanskrit being a sister language to ancient Greek. Their religion was Animistic and naturistic in character as evidenced by their earliest sacred writings, the *Vedas.* They worshiped a pantheon of nature gods much like the ancient Greek gods.

The Caste System. The conquest of the Dravidians was reinforced and institutionalized by the caste system which developed over the centuries. (Aryan means 'noble', and the word for caste is *varna,* which means 'color'.) Four major caste groupings developed (with hundreds of subcastes): the **Brahmins** were the priestly caste; the *Kshatriyas*, the warriors; the *Vaisyas*, the merchants and artisans; and the *Shudras* were the serfs. These are not strictly followed today. Not all Brahmins are priests, but they do tend to be the leaders in Indian society. Nevertheless, this system has produced a rigid hierarchy in Indian culture which governs one's status and occupation. Outside this caste system are more than 100 million outcastes or untouchables, who perform the lowest and most degrading tasks in society. Lewis explains:

> The caste system is closely bound up with the doctrine of *Karma*, according to which the nature of one's rebirth after death is determined by one's thoughts, words, or deeds during life. One may move up or down in the scale, a man of low caste may be reborn as a member of a higher caste, or vice versa. Thus the inequalities of the caste system—and all the differences in human life—are both explained and justified. Poverty and riches, health

and disease are ascribed to *Karma.*[4]

Hindu philosophy: achieving oneness with the World-Force

Although much of Hindu practice cannot be directly related to its abstruse philosophy, there is a common thread of ideas which are dominant. Although there is considerable diversity, essentially Hindu thought is monistic or pantheistic. That is, the Ultimate Reality has but one principle, called **Brahman(a).** This is not a personal God who has created the universe. It is the impersonal 'Force' which pervades the universe and is not at all distinguished from the universe. It could be called the 'World-soul.'

Since there is but one principle to reality, our individual existence is only a temporary illusion (*maya*), as is the physical world. Thus our individual soul or self (*atman*) is ultimately only a part of the universal World-soul *(Brahman).*[a] Time is viewed as an endless cycle of reincarnations, symbolized in the wheel of life (*samsara*). Life in this physical world is only an evil illusion which obscures our real unity with Brahman. So the goal of life is to be liberated from this cycle of existence. This 'liberation' is called **Moksha** or sometimes the Buddhist term *Nirvana* is used.

Since there is no forgiveness or escape from the inevitable law of karma (strictly translated 'deeds'), the path to Liberation is discouragingly difficult and rigorous. Indeed, Hindus are not at all agreed as to how it is attained. There are six major philosophical schools explaining how the individual is to achieve oneness (*yoga* ='yoking') with the infinite. All are agreed, however, that the goal is for one's individual self (*atman*) to be merged with the universal World-soul (*Brahman*). Hindus use the illustration of a jar to represent our body. The air in the jar is really one with the universal air outside, but the jar (body) hinders its unity. Thus through yoga we are liberated from the illusion of our individual physical self and we merge into the Infinite. The person who knows this can say, "I am Brahman" and becomes the 'All'.

There are four major ways of yoga emphasized by the various schools of thought: 1) the way of mental/spiritual/physical discipline, 2) the way of works (karma), 3) the way of knowledge, and 4) the way of devotion or ritual (*bhakti*). One who attains proficiency in yoga is called a *yogi*. One who attains a high measure of world-denial is called a **sadhu** (simple).

---

a The word *Brahman* can also be rendered *Brahman(a)* because of the hard 'n' ending. It is also referred to as *paramatman.* It is to be distinguished from the name of the caste *Brahmin* and the word for 'prayer' (*Brahma*).

Hindu scriptures: the *Vedas* and *Upanishads*

The Sanskrit **Vedas** are a complex body of literature written over many centuries, probably beginning about 1200 B.C. and completed by the writing of the Upanishads about 600 B.C. The dating is very uncertain since there are no historical connections in these writings. They rather consist of hymns, prayers, formulas and incantations, myths, and legends. The first indications of karma and reincarnation are found in the *Upanishads.* After the Vedas came a massive body of literature called the *Vedanga*, which includes the *Mahabharata* of which the *Bhagavad Gita* (A.D. 350) is especially revered by Hindus today because it emphasizes Karma Yoga and the ten incarnations of Vishnu, especially as Lord Krishna.

Popular Hinduism today

Popular Hinduism is in distinct contrast with the obscure philosophy explained above. The average Hindu probably understands little of this complex philosophy. The life of the Hindu is strongly governed by customs (*dastur*) passed down from past ages. The caste system and the veneration of the cow are at the core of things. The worship of the many (33 million) gods of Hinduism is an important part of life.

Polytheism. Central to that worship is a triad of deities among the vast pantheon: Brahma—the creator; Vishnu—the preserver; and Shiva—the destroyer. Especially important is the idea that Vishnu, in the form of Krishna, is reincarnated from age to age in many different forms (*avatar*). There is a vast mythology surrounding the gods and goddesses. Most Hindus are especially devoted to the worship of one of these deities. The relationship of the abstruse philosophy to the mythology and worship of the deities is difficult to discern.

India is filled with a multitude of temples and shrines, some ancient and covered with obscene carvings, while others are more modern and attractive. The temples are seen as the abode of the gods and are not for congregational worship. The Brahmin temple priests serve the gods, as worshipers bring their offerings.

The position of women in Hindu culture has been especially bad. Originally widows would be coerced to throw themselves upon the funeral pyre of their husbands, and little girls were given to the priests as temple prostitutes. The British government outlawed these practices in 1829 due to missionary pressure, and today the influence of western education and Christianity is improving the lot of women somewhat.

Summary and conclusion

Hinduism is a complex of philosophies, mythology, custom, and religious practices which are both pantheistic and polytheistic. Although distinctively Indian in its background, it has spread to the West in modified forms in recent years through a variety of sects and teachers (e.g., Hari Krishnas and Divine Light Mission), but its main strength is in India and among overseas Indians. It is important to realize that Buddhism and the Jain religion became offshoots of Hinduism more than two thousand years ago. About 500 years ago an attempt to reform Hinduism with Islamic ideas resulted in the Sikh religion of Guru Nanak.

BUDDHISM: HINDUISM'S OFFSPRING SPREADS EAST

Introduction

During the time that Hinduism was in its formative stages, a new religion came out of it which was to dominate the Far East, even though it perished in India, the land of its origin. Unlike Hinduism, which had no personal founder, Buddhism is attributable to one man, **Siddharta Gautama,** who was born a Hindu prince about 563 B.C. in the northeast of India near the Nepal border. Since then its traditional form (*Theravada*) has become the major religion of about 150 million people of Southeast Asia and Sri Lanka, and a broader form (*Maha-yana*) is a part of the multireligion of more than 450 million in China, Korea, Japan, and Tibet.[5] Like Hinduism, Buddhism is essentially monistic pantheism with idolatrous manifestations. Like Hinduism there is a tremendous diversity of beliefs and practices within Buddhism, ranging from atheism to polytheism. However, the major common unifying element among all forms is the illumination experience of Gautama the Buddha.

The life and illumination of Gautama the Buddha (563-483 BC)

Siddharta Gautama was the son of a Hindu clan ruler of the Kshatriya caste. His upbringing in the palace was sheltered from the harshness of real life outside even until after his marriage. But seeing death, disease, and poverty in the outside world for the first time so shook him that he left his wife and infant son and went out to find the meaning of life. At first he tried the rigorous asceticism of Hindu Brahmin teaching. After years of extreme self-mortification during which he starved himself almost to a skeleton, he realized that this did not lead to self-realization. He devoted himself to intense mental activity which culminated in a flash of enlightenment while sitting under a sycamore fig tree (**the *Bo* or wisdom tree**). This is the central, unifying event of all Buddhism since it made Gautama a 'Buddha' or 'enlightened one'.

What was the idea that flashed into Gautama's mind, which has so dominated the Far East? It has to do with suffering, its cause and cure.

He concluded that suffering is intrinsic to human existence and comes from desire—"desire for possession and selfish enjoyment of any and every kind, but particularly the desire for separate, individual, existence." The solution is to eliminate desire. "Suffering ceases when desire ceases, when this selfish craving, this lust for life, has been renounced and destroyed." This is accomplished by what Gautama called the **Middle Way.** It is not by extreme asceticism or by fleshly self-gratification, both of which Gautama had tried. Starting with the Hindu teaching of Karma, that people are reborn according to their behavior in a previous lifetime, Gautama taught that "only by complete detachment could a man's thoughts, words, and actions be deprived of their power to bind him to the inexorable wheel of life and death."[6]

The order of monks. Gautama's first converts were the five ascetic Hindu companions in Deer Park, Benares (Veranasi) with whom he had been seeking Liberation. He soon established the Order (*Sangha*) of monks, which is the main propagator of traditional Buddhist teaching in Southeast Asia today. The monks in the Buddhist Order are not priests, but are seeking *Nirvana* (oblivion) for themselves while seeking to teach and exemplify the teaching to the world. After making many converts as a mendicant preacher for over forty years Gautama the Buddha died at the age of eighty.

Buddhist philosophy: the Middle Way

The Buddhist philosophy taught by traditional Theravada Buddhism in southeast Asia draws heavily from its Hindu roots, but with significant changes. It is not concerned with a personal God or with the gods. It could better be described as a psychological philosophy of personal release from suffering. Kraemer called it "a nontheistic ethical discipline."[7]

Gautama kept the Hindu doctrine of karma intact, but he modified the concept of reincarnation to become his teaching of 'rebirth'. The difference is that Gautama did not accept the Hindu idea of soul-self (atman). Thus there is no soul to be reincarnated. The only connection between the rebirths is the karma. He illustrated this by the example of lighting one candle from another. No substance is passed from one to the other, but something is transferred nevertheless.

The goal of Gautama's teaching is to escape from this endless cycle of rebirths to 'oblivion' (Nirvana). "The dew-drop slips into the shining sea." Gautama insisted that Nirvana was neither existence nor nonexistence. Like Hinduism, Gautama taught that the world of phenomena is impermanent illusion (maya). There is nothing eternal inside a man's body. Separate individual existence is an illusion. Nirvana can best be understood against this background. How does the Buddhist accomplish this goal? **The Noble Eightfold Path of the Middle Way** may be summarized as follows:

1) **Right Views:** Acceptance of the Teaching and rejection of unworthy attitudes and acts;
2) **Right Desires:** free from lust, ill will, and cruelty;
3) **Right Speech:** plain, truthful, free from gossip and harshness;
4) **Right Conduct:** charity and abstention from killing any living being (including eggs and insects);
5) **Right Mode of Livelihood:** harming no one and free from luxury;
6) **Right Effort:** always pressing on to overcome evil and develop and maintain meritorious conditions;
7) **Right Awareness:** of the implications of the Teaching in life situations;
8) **Right Meditation:** This emphasis upon arduous mind development is central to Buddhist practice.

Although this seems like a fairly simple summary, actually walking the eightfold path involves passing through Four Stages in which Ten Fetters are successively broken. Thus traditional Buddhism has proved to be a most radical system of self-deliverance and puts the total responsibility upon the individual. The Scripture of traditional Theravada Buddhism is called the *Tripitaka* **(three baskets),** a massive book committed to writing in the ancient Pali language of northern India several centuries after Gautama. The similarities and differences of traditional Buddhism with Hinduism are as follows:[8]

Gautama's Borrowings from and Modifications of Hinduism

Hindu Concept	Gautama's Buddhism
Wheel of Life (cyclical time line)	Wheel of Life (unmodified)
Karma (consequence of deeds)	Karma (unmodified)
Maya (illusion)	Maya (unmodified)
Asceticism	The Middle Way
Atman (individual soul)	No Atman
Reincarnation of soul	Rebirth without reincarnation
Moksha (realization)	Nirvana (oblivion)
Pantheistic	Atheistic > Pantheistic
Caste System	No Caste System

Later development: Mahayana Buddhism

Traditional Theravada Buddhism spread throughout Southeast Asia and is today the dominant religion of Burma, Sri Lanka (Ceylon), Thailand, Vietnam, Laos, and Cambodia (precommunist). By the seventh century A.D. it had declined badly in India and was wiped out by the later Muslim conquests. But sometime before the time of Christ another broader form of Buddhism developed in India, later to spread to China, Korea, Japan, and Tibet. It saw traditional Buddhism as too narrow, rigorous, and individualistic, and came to be called *Mahayana* (the Broader Vessel) in contrast to traditional *Hinayana* (the Narrower Vessel), as they called it. There are many different forms of Mahayana Buddhism today, and on the surface some don't seem to relate much to Gautama's original teaching. However, they all stress Gautama's enlightenment under the Bo tree and build on that in different ways.

As the more liberal type of Mahayana Buddhism spread to China in the first century after Christ, the practical Chinese modification became highly successful, especially in the Tang Dynasty (A.D. 620-907). This was because the austere teaching of Gautama was replaced by a more easily understood concept of salvation for all. This was brought about by the concept of Buddhist saints, *Bodhisattvas* (wisdom beings), who gave up Nirvana and the merit of their own good deeds to become saviors of others. This was linked with a more physical concept of heaven which could be attained by all through faith in the saints. Although Gautama had nothing to say about God, Mahayana Buddhism introduced a supreme Reality from which the universe emanated. It deified Gautama and the Bodhisattvas and made individual immortality the hope of the devotee. Images were introduced and the worship of 'the Goddess of Mercy' (Kwan-yin) became very common as Mahayana spread to Japan in the sixth century A.D.

In addition to the *Amida* or 'Pure Land' Sect, the Chinese developed the *Ch'an* Sect from the teachings of an Indian teacher. It is known as *Zen* Buddhism in Japan. Zen is the existential form of Buddhism, and stresses 'Enlightenment' through a flash of intuition. This is not attained through study, knowledge, or reason, but rather by a discipline which precipitates this mystic enlightenment. Zen and other sects of Buddhism have become a major molding force in Japanese culture and society. It has been in competition with Shintoism since the sixth century, so that there has come to be a mixture of the two religions there.

When Mahayana Buddhism spread to Tibet in the seventh century A.D. it was combined with local spiritistic religion to form **Lamaism**, the national religion of Tibet and Mongolia. The Communist conquest of Tibet in 1951 forced their leader, the Dalai Lama, to flee to India with many of his followers. He is believed to be a reincarnation of a Bodhisattva. Lamaism has been called the Esoteric Sect of Buddhism since it stresses secrecy.

Summary and conclusion

Buddhism is thus, like Hinduism from which it came, a complex of philosophies, mythology, custom and religious practices which are both pantheistic and polytheistic. More missionary than Hinduism, it spread through eastern Asia. Although Gautama did not include deity in his philosophical scheme to escape suffering, later forms of Buddhism incorporated deity as modifications were made by the Chinese and Japanese. Thus the major remaining common element in traditional and Mahayana Buddhism would be Gautama's experience of enlightenment under the Bo tree. Most outstanding about Mahayana has been its ability to coexist and even integrate with other religions in China and Japan. This has led to the phenomenon called 'multireligion', to which we shall now proceed.

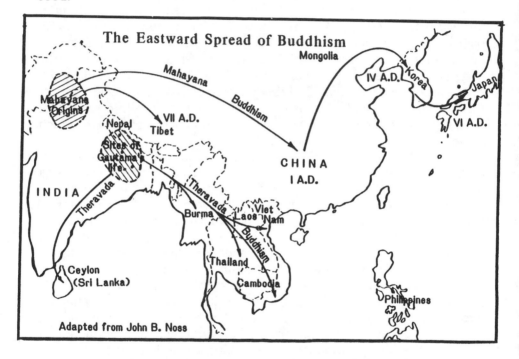

The Eastward Spread of Buddhism

Adapted from John B. Noss

MULTIRELIGION IN CHINA: TAOISM, CONFUCIANISM, AND BUDDHISM

We have seen how the pragmatic Chinese contributed to the modification of Mahayana Buddhism. But Buddhism never became the exclusive religion of the Chinese people. Before Buddhism arrived in China, Confucianism and Taoism were well established, and Buddhism simply became the third religion which most Chinese adopted. The term for religion in China is *Chiao,* which really includes the idea of education and culture, as well as religion. Thus a good Chinese can be simultaneously Taoist, Confucianist, and Buddhist. Each makes its own contribution to the Chiao of the Chinese. We call this phenomenon 'multireligion.' The ethical teachings of Confucius focus upon human interpersonal and societal relations and strictly speaking is not a religion at all.

Taoism is more spiritistic and naturistic and is mostly concerned with man's relationship with the natural world around him.

The animistic religion of China before Confucius already involved ancestor worship and the concept of *yin* and *yang*. These have persisted to the present day, although the Communists have had great success is rooting out traditional Chinese religion from Red China. The concepts of yin and yang involve contrasting, yet harmonious opposites in nature. Yin stands for earth, the moon, darkness, evil, the female sex, etc. Yang stands for heaven, the sun, light, fire, goodness, and the male sex. The gods are yang; evil spirits are yin. These primeval notions have been incorporated into the multireligion of Chinese culture.

Taoism

Tao (the way) may be traced back to **Lao Tsu (Lao Tse)**, who lived in the sixth century B.C. We know very little about him other than that he was keeper of the royal archives. He grew weary of society at the seat of government, and deciding to become a recluse, he headed for the mountains. The warden of the pass begged him to leave a record of his teachings. Thus he wrote the ***Tao Teh Ching***. Taoism has very little to say about God and heaven. Baker has summarized it well:

> The theme of the Taoist classic briefly is that man in his quest for the good life should cease from preoccupation with 'externals' and from fretful effort. He should relax and let Nature have her way. Nature, or the Universal Principle, perhaps best translates the elusive concept of Tao as used in the Tao Teh Ching. The way of the Tao expresses itself in natural spontaneity: everything is accomplished by not striving for anything—'a perpetual accommodation of self to one's surroundings, with a minimum of effort'. Taoism, in terms of the Tao Teh Ching, is the Chinese brand of mystical quietism.[9]

Confucianism

We know more about **K'ung Fu-tsu** (which was latinized to Confucius by Jesuit missionaries) who was born half a century after Lao Tsu in 551 B.C. He became Minister of Justice in the government, but when his counsel was not heeded he resigned and gathered about him a group of disciples. A precise and fastidious man, he got very little hearing outside the circle of his disciples. After his death his writings and some important disciples over the following centuries perpetuated his teachings. Most important among his *Five Classics* and the *Four Books* is the *Analects*. Later his teachings were so revered that imperial sacrifices were instituted at his tomb. Thus what started out to be an ethical philosophy developed into a religion.

Confucian philosophy is really a system of utilitarian ethics. Confucius only mentioned God once in his writings but rather stressed the Superior Man and the way he should behave in his family and public relationships. Thus he was much concerned with the idea of the ideal social community. He expounded **Five Virtues:** Goodness, Righteousness, Propriety, Knowledge, and Sincerity. He taught that these moral qualities should be manifested in **Five Relationships:** Prince and Minister, Father and Son, Husband and Wife, Elder Brother and Younger Brother, Friend and Friend.

Chinese Buddhism

As we have seen, Chinese Buddhism is of the Mahayana variety and somehow interacts in harmony with Taoism and Confucianism. Indeed, Chinese religion is a classic example of religious syncretism, that is, the combining of diverse religious ideas and practices into one. The teaching of Nirvana was too abstruse and intuitional for the Chinese mindset, so that Chinese Buddhism substituted a more earthy worldview for the abstract philosophy of Gautama. This included the introduction of images for the illiterate. In China one Buddhist Saint assumes female form as the Goddess of Mercy, Kwan-yin, known as Kwannon in Japan. "To most who worship at the temples, Buddha and the Bodhisattvas are quite indistinguishable from the pantheon of polytheistic deities worshiped in the popular religion."[10]

Summary and conclusion

We have been describing the traditional Chinese religion of precommunist China and of the overseas Chinese. The communist crusade against religion on the mainland has had a tremendous impact upon the beliefs of the people. Perhaps Taoism and Confucianism have suffered the greatest loss. Ancestor worship has to some extent been rooted out of Chinese culture. Thus traditional Chinese religion survives mainly in Taiwan, Hong Kong, Singapore, and the many other places to which Chinese have emigrated. But even there religion is more a cultural thing than a deeply held faith, as most Chinese people have been caught up in a materialistic struggle for advancement.

MULTIRELIGION IN JAPAN: SHINTO AND BUDDHISM

The religious beliefs of the Japanese are a complex mixture of religion, culture, nationalism, traditions, myths, and custom. Specifically, it is a mixture of nationalistic animism called Shinto and various forms of Mahayana Buddhism which arrived in the sixth century A.D., some sects of which are uniquely Japanese. For centuries the two religions were interwoven in what was called, "the Twofold Way of the Gods." After a revival of Shinto, the Emperor Meiji in 1882 disestablished Buddhism and made Shinto the state religion. This strengthened emperor worship and led to Japanese militarism in modern history. The American occupation disestablished State Shinto in 1945, but various sects of Shinto have flourished since then.

The feudal history of Japan has conditioned the people to put nation and family first and to repress individual decision. Thus religion is primarily a matter of rigid custom, not of personal faith. Today Shinto is more prominent in everyday life, but Buddhism takes over after death. Others contrast Shinto as the religion of public life; Buddhism as especially pertaining to private life. Nevertheless, Japanese households have both Shinto and Buddhist shrines. The public Buddhist temples show Shinto influence and Shinto shrines show Buddhist influence. Let us focus first on Shinto.

Shinto

Shinto comes from Chinese *shen*=god and *tao*=way, thus 'Way of the gods'. The word for deity is **Kami**, which is so vague in meaning that it is probably equivalent to the mana of animism. It is connected with natural forces, with agriculture, with fertility, with sacred objects, and with virtually anything Japanese. Hundreds of thousands of shrines are approached through a unique wooden gateway called a *torii*.

Shinto is supported by complex myths which were recorded in the **Kojiki** in A.D. 712. The stories tell of many gods and goddesses who appear and disappear in a pre-existing universe likened to an ocean of mud veiled in darkness. They produce offspring in a succession of legends and myths coming down to Jimmu Tenno, who is claimed to be the first human emperor and founder of the Imperial Dynasty about 660 B.C. This is the basis for the claim that the emperor is of divine origin. Shinto shrines are not for congregational worship, but for individual ritual worship overseen by a hereditary priesthood. On days of national festivals and shrine anniversaries, public ceremonies are held. Otherwise the worshiper comes at his own convenience with an offering of food, which is accepted by the priest in a brief ceremony.

In addition to state and shrine Shinto, many Shinto sects have multiplied and prospered since World War II. Of the thirteen major sects, Tenrikyo is perhaps the most popular. Other sects emphasize faith-healing or the worship of some major kami such as Mt. Fuji.

Japanese Buddhism

The Mahayana Buddhism which came to Japan in the sixth century A.D. was influenced greatly by Confucianism and Taoism. Shinto favored the ruling classes, but Buddhism offered salvation for all and met felt needs. In the home the **Butsudan** (family altar) symbolizes the rule of the dead over Japan as departed ancestors are worshiped daily.

The main strength of Buddhism in Japan is in the sects, of which there are six major schools with many subsects. As in China, Amida and Zen Buddhism are very popular. To these are added distinctively Japanese sects, such as **Tendai, Shingon, and Nichiren.** Although statistics for Buddhist and Shinto sects are hard to verify, undoubtedly tens of millions of Japanese can be counted. Many of the sects have a more congregational emphasis like Christianity.

Summary and conclusion

Japanese religion is both an enigma and a paradox. Just as vague as is the meaning of Kami, just so is the vagueness of Japanese religious thinking, which is more culture, custom, and decree than conviction. And yet the Japanese are the most literate people on the face of the earth, and their technological prowess has put them at the forefront. William Pape's summary is penetrating:

> In these postwar years two opposite trends are clearly discernible: less religion, and more religion. A skepticism that regards all religions, including the Gospel, as unscientific and superstitious is the fashion for many intellectuals who, unhappily, include a large number of professors and teachers responsible for the education of a new generation. On the other hand, many people who became disillusioned with the failure of traditional forms of religion are turning with pathetic eagerness to the innumerable sects springing up all over the country. [11]

1. A. T. Houghton, "Animism" in *The World's Religions,* ed. J. N. D. Anderson, 1st ed. (1951), p. 9.
2. William Paton, *Jesus Christ and the World's Religions* (1916), p. 19.
3. Houghton, "Animism," in *Religions,* ed. Anderson, p. 23.
4. John Lewis, *Religions of the World Made Simple.*, p. 29.
5. Johnstone, *Operation World*, p. 50.
6. David Bentley-Taylor, "Buddhism" in Anderson, pp. 120-21.
7. Hendrick Kraemer, *The Christian Message in a Non-Christian World* (1938), cited in ibid, p. 126.
8. Bentley-Taylor, "Buddhism" in ibid, pp. 121-22.
9. Norman Baker, "Confucianism" in ibid, p. 182.
10. David Adeney, "China," in *Religions in a Changing World,* ed. Howard F. Vos (1959), p. 133.
11. William H. Pape, "Japan," in Vos, p. 94-95.

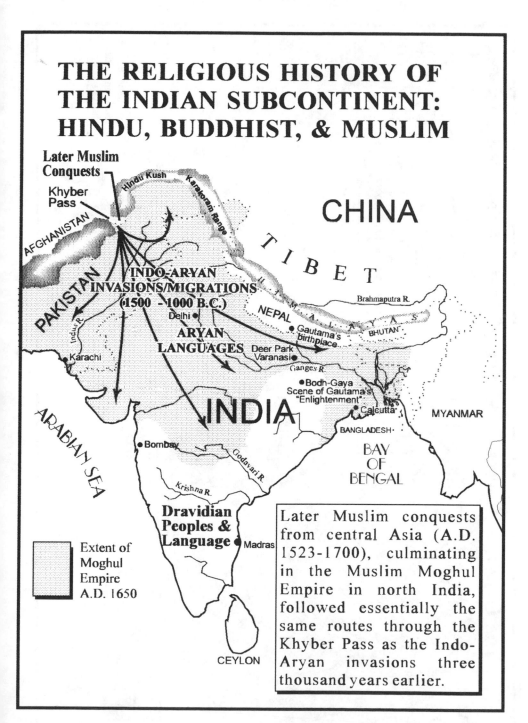

THE RELIGIOUS HISTORY OF THE INDIAN SUBCONTINENT: HINDU, BUDDHIST, & MUSLIM

Later Muslim Conquests

Khyber Pass

Hindu Kush

Karakoram Range

AFGHANISTAN

CHINA

TIBET

PAKISTAN

INDO-ARYAN INVASIONS/MIGRATIONS (1500 – 1000 B.C.)

HIMALAYAS

NEPAL

BHUTAN

Brahmaputra R.

Indus R.

Karachi

Delhi

ARYAN LANGUAGES

Gautama's birthplace

Deer Park
Varanasi

Ganges R.

●Bodh-Gaya
Scene of Gautama's
"Enlightenment"

Calcutta

MYANMAR

INDIA

BANGLADESH

ARABIAN SEA

● Bombay

Godavari R.

BAY OF BENGAL

Krishna R.

Dravidian Peoples & Language

● Madras

Extent of Moghul Empire A.D. 1650

Later Muslim conquests from central Asia (A.D. 1523-1700), culminating in the Muslim Moghul Empire in north India, followed essentially the same routes through the Khyber Pass as the Indo-Aryan invasions three thousand years earlier.

CEYLON

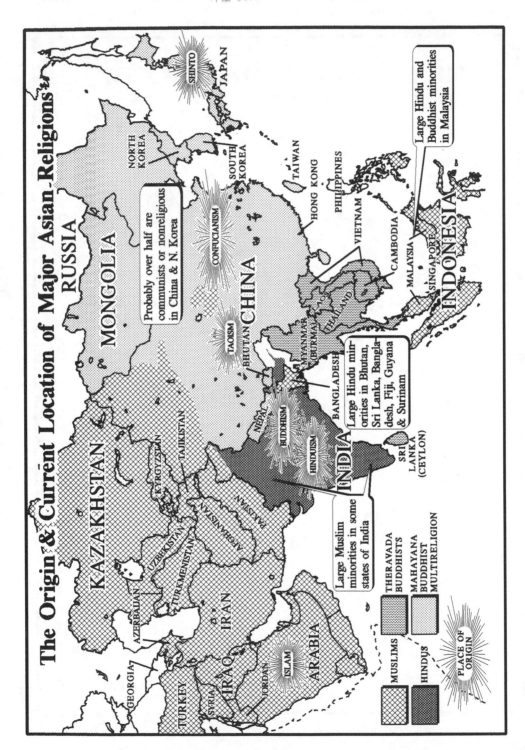

The Origin & Current Location of Major Asian Religions

Probably over half are communists or nonreligious in China & N. Korea

Large Hindu and Buddhist minorities in Malaysia

Large Hindu minorities in Bhutan, Sri Lanka, Bangladesh, Fiji, Guyana & Surinam

Large Muslim minorities in some states of India

THERAVADA BUDDHISTS

MAHAYANA BUDDHIST MULTIRELIGION

MUSLIMS

HINDUS

PLACE OF ORIGIN

RUSSIA
MONGOLIA
KAZAKHSTAN
NORTH KOREA
SOUTH KOREA
JAPAN
SHINTO
CONFUCIANISM
TAOISM
CHINA
TAIWAN
HONG KONG
PHILIPPINES
VIETNAM
CAMBODIA
MALAYSIA
SINGAPORE
INDONESIA
BHUTAN
MYANMAR (BURMA)
THAILAND
BANGLADESH
NEPAL
BUDDHISM
HINDUISM
INDIA
SRI LANKA (CEYLON)
TAJIKISTAN
KYRGYZSTAN
UZBEKISTAN
TURKMENISTAN
AFGHANISTAN
PAKISTAN
AZERBAIJAN
IRAN
IRAQ
ARABIA
ISLAM
JORDAN
SYRIA
TURKEY
GEORGIA

"Jesus replied, 'And why do you break the command of God for the sake of your tradition? . . . Thus you nullify the word of God for the sake of your tradition'"
  —Matthew 15:3, 6, NIV

THEISTIC RELIGIOUS CONTEXTS: CORRUPTED TRADITIONS

JUDAISM: A NATION'S TRADITIONS

Introduction

Many people might assume that Judaism is the religion of the Old Testament. However, it is clear from the critique of contemporary Judaism by the Lord Jesus that it had become a religion of the tradition of the elders, not of the word of God. The intervening two millennia have seen Judaism become even more a religion of tradition, especially as crystallized in the Talmud, the encyclopedic compendium of Jewish laws, interpretations, and traditions originating in the first through fifth centuries after Christ. Indeed, the destruction of Jerusalem and the Temple in AD 70 by the Romans was a major paradigm shift, which radically changed its essential nature from the core sacrificial system to a mass of traditions.

Judaism has been called a conglomeration and is a religion of practice, not doctrine.[1] It involves birth and race, although now the state of Israel still struggles to define a Jew. The Orthodox in Israel refuse to recognize Reform and Conservatives as true Jews, even though worldwide they are numerically significant. I will assume that readers are familiar with Old Testament history and will pick up our survey with its close.

Judaism's origin and development.

Judaism is the first of three great monotheistic religions. Although the one true God revealed Himself to the patriarchs and Abraham, monotheism was not consistently practiced by Israel until the post-exilic period because of the continuing compromises and apostasy. In exile, isolated from Jerusalem, the synagogue was developed and perpetuated as a center for monotheistic faith, not only in the continuing diaspora, but also back in Judea. Despite the corruptions and fragmentation of Judaism, it was so far superior to the heathen religions, that the synagogue drew in many Gentile inquirers.

The intertestamental period. With the conquest of Israel by Alexander the Great (332 BC), a period of hellenization began. This was evidenced by the **Septuagint** translation of the Old Testament into Greek in the third century BC by the large colony of Jews in Alexandria, Egypt and the philosophical writings of **Philo** there three centuries later. Out of such attempts to merge Greek philosophy with the Bible arose the sect of the **Sadducees,** which had modified revelation with Greek rationalism. Out of the Maccabean revolt against Antiochus Epiphanes' repression came the **Hasidim,** the antecedents of the **Pharisees.** By Christ's day the Herodians, the Zealots and the Essenes had developed as rival sects.

The great dispersion and the Talmud. The failure of the Jewish revolt against Rome in AD 66 and the destruction of the temple threatened the survival of Judaism. Of the sects only Phariseeism survived, and Rabbi Johanan ben Zakkai made Jabneh (Jamnia) on the coast a center for writing down the oral traditions and laws, which under his successors developed into the **Palestinian Talmud** (Mishneh) by about AD 220. After the failure of the Bar Cochba revolt (135), Babylon became the center of Jewish population and scholarship, resulting in the **Babylonian Talmud** (Gemara) by the fifth century. Together these massive compilations of up to 63 volumes has become central to Judaism's survival over the centuries.[2]

Medieval persecution. Although 'Christian' treatment of Jews deteriorated after Constantine, at first the Muslims were more tolerant. Jews prospered in Baghdad until the 11th century, when the Turks began to oppress them. Settling in Spain under the Moors, they saw the flowering of a 'golden age' of science, religion, and philosophy. There the **Karaite** movement developed as an attempt to return to the Old Testament. In the 12th century, the great scholar, **Moses Maimonides,** systematized the Mishneh into thirteen cardinal principles, now in the Jewish prayer book (although not accepted by all). In this period also a mystical teaching called the **Kaballa** arose, with hellenistic and Gnostic origins. But the Crusades revived the persecution of the Jews and forced them east again as they were expelled from Britain (1290), France (1394), and Spain (1492). The Sephardic Jews fled to the Middle East and the Ashkenazis to Poland and Russia.

Modern persecution. Unfortunately Martin Luther, although at first favorable to winning Jews to Christ hardened in his attitude, which resulted in persecution in Germany. The Cossack **pogroms** in Poland slaughtered half a million. It wasn't until the enlightenment and changed political circumstances in 1848 that Jews were released from their ghettos and integrated back into European society. Up until this point they were in the main absorbed in Talmudic study. But now influenced by the enlightenment, **Reform Judaism** began to repudiate the Talmud and Messianism and flourished in the West. Continuing adverse circumstances of anti-Semitism caused Theodore Hertzl to advocate **Zionism** by 1896, which was reinforced by the British Balfour Declaration during World War I, recognizing Palestine as the national home for Jews. The Nazi holocaust accelerated this return, and the UN recognition of the State of Israel in 1948 was another incredible pivotal event for Judaism.[3]

Contemporary Judaism

Doctrines of Judaism. Although Judaism is a religion of practice, not doctrine, some generalizations are possible. The **Torah** is generally understood to be essentially the books of Moses, and in a broader sense the whole body of Jewish teaching, legislation, practices, and tradition. The rest of the Old Testament is not seen as more authoritative than the whole bulk of rabbinic teachings or the Talmud, which explains the general ignorance of it among Jewish people. Their understanding of God is really a unitarian concept, emphasizing His singleness, through misunderstanding the composite unity of Deuteronomy 6:4. He is the God of all creation, but in a special way He is Israel's God.[4]

Judaism does not see humanity as fallen, but emphasizes original righteousness. Although it acknowledges an evil inclination and individual sins, it does not accept the idea of original sin as held by Christians. Sin is a deficiency which can be remedied. Since the sacrificial system is no longer operative, repentance, prayer, and active kindness are seen as substitutes. The **Day of Atonement** (Yom Kippur) is the focal point for repentance and confession of sins. Human initiative is essential to progress toward perfection. Except for Orthodox Jews, the expectation of a personal Messiah has been abandoned for a belief in progress and hope. Life is the most precious gift to the Jew, and death the greatest calamity. Life after death is very vague in Jewish thinking, without a clear concept of bodily resurrection. The Jew inherits heaven by right through the covenant with Abraham. Salvation is an entirely foreign concept.[5]

The practices of Judaism. Religious Jews decry the fact that the majority of the upward of eighteen million Jews worldwide are non-religious. Broadly speaking the religious fall into three categories: Orthodox, Conservative, and Reform. **Orthodoxy** is the religion of the Talmud and tradition; Reform Judaism is a modernizing repudiation of the Talmud akin to Protestant liberalism; **Conservatism** attempts a compromise between the two.

Although the synagogue is the center of worship, the home has a special place in Judaism, with its Sabbath and Passover *Seder* (order) rituals. The roots of the festivals of the Jewish sacred year are in the books of Moses. *Rosh Hashanah* (New Year) inaugurates the ten Solemn Days which end with the Day of Atonement in the fall. The three pilgrim feasts of the Old Testament are perpetuated: Tabernacles (*Succoth*) in the fall, Passover (*Pesach*) in the spring, and the Feast of Weeks (*Shabuoth*) fifty days later. *Hanukkah* (Dedication) and *Purim*, although not instituted by Moses, have basis in pre-Christian history.

Summary and conclusion

Judaism has always been struggling to survive, as an ethnic people, as a religion, and now as a nation. The paradox is that while possessors of the most ancient revelation of the true God, modern Jews are in search of new values and new spiritual insights, frequently far removed from their ancient faith. Having survived the persecutions, the pogroms, the holocaust, they are still not sure what Judaism really is and who a Jew really is. As Christians, we believe their only real fulfillment is in the Messiah, the Lord Jesus Christ.

ROMAN CATHOLICISM: PROGRESSIVE APOSTASY

Introduction

When and how did Roman Catholicism begin? Did Christ found the Roman Catholic Church, and did He found it upon the Apostle Peter? Why do Evangelicals consider Roman Catholic countries to be mission fields? In the light of the claim of Roman Catholicism to be the only true church, these are vital questions foundational to missions today. There are almost 900 million nominal Roman Catholics in the world today. Are they a valid mission field? Let us examine the data. We would suggest that Roman Catholicism is a gradual development over the centuries and did not have any one point of beginning. It has moved so far away from true Christianity that Catholic peoples need to be evangelized.

The origins of Roman Catholicism

The claims of Rome. The Catholic Church claims that at Caesarea Philippi the Lord Jesus made the Apostle Peter the first Pope by giving him the keys of heaven, calling him the Rock upon which the church was to be founded, and thus giving him the power of absolution from sins to be delegated to his priests (Matt. 16:18-20). They believe that Christ confirmed this after His resurrection when He three times commanded Peter to feed His sheep (John 21:15-19), and that Peter passed this authority on down to His successors by 'apostolic succession'.

However, careful study of the whole of Biblical teaching indicates that Christ himself is the Rock upon which He is building His church, and that the keys are not the keys of heaven, but rather the keys to the kingdom. Peter used these keys on three occasions to open the door of faith to the Jews (Acts 2), the Samaritans (Acts 8) and the Gentiles (Acts 10) through preaching the Gospel. Space does not allow a thorough refutation of Rome's claims. But a correct translation of the Greek tenses of Matthew 16:20 shows that Christ is charging Peter to make sure that as he proclaims the message of forgiveness, he must be careful to tell the message based on heaven's terms. That is, what is declared forgiven on earth must have been already forgiven (perfect participle) in heaven. The Amplified Version is most helpful: "whatever you bind—that is, declare to be improper and unlawful—on earth must be already bound in heaven; and whatever you loose on earth—declare lawful—must be what is already loosed in heaven."

OF COURSE OUR CHURCH IS THE TRUE CHURCH! JESUS MADE PETER THE FIRST POPE...IT SAYS SO... IN THE BIBLE!!

Ultimately, the Roman Catholic Church does not allow individuals to interpret these or any other biblical passages. They argue that the Bible is a product of the Roman Church and it alone has the right to interpret it. The Bible is just part of the traditions of the church and not superior to them. The Pope has the final say as to what church doctrine is to be.

The historical development. The origins of Romanism not only go back to a misinterpretation of these passages, but can be traced back to corruption of apostolic doctrine that began in the centuries right after the apostles. According to Newman, the earliest corruptions evident in the writings of the church fathers were many: 1) loss of the purity of grace in salvation and reversion to the Jewish error of the meritoriousness of external works; 2) fetishism; 3) sacerdotalism (seeing the pastor as priest); 4) ritualism; 5) allegorical interpretation of the Bible; and 6) the bishop's right of absolution.[6]

A most significant event in the development of Romanism was the Edict of Toleration of A.D. 313 and the 'conversion' of the Roman Emperor **Constantine** a decade later. Although a seeming victory for Christianity after ten periods of intense persecution, it opened the church to secularization, paganization (images, saints, mariolatry), and politicization. It was the beginning of the union of church and state, as ultimately Christianity became the official religion of the Roman Empire. This stimulated the power of the already-developing church hierarchy, and eventually the tables turned with the church becoming the persecuting power! Many sincere people reacted to this flood of worldliness in the church by turning to monasticism and asceticism as the solution.

A century later **Leo the Great,** who was bishop of Rome from A.D.

440-61 marked a significant stage in the evolution of the papacy. The Council of Chalcedon was favorable to his papal pretensions and yet gave the bishop of Constantinople equal authority with the bishop of Rome. Another giant step was made by **Gregory the Great** (A.D. 590-604) who secured the allegiance of the weakened Roman Emperor to the bishop of Rome, pressed for uniformity of worship, and subjugated the British and German churches to the authority of Rome.

In the eleventh century **Hildebrand** was a maker and ruler of popes who eventually became Pope himself as Gregory VII (A.D. 1073-85). His plan to free the church from interference of laymen, to subject all clergy to the pope, and to force civil rulers to act in the interest of the papacy, reached its greatest success when he forced the Emperor Henry IV to humiliate himself by coming to him barefoot in the snow at Canossa.

After the Protestant Reformation the Roman Church started a Counter-Reformation to recoup the losses from and lessen the impact of Protestantism. The Pope convened the **Council of Trent (A.D. 1546-47)** which decided to make tradition equal to the Scripture, declared the Apocryphal books to be part of the Biblical canon, and crystallized many traditional accretions of the centuries. However, this did not end the development and accretions of the Roman Church. For example, in 1854 Pope Pius IX issued a papal bull declaring the Immaculate Conception of Mary (not the virgin birth of Christ), and in 1950 Pius XII defined the bodily assumption of Mary into heaven as a church dogma.

Vatican II Council. The changes in Romanism in the last thirty years have been most radical. Most came about as a result of the Vatican II Ecumenical Council of 1962-65. Liberal voices in the church were heard by Pope John XXIII in convening the council to open windows to change in the church. Not only have there been external changes, but the church has been torn in three directions: traditional, liberal, and charismatic factions. Many Roman Catholics no longer submit unquestioningly to the authority of the Pope and the hierarchy.

Faith and practice

We have already noted that the Catholic view of the place of the Bible is clearly distinct from the evangelical view. Although all three branches of Christendom (Romanism, Orthodoxy, and Evangelicalism) agree on the doctrines of the Trinity and the person of Christ, the concepts of salvation are radically different. Although there are a multitude of other differences, such as in reference to Mary, the saints, etc., we will focus on the essential area which relates to salvation and on the sacraments.

Sacramental salvation. The Roman Catholic concept of salvation is essentially a piecemeal salvation, merited by a succession of human good works. Although the word 'grace' is frequently on the lips of Catholics, they do not understand it as 'unmerited favor' and are trying to earn salvation. Thus the Catholic is in the process of being saved, but can never say that one has been saved. Salvation is mediated by the church through the sacraments. Let us focus on the sacraments.

Five of the seven sacraments have to do with salvation: Marriage and Ordination having special functions. **Baptism** is viewed as giving new birth and cleansing the infant of original, Adamic sin. **Confirmation** is seen as a reaffirmation of baptism and the sealing of the Holy Spirit. The sacrament of **Penance** relates to the powers of absolution from sin which the priest gives in the confessional.

The **Mass or Eucharist** is the core of Roman theology. The belief in **Transubstantiation** means that in the Mass the bread and wine are actually transformed into the literal body and blood of Christ. It is thus seen as a perpetual, unbloody sacrifice of Christ each time the

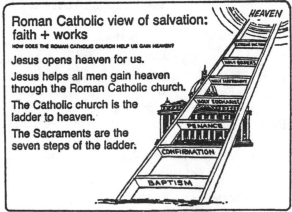

Roman Catholic view of salvation: faith + works

HOW DOES THE ROMAN CATHOLIC CHURCH HELP US GAIN HEAVEN?

Jesus opens heaven for us.

Jesus helps all men gain heaven through the Roman Catholic church.

The Catholic church is the ladder to heaven.

The Sacraments are the seven steps of the ladder.

mass is offered. This builds up the treasury of merit which is available to the Catholic who attends. **Extreme Unction** means the last rites administered just before death, if possible. Even this does not guarantee the salvation of the faithful, however, since masses must be said to help release the dead from purgatory. Thus salvation is mediated directly by the priestly representatives of Peter's successor, the Pope.[7]

Today's diversity. Charismatic Catholics hold these beliefs along with traditional Catholics. They see charismatic phenomena as a confirmation of their infant baptism. The third movement in the Roman church today is the liberal theology which has mushroomed since Vatican II. Some of it is borrowed from the Protestant liberals, but the evolutionary philosophy of the late Jesuit writer, **Pierre Tielhard de Chardin** has been the most influential today. Another movement which arises from the more liberal Catholic theology is **Liberation Theology** started in Latin America by **Gustavo Gutierrez** in the early 1970s. It is a revolutionary Marxist movement which strives to overthrow oppressive governments, but is disguised by a thin veneer of Biblical quotations as being Christianity. It is spreading from Latin America to other Catholic countries like the Philippines.

Summary and conclusion

Evangelicals view Roman Catholic countries as mission fields because the Roman Catholic church is not apostolic Christianity in its teaching of salvation, but rather is a mass of unbiblical traditions of men which developed in the centuries after the apostles. In this regard it is closer to the Pharisees' legalism, which Christ exposed so clearly during His ministry. Like Phariseeism, Romanism puts the human tradition above the word of God (Matt. 15:1-9). This is not to deny that Catholics are studying their Bibles more than before, and some may be born-again Christians. But they would be saved despite their church, not because of it.

EASTERN ORTHODOXY: CATHOLICISM'S SISTER

Introduction

Eastern Orthodoxy is the third largest branch of Christendom, with about 215 million adherents. It is predominant in eastern Europe, Russia, and northeastern Africa. This includes the Greek Orthodox, the Russian Orthodox, Armenian, Syrian, and Coptic churches which arose from the Eastern Roman Empire and became separate from the evolving Roman Catholic Church in a series of events over seven centuries. It has many similarities with Roman Catholicism, but has developed in its own unique way over the centuries.

Its history

The churches in the western part of the Empire used Latin; the eastern, Greek. So when the Emperor Constantine founded Constantinople in the east as a second capital of the Empire (330), he began the long process of alienation. Two centuries later, the Emperor Justinian made the city the focus of the eastern church by building the massive Church of Hagia Sophia (now a Muslim mosque/museum). Seven Ecumenical Councils were held in the East, and it was the Eastern Church which had to confront the inroads of Islam in the seventh century. The Muslims' hatred of idolatry stirred up the **Iconoclastic Controversy** between East and West. Many eastern church leaders tried to minimize the use of images in worship. "The Popes of Rome had no sympathy with the image-breaking of the emperors of the East."[8] The coronation of Charlemagne (800) by Pope Leo III destroyed the political unity of the Empire. An inconsequential theological difference relating to the use of the *filioque* ('from the Son') clause in the "procession of the Holy Spirit" was used as the excuse for further alienation. But the last straw was the sacking of Constantinople by the Crusaders of the Fourth Crusade in 1204. This so weakened the eastern Empire that the city fell to the Muslim Ottoman Turks in 1453. This put much of the Eastern Church under Muslim domination until World War I. The continuing conflict between Muslims, Catholics, and Orthodox in the Balkans arises out of those tragic events.

During these centuries the most positive event was the conversion of the Slavic people to Christianity through the efforts of Cyril and Methodius, as already outlined in chapter 7. This includes the Russians, Ukrainians, Bulgarians, and the Serbs, who are in the main the adherents of the Russian Orthodox Church. Unlike the Roman Catholic Church, Orthodoxy did not go through a struggle of reformation and counter-reformation. However, there was an unsuccessful attempt at reformation through Cyril Loukaris, the Patriarch of Alexandria and Constantinople in the 17th century, who came to essentially evangelical views. But he was opposed within Orthodoxy and by the Catholic Jesuits and ultimately assassinated by the Turkish Sultan's orders.

The doctrines of Orthodoxy

All three branches of Christendom traditionally accept the doctrine of the Trinity and the deity of Christ set forth in the Nicene Creed (325). Beyond that, however, Orthodoxy is very defective on the doctrine of man and the plan of salvation—that is, the significance of the passion of Christ, justification, conversion, and regeneration have not been considered. It would be helpful to outline the major differences with Roman Catholicism: 1) Rejection of the papacy and papal infallibility; 2) Marriage of lower clergy; 3) Communion in both kinds; 4) Threefold immersion of infants; 5) Use of the vernacular languages in worship; 6) Rejection of the Immaculate Conception of Mary; 7) Rejection of purgatory.[9] There are many more subtle differences which result from the differing cultural backgrounds and philosophical approaches of east and west. The ultimate outcome of the Iconoclastic Controversy was that icons are rendered in bas-relief in Orthodoxy while they are represented in the round in Catholicism.[10] In general we could say that the Eastern Church has been "esoteric, mystical, and speculative, rather than logical, dialectical, or practical."[11]

Although the Greek Church suffered for centuries under Islam, and the Russian Church for seventy years under Communism, with the demise of the Soviet Union Orthodoxy is experiencing a resurgence. In 1961 it joined the World Council of Churches in New Delhi and in 1962 effected a mutual reversal with Roman Catholicism of the excommunications of 1054.

Summary and conclusion

What has been said in the section on Catholicism regarding its erroneous teaching on salvation can also be said of Orthodoxy. It is a sacramental salvation through the church, not a personal relationship with Jesus Christ by simple repentant faith, as the Bible teaches. As in Romanism the practice of Mariolatry, veneration of relics, etc. are in total contradiction to orthodox doctrine. Thus Orthodoxy ought to be considered a mission field rather than a true Christian church.

ISLAM: MILITANT UNITARIANISM'S
ULTIMATE CLAIMS

Introduction

Islam presents a unique challenge to missions in a number of ways:

1) It is the only major post-Christian religion, having been founded by the 'prophet' Muhammad about A.D. 610.

2) It has borrowed heavily from Judaism and Christianity.

3) It is second to Christianity, with over one billion followers.

4) It is now aggressively expanding into Africa, Europe, and North America with oil-money backing.

5) It is the most resistant to evangelization.

6) It is the only religion to have conquered 'Christian' regions militarily with little retrenchment.

Islam is the religion of the prophet **Muhammad**, wrongly called Muhammadanism. The word 'Islam' means 'submission', and its followers are called **Muslims** (or as some spell it, Moslems), which means 'those who submit'. It could be characterized as a militant deistic unitarianism, which claims to be the original and final religion. Muslims believe that the books of the Prophets (Bible) were corrupted and that Muhammad was given the original message again in the **Qur'an (Koran)**, which can never be corrupted. They believe that Muhammad is 'the capstone of the Prophets', that is, the greatest and last. Like Judaism and Christianity it is a religion of a holy book, the Qur'an. Since Muhammad borrowed so much from the Bible, some have even called it a "Christian heresy." While recognizing Jesus as a prophet, Islam denies His deity and saving death and ends up being a very legalistic scheme of salvation by human merit! Islam is not just a religion, but a whole way of life including political, social, and cultural aspects.

Muhammad, 'Capstone of the prophets'

Muhammad was born about A.D. 570 and raised in the city of Mecca, Arabia, in an animistic and idolatrous desert culture. An orphan raised by his uncle, Muhammad came into contact with Jews and 'Christians' while on caravan trips into Palestine and Syria. This exposure to monotheism led him to question many Arab beliefs and practices. He was troubled by the idolatry, immorality, tribal warfare, and cruel practices like burying alive unwanted baby girls. At the age of twenty-five he was employed in the caravan trade by a rich widow named Khadijah, whom he subsequently married.

He also was exposed to Judaism and Christianity through foreign merchants trading in Mecca and through some personal contacts. Unfortunately the form of Christianity he was exposed to was quite corrupt.

Although he was impressed with the teaching of the last judgment and punishment of idolatry, he reacted against the misimpressions he had of Judaism and Christianity. For instance, he thought the virgin birth of Christ involved sexual procreation by God.

At the age of forty he claimed to have received a revelation from God through an angel in a cave near Mecca. The angel told him to recite, and the 114 memorized recitations supposedly given him over the next twenty years form the Qur'an (recitation), the holy book of Islam. "After repeated visions, he believed himself called to preach the religion of one absolute God (*Allah*), the Creator, Ruler, and Judge of the universe. Opposition in Mecca finally caused his migration [withdrawal] to Medina in 622. This flight, known as the *Hegira,* marks the beginning of the Islamic Era."[12] Although Muhammad hoped that the large community of Jews in Medina would convert to his brand of monotheism, they began to ridicule his modifications of Old Testament accounts of Abraham, Moses, and the prophets that were included in the Qur'an. Nevertheless, he was able to establish a religious and political power base in Medina and in eight years was able to come back with an army and conquer Mecca. By conquest, persuasion, and even trickery, Muhammad was able to gain both political and religious supremacy over all Arabia before he died in A.D. 632.

Islam spreads and splits

Following Muhammad's death, Islam continued to spread through conquest. Within a few years Jerusalem fell, then Egypt, Iraq, Persia, and most of Asia Minor within twenty years. In less than a century all of North Africa and part of Spain came under Muslim control, and the Battle of Tours in France (A.D. 732) checked Muslim expansion into Europe. Later conquests and propagandizing spread Islam into the Balkan states of Europe, large sections of Africa, India, central Asia, China, Malaya, Indonesia, and the southern Philippines.

Muhammad did not designate a successor, and the first two Caliphs who succeeded him were not disputed. However, the third was murdered, and Muhammad's cousin and son-in-law, **Ali**, was designated as the fourth Caliph. Out of a confused political struggle, Ali and his son, **Hussain** were murdered, and Islam split. The majority (about 90 percent) are called **Sunnites** (traditional), and the minority who feel that Ali was the divinely appointed Caliph from the start are called **Shi'a** (the party, sect). The Shi'ites are a majority in Iran and Iraq and have large minorities in other countries as well. Outstanding among the sects of Muslims are the *Ahmadiyyas*, a modern sect from the Punjab of India/Pakistan, considered heretical by the majority, who are the most zealous in making converts, especially in Africa and the West. They especially target Christians.

Islamic faith: deistic unitarian legalism

Although Islam stresses practice over doctrine, it cannot be understood apart from a core of Muhammad's passionate teachings:

1. "First and foremost comes the message that God is one and absolute, a God of stark, absolute, transcendent power. His will is entirely arbitrary and can be changed at his pleasure in a contrary direction."[13] The transcendence of Allah is so stressed that he becomes virtually unknowable. He cannot be likened to anything or anyone. His majesty and power are emphasized; love is seen as a human emotion unworthy of God; holiness is not mentioned. Therefore the doctrine of absolute predestination becomes very fatalistic: the Muslim is to submit to the will of an arbitrary Sovereign. The doctrine of the Trinity was very abhorrent to Muhammad, probably

Surah 4:171 in the Koran directly contradicts the Bible and states that God has no son. Mohammed was reacting strongly against polytheism among his own people. He wanted to teach that God was one and one only. The second hand instruction on Christianity that he received from family and friends (he could not read or write) probably confused him on the meaning of the Trinity. To make Jesus the "son of God" must have sounded like polytheism to Mohammed, who taught that "there is no God but Allah."

Mohammed places the burden of earning salvation upon the believer in Islam. The Pillars of Faith and other disciplines imposed by the Koran help, but the Moslem is left to strive on his own to live a life free from sin. He has no assurance of salvation.

because he misunderstood that Christians believed Mary to be part of the Trinity. To say that any man could be the Son of God was blasphemy to him, since "God is not begotten, neither does He beget" (Surah 4:171).

2. Salvation is by human merit. Somehow this is harmonized with predestination. Islam is a religion of laws which are intended to govern all of life. The core is summarized in the five pillars of Muslim practice (see below). Religious Muslim society thus is very legalistic, much like the ancient Pharisees in many ways.

3. Muhammad was the final and greatest of the many prophets that Allah has sent to mankind. Abraham, Moses, David, and Jesus (*Hazrat Isa*) are recognized as prophets of Allah to the Jews and the channels of the *Taurat* (Law), *Zabur* (Psalms), and *Injil* (Gospel). But Muslims believe that

Muhammad supersedes all the prophets, and that the Qur'an supersedes and replaces the Bible. In addition they believe that Jews and Christians have changed and corrupted the Bible, especially taking out of it all the prophecies about Muhammad. Muhammad is not seen as a savior, although he is highly revered and slavishly imitated. While Muhammad claimed to be no more than a man, many Muslims see him as the most perfect of God's creatures.

4. Muhammad preached a bodily resurrection, followed by judgment based upon human merit. God will weigh men's good and bad works in a great pair of scales. Muslims hope to go to a sensual paradise; unbelievers and faithless Muslims will go to one of seven hells. There is no dualism between the world of the flesh and of the spirit—thus paradise is viewed very materialistically.

Five pillars of Islamic practice:
salvation by works

Although Islamic law is a complex code, there are five practices which are obligatory upon all. Muhammad made the essentials easy enough for his religion to gain widespread acceptance.

1. Recitation of the creed *(Shahada)*. The Muslim must recite the Creed daily in Arabic. "Allah is great. There is no God but Allah. Muhammad is the apostle of Allah." This is also called 'the Witness' since the Muslim is bearing witness to his belief.

2. Ritual prayers *(Salaah)*. Muslims must recite set prayers in Arabic while doing stipulated postures and prostrations facing Mecca. The faithful are called to prayer five times a day by the religious teacher (Mullah, Imam, Maulvi, etc.), who calls from the minaret of the mosque in a loud and penetrating voice. On Friday, congregational prayers are held in the mosque following a sermon by the leader/teacher.

3. Month-long fast *(Sawm)*. During the month of *Ramadan (Ramazan)* Muslims must refrain from food, water, smoking, and sex from sunrise to sunset. The fast is enforced by social pressure in Muslim lands..

4. Almsgiving *(Zakaat)*. Two-and-a-half percent of a Muslim's assets must be given annually to the poor, homeless, debtors, and for the spread of Islam. This tends to encourage beggars in Muslim lands.

5. Pilgrimage to Mecca *(Hajj)*. Once in a lifetime a Muslim must make a pilgrimage to the sacred city of Islam and perform certain rituals there, including going around the Kaaba (a cube shaped building) seven times. Upon return they may affect the title *Hajji*. The farther a Muslim lives from Arabia, the more difficult and expensive this becomes, although they are excused if it is financially impossible.

Situational factors mentioned in the Qur'an effectively remove any great moral demands from Muslims, as far as honesty, sexual purity, etc. are concerned. Muslim men may have four wives, although Muhammad was given special permission to have twelve. Other important practices include circumcision, abstaining from pork and alcohol, participation in *Jihad* (holy war) against infidels, veiling of women, and various festivals.

The Qur'an and the traditions

Since Muhammad was possibly illiterate,[14] the Qur'an was memorized by his first followers and not written down until after his death when some of those who had memorized it were killed in battle. The earlier of the 114 *Surahs* (chapters) are short and emphasize judgment against idolatry. Later Muhammad wove more of the Old Testament stories into the longer Surahs. However, he has Abraham offer up Ishmael (the father of the Arabs), not Isaac. Although Jesus is mentioned in 93 verses and given exalted titles, someone else was crucified in his place because Allah would not allow His holy prophet to be crucified. Paradoxically Jesus is now alive in heaven and will come back to establish Islam on earth. Muslims believe that only the original Arabic is really the Qur'an and have not been favorable to translation into other languages.

There are also a mass of Traditions *(Hadith)* about what Muhammad did or said, which are viewed in diverse ways by different Muslim sects. They were passed down from generation to generation with the name of the various witnesses affixed. Some are undoubtedly genuine, many probably spurious. However, no Muslim sect gives them equal authority with the Qur'an although they have a vast influence upon Muslim thought.

THE ORIGIN OF RELIGIONS

There are basically only two approaches to the origin of the diverse religions of man: the biblical view and the evolutionary explanation.

The evolutionary scenario. Following the widespread acceptance of Darwin's theory of organic evolution, the evolutionists began to apply the evolutionary principle to other academic disciplines, including religion. The principle would have to be that religions started in simple form among evolving ape-like humans and over the ages evolved into the present "higher forms" of religion. Thus J. G. Frazer suggested that magic is the origin and root of all religions. H. Spencer argued that ancestor worship, including the hero cult, is the root of all religion. F. B. Jevons focused on totemism as the source. The most common construct is that out of primitive animism and the evolving tribal cultic idol worship, a synthesis of tribalistic polytheism developed in Babylon, Egypt, and the Mediteranean area. Lewis Browne saw much of the idolatrous pantheon originating from Babylon and spreading. Then out of this polytheism, monotheism ultimately evolved. They would also reconstruct the Old Testament into an evolutionary framework.

The biblical data. The Bible does not directly give a theology of the origin of man's religions. But there is enough clear data to construct a satisfying explanation. Of course, as to Old Testament religion and Christianity, it is crystal clear that it is the product of God's self-revelation over the ages (Heb. 1:1-2). But what of the other world religions?

Genesis 11 gives us the first clue. The tower of Babel was undoubtedly a ziggurat, which we know were common in the area of Babylon as artificial 'high places' for the worship of idols. This then explains adequately the severity of God's judgment of the confusion of languages. And even though Browne takes an evolutionary view, he does see Babylon as the fountainhead of idolatry. He has a map showing how the worship of the Babylonian goddess Ishtar spread to Canaan as Ashtoreth, Isis in Egypt, Astarte and Ammas in Asia Minor, Aphrodite and Venus in Greece, and Cybele in Rome.[15] Alexander Hislop showed in great detail the origin of emperor worship under Nimrod in that locale, along with the worship of the mother-child idolatry of his wife and son. The worship of Tammuz (Adonis in Greece) is mentioned as an abomination in Ezek. 8:14.

Ultimately, Paul gives the description of God's wrath upon idolatry and naturism in Romans 1:18 ff, portraying it as a devolution, not an evolution. God gave the patriarchs the true knowledge of Himself, but the descendants of Noah's sons lost that knowledge and lapsed into the diverse religions we see today. Certainly Satan is behind the absolute confusion of even the highest religions. For example, Salman Rushdie's reference to the Satanic Verses in the title of his novel was embarrassing to Muslims because there is a strong thread of allusions to demonic influence in the Qur'an and the traditions of Islam.[16] Much more could be said.

---

1. H. D. Leuner, in Anderson, *Religions* (1951), p. 25.
2. Noss, *Religions* (1974), pp. 400-13.
3. Ibid, pp. 413-7
4. Jacob Jocz, in Vos, *Religions (1959)*, pp. 43-46.
5. Leuner, pp. 30-35.
6. Albert Henry Newman, *A Manual of Church History*, 1:292-93.
7. Loraine Boettner, *Roman Catholicism*, pp. 168-269.
8. George Yphantis, "Eastern Orthodoxy," in Vos, p. 345.
9. New Schaff-Herzog Encyclopedia of Religious Knowledge, "Eastern Church," vol. IV.
10. Noss, pp. 470-1.
11. Yphantis, p. 340.
12. Irvine Robertson, "World Religions Study-Graph."
13. Lewis, *Religions Made Simple*, p. 85.
14. Anis A. Shorrosh, *Islam Revealed*, pp. 52-3, gives convincing evidence against the traditional view that Muhammad was illiterate. He suggests the myth of his illiteracy was an attempt to magnify the miracle of the Quran.
15 Lewis Browne, *This Believing World* (1926), p. 61.
16. Some years ago a Pakistani with a degree in Islamic theology took me through a host of references in the Qur'an and the Hadith describing these demonic influences.

THE MAJOR FEATURES OF THE MAJOR RELIGIONS

RELIGION	FOUNDER	DATE FOUNDED	PLACE FOUNDED	ADHERENT LOCALE	NUMBER	HOLY BOOK	WORLD VIEW
HINDUISM	None	1500 BC to I AD	India	East Indians	825 million	Vedas Upanishads	Pantheism/ Polytheism
THERAVADA BUDDHISM	Gautama the Buddha	VI BC	Northeast India	Southeast Asia	180 million	Tripitaka	Atheism > Pantheism
MAHAYANA BUDDHISM	Gautama?	III - I BC	Northwest India	Central & East Asia	475 million	Sanskrit Writings	Pantheism
TAOISM	Lao Tse	VI BC	China	Chinese	N/A	Tao Teh Ching	Naturistic
CONFUCIAN-ISM	Confucius	VI BC	China	Chinese & Korean	N/A	Analects	Ethical Humanism
SHINTO	None	V-VII AD	Japan	Japanese	100 million	Kojiki	Naturistic /Pantheistic
ISLAM	Muhammad	622 AD	Arabia	Middle East	1.1 billion	Qur'an	Unitarian Monotheism

"But Paul said, I am a Jew of Tarsus in
Cilicia, a citizen of no insignificant city;"
~Acts 21:39

"For our citizenship is in heaven."
~ Phil. 3:20

THE SECULAR CONTEXT OF MISSIONS

The new missionary quickly becomes aware of the various contexts into which he travels. Medical inoculations remind one of the health context. The sights, sounds, and smells alert one to the cultural context to some extent. Seeing the pervasive economic disparity, it doesn't take long to become aware of the socio-economic context. As one gets to know the people the educational context comes into view. But one must check out the media to find out the political context. Hu Shih, the great Chinese philosopher, once said that China has five great enemies: Poverty, disease, ignorance, greed, and disorder.[1] These are key factors in the world's misery into which we go. Let us look at the causes of disorder first.

THE POLITICAL CONTEXT

Although the missionary arrives on the field with a Bible very conscious of the religious context of our ministry, he also carries a passport, which reminds us of the political context of our target people. Our nationality is a fact of life, and we come as foreigners; in some countries very obviously so, in others not so markedly.

When I arrived in Pakistan in 1956, the Independence Day celebration reminded me that this was a new nation nine years from independence from the British Empire and separation from India as a Muslim nation. A constitutional convention was in progress in Karachi as I arrived, since for nine years they had carried on under the British form of government. A few months later the Suez Canal invasion by Britain and France stirred up hostility to anybody who looked British, and my Pakistani friends told me to stay off the streets for a few days. Two years later a military coup d'etat swept that all away, and imports came to an abrupt halt for a while. Like Adoniram Judson, many missionaries experience war situations or hostility to their home countries which radically affect their ministries. So how are we to relate to governments and the political context into which we go? How are national believers to relate? These are not easy questions to answer.

We know from Scripture that governments were ordained by God. By making a covenant with Noah and his sons (our ancestors) and the remnant human race and including in it capital punishment for murder (Gen. 9:6), God by so much was establishing the foundation of civil government. He strengthened and amplified it through the Mosaic Law for the nation Israel. He confirmed it through the teaching of the Lord Jesus (Mt. 22:15-22) and the Apostle Paul (Rom. 13:1-7).

On the other hand we know that Satan uses civil governments to his own ends. The satanic character of the governments of Babylon (Isa. 14) and Tyre (Ez. 28) is quite clear. Daniel was given to see the demonic warfare raging around government power (Dan. 10:1, 12-13). Christ called Satan the "prince of this world" (Jn. 12:31; 14:30; 16:11), and Paul confirmed his continuing activity as the "god of this world" (2 Cor. 4:4). The Apostle Peter concluded that normally we are to obey governments, except when they command us to stop proclaiming the gospel (Acts 4:19-20; 5:29).

Another factor to consider is that frequently opposition to the gospel comes from government bureaucrats who sometimes make up their own rules as they go, even if contrary to a constitution or written laws, or even misinterpret the law too narrowly or prejudicially. This is true in our own country as well as in the two-thirds world, as cases regularly coming into the Christian media attest.

Colonialism. We have already discussed colonialism in chapter 10. Coming into newly independent Pakistan, I found that colonialism was still prominently on the minds of the people. I was surprised to find that attitudes were not all negative, however. Some would say, "We had it better under the British." But most were hopeful that their newfound freedom would improve their lot. Over the years I also learned that Pakistan (also India, Bangladesh, and Sri Lanka) was irreversibly affected by centuries of British Raj (rule). In any case I took great pains to disassociate myself from this colonialism. This was not so easy, however, since people would see my white face, call me "Sahib," and show me undue deference as a Westerner. This unearned status was a hindrance to the ministry to which God had called me, even though it did make life easier in many ways.

Space does not permit a full appraisal of colonialism and its attendant imperialism. Herbert Kane has given a full discussion. A number of his key points as to the missionaries' involvements are worth noting:

1. In those days imperialism was a way of international life.
2. Even those missionaries who had misgivings tended to regard colonialism as the less of two evils.
3. Many missionaries regarded colonialism, evil though it was, as an instrument by which God was working out His sovereign purpose in the world.

4. The missionaries were among the first to detect and detest the evils of the colonial system under which they lived.
5. The missionaries always believed that their first allegiance was to Jesus Christ and not to any government, good or bad.[2]

The successor countries to British India have just celebrated their fiftieth anniversary and most African nations are about that far out of colonialism. The track record of these independent nations over the half century has been very varied, but mostly disappointing, and in some cases (like Congo/Zaire) disastrous. Thus in varying ways missionaries still find themselves living with the consequences of colonialism, for better or for worse.

Tribalism/nationalism. "If colonialism was the greatest force in the nineteenth century, surely nationalism has been the most potent force in the twentieth century." This apt generalization by Kane is more accurate regarding the earlier part of the twentieth century than the latter part in which internationalism has become a force (even since he wrote). But certainly tribalism and nationalism have been dominant in their diverse ways. Tribalism has consistently undermined the success of nationalism. This has been especially characteristic of African nations as exemplified by the recent genocide of the dominant Tutus by the majority Hutus in Rwanda. In reality the term 'tribalism' is too narrow since the same phenomenon is manifest between ethnic groups which could hardly be called tribal. In the Balkans we see the ongoing ethnic conflict between the Catholic Croats, Muslim Bosnians, and Orthodox Serbs. There the term "ethnic cleansing" was coined. In Sudan it is the Arab Muslims from the north persecuting the non-Muslim tribal peoples of the south. In former Pakistan it was the Punjabis and Pathans of the west repressing the Bengalis of the east, which caused the split-off of Bangladesh.

However, in the main with the demise of western empires scores of new nations came into being, and despite the ethnic strife have become a major factor in the world political situation.

Kane, with his inclination to historical analysis, makes the point that in the first place the missionaries sowed the seeds of nationalism in the minds of the nationals:

> By opening schools, reducing hundreds of languages to writing, translating books, especially the Bible, they did more than anyone else to promote the ideas and ideals of democracy, including such concepts as the dignity of labor, the worth of the individual, social justice, personal integrity, freedom of thought and speech, etc. Their educational institutions produced the intellectual elite who eventually provided leadership for the independence movement.[3]

Communism. Communism proved to be the greatest threat to the progress of the gospel during most of the twentieth century, but by the end of the century its impact has diminished incredibly. Back in the 1950s and 60s over a third of the world population was under communist control and looked to expand even further. However, the end of the century saw an astonishing demise of communist political power, which we could hardly have imagined. The West won the cold war! Now only a few small communist regimes remain, and mainland China now seems more capitalistic than communistic, although it is still totalitarian. With the breakup of the Soviet Union, communists are no longer running the government in Russia, although many communists still sit in their parliament. Some Marxist guerrillas are still active in Latin America, but even their power is waning. But we must not count them out prematurely.

Totalitarianism. Since the days of the Roman Empire the major opposition to the gospel has come from totalitarian governments. There were the ten periods of persecution in the first three centuries of the church. And yet the "blood of the martyrs was the seed of the church." In this century Hitler's Nazi brand of fascistic totalitarianism greatly impacted Christians in Europe. Now Russia is moving away from totalitarianism but still ambivalent about keeping open doors for missionaries. China's shift toward capitalism has only temporarily relieved the pressure on the Christians since in various provinces Christian workers are being persecuted again on a regular basis. The national church needs to be prepared to face such persecution since it has been said that the age of martyrs is now.

THE HEALTH CONTEXT

Tourists go abroad with an awareness of the difficult health environment into which they may travel and are given warnings about food and water in addition to the many and complex inoculations they get. Missionaries, staying for longer periods, must take greater precautions. Additionally, missionaries must be concerned not just for their own health, but also for that of the people to whom they go, especially of believers. This is, of course, the basis of medical missions (to be discussed in ch. 23).

The pioneer missionaries of past centuries found disease a major obstacle, as has already been noted. With the incredible advances of modern medicine, although we still have concerns, we also have many more resources for avoiding disease. But for the major populace many of the health scourges continue endemic despite modern medicine, either because of ignorance, poverty, or lack of access to medical help. Dysentery, malaria, typhoid, and a number of others are far from conquered. In addition, AIDS is endemic in Africa, spreading in Asia, and a serious problem here at home. Drug abuse is also a health concern around the world.

David Woodward saw health concerns as a part of God's "call to the world's misery," and quotes Dr. Douglas Gibson, an former missionary to China: "The relief of suffering is so essentially a part of the practice of Christianity, that to omit it would invalidate the gospel message and make it as sounding brass and tinkling cymbals."[4]

THE SOCIO-ECONOMIC CONTEXT

The socio-economic context also hits the newcomer full in the face. The poor and disenfranchised are found in every country, but they are more obvious in most two-thirds-world countries. Here in North America we have our share (cf. ch. 15). Poverty and famine are a part of the world's misery just alluded to. Its causes are many: political oppression, incompetence, wrong-headedness, lack of education, discrimination, social marginalization, corruption, etc.[a] For example, recent famines in North Korea have a clear political cause. On my recent visit to South Asia I learned a new Urdu/Punjabi loan word from English, *corupshun:* a word widely used because the practice is so common. It most definitely contributes to the widespread poverty there.

How does the Christian relate to it? We reject the 'prosperity gospel' which says that God has promised economic (and health) prosperity to believers as our right. Yes, God did promise national prosperity for Israel if they would walk in His ways. But in the New Testament we find no comparable promises of prosperity for individual Christians. On the other hand we find that in many ways grinding poverty hinders the progress of the gospel. Ignorance, illiteracy, disease, and early death are the results of poverty and in some cases the causes. The Christian cannot be unmoved by such misery. And we know the first step in social uplift is personal redemption in Christ. Over the years missionaries have had a good track record in compassionate ministries to help relieve such misery.

One of the great paradoxes the missionary faces is the responsiveness of the poor. Some have drawn a false dichotomy by stating that a hungry man cannot listen to or respond to the gospel. The apostle Paul indicated that the response of the poor is part of God's plan: "For consider your calling, brethren, that there were not many wise according to the flesh, not many mighty, not many noble; for God has chosen the foolish things of the world to shame the wise, and God has chosen the weak things of the world to shame the wise, . . ." (1 Cor.

---

[a]   In Pakistan there is a unique situation in which most of the Christians come from the outcaste classes of Hinduism, even though the majority of the populace is Muslim. Thus apart from the ongoing Muslim oppression, the Christians start from a poor economic condition.

1:26-7). But frequently it is as men come to the end of themselves that they turn to Christ. This is borne out by statistics from many parts of the world. The sociological standing of Brazil's Christians has been carefully researched, and has confirmed that the vast majority are from the lower classes. In India it is the lower castes who have been most responsive. In general we have not been so successful in reaching the upper classes, although there are some notable exceptions. Some missiologists have suggested that the reason is because most missionaries come from the middle class or lower middle stratum. This is undoubtedly true.

Indeed, this is one of the great dilemmas of the missionary. Where do we fit into the sociological mosaic? Where can we be most effective? My own primary ministry was among university students, but even many of them were coming up from the lower classes. Secondarily, I was working with a group of indigenous brethren assemblies, and some of our ministry was among the very poorest. Coming from the affluent West we seem rich to the people in most two-thirds-world countries. But that only heightens the paradox. This leads us immediately into issues that are also cultural.

THE CULTURAL CONTEXT

Far more subtle than the above discussed contexts is the cultural environment into which the missionary comes. We have already defined the missionary as a cross-cultural proclaimer of the message. Thus it is clear that culture is at the heart of all the missionary does. But what do we mean by culture? Paul Hiebert gives us a definition: "the more or less integrated systems of ideas, feelings, and values and their associated patterns of behavior and products shared by a group of people who organize and regulate what they think, feel, and do."[5]

Relating to cultures

Culture shock. The missionary's first confrontation with major cultural differences has been termed 'culture shock.' Actually at first things seem very exciting in a new culture. There is so much to see and learn. But then in a little while the newness wears off, and there begins to be a revulsion at the sights, sounds, smells, and experiences. It is not just the poverty and dirt or the fear of disease. "Culture shock is the disorientation we experience when all the cultural maps and guidelines we learned as children no longer work. Stripped of our normal ways of coping with life, we are confused, afraid, and angry. We rarely know what has gone wrong, much less what to do about it."[6] Hiebert lists a number of factors: language shock, changes in routine, changes in relationships, loss of understanding, and emotional and evaluative disorientation. I have a suspicion that John Mark experienced culture shock when, as a monocultural Judean Jew, he arrived with Paul and Barnabas among idolatrous pagan in Perga of Pamphylia. Paul and Barnabas as bicultural Jews had less problem with the cultural context.

Identification. Coping with culture shock is only the beginning of the missionary's struggle with culture change. As we have just intimated, the missionary wonders how and where he can fit into the cultural mosaic— economically, socially, in dress, in physical appearance, etc. Hudson Taylor was a pioneer in the process we call identification (cf. c. 10). I sought to follow his example in Pakistan. Since my ministry was among college students who wore blazers and ties like westerners, it would have made little sense for me to wear the dress of village men (*shilvar-kameze*). Before I married I lived with Pakistanis in several different situations over 2½ years, which not only was valuable linguistically, but also gave me a most valuable insight into the culture, their way of think-ing, the condition of the churches, and even many contacts in the Chris-tian community I would not otherwise have made. But after marriage I found this was much more difficult. In regard to economic level we sought a median, a compromise which we hoped would not be a stum-bling block to those below or above. Since the gap between rich and poor is so much greater in the two-thirds world, such issues are height-ened. Amazingly some 'old school' missionaries were offended that I lived with nationals.[b] The social hangover of colonialism was a major obstacle to identification. Since the essence of gospel communication is building personal relationships, identification is absolutely essential. Each generation of new missionaries needs to shed our cultural arrogance and learn how to identify with the people to whom God sends us.

We have a solid biblical basis for identification. The incarnation of the Lord Jesus was an incredible identification with the human race. He not only looked human, but He was perfectly human (Jn 1:14; Rom. 8:3; Gal. 4; Phil. 2:6-7; Heb. 2:17). Even more He became a servant of men. "Just as the Son of Man did not come to be served, but to serve, and to give His life a ransom for many" (Mt. 20:28). In the Indian subcontinent a question always asked of the stranger or foreigner is, *"Koi khidmat hai?* (Is there any service I can render to you?)."* In our seeking to identify, this verse and cultural pattern becomes a real challenge to the mission-ary from the affluent West. Are we willing to become servants of the people to whom we go? Paul well understood and practiced the princi-ple of identification:

> And to the Jews I became as a Jew, that I might win Jews; to those who are under the Law, as under the Law, though not being myself under the Law, that I might win those who are un-

---

[b]   One high-church Anglican was heard to comment when I was in the hospital with a near-fatal illness, that "it serves him right for living with Pakistanis."

der the Law; to those who are without law, as without law,
though not being without the law of God, but under the law of
Christ, that I might win those who are without law. . . . I have
become all things to all men, that I by all means may save some
(1 Cor. 9:20-22).

Yet in Paul's cultural flexibility he did not ever compromise the absolutes
of the gospel message (Gal. 1:6-9). Some scholars have felt that there is
a disparity between Paul's principles and his practice as recorded in Acts.
But I am convinced that in merely cultural matters he was flexible to
avoid offense to the gospel and totally consistent with his principles as
stated above (cf. Acts 21:17-26).

I think there are a number of factors which will help in the process
of identification. First off we must recognize that missionaries, especially
before World War II, did not exemplify identification well. The root of
the problem was ethnocentrism, a false concept of the 'white man's
burden,' and an attitude of cultural superiority. Let's face it: there are
good and bad aspects of all cultures, even our own. For example, a
strong emphasis upon hospitality permeates the south Asian and Middle
Eastern cultures. This is an area where western cultures are very weak
and defective.

Other expatriates do not have the same motivation to identify as the
missionary does, and it is all too easy to slip into their erroneous pattern.
Kane points out that identification is more difficult in some cultures than
in others and concludes: "But in the more advanced countries of Asia
with their rich and ancient civilizations the missionaries might easily have
done a better job of identification."[7] We realize that identification can
never be total. Even people of European descent going to Europe may
never get the accent and the subtleties of the culture right. Africans
wonder why Afro-American missionaries can't speak their language properly. Our physical appearance may betray us as foreigners. But we must
not fall into a defeatist attitude and give up trying. Although the nationals
may not appreciate the difficulties of identifying, they certainly appreciate
the effort we make to bridge the cultural gap. Kane lists a number of
obstacles to identification: a stratified society, domestic family life situations, multiracial situations, economic disparity, non-Christian value systems, and religious rites contrary to the word of God.[8]

Communicating the message

There are a number of terms which come into play in seeking to
communicate the gospel message to the receptor people. The discipline
of cross-cultural communication has been advanced by light years in just
the present generation. The term contextualization is relatively new and
controversial, but without doubt absolutely essential to the planting of
indigenous churches. And the focus upon distinct people groups was a

foundational concept, popularized by Donald McGavran's 'church growth movement.'

Cross-cultural communication. David Hesselgrave, in his classic text, has given the basis for communicating in a cultural way:

> In the first place, the missionary cannot *communicate* without concerning himself with culture because communication is inextricable from culture. Just as Christ became flesh and dwelt among men, so propositional truth must have a cultural incarnation to be meaningful. In the second place, the missionary cannot communicate *Christianity* without concerning himself with culture because, though Christianity is supracultural in its origin and truth, it is cultural in its application.[9]

Hesselgrave sees seven dimensions of cross-cultural communication: world views (ways of perceiving the world), cognitive processes (ways of thinking), linguistic forms (ways of expressing ideas), behavioral patterns (ways of acting), social structure (ways of interacting), media influence (ways of channeling the message), and motivational resources (ways of deciding). Considering our target cultures from these distinct perspectives, we become vastly better equipped to bridge the cultural chasms in our communication of the eternal word of God into sinful human cultures.

Contextualization. We need to define contextualization, but it is hard to get a consensus on its meaning. Sherwood Lingenfelter's definition is helpful: "The idea of contextualization is to frame the gospel message in language and communication forms appropriate and meaningful to the local culture, and to focus the message upon crucial issues in the lives of the people."[10] The term began to be used by ecumenical Protestants by 1972 in an attempt to restructure theology to harmonize with the diverse cultures of mankind. Evangelicals at first were hesitant to utilize this concept because of its connection with a liberal agenda. But increasingly evangelical missiologists saw a biblical basis for couching the message in "forms appropriate and meaningful to the local culture" and found additional support from the disciplines of anthropology, sociology, and linguistics.[11]

Although the validity of contextualization is now well accepted by evangelical missiologists, there is considerable discussion as to how far we may go in contextualizing the gospel without lapsing into syncretistic compromise of the gospel with non-Christian cultural elements. It must start with culturally sensitive Bible translation and carry right on through to a contextualized agenda for teaching theology to new Christians, with many other dimensions in between.

Foundational to the process is the recognition that the eternal word of God was revealed to people in a number of diverse cultures. Moses was coming out of an idolatrous Egyptian culture, and the rest of the Old Testament came into ancient near-eastern cultures—some Hebrew, some Babylonian, some Persian, while the New came into Graeco-Romanized Jewish and Gentile cultures. We have to understand the Bible in its cultural context, which is so different from our own. Then we have to transfer the eternal, abiding truth into a target cultural context. The irony is that frequently the culture of the target people is closer to the biblical cultures than to our own culture. However, in contextualizing the form of the message we must be very careful not to compromise the transcultural absolutes of God's revelation.

Indigenization. The most venerable term for our consideration is the 'indigenous church.' Of course, indigenous means 'native.' In the nineteenth century Henry Venn and Rufus Anderson set out what have been called the indigenous principles of missions. Subsequently John Nevius, a Presbyterian missionary to China applied these principles when he was transferred to Korea when it opened up to missionaries. He concluded from his experience in China that the churches must be developed from the earliest possible time on an indigenous basis. Roland Allen spelled this out with the three selves: self-supporting, self-propagating, and self-governing. In essence it involves contextualizing the church to the indigenous culture, thus keeping it from dependency upon the missionary.

THE EDUCATIONAL CONTEXT

So much of the world's misery is caused by ignorance. Much of the disease of the two-thirds world is caused by ignorance of the most elementary sanitary precautions given to Israel in the Mosaic Law (cf. Num. 19, Deut. 23:12-3). Lack of education is a major cause of the poor economic conditions in many countries. But the ultimate ignorance as to its eternal consequence is the ignorance of the word of God and the message of salvation. Paul spoke of the condition of the mass of humanity when he wrote: ". . . you must no longer live as the Gentiles do, in the futility of their thinking. They are darkened in their understanding and separated from the life of God because of the ignorance that is in them due to the hardening of their hearts" (Eph. 4:17-18 NIV). Even if the missionary goes to a highly literate country like Japan or Europe, it is the ignorance of the gospel which is most significant.

In some areas illiteracy is a major obstacle to the spread of the message. Literature ministry is thus restricted, and the converts then are hindered in the discipleship process. Early missionaries put great stress on educational ministries in order to meet the needs, and that continues to this day (cf. c. 23). However, coming from the educated West, we must not suppose that illiterate people are stupid or unable to become mature Christians. Education is not a panacea. Illiterate people have great retentive powers, and in Pakistan I have seen totally illiterate preachers who were able to plant a church. They had memorized Scripture and were able to relate it to the people, frequently using a literate child to read the passage before preaching on it. But all things being equal, God can use a sharp tool better than a dull one. So to build strong churches and lift the people out of their poverty, disease, and other problems, education is a basic tool of the missionary. It starts with literacy work, moves on to elementary education and Bible schools, leading ultimately to seminary level in many cases. This is all in perfect harmony with the Lord's words in the Great Commission to teach them whatever He has commanded us (Mt. 28:18) and Paul's instruction in 2 Timothy 2:2: "And the things which you have heard from me in the presence of many witnesses, these entrust to faithful men, who will be able to teach others also."

CONCLUSIONS

We have examined both the religious and secular contexts of the world to which we are sent. The world is absorbed in its own concerns, in bondage to the religious and nonreligious systems to which they adhere. They are not usually eager to turn from what they have to something new. They are much taken up with the political issues of their country, province, or locale. They are absorbed in the struggle to maintain physical health in a world full of disease. They are mostly caught up in materialism, either from the perspective of the have-nots or of the affluent. The societal mosaic may find them isolated from the truth of the gospel of Christ. Their culture makes the missionary and his message seem so foreign to them, so incomprehensible. Who can bridge that cultural gap for them? Who can identify with them? Who can make the gospel seem less foreign? Who can plant an indigenous church in which they will feel at home?

David Woodward has put it so aptly in poetic form:

When you came to answer the heathen cry
And thought you would hear a piteous sigh,
    You never expected this–
Men with a satisfied, comfortable air,
Women too busy with gossip to care
    For a truth they do not miss.
Did you dream of a host of upraised arms
Beseeching release from pagan alarms,
    Only to wake with a start?
Now that you know they are passing your door,
Preferring an idol's parade much more,
    What does it do to your heart?

You are so earnestly giving the Word,
But listening ears seem not to have heard,
    No matter how much you repeat.
Strong in the grip of tradition, they sit,
Almost defying you ever to fit
    Your shoes on their mental feet.
Patience, my brother, before you will learn
Where the silent ache and the anguish turn
    To an unknown God to pray.
Bringing the sheaves from the harvest will wait
On sowing and growing at God's own rate,
    A thousand years or a day.
As sure as there's sin in old Adam's breed,
So certain it is that you'll find a lead
    Into the devil's domain.
Keep on believing that He who has won
Your full allegiance has also begun
    Seeking the lost who remain.[12]

Enrichment from *Perspectives*:

All of Section C (Chapters 1-20), also Section D, Chapters 32-34.

1. David Brainerd Woodward, *God, Men, and Missions* (1964), p. 78.
2. Kane, *Understanding Christian Missions*, pp. 246-55.
3. Ibid, p. 257.
4. Woodward, pp. 71, 68-77.
5. Paul G. Hiebert, *Anthropological Insights for Missionaries* (1985), p. 30.
6. Ibid, p. 66.
7. Kane, pp. 341-2.
8. Ibid, pp. 344-5.
9. David J. Hesselgrave, *Communicating Christ Cross-culturally* (1978), p. 82.
10. Sherwood Lingenfelter, *Transforming Culture: A Challenge for Christian Mission* (1992), p. 15.
11. David J. Hesselgrave and Edward Rommen, *Contextualization: Meanings, Methods, and Models* (1989), pp. 27-35; Warren Chastain, "Contextualization: Some Cautions and Criticisms," *Seedbed* VIII:3, pp. 39-40.
12. Woodward, p.92..

PART IV

HIS GEOGRAPHIC SOCIETY:

THE REGIONAL DIMENSION

Western	Tribal/Animist	Other Buddhists*	Chinese	Hindu	Muslim
100 million	150 million	250 million	500 million	700 million	1 billion

*Japan, South East Asia

Unreached Groups

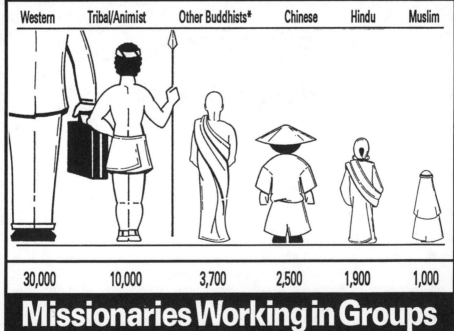

Western	Tribal/Animist	Other Buddhists*	Chinese	Hindu	Muslim
30,000	10,000	3,700	2,500	1,900	1,000

Missionaries Working in Groups

"For Jews have no dealings with Samaritans."

~John 4:9

"And Philip went down to the city of Samaria and began proclaiming Christ to them."

~Acts 8:5

NORTH AMERICA: OUR SAMARIA

IS NORTH AMERICA A MISSION FIELD?

Global missions from North America had its origin right here with home missions. It was success in the evangelization of native Americans which convinced William Carey that evangelizing the heathen was viable. In 1646 John Eliot began missionary witness to the Indians of Massachusetts. Sporadically until 1810, when foreign missions effort started here, a diversity of home missions ministries was carried on. But since then, as foreign missions increasingly came into the focus of American Christians, home missions ministry was greatly neglected. This left large segments of North Americans without the gospel.

Many might challenge this statement by exclaiming, "Haven't most Americans heard the gospel over and over and had abundant opportunity to accept Christ? Aren't there two million religious programs each year over several thousand radio and TV stations? Aren't there hundreds of home missions agencies blanketing North America with the gospel of Christ?" There is some truth to this reaction, of course. But the reality is that although American evangelical churches have been among the most successful in evangelizing large segments of our society, there are vast pockets of totally unreached people all over North America. Although 28% of North Americans are considered evangelical, most of the population is part of that mosaic of distinct peoples who are culturally, religiously, or sociologically isolated from evangelical Christians, churches, and ministries. Earl Parvin has gotten the nub of the matter when he states, "The disquieting fact of the matter is that there are vast multitudes of Americans who will live and die in North America without ever once hearing the gospel."[1]

As an example, Brooklyn was called the "city of churches" before it became a borough of New York City. Yet a missionary colleague who is planting a Chinese church there told me that a significant number of the immigrants whom he has won to Christ had never even heard the name of Jesus before receiving his witness. Similar stories could be multiplied across North America from the native Americans, Afro-Americans, Jews, immigrant ethnic/religious groups, or pockets of alienated, isolated kinds of people. Even worse might be the stories of millions of people who are familiar with the name of Christ and with professing Christians whose unchristian lifestyle or treatment of them has radically alienated them from the gospel, whether contemporaneously or in the history of their people. This would be true of most native Americans, many Afro-Americans, most Muslims, Jews, and homosexuals, to name a few.

Certainly the vast majority of evangelical churches are not effectively reaching such groups, and our home mission agencies are only scratching the surface. Indeed, Christians have barely recognized the majority of these people as a mission field at our doorstep. In truth they are part of the 'hidden peoples' to which Ralph Winter alerted us in the Lausanne Congress in 1974. Perhaps he and most of us were thinking of the hidden peoples abroad: the billion Muslims, hundreds of millions of Hindus, Buddhists, atheists, etc. But we must also focus upon the 'hidden peoples' of North America, who although geographically not necessarily far from us, are nevertheless invisible to most Christians. And even if they are visible to us, we are not concerned to reach them for a number of reasons: ignorance, fear, prejudice, inertia, or whatever.

Home vs. foreign? The distinction between home and foreign missions is not as sharp, clear, and biblical as most of us have imagined. We have already focused upon the basic imperative in the Greatest Commission to "make disciples of all peoples (*ethnē*)," and that includes ethnic groups here at home. However, in the Acts form of the Commission, the Lord Jesus spelled it out more explicitly so that there is no room for misunderstanding: "but you shall receive power when the Holy Spirit has come upon you; and you shall be My witnesses both in Jerusalem, and in all Judea and Samaria, and even to the remotest part of the earth" (Acts 1:8). The Lord started with Jerusalem and Judea, which represents the evangelism of people like us locally and throughout our nation. This we are doing to some extent and with some success. But we have neglected our Samaria. A century ago, C. I. Scofield (of reference Bible fame), the founder of the Central America Mission, called Central America "our Samaria," since in the end of the nineteenth century missionaries were sailing by it to reach South America. But he was only partly right, because our Samaria is really much closer to home.

Historically the Samaritans were that religio-ethnic group which had become alienated from the mainstream of Judaism and was despised by the Jews. In chapter 5 we looked at the difficulty the early church had in bridging the gap into the Samaritan community because of deep-rooted prejudice and hatred among good, kosher Jewish people. Christ went out of His way to expose that prejudice for what it was: e.g., the parable of the Good Samaritan and the healing of the ten lepers. In a similar way our Samaritans are those peoples who have been marginalized because of language, culture, religion, race, morality, or social status. In some cases we have a fairly good record of seeking to reach out to a particular group, such as alcoholics and Jewish people, especially in the last century or so. But in most cases our record is abysmal!

It is not a matter of either/or between home and foreign missions. The Lord Jesus mentioned home missions before foreign missions because home missions is foundational to our outreach to the "remotest part of the earth." Remember our discussion of the Antioch church in chapter 4—how that one secret to the missionary vision of that church was the evangelism of Gentiles at home before they sent out Paul and Barnabas as the first foreign missionaries. Cross-cultural outreach here at home is foundational to foreign missions, which is almost totally cross-cultural in nature. We must have strong multi-ethnic churches at home as the best launching pad for foreign missions. Also we can best train missionaries in cross-cultural witness here at home before we send them abroad. Thus home and foreign missions are complementary. Some mission agencies recognize this and have both home and foreign missionaries in their membership. However, we now have the ironic situation in which some foreign mission boards will not allow returning foreign missionaries to work as home missionaries among the immigrants from their foreign field (perhaps out of the unjustified fear that many will stay home). There should be no competition. Acts 1:8 is clear evidence that both must be done simultaneously. Parvin's statement is to the point:

> It is to be noted that in recent years many citizens of the "mission" world have come to visit or reside in the United States. The newcomers have become one of the larger gospel-neglected segments of American society. The time has come for the church to realize that her mission includes more than her primary targeted peoples in her near community and her "foreign" interests. Peter Gunther suggests that those people in between are "completely ignored" and then calls them the "important gap, national missions."[2]

Ralph Winter has suggested that it might clarify matters if we talked about "domestic missions" to be contrasted with "frontier missions," since much of foreign mission activity is really domestic to the indigenous churches abroad. And in reality there are many unreached frontiers right here in North America today.

Many years ago Homer Payne said that "missions has become an alibi for many American Christians." What could he have meant by that? Just this, that for most of us it is easier to write a check to support foreign missionaries than to be engaged personally in aggressive evangelism here at home. His statement is especially relevant to our lack of witness to the Samaritans among us.

How can we reach our Samaria?   Parvin has put it succinctly: "There is a disturbing misconception within the evangelical community that with all of the evangelistic activity going on, the millions of un-churched Americans can be reached by means of the evangelistic pro-grams already in place."[3] Ideally it would seem simpler if the local chur-ches would simply reach out to the Samaritans among us, win them, and enfold them. But if our track record is any measure, this is just not hap-pening on a scale adequate to make any satisfying penetration of these 'hidden peoples' at our doorstep. And then there is the geographical distance of some of these people from evangelical churches, and more importantly the cultural, religious, and in many cases linguistic distance. Here is where the 'sent-out' missionary come in. The missionary is es-sential both to go to them physically and to learn their language (if advis-able), religion, and culture. Here in North America, as abroad, the para-church mission agency is essential to mobilize, train, and stand behind such missionaries.

Parvin suggests steps which churches can take to meet the needs:

1. The church must become aware of the spiritual needs of all segments of society. . . .
2. The church must determine what can be realistically accom-plished within the framework of the in-house evangelistic pro-grams already in place or those that can realistically be devel-oped to reach the total community.
3. The church must develop a realistic definition of missions that recognizes that any people she cannot service with the gospel through her in-house programs of evangelism are a bona fide mission field, whether at home or abroad. . . .
4. The church must alert her people concerning the community needs that are beyond her in-house programs and send those who are gifted and respond to those needs, . . .
5. The church must call for her training institutions to initiate programs to alert and prepare her students for missionary service to evangelize at home as well as abroad.
6. The church must prepare internship programs for her gradu-ates to mature and display their spiritual gifts . . .
7. The church should encourage foreign missions to develop home departments to assist her to reach foreign citizens resident here. . . .
8. The church should recognize national missions to be as valid as foreign missions.[4]

THE HISTORICAL BACKGROUND

We have already taken note in Chapter Eight of the ministry of John

Eliot to the Algonquin Indians in 1646 and the founding of the **Society for the Propagation of the Gospel in New England** in 1649. We should also note that five generations of Mayhews gave themselves to the evangelization of the Indians on the coastal islands of eastern Massachusetts.

The Moravian missions were the major factor in the evangelization of native Americans in the 18th century. Their leader, Nicholas Zinzendorf came to Pennsylvania in 1741 to organize German immigrants into churches and to start work among the Indians. David Zeisberger moved a group of Moravians to Ohio to establish Christian communities and to evangelize the Indians, in which they were very successful. The Great Awakening of 1734 stirred up interest in Indian evangelism. Henry Barclay saw fruit among the Indians of New York beginning in 1741. About that time David Brainerd began his fruitful witness to the Indians of New Jersey and Pennsylvania (cf. ch. 9). It is not widely known that one of the ministries of Jonathan Edwards was as a missionary to Indians at Stockbridge, Massachusetts along with John Sergeant. Dartmouth College was founded by Eleazer Wheelock to train Indians and colonists for missionary service. By 1761 the Presbyterians sent Samuel Kirkland, James Davenport, and Simon Horton to work among the Indians and black people. The Quakers also developed an extensive work.

After the Revolutionary War, the Second Awakening of the 1780's revived interest in missions. The formation of the Missionary Society of Connecticut in 1798 was the first of a sequence of a number of denominational missions agencies. The uniting of many denominational Bible societies into the American Bible Society in 1816, the founding of the American Sunday School Union in 1824, the American Tract Society, and the American Home Mission Society, both in 1826, were the beginnings of interdenominational efforts, even though not clearly targeted to Indian, black, or Hispanic minorities.

The slavery issue, the Civil War (1861-5), and the post-war expansion of the nation into the west put a damper on cross-cultural missionary activity for a while. The growing foreign missions movement toward the end of the nineteenth century possibly detracted from the home missions thrust. The Student Volunteer Movement started in 1886 had no counterpart to stir up interest in home missions. However, work among alcoholics was started with the **McAuley Water Street Mission** in New York (1872), the **Pacific Garden Mission** in Chicago (1877), and the **American Rescue Workers Mission** (1896). **Christ's Mission** was founded in 1891 to reach Roman Catholics and the **American Board of Missions to the Jews** (now Chosen People Ministries) in 1894.[5]

The twentieth century has seen the development of well over 500 national missions agencies, most in the thirty years after 1930. This includes about 40 foreign missions with work here at home.. The number of missionaries can only be estimated from a 1980 survey which indicated 12,000 workers in responding agencies: perhaps the total is double that. The Southern Baptists listed 2,800 workers and the Assemblies of God, 660. But little other denominational statistics are available. Campus Crusade for Christ fields over 3,000 workers; Youth For Christ, 1000; Child Evangelism Fellowship, 600; and three other agencies have over 400. But in the main most agencies are small with slow numerical growth.

One of the difficulties home missions have faced is lack of organization. It wasn't until 1941 that H. A. Ironside stimulated the formation of the **National Home Missions Fellowship** (now called the Association of North American Missions) at Moody Memorial Church. It has 24 member missions, representing 700 missionaries. Apparently many other national mission agencies are not organized into any associational relationship.[6]

ETHNIC MINISTRIES

Missions in North America began with ethnic ministry to native Americans. Then it expanded to Negroes (as they were then called). The Hispanic influence began in the Southwest long before the Pilgrim fathers arrived, but has not been the focus of missions until more recently. Hundreds of different ethnic groups have immigrated over the centuries; some have been given a witness, but the majority have been totally overlooked. Most of the immigrants in the ninteenth and first half of the twentieth centuries have been Europeans, with the exception of mainly Chinese and Japanese communities. But with the new immigration laws of the 1960s a radical shift began. Vast numbers of other Asians, Middle Easterners, Africans, Latin Americans, and peoples from the Caribbean have been coming. In a real sense the two-thirds world has been coming here. Let us look at the diverse ethnic ministries of North America.

Native Americans

The present generation of native Americans has not been reached effectively with the gospel as evidenced by the statistic that over 92% do not attend church services at all, even though about 17% have some affiliation with churches of all kinds. But "syncretistic indigenous sects and cults as well as reversions to pre-Christian beliefs are widespread." Most are isolated from evangelical churches in many ways. Geographically they are scattered on many reservations, some incredibly large and inaccessible and others small, or in inner cities over the continent. Their animistic culture and religion is very naturistic with little concept of a personal God. Tribal and linguistic diversity isolates them from each other and from the gospel. For example, the Navajos are one of the largest groups (about 200,000 out of 1.8 million), but few missionaries have really mastered the language.[7]

But the most serious factor is the alienation resulting from the outrageous treatment by the white man. Johnstone has put it well:

Native Americans have suffered intensely in their encounter with centuries of European immigrants. They have lost almost all their lands, their self-respect and much of their culture, and they still face prejudice and insensitivity to their plight. Poverty, disease and unemployment are common among those on Indian reservations and among the 50% or so who have migrated to the cities. There is a vigorous movement across the country to revive the indigenous culture; this is successfully demanding the honouring of treaties protecting Indian lands and rights that have rarely been kept by the government in the past.[8]

Of the 300 languages which have been identified, only about 50 are in common use today. Parts of the Bible are available in 35 languages, New Testaments are available in six, and the whole Bible is only in Navajo. Although over 40% of native Americans consider themselves christianized, probably only 3 to 5% are evangelical Christians. The Southern Baptists and the Assemblies of God have the largest evangelical ministries, with about 500 churches between them. Also there are 22 interdenominational agencies with over 300 missionaries and 26 churches. There is a dearth of Indian pastors for those churches.[9]

The needs among native Americans remain exceedingly great, whether spiritual, moral, economic, educational, or social. It has been suggested that the most strategic ministry today is to train indigenous Christian workers for church planting and development.

Afro-Americans

In view of the abysmal treatment of black people by professing Christians, it is astonishing that there are as many Christians among Afro-Americans as there are. Nevertheless, only about sixty percent of Afro-Americans are affiliated with any Protestant church, with active involvement considerably less. It is very difficult to appraise the percentage who are actually born-again Evangelicals because many black churches have a different agenda in which evangelism in the classic sense is not a high priority. In many cases (as in far too many white churches) baptism is taken as a synonym for salvation. Thus the stereotype of Afro-Americans as Bible-believing Christians is far from accurate.

Liberalism has made extensive penetration into the black pastorate, especially since most evangelical colleges and seminaries were closed to blacks until recent decades. Moveover, at present only a quarter of black seminarians are in evangelical institutions. Just as with white churches there has been a paradigm shift in the last century (as explained in chs. 10 & 11). Although in white churches there was a significant separatist movement which has re-established an evangelical base, both as to churches, denominations, and institutions, in the Afro-American community no such movement exists. So although a century ago Lawrence Jones' statement that "blacks were clearly at one with the dominant religious community in affirming the divine inspiration of the Bible,"[10] today such is not the case. A number of organizations have been formed to reinforce an evangelical stance in the black community: the National Black Evangelical Association in 1963, the Mission Association of Negro Evangelicals, and the Fundamental Baptist Fellowship Association.

Further complicating the situation in black churches is the institutionalization. Parvin states, "It has so many auxiliary programs that the people become too busy to have time for evangelism."[11] Black evangelical leaders have varying opinions about the evangelical credentials of the average black church, but probably all would agree with Richard Mattox that the churches are in the main untaught and unaware that they should be evangelizing.[12] William L. Banks states it bluntly: "A black person even now has to prayerfully seek a local assembly which is without gospel jazz, fashion shows, money-raising gimmicks, and condoned immorality, and positively speaking, a church which stresses clean living, preaching of the Word, and the saving blood of Jesus Christ! To find such an assembly is no easy task."[13]

Missions to Afro-Americans. Considering the size of the Afro-American community, relatively little missions outreach has been carried on, either historically or currently. Howard Jones points up the fault: "If white fundamentalist and evangelical churches would have been just as dedicated in evangelizing black America and other non-Caucasians as they have been in evangelizing the great masses of people on the mission fields abroad, America would probably be a different nation today."[14] The proof of the failure can be seen in the growth of Islam among Afro-Americans and in the horrendous social problems in the inner city. The white flight from the urban scene reflected the churches' failure to win their neighbors of different ethnicity and to make an effort to achieve the multiethnic ideal represented by the Antioch church (Acts 11:19-26; 13:1-3). There are a number of churches which have succeeded, but they are far too few in number. (My experience in a multiethnic urban church shows that racial fears are unjustified.) Now missions to the Afro-American community are farther behind than if they had started a generation or two ago. Despite the successes of integration in American society, the sense of alienation, anger, and frustration in a large segment of the black community is a major obstacle to evangelization.

How then can the task be accomplished? Are whites disqualified from involvement? A generation ago Tom Skinner addressed that question directly. He said that white Christians who come with a condescending attitude cannot be effective. "When a white man approaches the Negro in honest friendship, Christian love and understanding sympathy, there will be good communications and results."[15] In addition he points out that white Christians need to support black evangelists and ministries targeting their own community.

One of the outstanding strategic issues is whether our energy should be focused on bringing more Afro-Americans into integrated churches or on the other hand, on going into the black community to evangelize and strengthen the black churches. Undoubtedly both should be done simultaneously because of internal subcultural differences within the Afro-American community. It is helpful to distinguish at least three black groups in America: those who are culturally black, those who fit into white culture, and the West Indian and African immigrants who have their own distinct cultures and/or languages.

Hispanic Americans

The Hispanic population of the USA is officially about ten percent of the total population, but the many illegal immigrants raise that number to over eleven percent, or about 29 million (1998). There is great diversity among Hispanics, with the Mexican-Americans (or Chicanos) at about 45% of the total, the Central and South Americans (Latinos) at about 9%, Puerto Ricans about 8%, and Cubans at about 4%. In general we could say that the Chicanos are mostly located in the 150 miles north of the Mexican border, the Puerto Ricans in Metropolitan New York and New England, and the Cubans in southern Florida. They are a definable minority which is only partially integrating into the larger American society.

Most are nominally Roman Catholic and have in the main been neglected by evangelical churches, since it is estimated that only ten percent are Evangelicals, which is less than the proportion back home. Parvin says that "by and large they have been neglected by their own espoused Roman Catholic church and more particularly by the evangelical church. In the opinion of Luis Palau, a well-known Latin American evangelist, they are largely unevangelized."[16] This neglect by the Catholic church provides a strategic opportunity for evangelism since they are already defecting to other ideologies and cults. As in Latin America, so here over 80% don't attend the Catholic church. Pentecostals have been among the most successful in reaching Hispanic communities. Parvin gives a good summary:

> Missionary activity among the Hispanics is widespread, but uncoordinated and scattered. Although most denominations have some Hispanic ministry, it has been limited primarily to the Baptist and the Pentecostals. The Southern Baptists have established 1,400 churches, most of which have Hispanic pastors, serving a Christian community of 150,000. The American Baptists report 300 congregations. The Assemblies of God list over 700 groups, while the Church of God (Cleveland, TN) has a membership of

10,000 and the Church of the Nazarene claims 89 churches.[17]

As with other ethnic minorities, the strategic question arises as to ordering our priorities. Obviously, planting Hispanic churches is essential for reaching the majority who prefer Spanish over English or may have limited facility in English. Another approach has been to establish a Hispanic adult Sunday School class as the starting point for a ministry in an integrated church. First Baptist Church of Flushing, NY has done this effectively. Alternatively we see an increasing number of bilingual Hispanics coming into English-speaking congregations, which does move toward the ideal. But in the meanwhile a distinct Hispanic outreach is essential. This will take missionaries who are fluent in the language and conversant with the culture. It is most strategic to use returned missionaries from Spanish-speaking countries in North American ministry. In addition, new missionaries should be recruited for local Hispanic church-planting work. In some cases Hispanic pastors have banded together to form a church-planting agency. This can also include area evangelistic crusades.

Spanish-language gospel radio programs are proving to be quite effective, both on Christian stations and networks and as broadcast on secular stations. Many denominations and interdenominational ministries have such programming. They concentrate, of course, in the areas in which there is a large Hispanic population.

Established ethnic groups

The designation of an ethnic group as 'established' doesn't tell the whole story since there is frequently a continuing immigration. Let us look first at those ethnic groups which have a long history of immigration. In such ethnic groups there are people in three stages: the new immigrants, those in a transitional phase, and those who are well established and settled into the American cultural mosaic. But frequently those in the cultural ghetto may either be new or long-term residents who are not integrating.

It is estimated that there are well over eleven million ethnic people in the USA, over and above the three large minorities we have already considered.[18] It is clear that the mission field has come to us today. Twenty years ago Don Bjork could say, "the sheer number and kind of newcomers is outpacing timely and effective response from existing churches and agencies. Most of the present waves of newcomers are from cultural groups previously unserved by home missions and churches of North America. Foreign missions have the intercultural expertise to reach them."[19] This statement is even more relevant today. The diversity of ethnic groups is expanding.

Jewish-Americans. Jews were among the earliest immigrants to the New World. When Roger Williams came to Baptist convictions and founded Providence, Rhode Island as a religiously tolerant refuge, Jews found that refuge. Many waves of Jews have come over the centuries: the Marranos from Spain and Portugal, from the European ghettos and from Russia in the last century, from Hitler's Germany, from Cuba, from the Middle East, and most recently from the former Soviet Union. Now there are about seven million in America, whose ancestors, and in many cases themselves, fled from anti-Semitism. They are an urban people, with over a million in New York City alone.

The question of 'who is a Jew?' makes it difficult to categorize them. The state of Israel has not resolved it. The reason is that the majority of American Jews are nonreligious. And the Orthodox do not accept Reform and Conservative Jews as being true Jews, and none accept Messianic Jews as true Jews. So from one point of view they are an ethnic group, but the religious identification is also essential. Ultimately, the apostle Paul made it clear that the only true Jew is the Messianic Jew (Rom. 2:17-29). Because of the persecution of Jews by professing Christians over the centuries, most Jews are not open to the gospel of the Messiah (cf. Ch. 13). We have already noted the failure of the Protestants to evangelize Jews. It was not until 1809 that the **Society for Promoting Christianity Amongst the Jews** was founded in London. And here it was not until 1885 that the **Chicago Hebrew Mission** (now the American Messianic Fellowship) was formed, followed in a decade by the **American Board of Missions to the Jews** (now Chosen People Ministries). With the revival of the premillennial view that Israel still has a place in the plan of God, many other agencies have been founded since then, most of them relatively small. The founding of **Jews for Jesus** in 1973 by Moishe Rosen was most significant, not only because it has become the second largest agency, but especially because it popularized a culturally sensitive approach to Jewish people. There is significant controversy as to how far to press this contextualized approach, but it has undoubtedly been a move in the right direction. There is no question that far more Jews are turning to Christ than fifty years ago, and some estimate that there are a hundred thousand Hebrew Christians in North America.

Chinese-Americans. A very conservative number for the Americans of Chinese descent would be 1,700,000. Some recent reports put the number much higher. Chinese began to immigrate to the west coast in great numbers in the middle of the last century. From 1882 to 1943 they were excluded by law. Since then there has been a continuing flow, both of legal and illegal immigrants. The events of the last half century in mainland China and Hong Kong have accelerated the flow. Although there are large Chinatowns in Manhattan, San Francisco, and Vancouver (with another developing in Brooklyn), most Chinese-Americans live out in the suburbs, and their academic successes are well known.

Although there are at least 1,000 Chinese churches (including 200 in Canada), they are far from reaching the whole community. The rapidly growing, more affluent American-born Chinese (ABCs) are not being effectively evangelized. Indeed, many of the ABC young people who attend church are more interested in education and good jobs than in Christian ministries. In addition, many of the new illegal immigrants do not understand English or a dialect used by a Chinese church nearby . In 1972 Chinese evangelical leaders formed the North American Congress of Chinese Evangelicals (NACOCE), and a number of other organizations were established to encourage and coordinate outreach. Unquestionably, mission organizations from the majority community need to work with these indigenous ministries to accelerate the evangelism.

Japanese-Americans. Japanese farmers first came to the west coast after 1885. Today there are upward of 3½ million Japanese-Americans, including a million in Hawaii. This would include many Japanese citizens who are here for business. Like the Japanese of the homeland, the immigrants are highly literate, and earn more than the average American. Other concentrations would be found in Los Angeles, and Ft. Lee, New Jersey. Most Japanese are Shinto/Buddhists and like Japanese in the homeland are little evangelized. Probably relatively little is being done to reach Japanese-Americans.

French-speaking Americans. The French were among the earliest explorers and settlers in North America. So it is not surprising that there are upward of ten million French-speaking people here, eight million in Canada, a million in New England, over a million Cajuns in Louisiana, and 300,000 Creole-speaking Haitians. Many of these are bilingual, almost all would be nominal Catholics, and very few would be evangelical Christians. Quebec has been called one of the least evangelized areas of North America. The same could probably be said of Cajun country. There are perhaps one hundred French evangelical churches in Canada, but just a few in Cajun country. However, among Haitian immigrants there is a fairly strong evangelical movement, since missions to Haiti proper have been quite fruitful.

Other European Immigrants. Today there are perhaps a million Portuguese-Americans concentrated in New England, New York, Newark, NJ, and California. There are also over a million Portuguese-speaking Brazilians. There are some evangelical churches, but little information is available. There are also several million Slavic-Americans from Eastern Europe. Both groups would be mainly Roman Catholic and relatively underevangelized.

New ethnic/religious groups from Asia/Africa

The mosaic of peoples flooding into our country in recent decades is difficult to simplify, analyze, or quantify. Perhaps a focus on their religious identity will best cut through the complexity. First we need to make a few observations. There are two possible ways of reaching these new immigrants, either through local church outreach or through missionaries especially dedicated to this ministry. Because of the language barrier it is highly unlikely that any local church can be effective in reaching these groups. This is because of the immigrants' lack of facility in English in general, heightened by the even more limited understanding of English by the wives. When we remember how a century ago most European immigrants were evangelized in their mother tongues, this is easy to grasp. Additionally, most of the European immigrants included large number of evangelical Christians, who then started churches among them. This is not the case with the current flow of immigrants. Few are professing Christians. Furthermore, even missionaries have a difficult time unless they learn the language. In some cases the missionary learned the language while working on the foreign field. In other cases it may be necessary for the missionary to go abroad to learn the language. (This is the present policy of the North America field of International Missions, Inc.)

One of the tremendous advantages of reaching these immigrant peoples is the incredibly strong linkage they maintain with their home country. This has a twofold advantage: it frequently gives the missionary abroad contacts for friendship evangelism, the relatives of their contacts here at home. Furthermore, converts here can become effective witnesses to their relatives and friends back home.

Muslims. The day is fast coming when there will be more Muslims than Jews in North America, if it has not already happened. Current totals run about six million. Not all are immigrants, since over 40% are Afro-Americans. About one-fourth are from South Asia: India, Pakistan, Bangladesh. The next largest group is from the Middle East: Iranians, Turks, Egyptians, Palestinians, Jordanians, etc., and then a concentration from the Muslim areas of West Africa: Nigeria, etc. There are easily over a hundred different Muslim ethnic groups here in North America. The main concentrations are in New York City, northern New Jersey, Chicago, Los Angeles, and Washington, DC. For example, there are well over hundred mosques in the Chicago area, almost as many in metropolitan New York, and over a dozen in Paterson, NJ alone, for a total of 1200.

Hindus. Even more recent than the Muslim immigrants are the Hindus, mostly Gujaratis from India, although many other linguistic groups of India are represented as well. The heaviest concentrations are in the metro New York area, including northern New Jersey. There are several hundred thousand Hindus in North America, but no accurate census figures are available. The Harvard Pluralism Project discovered some 400

Hindu temples in North America, and as I write, the largest one of all has just been consecrated in Bridgewater, NJ. There is a large annual Indian (Hindu) festival in Middlesex county, where at least 65,000 Indians live. The India parade in Manhattan annually draws over 100,000 people. There are very few missionaries to these Hindus.

Sikhs. Sikhs are the followers of a sixteenth century Hindu reformer named Guru Nanak, who being influenced by Islam and impressed with the hypocrisy of both the Hindus and Muslims of northwest India, developed a syncretistic religion with over 20 million adherents, mostly in the Punjab of India. Over 350,000 Sikh immigrants are scattered over North America, from Vancouver (200,000), Toronto (80,000), with significant numbers in Washington, DC, New York, California, New Mexico, Oregon, etc. There have been some outstanding Sikh converts to Christ, such as Sadhu Sunder Singh (around WW I) and Bakht Singh, who was converted in Canada in the 1930s. There are some scattered ministries to the Sikh immigrants, but obviously much more needs to be done.

Buddhists. In addition to the Japanese immigrants already referred to, there are upward of one million other Buddhists in North America: Koreans, Vietnamese, Laotians, Thais, Cambodians, and Tibetans, with 1500 temples. As a consequence of the strong Christian movement in Korea, the Korean-Americans may well be the most evangelized recent ethnic group. Korean churches are numerous, the majority Presbyterians meeting in Anglo church buildings, and there is a great missionary interest among them. There seems to be little missions ministry among the other Buddhist ethnic peoples. Contrariwise, some of the Buddhist sects have been very active in making converts among Asian-Americans.

QUASI-CHRISTIAN RELIGIONS AND CULTS

Roman Catholics

Evangelical Christians have seriously neglected their responsibility to reach Roman Catholics with the gospel of God's grace. They are the largest religious group in North America (about 80 million), and yet there are only a few struggling agencies focusing on reaching them. Granted that today many Catholics are being reached directly by local churches, but in a real sense they are our largest North American mission field.

Since the Vatican II Council (1962-5), Catholics worldwide have been far more open to the gospel. Indeed, Catholics are being exposed to the Bible far more in their own churches. They are even singing some of our evangelical songs. But the vast majority of them still do not know Christ personally. Unfortunately many Evangelicals have not been willing to admit that Catholics are a mission field. Now the issue has been muddied even more by the Evangelical and Catholics Together (ECT) consultation, in which twenty key leaders from each side have made a statement on common doctrine, which they have all signed. What the evangelical leaders have naively overlooked are the many Catholic doctrines not mentioned in the document which directly contradict evangelical faith (cf. ch. 13). Even Parvin's *Missions in North America* only devotes half a page to work among Catholics. We need to wake up to our responsibility.

Eastern Orthodox Americans.

Greek and Russian Orthodox Americans represent about three percent of the population, or more than eight million people. Most of what has been said about Roman Catholics applies to the Orthodox as well. The tragedy is that we do not have missions to the Orthodox. As we noted in chapter 13, Orthodoxy never had a reformation movement of significance. It may well be that its very mystical, esoteric approach to the faith has left the Orthodox farther from a personal relationship with Christ. This is another great area of concern.

Cultic Groups

About four percent of North Americans are in one of the 358 marginal, cultic religious groups, which means about eleven million people. The largest by far are the Mormons, with about ten million worldwide and somewhat less than half of that here. Their use of young short-term missionaries has made them one of the fastest-growing religious groups in the world. Unfortunately, they find millions of biblically ignorant nominal Christians as plums ripe for the picking. Von Baalen once said that the cults are the unpaid debts of the church, and this is certainly true.

The Jehovah's Witnesses are way behind the Mormons, with less than a million adherents, in part caused by their continuing fiascos of predicting the kingdom to begin, most recently in 1975. But they, like the Mormons, follow a biblical method of evangelism, door-to-door witness (Acts 20:20), while proclaiming a cultic heresy. True Christians need to take back the biblical methodology which the cultists have usurped. Indeed, we need to become more aggressive in missions to the cultists. Encouragingly, a growing number of churches and agencies are doing so with considerable success.

There are hundreds of other quasi-Christian cults. Christian Science has been in decline. The Unification Church of Sun Myung Moon stands at about one-half million adherents. The one million Seventh Day Adventists are hard to classify. Although years ago some specialists felt that they should be recognized as essentially evangelical, my experience shows that they are very diverse. Some Adventists seem to be trusting in the blood of Christ for salvation, and some seem to be trusting in their law-keeping. The offshoot Worldwide Church of God, founded by Herbert W. Armstrong, has moved to a more evangelical stance since his death. There are many organizations providing materials and services for witness to cultists.

OCCULT RELIGIOUS GROUPS

It is hard to classify the various occult groups, which have exploded in recent years. Astrology, witchcraft, new age, Scientology, satanism, and Spiritualists are the most numerous. Then there are many which more directly can be traced to Asian religions, such as Bahai, Hare Krishna, Divine Light Mission, Transcendental Meditation, etc. Evangelical Christians have responded with significant literature exposing the errors of these groups, but much more needs to be done to liberate their adherents through the gospel.

INSTITUTIONAL/SPECIAL MINISTRIES

Prison/Jail ministries. Ministry to prisoners requires a special focus since they tend to be a subculture within themselves, out of reach of most churches and in fact mostly unchurched. The number of prisoners is escalating currently to about 1.6 million, with five million passing through the penal system annually. Scripture enjoins us to "remember the prisoners, as though in prison with them" (Heb. 13:3), and prisoners are mentioned in both testaments 130 times. The Wesleys began to preach in the jails of England in 1730. Since then many prison ministries have been formed, the most famous being Prison Fellowship, founded by Chuck Colson. Many local churches and individuals are directly involved, with considerable impact. Another entre is through prison chaplaincy, although the burden of administrative work limits direct witness.

Institutions of mercy. There are a host of diverse institutions of mercy which provide great opportunity for witness. Rescue missions were among the earliest, and today there are about 250 such ministries to chemically-dependent people with about 1,500 workers. The **International Union of Gospel Missions** was founded in 1913 as a fellowship of such missions. The widespread alcohol and drug abuse has given such missions a growing responsibility.

Years ago the major ministry to abandoned children was in orphanages, but today most children in children's homes have been either abused or abandoned. Some are special needs children, such as the handicapped or retarded. Only a small percentage of child-care facilities are run by evangelical Christians, and little is being done to reach those in the other institutions. Institutions ministering to the handicapped work with both adults and children. Many involve camps and ranches.

Local churches tend to be heavily involved in nursing-home ministries and in a whole spectrum of homes for those with different levels of medical need. About eight percent of seniors are in such homes.

Ministries to distinct categories of people. There are a great number of people who are best reached in their unique situations. This would include the military, the educational community, children, mobile people, and bikers (motorcyclists).

Military personnel number about two million in North America, with family members near bases making the total field over five million. During World War II a number of agencies were formed to focus on the military; **Christian Servicemen's Centers** (1941), the **Navigators** (1933), **Officers' Christian Fellowship** (1943), **Overseas Christian Servicemen's Centers** (1954, now Cadence, Int.), and many others. These organizations have had a great impact since service people have proved to be quite open to the gospel witness.

College-student ministry began in England in 1877 with the Cambridge Inter-Collegiate Christian Union. From there **InterVarsity Christian Fellowship** was brought into Canada in 1928 and into the USA in 1938. As this student movement spread worldwide, the International Fellowship of Evangelical Students was organized. Subsequently the **Navigators** expanded its ministry to the college campus, and in 1951 Bill Bright founded **Campus Crusade for Christ. International Students, Inc.** (1953) has a more clearly cross-cultural focus since it is a ministry to the half-million foreign students here, with 137 missionaries to 278 campuses.

Ministries to students in high schools includes Young Life, Youth for Christ, Word of Life, Hi-BA Clubs, etc. At lower levels the Bible Club Movement, Child Evangelism Fellowship, Boys Brigade, Pioneer Girls, and Awana have effective ministries, usually connected to the local church.

GEOGRAPHIC MINISTRIES

Rural/mountain ministries. The one-quarter of North Americans who live in rural areas are a vast mission field because rural churches are struggling to survive and many communities do not have an evangelical church. The **American Sunday School Union** (now American Missionary Fellowship) was founded in 1871 to reach this field. The Southern Baptist Convention has been very active in rural church planting. Now there are dozens of agencies focusing on rural and mountain areas: American Mission for Opening Churches, Village Missions, and Rural Home Missionary Association, among the larger ones.

Urban ministries. Most urban ministry is really ethnic ministry which we have already discussed. This is a result of the 'white flight' to the suburbs, the migration of rural southern blacks, and the accelerating flow of immigrants and refugees. Tragically, the white churches fled to the suburbs, thus failing to reach their geographic constituency (responsibili-ty?). In addition, many of the urban churches have gone liberal or be-come ineffective because of entrenched leadership. Urban church-plan-ing ministries are desperately needed to fill the gap.

Alaska and Hawaii. Alaska has been recognized as a mission field for some time because of the significant number of Eskimos, Indians, and Aleuts there. But the majority population is also in the main un-churched, at most ten percent evangelical. Although Hawaii has a longer history of missionary activity, only two percent of its population are Chris-tians. It is a uniquely diverse interracial society, 74% Asian in character. The churches of Hawaii do not seem to be strong and evangelistically in-clined.

CONCLUSION

It is obvious from this brief overview that home missions needs and activities are so diverse that vast pockets of unreached and minimally reached people are to be found all over North America.

---

1. A. Earl Parvin, *Missions USA* (1985), p. 12.
2. Ibid, p. 15.
3. Parvin, "Missions in North America" (1997), p. 1/3.
4. Parvin, *Missions USA*, pp. 18-20.
5. Ibid, p. 30.
6. Parvin, "North America," pp. 2/7,8.
7. Parvin, *Missions USA*, pp. 45-7.
8. Johnstone, *Operation World,* 5th ed., p. 566.
9. Parvin, *Missions USA*, pp. 59-65.
10. Lawrence A. Jones, "They Sought a City," cited by Parvin, p. 93.
11. Ibid, p. 93-4.
12. Quoted in Ibid, p. 94.
13. Quoted by Melvin C. Banks, "The Black Sunday School: Its Strengths, Its Needs," *Christianity Today*, July 1974, p. 10.
14. Howard Jones, "The Black Church in America," *The Good News Broadcaster*, March 1973, p. 9.
15. Tom Skinner, *Black and Free* (GR: Zondervan, 1968), pp. 139-40.
16. Cited in *Missions USA*, p. 108.
17. Parvin, "Missions in North America," p. 5/10.
18. Johnstone, *Operation World*, p. 563.
19. Don Bjork, "Reaching Newcomers in North America," a paper presented at joint NAE/EFMA conference, Orlando, March 1979.

"... the church began in Asia. Its earliest history, its first centers were Asian. Asia produced the first known church building, the first New Testament translation, perhaps the first Christian king, the first Christian poets, and even arguably the first Christian state."

~Samuel Hugh Moffett

16

ASIA: THE FIRST AND VASTEST CHALLENGE

Asia is in many ways the most fascinating of the world continents. Even though it is a continent of great ancient civilizations, Europeans for centuries in the Medieval period were vastly ignorant of Asia. In the age of exploration Europeans began to explore the mysteries of this vast and intriguing continent. As more became known, God stirred up missionary pioneers to penetrate Asia with the gospel of Christ. Response has been uneven: some of the most evangelized and some of the most unevangelized peoples on the face of the earth are found in Asia. Asia cannot be ignored. With the economic and technological rise and recent crisis of the Pacific rim nations (Japan, Korea, Taiwan, Hong Kong, Singapore), Westerners are being forced to come to terms with Asia. As Christians, especially, we too must come to terms with the great spiritual need of Asia. Let us get an overview of Asia before we examine penetration of the gospel on this continent.

THE DISTINCTIVES OF ASIA

Continent of ancient civilizations

It would be very difficult to prove which of the great Asian civilizations was the earliest. But of this we can be sure: the most ancient civilizations were planted in Asia up to five thousand years ago. Chinese civilization is undoubtedly very ancient and continuous up to the present. Evidences of even older civilization in Vietnam have recently been uncovered.[1] Archaeological remains of the ancient Indus River civilization in Pakistan of the Indian subcontinent have long been excavated and point to a time before 1500 B.C. Closer to Old Testament history were the ancient Mesopotamian civilizations out of which Abram came and the ruins of Ebla in Syria which clearly predate Abram's day.

Chinese repugnance for foreigners is attributable to their pride in their ancient civilization, as Kane points out:

> So far as the Chinese were concerned there was only one
> civilized country in the world, the Middle Kingdom. All others
> were beyond the pale of civilization; hence they were called "bar-
> barians." China's civilization reached its highest point during the
> Dark Ages, when the lights all over Europe were going out.
> Changan, the capital of the T'ang Dynasty, was probably the most
> sophisticated city in the world of that day. With such a history and
> such a civilization, China can be forgiven if she entertained ideas
> of her own greatness.[2]

The most populous continent

Although greater Asia encompasses one-third of the world's land area,
unevenly compressed into that land mass is about five-eights of the
world's population. Six of the world's eight most populous nations are in
Asia: China and India alone comprise one-third of the world's population.
Many of the world's greatest cities are in Asia: Tokyo, the largest;
Shanghai, Bombay, Calcutta, and others are right behind. Although Asia
is still mostly rural, its cities are mushrooming in the urbanization so
common in two-thirds-world countries. And overall, population is
growing at an alarming rate. One striking factor in the population mosaic
of Asia is the large number of overseas Chinese who are scattered
through the countries of Southeast Asia, in countries like Singapore,
Malaysia, the Philippines, Indonesia, etc.

That population, however, is not evenly distributed because of the vast
areas of mountain and desert in Asia. The Himalayas are the vastest and
highest mountain chain in the world. Reaching out from the Tibetan
triangle are massive spurs running down into Southeast Asia and
Afghanistan in the West. These areas are more lightly populated, but the
mountains have provided a barrier which isolates the cultures in the
different areas of Asia and explains their great differences.

Home of the major world religions

All of the major world religions originated in Asia, and even though
some have shifted in their area of dominance, all are still prominent in
Asia. As we have surveyed in the previous section, Hinduism is the
dominant religion of India, with some influence in Southeast Asia. Out of
it arose Buddhism in India, which has become the dominant religion of
all of eastern Asia in its two major forms. Confucianism and Taoism are
native to China and Shinto to Japan. Islam is the 'Johnny-come-lately' of
Asian religions, arising in the Arabian peninsula about A.D. 610 and
spreading east all the way to Indonesia and the Philippines.

These religions have had a tremendous hold upon their adherents—
much more so than that of Animism upon tribal populations. Being

considered more 'developed' religions, their complex philosophies and strongly enculturated religious practices, have made them dominant features in the life of most Asians. The result is that it has been much more difficult for the gospel of Christ to penetrate these cultures over the centuries. However, today there are a number of factors which are beginning to make more Asians open to the gospel as never before. We will discuss them below.

Continent of incredible change and contrast

Rudyard Kipling could not have been more wrong when he wrote, "East is East and West is West, and never the twain shall meet!" The fact is that Asia is westernizing and changing at a rapid rate. Don Hoke testified from personal experience:

> After twenty-one years in Asia, I feel that particularly in the growing urban centers we are witnessing the spread of a great, gray, materialistic, secular uniculture across the entire continent. Jet down into any city of Asia and the sights are the same: glaring neon advertisements (usually of Japanese products!); movies from every country of the world (many of them pornographic); standard-looking taxis, clothing, recreation and central shops. . . .under the surface lies the same meaninglessness, the same search for pleasure, the same indifference to old religions (except for marriage and death ceremonies), the same practical agnosticism, and the same openness toward Western "improvements." This is the real Asia of today.[3]

Much of the change has been fueled by the economic and technological revolution of the Pacific rim countries: Japan, Korea, Taiwan, Hong Kong, and Singapore. This has resulted in vast contrasts in Asia economically and technologically. At the opposite end of the spectrum is Bangladesh, once referred to as a "basket case among nations" because of the overpopulation, poverty, lack of resources, and dim future of that nation. The Philippines is struggling to come out of the mismanagement and exploitation of the dictatorial former Marcos regime and experiencing grinding poverty and political, religious, and social upheaval. Even within one country, like India, one finds incredible contrast between the wealth of a few and the poverty of the many. This is especially evident in the great cities.

Politically also Asia is undergoing vast change. From the dominance of the colonial powers in the earlier part of the century, many Asian nations have become independent. But mainland China has gone through thirty-five years of xenophobic and doctrinaire Communism, followed now by a more open and western-leaning Communistic government for over a decade. Hong Kong and Macao are looking forward (with great trepidation) to becoming part of that picture in 1997.

The Indo-Chinese countries of Vietnam, Laos, and Cambodia (Kampuchea) are in their third decade under fanatical Communist rule and warfare to determine which kind of Communists will dominate. Afghanistan rebels struggled to throw off the oppression and genocide of their Communist Russian masters, and in doing so millions became refugees. The overthrow of the Shah of Iran and the rise of Muslim 'Fundamentalism' (really legalism) resulted in a disastrous war with Iraq, with millions of casualties in the process. Relatively speaking only the Indian subcontinent seems to be relatively less changing. But especially in the great cities change is very evident, as are the contrasts.

Scene of colonialism's demise

In all of Asia only Japan, Thailand, Afghanistan, and Iran escaped totally from being made colonies of some Western empire. Even Japan was forced to open up to foreign trade by Commodore Perry and came under American military rule after World War II. And recently Afghanistan had its 'imperial lords'. Some colonial governments were relatively enlightened and left a legacy of governmental infrastructure (laws, courts, railroads, postal systems, etc.) that continues to this day. Residents in the countries of the Indian subcontinent are sometimes heard to say, "We had it better under the British." But the departure of most of the colonial powers was not mourned by their erstwhile subjects. Whether hated or appreciated, the colonial impact upon Asia is irreversible. The dominance of the British Empire established English as the closest thing to a world language today, with French running quite far behind. The impact of Western education upon the intelligentsia of Asia has also brought about irreversible changes. As Hoke noted, Western materialism has undermined the religious allegiance of many Asians. For example, Muslim college students in many parts of the Muslim world are far less likely to say their prayers and attend the mosque for Friday prayers. This gives great opportunity for the entrance of the gospel.

Continent of 'hidden frontiers'

It was in the 1974 Lausanne Congress of World Evangelism that Ralph Winter first emphasized the 'hidden frontiers' of missions among the over three billion Chinese, Hindus, and Muslims who are not effectively being reached for Christ by missionaries or living churches. (We could well add Theravada Buddhists and Shintoists to this list.) All of these are dominant in Asia. Others have taken his analysis and made it a watchword of missionary effort. Indeed, new mission organizations with words like 'frontiers' and 'pioneers' in their names have been established with these new frontiers in mind. So not only is Asia the most populous continent, but it is also the continent with the greatest number of unreached people by far. This is not to say that these people do not know the name of Christ or could not hear the gospel somewhere (even on the radio). Winter has been saying that they cannot hear the gospel in a culturally understandable way from an effective cross-cultural witness. They have no contact with Christians. Thus they are not being effectively reached for Christ. A few are turning to Christ here and there, but the cultural and geographical barriers are still very great. This fact now moves us to consider the realities of gospel penetration in Asia up to the present.

GOSPEL PENETRATION IN ASIA

Early evangelism in Asia

Did Christianity penetrate Asia in the days of the Apostles? Although the Mar Thoma Church of India has the tradition of being founded by the Apostle Thomas, this is controversial. Don Hoke is positive, "But a careful review of the historical evidence now inclines me to believe that it is at least 50 percent likely that the church of Christ was initially planted in India, Turkestan, Afghanistan, Mongolia, and probably Tibet within the first two centuries of the Christian era."[4] The early evangelization of Persia (Iran) is quite clear. The Syrian churches (wrongly called Nestorian?) undoubtedly did reach on into South India in early centuries. We also know that these churches did send missionaries into China in the seventh century as proved by the Changan stone stele, dated A.D. 781. The church was not influential, and was repressed by the Emperor Wu Tsung by decree of A.D. 845.[5] Did it not survive because of a weak view of the person of Christ? We can only guess.

Actually Christianity came to China on four distinct occasions, and only the fourth succeeded. The second was the attempt of the Franciscans under John of Monte Corvino about 1294. Although there were about 100,000 converts, after the missionaries were expelled by the Ming rulers in 1368, the churches disappeared. The third attempt was by Jesuit missionary Matteo Ricci in 1601. As many as a quarter million were converted, but a century later the pope's intervention in a dispute over the proper name for God offended the Emperor, who then began persecution of Christians and expulsion of missionaries. The fourth was the modern evangelization by Protestant and Catholic missionaries, which has been relatively successful.

Modern evangelization of Asia

Asia was also the field first penetrated by both Roman Catholic and Protestant missionaries in modern times (see chs. 8 & 9). Little known was the founding of a small Protestant church in Molucca by Dutch Protestants in the early sixteenth century.[6] Jesuit missionaries began to penetrate Asia in 1540, outstanding among whom was Francis Xavier. They made converts in India, China, Japan and Indonesia. They were followed by other Dutch Calvinist chaplains in the East Indies and Ceylon by the end of the sixteenth century. Most of the great Protestant pioneers started work in Asia: the Danish-Halle Mission in south India, William Carey in the Bengal of northeast India; Adoniram Judson in Burma, Henry Nott in the South Sea Islands, and Robert Morrison in China.

THE RELIGIOUS STATUS OF MAJOR ASIAN COUNTRIES

COUNTRY	Population 1995	Professing Christ'n %	Evangel- icals %	Majority Religion
China	1135.5	6.1	5.0	Non-religious
India	853.4	3.9	1.0	Hinduism
Indonesia	181.3	12.6	4.5	Islam
Japan	123.5	1.6	0.3	Shinto/Buddhism
Pakistan	122.7	1.7	0.2	Islam
Bangladesh	115.6	0.4	0.1	Islam
Vietnam	67.2	9.8	0.8	Thera Buddhism
Philippines	62.4	88.5	5.1	Roman Cath.
Thailand	55.7	0.8	0.3	Thera Buddhism
5 CIS Reps.*	55.4	5.3	0.2	Islam
Korea, So.	44.9	34.6	21.1	Buddhism\Conf.
Myanmar	41.7	6.3	3.6	Thera Buddhism
Korea, N.	22.9	0.6	0.4	Non-religious
Taiwan	20.3	4.8	2.1	Multireligion
Nepal	19.1	0.6	0.6	Hinduism
Malaysia	17.3	7.3	3.1	Islam
Sri Lanka	17.2	7.6	0.4	Thera Buddhism
Afghanistan	16.6	0.0	0.0	Islam

*Uzbekistan, Kazakhstan, Tajikistan, Kyrgyzstan, Turkmenistan

The diversity of results

Considered overall, Asia has not been a particularly fruitful area for missions compared with Africa and Latin America. About 7 percent of Asia's population today are professing Christians; about 3.1 percent are Evangelicals. There has been a vast diversity of results, from a low of about 0.1 percent Evangelicals in Bangladesh to a high of 21 in South Korea. The largest concentrations of Evangelicals would be mainland China with roughly 57 million (according to recent reports); South Korea with 9.2; Indonesia with 8.2; south India with 8.5; and the Philippines with three million. With the exception of Myanmar (Burma), Hong Kong, Singapore, and Taiwan, most of Buddhist southeast Asia has significantly less than one percent Evangelicals.[7]

Looking into the mosaic of population within countries, we note a diversity of results. Muslims have been the least responsive; traditional (Theravada) Buddhists have also been hard to win in large numbers; upper caste Hindus have not been open; and Shinto seems to be the factor in hardening the Japanese to the gospel. Animistic tribes have, as elsewhere, generally been very responsive. Whether the Dani of New Guinea or the Nagas of northeast India, the response has been overwhelming. Outcaste Hindus have also been very responsive. While response to the gospel in pre-Communist China was not great, the most recent good news is that disillusioned Communistic Chinese have been turning to Christ in great numbers in the last decade. Church growth in South Korea, somewhat uniquely for its setting, has been extremely encouraging. And centuries of Roman Catholicism in the Philippines seem to have broken the ground for the germination of the true word of God.

Why the unevenness of response?

Perhaps the diversity of Asia itself explains to some extent the diversity of results from missionary work there. However, there are many enigmas in the mosaic of response. Herbert Kane has given us an excellent analysis as to why Asia generally has not been highly productive. He cites five reasons for the paucity of results:

1. In this part of the world the Christian missionaries encountered ancient, well-developed civilizations. . . .

2. The Christian missionaries came into direct conflict with ancient, highly developed religious systems which antedated Christianity.

3. The missionaries encountered deep-seated, longstanding social and religious practices and prejudices which were inimical to the Christian gospel.

4. Christianity was closely identified with colonialism, and nobody liked colonialism.

5. The exclusiveness of Christianity made it unacceptable to the Asians.[8]

We have already discussed three of these factors in our survey of Asia's distinctives: civilizations, religions, and colonialism. Let us focus upon Kane's third and fifth points.

Ancient, deeply rooted socio-religious cultural practices

There are five main practices and beliefs which are most significant here: the caste system of Hinduism; karma of Hinduism and Buddhism; the ancestor worship of Chinese Confucian culture, which also influenced Korea and Japan; ethnocentric emperor worship of Japan; and laws of apostasy in Islamic lands. The last we shall discuss in a later chapter devoted to the Muslim world. The reader has already been introduced to the others in the preceding chapter. But let us clarify just what is involved.

The caste system. The caste system of Hinduism goes back to the Aryan invasions and conquest of the Indian subcontinent in the 1500 to 500 B.C. period. The caste system which began to develop at that time proved to be a valuable religious and cultural means by which the Aryans were able to maintain their dominance over the Dravidians. Hindu society is divided into the four main castes, with millions of untouchables below this caste structure. There are hundreds of subcastes as well. Hindus are locked into a particular caste for life as a consequence of a previous incarnation. Caste rigidly governs one's occupation, social status, marriage, and innumerable details of life. Different castes are viewed as distinct species, as distinct as animal species are from each other. Certainly the unity and equality of the human race is denied thereby.

The higher on the caste scale, the more a Hindu has to lose by becoming a Christian. If he has eons of merit (karma) accumulated in previous incarnations, that is a lot to give up to become a Christian. To make matters worse, since most Christians in India have come from lower caste and even untouchable background, the upper caste Hindu would have to swallow a lot of pride and prejudice to turn to Christ.

The irrevocable law of karma. Karma means the inevitable law of the consequences of human deeds. Sin is irreversible and unforgivable. Not only does this law govern Hindu philosophy and practice, but it is the major feature that Gautama the Buddha carried over into Buddhism as well. Although Buddhism does not have the caste system, the law of karma consistently followed leads to a fatalism and hopelessness in both Hinduism and Theravada (traditional) Buddhism. The consequence is that both caste Hindus and traditional Buddhists in southeast Asia have been historically hard to reach for Christ. Only among the broader Mahayana form of Buddhists in China and Korea has there been a substantial response to the Christian gospel. And in mainland China another factor had to be dealt with before millions began turning to Christ. That was ancestor worship.

Ancestor worship. Ancestor worship was already found in China before the sixth century B.C., when Confucianism and Taoism were founded. Confucius' teachings clearly reinforced it by emphasis upon 'filial piety'. It is not just living parents and grandparents who are to be revered, but also the dead. Thus for a Chinese Christian convert to stop ancestor worship is to disgrace the family, especially the ancestors. "For a son to neglect his father, living or dead, was to commit the unpardonable sin in the eyes of the Chinese."

Emperor worship. "The Japanese added emperor worship to ancestor worship and thereby compounded the difficulty."[9] Japanese Shinto
culture puts great stress upon ethnic and national identity. In the Shinto
scriptures, the Emperor is seen as a descendant of the gods. In a real
sense the Japanese themselves are seen as a divine, superior people. To
become a Christian is to deny all this heritage. With the defeat of Japan
in World War II, it was hoped that Shinto would decline and that
Japanese would be disillusioned with these ideas and turn to Christ.
Rather it would seem that the Japanese have drawn back within
themselves and tried to prove their superiority in another way. The
Japanese economic 'miracle' has not helped to turn people away from
this idolatrous ethnocentrism toward acknowledging their own sinfulness
and need of a transcendent Creator God.

The exclusiveness of Christianity

Generally speaking, the east Asian religions are very inclusivistic. Only
Islam makes strong exclusive claims like Christianity. But the monistic,
pantheistic religions like Hinduism and Buddhism tend to feel that no
one religion or school of religion has the whole truth. There are many
paths up Mt. Fuji and they all lead to the top. Hindus have no problem
accepting Jesus into their pantheon of deities along with Krishna and
even Gautama. Mahatma Gandhi saw the different religions as beautiful
flowers from the same garden or branches of the same majestic tree.
This is all possible because these religions tend to see man as good, not
sinful. So the idea of a unique salvation from sin and depravity is
repugnant to them.

Why such great success in some areas?

There is no easy answer to the unevenness of response to the gospel
in Asia. Missionaries have struggled over the centuries to understand the
factors. Modern missiologists have researched the evidence. Here are
some suggested answers:

Korea. The first Protestant church in Korea was planted just a
century ago in 1884. And yet within a century, 35 percent profess some
form of Christianity, 27 percent are Protestants, and 21 percent can be
counted as Evangelicals. The largest congregation in the world is in
Seoul (Full Gospel Central Church), and the largest Presbyterian and
Methodist congregations in the world are also there. Some campaigns
and rallies have drawn a record up to 2.7 million in one meeting (Explo
'74 and World Evangelization Crusade '80). The Billy Graham Crusade
was the greatest that Dr. Graham had ever experienced, with 4 million
attending in six cities. There are several theological seminaries with over
a thousand students each, and over 500 per year graduate from 38

seminaries.   Church growth seems to be continuing at an impressive rate.

This is all in contrast to Japan, less than 100 miles away, where only one-half percent are Protestants and only 0.3 percent are considered Evangelicals.   Both are predominantly Buddhist countries.   Why the striking difference?   Samuel H. Moffett, son of one of the pioneer Presbyterian missionaries, gives his helpful analysis:

> The most important reasons seem to have been a stress on people-to-people evangelism, Bible training for the entire church membership, the adaptation of the Nevius method (which pro-moted self-support, self-government and self-propagation), and the unique outpouring of the Holy Spirit in revival.   Presbyterians also strategically deployed their missionaries to take advantage of and to follow up areas of growth, . . .[10]

The contrasting church growth among the Presbyterians and Methodists would support Moffett's analysis.   It would also seem that Korean Buddhism and Confucianism were not as deep-rooted in the populace when Christianity arrived.   Animistic Shamanism was predominant and still is significant today.

Animistic peoples of Oceania, India, Burma, Laos, Taiwan, etc.   In our survey of the history of missions we noted the remarkable response to the gospel among some of the Animistic peoples of Burma and Oceania (the islands of the south Pacific).   That same phenomenon has occurred in numerous places around the world, including many in Asia. The Karen, Kachin, Lahu, Wa, and Lisu of Burma and the bordering areas of Laos and China were mentioned.   The Santal, the Nagas, the Mizos, of northeast India have turned to Christ in the majority (Nagaland is the only predominantly Baptist ethnic state in the world!). Approximately ten to thirty percent of Animistic peoples of the south Pacific are counted as Evangelicals (average 16%).   Many tribes of New Guinea have turned to Christ by the tens of thousands (both in Papua and Irian Jaya, Indonesia).

There are a number of factors which can be mentioned to account for the good response in this sector of Asia.   In some cases the fact that missionaries arrived early and persisted with great sacrifice explains a lot. In other productive areas, the missionaries arrived after the Second World War and have already seen unbelievable results.   There we note the same persistence and sacrifice, including martyrdom.   In Burma we saw the traditions of a Creator God and man's alienation from Him which contributed very significantly to the great response (also true in northeast Indian tribes).   Whatever the causes, we can praise God for this encouraging fruit.

The Philippines.   A unique situation in Asia is seen in the Philippine

Islands. This is the only Roman Catholic country in Asia, and is second only to Korea in the responsiveness of the people to the gospel. About five percent of the population may be counted as evangelical Christians out of 7.5 percent Protestants. The roots go back to 377 years of Spanish rule, during which the Catholic missionaries brought about a nominal conversion to Romanism. However, church attendance is very low because of the small number of priests. So when American rule began in 1898 and American Protestant missionaries began their work, the opportunity was incredible. Evangelical church growth did not really begin to mushroom until the '60s and '70s, however, but since then Filipino church growth has been most encouraging. A number of Filipino mission organizations have sent out 670 missionaries, 180 of which are in other lands. There are still many tribal peoples and about five million Muslim peoples who are unreached with the gospel, as well as the majority of nominal Catholics, who know very little about Christianity.

South India. In the Hindu environment of India, the two southern-most states of Kerala and Tamil Nadu have seen the greatest penetration of the gospel. This is partly because of the ancient Mar Thoma church and the early efforts of the Danish-Halle mission in that area. In Kerala over 20 percent are professing Christians. Although India is closed to new overt missionaries, and with most of the remaining ones already retired, few are left. However, a significant number of bi-professional workers (tentmakers) are making an impact. Even more encouraging are the thousands of south Indians who are going to the much needier areas of north India as missionaries. They are cross-cultural missionaries in the fullest sense since the languages and culture are quite different. In addition, tentmaker missionaries have been successful in coming in and planting churches. Gospel radio is also having a great impact, both from TWR Sri Lanka transmitter, but also from an exciting new central Asian location in Irkutsk.

Mainland China. The most thrilling story of modern times is the last decade of church growth in mainland China. How can we account for the fact that when the missionaries left after the Communist takeover in 1950 there were less than a million Protestants, while now the latest reports seem to indicate over 56 million Evangelicals? Clearly the excesses of the Maoist Communist government over most of those years were a major factor. An important part of the cultural revolution of the sixties was a crusade against all religion. Mao especially hated Confucianism as being antiquated and obsolete. Since almost all Chinese were adherents of the three religions, the Communist invective focused upon them. It is clear that Mao Zedong broke the back of the ancestor worship which was so ingrained in the Chinese culture. Just as God used the wicked Assyrians to judge the Israelites, so God used the wicked Communists to judge the multireligion of China. Knowledgeable

China watchers report that upon the death of Mao Zedong there was a disillusionment and spiritual vacuum in Red China, which began to be filled with the gospel. With the new freedoms that came in the ensuing years, pastors were let out of prison and saw house churches mushroom within a few months. Christians became bolder to witness. Missionary radio was beaming in from many directions. Bibles were smuggled in to be distributed to eager Christians. Many factors conspired together to bring about the incredible church growth. There is controversy, it is true, as to whether the right way is for the Christians to be in the government approved Three-Self churches or in the underground churches. But God is sovereign and is at work in many different structures in mainland China today. Although the government has abandoned Communism, it is still totalitarian and represses Christian witness. Not only are the house churches thriving, but tentmaker missionaries are able to have an effective witness in China today. And Hong Kong still retains the greater freedom they had before its return to the central government in 1997.

The big picture today

Despite the most encouraging progress in some areas, there are a number of significant concerns in Asia today, which Johnstone targets:

Areas of decline. For decades the church in Sri Lanka has been steadily going down as a percentage of the population—only recently reversed. Hong Kong is losing as many Christians through emigration as it is gaining through conversion. North India has a small Christian presence, but this is nominal and in decline in many areas. Pray for this to be reversed.

Nominalism. This has become a problem in some Christian communities in Indonesia, India, [Pakistan], Myanmar and Philippines; yet in these same countries many denominations are growing vigorously. Pray for revival.

Syncretism. Evangelical theological education has expanded as nowhere else in the world in east and southeast Asia. Theology is being indigenized and losing some of the Western emphases, but is in danger of compromise—in universalism, evolution and veneration of ancestors and other areas.

Persecution. The collapse of Communism in other parts of the world has less affected Asia. Persecution of all believers is still acute in North Korea and persecution of unofficial Christianity in China and Vietnam remains harsh. Persecution of Christian by Muslims in Indonesia, Pakistan, Malaysia and Brunei has increased during the '80s. Buddhists in Bhutan and Sri Lanka have stepped up pressure on Christians. There is greater freedom in Hindu Nepal, but persecution of Christians has increased in some areas of India.

Missions vision. This has grown spectacularly during the '80s. At first most of this vision was for unreached ethnic groups within their own nations (especially India, Philippines, Myanmar, Indonesia) or to their own ethnic communities in other lands (Japanese, Koreans and Chinese especially). However, this has changed and the cross-cultural foreign missionary force is growing fast.[11]

The unfinished task in Asia today

Little-evangelized areas. There are over a dozen areas or countries with less than one-half percent Evangelicals. Although India with its 850 million people has one percent Evangelicals overall, at least eleven states of India (mostly north) are in this very needy category (Bihar, Gujarat, Haryana, Himachal Pradesh, Jammu & Kashmir, Madhya Pradesh, Maharashtra, Punjab, Rajasthan, Uttar Pradesh, and Bengal). The five Asian Muslim republics of the former Soviet Union have differing Christian presence, but all are under half of a percent.[12] Starting from the virtually unevangelized countries in order they are: Afghanistan, Maldives, Mongolia, Bangladesh, Cambodia, Pakistan, Bhutan, Thailand, Japan, N. Korea, and Sri Lanka. We should also mention Laos, Nepal, and Vietnam as having less than 0.8 percent Evangelicals. There is a missionary presence moving into newly opened areas, esp. Mongolia, the five CIS republics, and Nepal. The many minorities of China, especially the Muslims of the northwestern provinces and the Buddhists of Tibet are especially needy. And other more limited-access countries desperately need creative 'tentmakers' to move in. A few are doing so, but far more are needed.

The hidden peoples. Since 1974 when Ralph Winter highlighted the "hidden peoples" of the Muslim world, the Hindus (especially upper castes), and the Buddhists as virtually unreached peoples, there has been some mobilization of personnel to reach these groups, The dissolution of the Soviet Union has given unprecedented opportunity to reach the Muslims of Central Asia. There has been a surge of interest, both on the part of prospective missionaries and mission boards, in Muslim work. But since Muslims have been neglected for so long, we have a long way to go to catch up.

Somehow interest in Hindu work has not caught fire. Perhaps the perception that all the Hindus are in India and that India is a "closed country" has dampened enthusiasm. In fact, there are vast numbers of reachable Hindus here in many western countries, as well as Africa and Asia. In addition, there are opportunities for tentmakers in Northern India and for creative partnerships with south Indian missions to the North.[13]

You will notice many Buddhist nations among the least reached. We have already pointed out the difficulty of reaching Theravada Buddhists in southeast Asia, but the Lamaistic Buddhists of Bhutan, Mongolia and former Tibet are also gospel-deprived. And although Protestant missions first arrived in Japan in 1858, it is still a lightly evangelized country, especially outside the major cities.[14]

Summary and perspective

It is unquestionable that the greatest challenges for world evangelism today are in Asia, both as far as great populations and lightly evangelized areas are concerned. But with a growing number of cross-cultural Asian missionaries coming forward from Korea, India, the Philippines, Myanmar, Indonesia, and Singapore, the need for creative ways of partnering with them is imperative. There will also need to be a shifting of western missionary resources from highly evangelized areas like the Pacific and Caribbean regions to the far needier areas of Asia. For restricted access countries like India, Indonesia, Myanmar, and Muslim countries, there needs to be creative strategies for non-residential and tentmaker missionaries as well.

Perspectives Enrichment: Chapter D-14

---

1. Donald E. Hoke, *The Church in Asia*, (1975), p. 47.
2. Kane, *Understanding Missions*, p. 199.
3. Hoke, ed., *Church in Asia*, p. 33.
4. Ibid, p. 50.
5. Ibid.; Kane, *Understanding Missions*, pp. 269-70.
6. Hoke, *Church in Asia*, p. 50 (undocumented statement).
7. Johnstone, *Operation World* 4th ed., pp. 49-50; update from 5th ed.
8. Kane, *Understanding Missions*, pp. 199-204 passim.
9. Ibid., p. 202.
10. Samuel Hugh Moffett, "Korea," in *The Church in Asia*, Hoke ed., p. 378.
11. Johnstone, 5th ed., pp. 40-45.
12. Ibid, p. 51.
13. A case in point would be the Summer Training and Outreach Program (STOP) of International Missions, Inc., of which I am the Academic Dean. Typically we get 20 to 40 trainees in the Muslim evangelism track, and 0 to 10 in the Hindu. (For information call Paul Troper at 973-427-5120.)
14. On a visit to southwestern Honshu in 1985, I was surprised at the number of cities of over 100,000 with no evangelical church.

We Live In An Asian World

The world drawn in
proportion to population

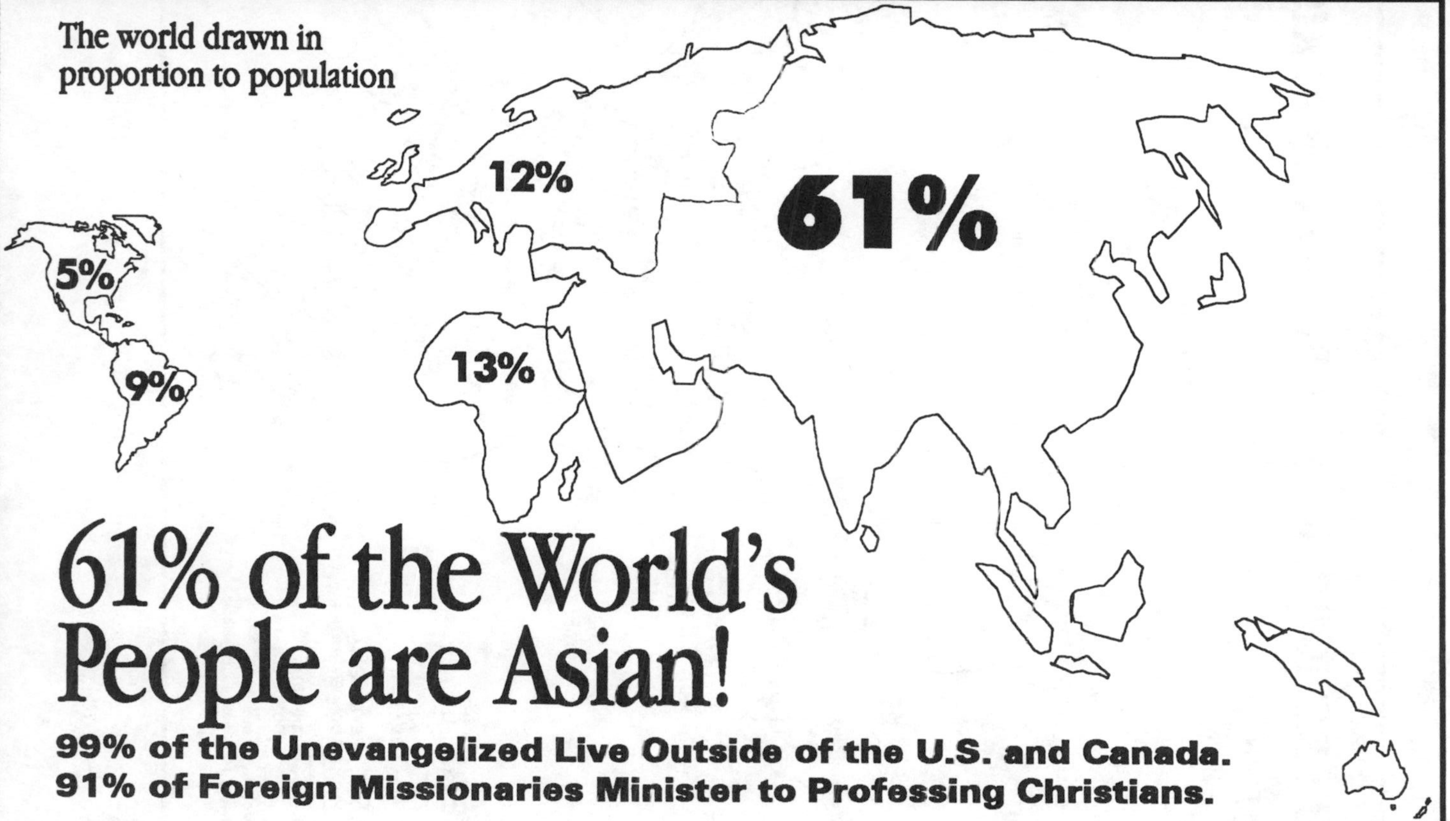

61%

12%

13%

5%

9%

61% of the World's
People are Asian!

99% of the Unevangelized Live Outside of the U.S. and Canada.
91% of Foreign Missionaries Minister to Professing Christians.

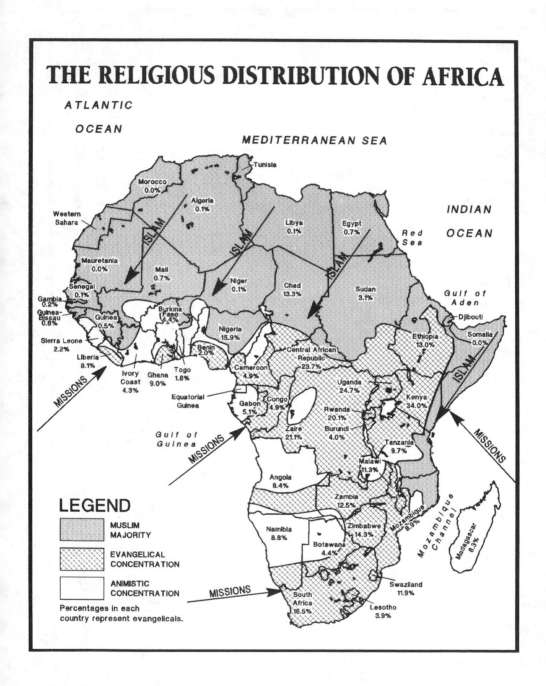

THE RELIGIOUS DISTRIBUTION OF AFRICA

ATLANTIC

OCEAN

MEDITERRANEAN SEA

INDIAN

OCEAN

Tunisia

Morocco
0.0%

Algeria
0.1%

Libya
0.1%

Egypt
0.7%

Red
Sea

Western
Sahara

Mauretania
0.0%

Mali
0.7%

Niger
0.1%

Chad
13.3%

Sudan
3.1%

Gulf of
Aden

Gambia
0.2%

Senegal
0.1%

Guinea-
Bissau
0.8%

Guinea
0.5%

Burkina
Faso
4.4%

Nigeria
15.9%

Djibouti

Ethiopia
13.0%

Somalia
0.0%

Sierra Leone
2.2%

Liberia
8.1%

Ivory
Coast
4.3%

Ghana
9.0%

Togo
1.8%

Benin
2.0%

Cameroon
4.9%

Central African
Republic
23.7%

Uganda
24.7%

Kenya
34.0%

MISSIONS

Equatorial
Guinea

Gabon
5.1%

Congo
4.9%

Zaire
21.1%

Rwanda
20.1%

Burundi
4.0%

Tanzania
9.7%

MISSIONS

Gulf of
Guinea

MISSIONS

Angola
8.4%

Malawi
11.3%

Zambia
12.5%

Mozambique
6.9%

Madagascar
6.3%

Mozambique Channel

Namibia
8.8%

Zimbabwe
14.3%

Botswana
4.4%

Swaziland
11.9%

MISSIONS

South
Africa
16.5%

Lesotho
3.9%

LEGEND

MUSLIM
MAJORITY

EVANGELICAL
CONCENTRATION

ANIMISTIC
CONCENTRATION

Percentages in each
country represent evangelicals.

"The expansion of Christianity in twentieth-century Africa has been so dramatic
that it has been called the fourth great age
of Christian expansion."

–Elizabeth Isichei

SUB-SAHARAN AFRICA:
GROWTH THROUGH STRUGGLE

Sub-Saharan Africa and North Africa are so diverse we must look at them separately. The Sahara Desert is a massive natural barrier between the two parts of Africa. The larger part of Africa south of the Sahara is not appropriately called 'black Africa' since there is a significant white population nor 'tropical Africa' since it is not all tropical. Although influenced by the Muslim north, sub-Saharan Africa is distinct. To understand contemporary Africa it is imperative to grasp something of its history. In earlier centuries Europeans called it the "dark continent" perhaps to indicate the complexion of the inhabitants and the cultural and religious conditions of the continent. In a sense, they were also admitting their ignorance of Africa, since there was a communication gap about the region south of the desert caused by the solid Islamic control of North Africa and the consequent blockage to Europeans until Portuguese ships began the age of exploration. Information about Africa directly across the Mediterranean Sea and North Africa was hard to come by. Christian missions penetrated Africa from four directions: 1) from the west in 1795 through Sierra Leone; 2) from the south through the Cape Colony in 1799; 3) from the east through Mombasa in 1844; and 4) from the southwest through the Congo River in 1878. We will need some background to understand this penetration.

EXPLORATION AND SLAVE TRADE

Portuguese exploration

Europeans had long wanted to find a way around the Muslim control of the Middle East to get to the Spice Islands of the Far East. It was Prince Henry (the Navigator) of Portugal who for forty years in the fifteenth century sent expedition after expedition down the African coast. In 1487 Bartholomew Diaz rounded the Cape of Good Hope, and in 1498

Vasco da Gama had explored the eastern coast and the route to Asia. Prince Henry was interested in evangelization as well as exploration, and the Catholic Church started missions at a number of places along the African coast. Congo was the most successful, but none of them survived until modern times. At first the Portuguese explorers and their missionaries had an excellent policy of trade and peaceful development, and a number of tribal kings with many subjects were baptized. However, their work was very superficial and did not survive.[1]

The infamous slave trade

The slave trade had an ancient history in Africa. Arab traders from the north would buy the captives from intertribal warfare. Slavery was an institution in the Muslim Middle East in the fifteenth and sixteenth centuries, Turks and Moors holding Europeans, Africans, and Arabs in slavery. The demand for slaves for their New World conquests motivated the Portuguese to reverse their altruistic policy and enter into the nefarious slave trade. This doomed their African missions to extinction. As Protestant nations like the Dutch and English followed up the Portuguese exploration and trade, they also got involved in the slave trade. The Dutch pushed the Portuguese out of many of their forts and trading posts both in Africa and Asia, and ultimately the British became dominant.

The Quakers (Society of Friends) were early objectors to the evils of slavery, first in Germantown, Pennsylvania in 1688 and then in England by 1772. Christians like Granville Sharp (of Greek grammar fame), John Newton, and William Wilberforce succeeded in getting an abolition bill through Parliament in 1807. The British ships began to aggressively cut off the slave trade by 1827 and persuaded other Western nations to give it up.[2]

FOUR ROUTES OF EARLY
GOSPEL PENETRATION

Via the Dutch Cape Colony

As the ships of the Dutch East India Company sailed around the Cape of Africa, they established a supply station in 1652, which quickly developed into a colony to provide the supplies needed. A trading relationship developed with the sparce Hottentot population in the area. In 1662 the first native convert was baptized and later married the settlement doctor. When Danish-Halle pioneers Ziegenbalg and Plutshau stopped at the Cape on their way to India in 1706, they sent letters back to Europe to appeal for missionaries to evangelize the Hottentots. **George Schmidt** of the Moravians did arrive at the Cape in 1737 and started a difficult mission. By 1799 the London Missionary Society sent four missionaries under the leadership of Johannes Vanderkemp to start work among the indigenous people.[3] The story of Robert Moffat's follow-up has already been told (see ch. 9).

Via colonies of liberated slaves in West Africa

In 1772 a legal judgment made free men of all slaves who set foot on English soil, and after the American War of Independence Negro slaves who had fought on the side of the British were homeless. The solution was a black colony in Sierra Leone in West Africa started in 1787. Increasingly after 1809 as British ships interdicted slave ships and freed the slaves, they were added to this colony. Many of the settlers were Christians and helped to facilitate Christian missions to the tribes of the area in ensuing years. The Baptist Missionary Society (of William Carey) started work in 1795, the Glasgow Missionary Society in 1796, the London Missionary Society by 1797, and the Church Missionary Society (of the Anglican church) sent two Germans in 1804 for their initial effort anywhere. By the 1850's the Anglicans of the West Indies made Sierra Leone their responsibility, and many other missions followed. Liberia was a similar colony of freed American slaves on the western coast and also a point of entry for foreign missionaries.[4]

From the east through Mombasa (Kenya)

In 1844 Swiss missionary **Johann Krapf,** serving with the Anglican CMS, got the permission of the Muslim sultan of the island of Zanzibar to begin work inland from the port of Mombasa. His travels and translation work laid the foundation for subsequent work by his colleagues and other missions which followed. David Livingstone was at the height of his explorations of inland Africa at this time, and seeing the evil slave trade he appealed for more missionaries to bring the gospel, for more legitimate trade, and for the end of the slave trade. Many responded to his appeal, but the results of the coming of commercial Europeans were usually harmful.[5]

By way of the Congo (Zaire) River

The Congo River basin was the least known and last penetrated major area of Africa. Livingstone devoted the last two years of his life to exploring the source of the Congo River, and upon his death in 1871 his protege, Henry Stanley, followed the Lualaba River to its mouth and established it as the source of the Congo. At this time the Baptist Missionary Society began to send missionaries into the Congo basin and together with missionaries from the Livingstone Inland Mission made substantial penetration. Many other missions followed over the next century to evangelize this vast tropical area.

The white man's grave

The early explorers and missionaries suffered incredible casualties through tropical disease. Few were killed by tribal peoples. Visitors to Africa today are astonished to see many graves of the pioneers. Typically fifty to ninety percent of the missionary teams fell to disease, either dying or returning home sick. The tendency was to blame the climate (malaria='bad air'). It was only as it was understood that the tropical diseases were caused by insects and unsanitary conditions that these diseases were conquered. The use of quinine and mosquito nets for malaria was major victory in the end of the last century. This paved the way for more substantial and lasting missionary penetration.

Three key 'faith missions'

In the beginning of the twentieth century three faith missions were among the vanguard of the inland thrust to reach new areas: Sudan Interior Mission (SIM), Africa Inland Mission (AIM), and South Africa General Mission (now Africa Evangelical Fellowship). In the 1890s a Canadian, **Rowland Bingham**, made two unsuccessful attempts to start a witness in Kano, Nigeria, his two colleagues dying in the effort. The third attempt by the SIM team was successful. Today the ECWA church arising from SIM's ministry has 700 thousand adult members. SIM has work in Niger, Burkina Faso, Benin, Ghana, Ivory Coast, and their largest in Ethiopia has about two million members. An AIM team under **Peter Cameron Scott** began ministry in Kenya in 1875, all but one of the first group dying in a short time. The third team to reenter in 1904 was successful. The Africa Inland Church there now has about a million members. Their work in Tanzania has about 300 thousand members, and lesser churches in Zaire, Uganda, Sudan, and Central African Republic. The Africa Evangelical Fellowship has work in South Africa, Zambia, Mozambique, Zimbabwe, and Angola, among others.

THE LEGACY OF COLONIALISM

In Asia we noted that by and large the missionaries followed the colonialists. The missionaries worked in areas where the colonialists had already established control (the cross followed the flag). In Africa the situation was the reverse: the missionaries were frequently the initial explorers (e.g. Livingstone), and the colonialists followed in their train (the flag followed the cross). In Livingstone's case he felt that the colonial governments would stop the slave trade and intertribal warfare. But in many other cases, the colonialists used the missionaries and the goodwill that they had established with the people as a means of gaining control of the areas. Thus the European powers carved up the whole of Africa into their own colonies: the Portuguese had Angola, Mozambique, and Guinea; the Dutch lost South Africa to the British, who also controlled a dozen more; the French had a dozen; the Belgians had Congo and Rwanda-Burundi; the Germans lost their two in World War I. Today most of Africa can be divided into Francophone (French- speaking) and Anglophone (English-speaking) countries. Of course, these were only the languages of government and higher education since the people continued to speak their own tribal languages and use trade languages like Swahili.

How do we evaluate the impact of colonialism? Herbert Kane takes a fairly positive approach and calls it a "blessing in disguise."

> It terminated the intertribal warfare and the slave trade, both of which were decimating the population, and imposed a much needed peace on the entire continent. Moreover, the colonial government favored missionary work in many ways. In the early years they made land grants for schools and mission stations and later on subsidized mission schools.[6]

After pointing up the tremendous developmental accomplishments of the colonialists, Peter Falk adopts a more negative viewpoint:

> The Africans were subjected to foreign rule and often did not understand the missionaries' motives for coming to their countries. Some missionaries tried to retain cordial relationships with the government agents, and they were suspected of being agents of the foreign powers. This suspicion did not provide a basis for communicating the gospel or for establishing fraternal relationships and the unity of the spirit in the body of Christ.[7]

The impact of colonialism became clearer after independence. The national boundaries related to the previous colonial masters and not to the indigenous tribal boundaries. This has caused serious problems up to the present. Those governments which followed a more enlightened altruism in their policies and trained the nationals for leadership, have left a legacy of stable democracies in many cases. Those who were more exploitive of the tribal peoples have left a terrible legacy of despotic dictators and countries ripe for Communism. For example, missionaries in Congo objected to the exploitive policies of the Belgian government, which has resulted in the almost total decay of society under dictator Mobutu.

The first World War forced the Germans out of Tanzania and Cameroon. It was distressing for the Africans to see the European 'Christians' fighting among themselves. Increasingly Africans saw Western 'Christians' living a lifestyle which was totally contrary to the Bible. The second World War reinforced their disillusionment with Western civilization and strengthened the movement toward independence. The French left in 1960; the British over a decade beginning with Ghana in 1957; the Portuguese in the '70s. Today over forty new African nations belong to the United Nations.

RAPID CHURCH GROWTH

Despite the difficult early years, rapid church growth began about the turn of the century. "From 1900 to 1950 the Christian population increased about sixty times. From 1950 to 1970 the growth rate has been even faster."[8] Apparently the departure of the colonial powers helped rather than hindered church growth. Today there are about eighty million Evangelicals (13% of the population) in Africa and the percentage of evangelical Christians in eight of the largest countries is over ten percent. Over half the people of Africa consider themselves Christian. Today,

> there are two remarkable 'Bible Belts' across Africa, one extends from Nigeria through Chad, Central Africa Republic, North Zaire, Rwanda and Uganda to Kenya with millions of evangelical believers. The other spans an arc of territory from Angola through Zambia, southern Zaire and Malawi to the Lomwe people in northern Mozambique.[9]

CONFRONTATION WITH ISLAM

From the time of its conquest of North Africa Islam has been gradually moving south through Africa to expand its area of influence. Originally Muslim traders came south across the desert trade routes. Also Muslim trading ships (dhows) came down the east coast much farther south to establish influence and control. The first Portuguese explorers to round the Cape confronted the Arabs along the east coast. Although in the main Islam was spread in sub-saharan Africa by the witness of these traders, as has been the pattern with Muslims there were some forced conversions.

The great competition between Christianity and Islam has continued to force animistic Africans to choose between them. This is the great religious struggle going on today in Africa. At the turn of the century three-quarters of Africans were still animistic; today less than one-sixth remain. They are turning to Christianity and Islam at an incredible rate. Which will win? A few decades ago it was being said that many more were turning to Islam than to Christianity. Either this was not accurate or the trend has been reversed, because today about one-fourth are Muslims—less than half the number of professing Christians. In any case far more are turning to Christ than to Muhammad today. The tension is especially sharp in Nigeria, where the northern half is Muslim and the southern half mostly Christian. The Muslims have started burning churches and using physical force to achieve their ends. Nevertheless, evangelism among the Muslims is bearing fruit.

What is the appeal of Islam to Africans? Kane's answer is good:

1) It poses as the "black man's religion"—supposedly indigenous to Africa, though it is not.

2) Islam was not identified with the European colonial system, even though it was connected through the Arabs with the slave trade of an earlier era.

3) Islam has made good use of lay missionaries, principally teachers and merchants who settle down and become part of the local community.

4) Islam makes fewer ethical and moral demands on its adherents. Polygamy, almost an insurmountable problem to the Christian church, is no problem at all to Islam, for all devout Muslims are permitted to have four wives at one time.

5) Some branches of Islam are now extensively engaged in social and humanitarian service, taking a leaf from the missionarys' book.[10]

THE CURRENT SITUATION

Out of the 1995 population of about 560 million, 48.1 percent are professing Christians (Evangelical, 13.2%; Roman Catholic, 16.7%; African Independent Churches, 6.7%; Coptic Orthodox, 3.9%; other Protestant, 6.9%; cults, 0.5%); Muslims, 26.7 percent; and traditional Animistic religions, 15.4 percent.

Four kinds of 'Christians'

There are four major kinds of professing Christians in Africa:

The Coptic Orthodox Church. The oldest 'Christian' community in Africa is the Coptic Orthodox Church, found in both Egypt and Ethiopia since the first century. It was the official state religion of Ethiopia before the Communist revolution (1974-76) and of a large minority in Egypt. It was very formalistic, monastic, superstitious, and dead, but Communist and Muslim pressures have forced it into a crisis. As a result there are stirrings and many Orthodox have come to a personal faith in Christ (both in Egypt and Ethiopia). Most numerous in Egypt and Ethiopia, they represent 3.9 percent of sub-Saharan Africa.

The Roman Catholic Church. Roman Catholics are the largest 'Christian' denomination in Africa with 16.7 percent of the population. The Catholics started early, and even though their sixteenth century mission did not survive, they have had the strong support of colonial governments from Catholic countries. The Catholics have seen substantial growth through the heavy investment of resources in Africa (mostly from Europe) and widespread institutional work. Their readiness to baptize people with a superficial understanding of their faith also accounts for the large numbers. There has also been a political and economic advantage for many Catholic converts. "Nominalism and a serious lack of African priests and leaders are key problems."[11]

Protestants. Protestants have overall numerically outstripped the Roman Catholics through recent church growth, bringing the total to 20.1 percent. However, only 13.2 percent of the population can really be counted as Evangelicals since there has been a significant impact of nominalism, liberalism, and neo-orthodoxy in Africa. This has been manifest especially among the African ecumenical leaders, who have espoused radical theologies. Some, like John Mbiti, have attempted to develop indigenous 'black theology' by incorporating features of the indigenous Animistic religions. At one time these ecumenical leaders called for a "moratorium on missions."

Evangelicals now number about 80 million and have experienced rapid church growth in recent years. In the past, church growth was hindered when converts were made part of an elite group in a mission compound. As the error of this nineteenth-century approach was recognized, and as greater responsibility was passed on to national evangelists, church growth began to accelerate. Revivals in the old-line denominations have brought millions to personal faith in Christ. Major church growth has taken place in the daughter churches of the faith missions. Since 1960 saturation evangelism programs like "New Life for All" in Nigeria have had significant impact there and in other countries. Indigenous Pentecostal denominations have grown dramatically in the last two decades. Theological Education by Extension has greatly helped to train national leaders. Mass media, including audio-visuals, literature, magazines, and radio, have been widely used. The advent of the transistor radio was a great boon to missionary broadcasting.

From the beginning Evangelicals have placed great stress upon using the vernacular and upon Bible translation. Robert Moffat's early error was not repeated in the main. In a continent with 1800 known languages, its importance can easily be seen. At present there are 107 complete Bibles, 196 New Testaments, and 277 other languages with portions completed, making a grand total of 580 languages.[12]

African Independent Churches. This is an extremely complex movement with up to seven thousand independent indigenous denominations having a total of about thirty-two million adherents. The largest is the church founded by Simon Kimbangu in Zaire in 1921. These churches are found all over Africa, but especially in South Africa, Nigeria, Zaire, Ghana, and Kenya. They usually were founded by a natural indigenous leader and seem to have sprung from a number of different causes. In many cases there was a strong desire to manifest their own African identity apart from the foreign missionary. Ethnic pride was a contributing factor at a time when nationalism was on the rise. Frequently a gifted national leader felt repressed by the missionaries, who often retained control too long. Sometimes it was part of a renewal movement within churches which had lost their vitality. Sometimes it was a leader who was disciplined by the church and 'took his marbles to play somewhere else'. Indeed, sometimes it was a desire to allow polygamy within the church, feeling that the missionary's version of Christianity was too legalistic. Frequently it was caused by the missionaries' failure to appreciate the valid features of African culture and attempts to force western culture upon the people. Some of the independent churches have elevated their 'prophet' to a blasphemous status, replacing Christ as Savior. Certainly some within the movement are fairly biblical in doctrine, but many have become syncretistic: combining Christian doctrine with animistic notions. They tend to have a very spirited, African form of worship, which includes hand-clapping, dancing, indigenous music, and faith healing.

THE RELIGIOUS STATUS OF MAJOR AFRICAN NATIONS

COUNTRY	POPULA. Million 1995	MUSLIM %	PROFES. CHRIST. %	EVAN- GELICAL %	EVANG. Million 1995
NIGERIA	100.1	40	40.9	15.9	15 9
ETHIOPIA	52.6	35	51.0	13.0	6.8
CONGO (Zaire)	42.3	1.4	92.3	21.1	8.9
SO. AFRICA	39.2	1.25	72.6	16.5	6.5
TANZANIA	32.9	35	36.6	9.7	2.6
SUDAN	29.1	70	14.4	3.1	0.9
KENYA	30.8	6	69.6	34.0	10.5
UGANDA	22.0	8	69.6	24.7	5.4
MOZAMBIQUE	17.9	13	27.8	8.9	1.6
GHANA	17.5	16	44.3	8.9	1.6
CAMEROON	12.9	24	46.2	4.9	0.6
ZIMBABWE	11.4	1.6	48.8	14.3	1.6
MALAWI	10.0	14.5	67.9	11.3	1.1
RWANDA	8.6	10	76.0	20.1	1.7

AN EVALUATION OF MISSIONS TO AFRICA

Why has the missionary movement in Africa been so productive? In what ways did the missionaries fail? What are the major problems the churches in Africa face today? What are the major unmet needs of Africa? It may seem arrogant to evaluate the tremendously sacrificial service of thousands of missionaries over almost two centuries. Since a number of writers have made suggestions, some attempt should be made to understand these things, so that we can improve and move ahead. Let us try.

Factors conducive to growth

The weakness of Animism. We have already noted the openness of Animistic tribal peoples around the world, to the Christian gospel. Their belief in a Creator God, even if they do not worship Him (as most certainly do not), predisposes the Animist to consider the gospel. There are other weaknesses of Animism which help. "Animism has no books and no temples; nor has it produced any great leaders, thinkers, or scholars."[13] Although the witch doctor or shaman was frequently a formidable opponent of the missionary, time and time again God worked in the ensuing power encounters either through medicine or by direct healing so that the gospel was victorious. So frequently the conversion of the shaman was the key to winning the tribe.

A substantial investment of resources. Somehow sub-Saharan Africa captured the imagination of the modern missionary movement. Possibly the drama, the adventure, and the physical dimensions of Africa's need contributed to the great flow of missionaries to Africa: currently over twelve thousand. From many different missions and denominations and many different countries they came: more per capita than anywhere else in the world, except the south Pacific and the Caribbean regions. Not just in personnel, but also in investment of money and institutions such as schools and hospitals, did Africa get a lion's share. Undoubtedly, it had to do with the total lack of such things before the arrival of the missionary. In any case, it has paid off. It might be argued as to whether those resources might have been better spent in direct evangelism. Possibly church growth might have been higher without so many institutions. But the missionaries saw the need for trained leadership, and indeed they provided leadership for the emerging nations. It is almost impossible for us now to second-guess the missionaries.

The cultural advantage of the missionary. The missionaries coming to the ancient civilizations of Asia were looked down upon, at least by the leaders. In Africa, however, the situation was quite the opposite. Coming from advanced technological societies, the missionary gained a lot of credibility with the people of 'preliterate societies'. Some may feel that this was unearned. But there is some basis for arguing that science and technology arose in 'Christian' cultures because the Christian worldview is conducive to them. It also might be argued that although Western technology did predispose the African to listen to the missionary's message, it might also have confused the issues as to what was God's truth and what was culture. In some ways this might have been counterpro-ductive, but it did open doors!

THE CURRENT CONTEXT FOR MISSIONS

Africa has suffered an unequalled sequence of natural, political, and economic disasters in the last few decades. To start with, 32 of the 40 poorest nations of the world are in Africa. Thirteen are in a state of eco-nomic collapse.

Many of the problems are at root political since most African nations have suffered from despotic leaders since independence from colonial-ism. Countries like Zaire, Somalia, and more recently Rwanda have been in political and economic chaos. Civil wars have left a legacy of famine and disorder. If anything, tribalism has been on the increase, exempli-fied by tragic tribal slaughter in Rwanda in 1994. In Sudan there is also a religious dimension since the Muslim government has been oppressing and waging war against the Christian and pagan tribal peoples in the south.

There are two political positives, however. Most significant is the ending of apartheid and the non-racial elections in the Republic of South Africa. The other is the greater religious freedom being experienced by Christians in the nine countries which were Marxist or Marxist-leaning in 1985 and have now rejected it. It was especially bad in Ethiopia, Eritrea, Angola, and Mozambique. These countries must now recoup from their disastrous past.

The second factor related to economic disaster is the famines that have been endemic to Africa, especially the Sahel areas south of the Sahara Desert. This has been exacerbated by the political chaos in some of these countries and in other areas. In 1992 sixty million people faced starvation.

Another disastrous factor affecting Christians in Africa today is the pandemic spread of AIDS in central and east Africa. Johnstone gives us the update:

> Villages and towns along road and river trade routes are being decimated by the disease. No one really knows the level of infec-tion with the virus — estimates in 1992 ranged from seven million to 20 million or more. Especially badly affected are Uganda, Zaire, Zambia, Zimbabwe and South Africa. The impact is already devas-tating.[14]

It is clear that Christians have not been exempted from any of these disasters. A strong emphasis on biblical morality will be needed to help the younger generation especially to escape from the AIDS catastrophe.

Most encouraging has been the opening of countries formerly closed to missionaries. Out of 14 formerly closed countries only 5 remain partly or fully closed: Angola, Comoros, Somalia, and parts of Liberia and Gabon. There are many opportunities in the newly opened countries: Mozambique, Ethiopia, Eritrea, Guinea, Guinea-Bissau, and Togo.

OVERCOMING OBSTACLES TO PROGRESS

We have already noted a number of serious obstacles to the further progress of the gospel in Africa, external to the churche: 1) political instability, 2) tribalism, 3) materialism, especially among the young people flooding into the cities, 4) Islam, 5) famine, and 6) the AIDS crisis.

We should also note a number of serious internal problems within the Christian community in Africa which hinder further progress.

1) Theological compromise and syncretism. The leadership of the old-line denominations shows the impact of western liberalism, which has resulted in nominalism, doctrinal compromise, and power struggles for leadership. Black theology is the term given to the African form of 'liberation theology' (which originated in Latin America). Perhaps, even more serious, are the African theologies, which are attempts to syncretize the old pagan (animistic) religions with Christianity. All of these lead to universalism.

2) Lack of trained leadership. The rapid church growth of recent decades has outstripped the development of properly trained leaders for the churches. There are two evangelical, interdenominational seminaries, one English-speaking and one French-speaking. The Association of Evangelicals of Africa and Madagascar (AEAM) accredits over 100 Bible schools. These are far from adequate for the evangelical churches.

3) A continued need for foreign missionaries. A generation ago some ecumenical African church leaders called for a "moratorium on missionaries." Although proportionately Africa has received a generous share of missionaries, there are still many unmet needs, especially for leadership training, but also for pioneer work.

4) A missionary vision for the African church. Ultimately the reaching of unreached peoples should be a partnership of African and Western missionaries. A significant number of cross-cultural missionaries have come from churches in Nigeria, South Africa, and Kenya. All the African churches need to share this vision.

We need to look also at some of the internal factors which have hindered sound progress in the past and may be lingering even now in the end of the twentieth century. The African independent churches should be a case study and a lesson to missionaries. Here are some suggestions: 1) encourage indigenous, not western forms of worship; 2) encourage, don't repress, the gifted-national leader; 3) cast off the last vestiges of attitudes derived from colonialism, to which missionaries sometimes fall prey; 4) set an example in regard to materialism by adopting a simple lifestyle; 5) keep praying and working for revival; 6) make sure we are not imposing Western legalisms; 7) work for true, not surface, indigeneity of churches; and 8) disciple (in the full sense of the word) national leadership.

The spiritual challenges of Africa today

Johnstone highlights some spiritual challenges for reaching Africa:[15]

Islam. There are 129 million Muslims in sub-Saharan Africa. Little penetration of the Muslim community with the gospel has been seen, except in Nigeria. The four major least-reached transnational peoples are all Muslim: the Fula, the Mandingo/Mande, the Hausa, and the Somali, and many of the nomadic peoples of the Sahel as well.

Animists. There are still 38 million Animists in the Sahel belt, who follow the traditional tribal religions.

Least-evangelized nations. In addition to the Muslim countries, there are still five nations with less than one percent Evangelicals.

Cities. Before the year 2000, Africa's cities may mushroom to 300 million. The gospel has penetrated better in rural areas and among the educated. The churches struggle to reach the poor flooding into the cities.

Bible translation. "Over 40 million Africans speaking 1,200 languages have nothing of the Scriptures, and nearly 200 million cannot read."

1. Peter Falk, *The Growth of the Church in Africa* (1979), pp. 73-80.

2. Ibid, pp. 96-101.

3. Ibid, pp. 143-55.

4. Ibid, pp. 103-117.

5. Ibid, pp. 233-86.

6. Kane, *Understanding Missions*, p. 219.

7. Falk, *Church in Africa*, p. 418.

8. Kane, *Understanding Missions*, p. 213.

9. Johnstone, *Operation World*, 4th ed., p. 45.

10. Kane, *Concise History*, p. 139.

11. Ibid.

12. Johnstone, *Operation World*, 5th ed.. p. 37

13. Kane, *Understanding Missions*, p. 220.

14. See Johnstone, 5th ed., pp. 34-39, for this whole update.

15. Ibid.

THE ETHNIC MOSAIC OF SOUTH AMERICA

CARRIBEAN SEA

GUYANA
15.5% SURINAM
2.9%

FRENCH GUIANA
3.9%

VENEZUELA
4.8%

COLUMBIA
3.1%

ECUADOR
3.4%

PERU
5.6%

BRAZIL
18%

BOLIVIA
8.4%

CHILE
27%

PARAGUAY
4.3%

ARGENTINA
6.9%

URUGUAY
2.2%

PACIFIC OCEAN

ATLANTIC OCEAN

NOTE:
Percentages
represent
evangelicals in
each country.

Falkland
Islands

KEY

	MOSTLY INDIAN
	MOSTLY EUROPEAN
	MIXED EUROPEAN & INDIAN
	MIXED EUROPEAN, INDIAN & AFRICAN
	MIXED AFRICAN & ASIAN
	MIXED EUROPEAN, AFRICAN & ASIAN
	MOSTLY ASIAN

"Latin America's racial rainbow is matched by its religious mosaic, with overlapping pieces that can periodically confuse the observer. . . In many ways that Christ was blended into the animistic beliefs, producing a syncretism evident today throughout the continent and particularly witnessed in popular Catholicism."

-William D. Taylor

LATIN AMERICA: EVANGELIZING A CHRISTO-PAGAN MELTING POT

The story of Protestant missions in Latin America is a most exciting one. Latin America is one of the great success stories of Evangelical missions. Although nominally a Roman Catholic continent, Latin America is the scene of some of the most rapid Evangelical church growth in the world. The impressive result is that on a given Sunday in Latin America today there are more Evangelicals than Catholics attending church. This highlights both the strengths of the Evangelicals and the weaknesses of Roman Catholicism in that part of the world. Although many nominal Roman Catholics may rightly be called Christo-pagans, there is a sense in which the Catholic missionaries were breaking the ground for the ultimate Evangelical advance. Protestant missions were slow to get started in Latin America, so most of this great advance has taken place since the turn of the century. Before we can understand the missionary advance we must look at the continent, past and present.

THE DIVERSE PEOPLES

The ethnic mosaic. Is Latin America really Latin? This might seem like a ridiculous question to most people. Especially since a missionary statesman was heard to say that Latin American culture is really European. Of course, 'Latin' refers to the Spanish and Portuguese cultures brought in by the conquistadors and it is true that these are the two dominant languages: Portuguese in Brazil and Spanish in most of the rest. However, there is a great diversity of ethnic groups in Latin America and not all are Latin by any means. It is true that the population is 41 percent European, but that includes large minorities of Italians, Germans, Ukrainians, Poles, and even British and Japanese. Some countries in the Caribbean area are Dutch-speaking, like Surinam; French-speaking, like Haiti and French Guiana; and English-speaking, like Belize and Guyana. Eleven percent of the population is still Amerindian; 7 percent is of African descent; 39 percent is of mixed race; and 1 percent are of Asian descent.

Ethnically speaking, there are really four kinds of countries: 1) There are the countries where European population is a majority: Uruguay (95%), Argentina (89%), Puerto Rico (75%), and Cuba (59%); 2) countries where Amerindians predominate: Bolivia (64%), Peru (54%), Ecuador (42%), and in Central America, Guatemala (42%); 3) countries where mixed races and diversity predominate: Brazil, the 'melting pot' has 54 percent European, 33 percent Mestizo and Mulatto, 11 percent African, 1.5 percent Asian, 0.1 percent Amerindian; 4) countries where African or Asian peoples predominate: most of the Caribbean has an African majority, and Guyana and Surinam are Asian (53%). Most of the countries are of the third category with a large mixed population. (Mestizos are mixed Hispanic and Amerindian while Mulattos are mixed African and European.)

Population of the whole area is 450 million and growing very rapidly (2.2% per year). Brazil with 165 million is the giant and Mexico with 93 million comes next. Latin America is rapidly being urbanized. Mexico City is in the process of becoming the largest city in the world, with Buenos Aires, Argentina and Sao Paulo and Rio de Janeiro, Brazil right behind as 'world-class' cities. Although the great cities of Latin America are modern and rich, there are millions of poverty-stricken people living in shanty towns on the outskirts of these cities.

The religious mosaic. Although the vast majority (80%) of the population of Latin America is nominally Roman Catholic, only a small minority are practicing Catholics (from a low of 10% in Uruguay to 20% in Costa Rica). A significant number of the European immigrants were Protestant, especially German Lutherans. But most Protestants today are the fruit of modern missions in the last 100 years, with Evangelicals now constituting about 11 percent of the population, the highest being in Chile (27%), Guatemala (23%), and Brazil (18%). **There are more evangelical Christians in Brazil than in all of Western Europe!**[1]

HOW DID IT ALL HAPPEN?

Although we consider the United States a 'melting pot', the Latin Americans have one up on us. The above statistics make it clear that Latin America has had a checkered history, ethnically and religiously. How did it all come about?

The Spanish conquistadors who followed the explorations of Columbus did not come alone. One of Columbus's goals was to evangelize the native population, and the conquistadors brought along priests, not only as chaplains but for that very purpose. The Franciscans came to Brazil in 1500; the Dominicans began work in Haiti in 1510, followed by the

Augustinians and the Jesuits. "By 1555 in the wake of the explorers and conquistadors, Roman Catholic missionaries had taken Christianity to the West Indies, Mexico, Central America, Colombia, Venezuela, Ecuador, Chile, Peru, and Brazil."[2]

Noteworthy about the missionary work in the New World was the use of the *patronato* system, by which the colonial governments were responsible to spread the Catholic faith among the Indians. It gave the Portuguese and Spanish governments all the patronage privileges in their designated areas with the right to appoint church officials and the responsibility to pay the cost as well. This was the root of the serious abuses which developed, because in their colonies the government was above the church. The Pope had no direct authority in the colonies.

The abuse of the Indians by the Conquistadors was legendary, as Latourette pointed out:

> In the West Indies the native populations died out within a few years after the advent of the Europeans. The cruelty, the exploitation, and the diseases of the white man accomplished their destruction before the Christian conscience could stir the home authorities to effective action. The populations which replaced them were white or Negro or a mixture of the two.[3]

Although some of the priests and even some of the government officials were high-minded and opposed to the oppression of the Indians, with the tremendous wealth of precious metals involved in the trade, the opportunity for abuse was just too great. The Indians were docile in obeying their new masters as they had their old, the tribal chiefs. Indians by the hundreds of thousands submitted to baptism. "In 1536 a missionary estimated the number of baptized at between four and nine millions. . . . By the end of the sixteenth century the pre-Christian pagan cults had disappeared in the more thickly settled portions of Mexico." However, the legacy of centuries of gross abuses and inhumanity ultimately dealt the church two serious blows.[4]

The first blow was the expulsion of the Jesuits from the colonies, beginning with Brazil in 1759. The reason lay in the ethical system adopted by the Jesuits called 'casuistry', which essentially means that 'the end justifies the means'. The behavior of the Jesuits was such that for centuries they were opposed by many Catholics. Whatever the cause, it left the Catholic missions in the New World badly depleted of personnel. The second setback was the sequence of wars of independence in various Latin American countries from 1810 to 1824. The new governments were hostile to the Church because of the Church's close association with the colonial governments. This caused a second exodus of Spanish and Portuguese missionaries and church administrators which left the Roman Catholic Church desperately short of leadership. They had not trained adequate national leadership and the lack of leaders has left the

Church weak right up to the present time. In a real sense this set the scene for the success of Protestant missions.

We are tempted to ask at this juncture how it was that, over a period of centuries, the conquistadors and the priests accompanying them could be party to such inhumanity in the name of 'Christianity?' Some did object to the treatment of the Indians and the Negroes, outstanding among whom was Las Casas who made several trips back to Spain to protest the treatment of the Indians. Pedro Claver is famous for his advocacy of and compassion for the black slaves. The root of the evil was the common view among Spanish Catholics that coercion in religion is justified in order to save the soul. This has been traced back to the fifth-century church father Augustine who so greatly influenced both Catholics and Protestants.[5] This idea of the use of force to bring people to faith was also prominent in the Spanish Inquisition of those days. It was an evil principle bearing an evil consequence.

AMERICAN PROTESTANT MISSIONS

A belated beginning

In chapter 10 we noted that Protestant missions to Latin America did not get started in the first era, as did missions to Asia and Africa. It was not until about the time of Hudson Taylor that an outreach to Latin America got underway. There were beginnings in the 1840s and '50s, but the 'Big Three' American denominational missions were the United Presbyterians in Colombia (1856), the Baptists (1864), and the Methodists in Argentina (1867). Why did the Protestant work here get off to such a late start?

A number of observations can be made. Certainly the Protestants had their hands full in initiating substantial missions to Asia and Africa and did not have resources to penetrate Latin America during the first era. Since the heaviest investment in missions in the first era came from Europe, the attitude of European Christians was significant. There was the opinion among many European Protestants that Latin America was already a 'Christian' continent and did not need evangelizing. This was especially true of the Anglicans, who consider themselves to be intermediate between Roman Catholicism and Protestantism. As late as the Edinburgh Conference of 1910, the Europeans strongly objected to the consideration of Latin America as a mission field.[6] It was only the more radical type of Protestantism found in the United States which did not see the Roman Catholic Church as essentially Christian. Thus it was missions from the United States which first penetrated Latin America on a significant basis. Remember that America had just gotten started in missions in 1810 and was a new nation with limited resources. Nevertheless, it was missions from North America that have carried the major burden of evangelizing Latin America right on up to the present. Kane characterized it as a "virtual monopoly."

Protestant colonial powers had begun to gain a foothold on the northern coast of South America in the middle of the seventeenth century and consolidated it in the Guianas in the next century. Moravian, Congregational, and Methodist missionary work in this whole Caribbean area bore considerable fruit, so that by 1900 the largest number of Protestants were in the Guianas, more than in Brazil, and almost triple the number in the rest of South America.

About the turn of the century hundreds of thousands of German Lutherans were migrating to Brazil, Argentina, Chile, and Uruguay. Although the church in Germany was slow to provide pastoral care for them, within a decade or two they were organized into churches and ministry arranged for. There were smaller numbers of other Protestant groups like the Waldensians of Italy.

Reaction to biblical evangelism

Translation of the Bible into the vernacular has been a basic Protestant principle. Under Catholic domination, the Bible was excluded.

> For almost three centuries after the European discovery of the New World the Bible was almost unknown in Latin America. The distribution of Bibles had been forbidden in the colonies by decree of the Pope and the King. The Roman Catholic Church intended to keep Latin America free from the "poison" of the Reformation and the Inquisition backed up its intent.[7]

In the early 1800's Bible distribution work began to penetrate. Bibles were shipped to merchants. A number of full-time workers began doing Bible colportage (distribution) work. The remarkable James Thomson traveled the whole length of Latin America distributing Bibles, beginning in 1817. There was always strong opposition to Bible distribution and evangelism. Unfortunately, the history of Protestant missions in Latin America is full of incidents of persecution and violence by the Catholics. Scenes of priests leading mobs to stone and burn Protestant churches were common right up to the 1950s, especially in Colombia. It is ironic that on a 'Christian' continent, Protestants experienced more actual martyrdom than on many 'heathen' fields. It was the Vatican II Council of the 1960s that caused a reversal of policy on the part of the Roman Catholic Church. The fruit of that reversal has been great as Catholics have begun to read and study the word of God. More recently it has been the Marxist revolutionaries who have been murdering Christians.

Patterns of church growth

As in Africa, in the last century missions in Latin America were building a base preparatory to the rapid church growth of the twentieth century. In 1900 in South America there were only about thirty thousand members of the churches planted by the missionaries (excluding the immigrants from Europe). By the Panama Congress (of missions) in 1916, membership had grown to ninety-three thousand, showing especial growth in Brazil. Although earliest missionary work started in the Caribbean area, this has not been the major area of recent church growth, which has been quite modest in the twentieth century. At the beginning of the twentieth century denominational missions began shifting their emphasis to educational institutions since the majority of the people were illiterate. The early part of the twentieth century also marked the arrival of Pentecostal missionaries, some fresh out of the origins of the movement in the United States. Although the 'faith missions' were just getting started in Latin America in this period, it was after the second World War that missionary personnel took a dramatic shift in their direction. By 1958 sixty percent of all missionaries in Latin America were in missions associated with the Interdenominational Foreign Mission Association or the Evangelical Fellowship of Mission Agencies.[8]

The figures.   Church growth in Latin America has been carefully studied because it has been so rapid. Although previously it was most encouraging, since 1960 there seems to have been a significant acceleration. This is especially striking in Colombia, where the opposition and persecution restrained growth. But with the new attitude toward the Bible since Vatican II Council, Colombian church growth has taken off. But because of the previous restraint there are still only 3.1 percent of Evangelicals in Colombia. Church growth in Brazil was 77 percent in the decade of the '60s and increased to 155 percent in the '70s. Brazil, Chile, and Guatemala are high in both the present percentage of evangelical Christians (18%, 27%, 23% resp.) and the rate of church growth. Four Caribbean nations have a large percentage of Evangelicals: Bahamas (33%), Puerto Rico (22%), Barbados (24%), and Jamaica (18%). Some of the countries with less than 5 percent of evangelical Christians are: Cuba (2.5%), Venezuela (4.8%), Surinam (2.9%), Mexico (4.3%), and Ecuador (3.4%). With its over 88 million population, accelerating church growth in Mexico in the last two decades is most encouraging. Despite guerilla warfare in some Central American countries churches have tripled in a decade.[9]

Marginal groups. When we analyze the current church statistics, we find some disturbing factors. When we note the number of Jehovah's Witnesses and Mormons (not included in above figures), we find them to be the largest denominations (excluding the Roman Catholics) in a number of countries like Mexico, Honduras, Panama, and Peru. Seventh-Day Adventists (included above) are the largest Protestant denomination in Venezuela and high on the list in a number of other countries.

Faith missions. Another disturbing factor is that while the faith missions have sent a lion's share of the missionaries since World War II, their churches represent only a relatively small part of the membership. Kane suggests three reasons for this: 1) they got a late start; 2) they have done extensive work among the Amerindians, who have proved to be much less responsive than the Latins; 3) Wycliffe Bible Translators is totally involved in tribal language reduction and translation work, which only indirectly contributes to church growth (and WBT is a large mission). [10] The fruit of the Amerindian work has been slow in coming. The ten million Quichua people (descendants of the ancient Incas) of the Andes Mountains were not very responsive to the gospel before 1970. During the seventies the Quichua church grew to thirty thousand and by the early eighties about eight hundred a month were turning to Christ and membership has risen to well over fifty thousand. [11]

Pentecostal growth. Pentecostals have seen incredible church growth throughout Latin America so that it is estimated that a majority of all Protestants are Pentecostal. Recognizing Pentecostals as fellow Evangelicals we rejoice, but are disturbed by the fact that one of the largest Pentecostal denominations is unitarian in theology, thus denying the Trinity. Peter Wagner has made an extensive study of Pentecostal church growth in Latin America and concluded that it is not their doctrine which has necessarily made them successful but rather their methods. [12] This is confirmed by the fact that cultic and marginal groups have also seen great church growth, and it cannot be attributed to their message, only their methods. Kane has summarized the results of this analysis. 1) Their "churches have been largely indigenous from the very beginning." Many other churches were run by the missionary for years before converting (belatedly) to indigenous principles. 2) They have not depended upon foreign funds. "3) They have made good use of lay witness. Every Christian is expected to share his faith with friends and neighbors. 4) Their lively and emotional church services, with plenty of indigenous music, hand-clapping, and testimonies, appeal to the emotional nature of the Latins. 5) They concentrate on the lower classes, who make up the bulk of the population," and make them feel accepted. 6) They have emphasized public witness: open-air meetings, Scripture distribution, and public parades and processions. 7) They have emphasized the experience of the Holy Spirit, not just as a doctrine to be believed. 8) They have stressed divine healing and the miraculous. [13] To these we could add the following observations. There is a sense in which Pentecostalism is the "unpaid debt" of Catholicism. It succeeds exactly where Catholicism failed. In place of the dead formalism of Romanism, Pentecostalism has stressed personal emotional involvement in worship. In place of a corpse hanging on a crucifix, the stress is on a living relationship with the Holy Spirit. In place of an artificial priesthood (now depleted of personnel), it stresses the priesthood of all believers. It has especially stressed practical training for its workers (the so-called 'street seminaries').

THE SPECTRUM OF BELIEFS

Among professing Christians there is a great spectrum of beliefs in Latin America. Let us survey that spectrum of viewpoints so that we might grasp the complexity of the situation today.

Contemporary Catholics

In the past Catholic scholars have identified four types of Latin American Catholics: formal, nominal, cultural, and folk. The formal Catholic is the serious, religious Catholic of the traditional kind. The nominal Catholic has some allegiance to the church, but rarely attends and makes little effort to practice the Catholic faith. The cultural Catholic, as the name suggests, appreciates the cultural aspects (art, music, literature), without the religious aspects. The folk Catholic blends Catholicism with native Animism, frequently referred to as Christo-paganism.

Among Catholics today the spectrum is far greater than ever. To a great extent the Papacy lost control after Vatican II Council. On the one hand, influenced by Pentecostalism there are millions of Catholics who have become charismatic and stayed within the Church. Although this has lost some momentum, it is still significant. On the other hand there are the liberal Catholics. They have borrowed liberal evolutionary theology from the liberal Protestants. A key writer is the late Jesuit philosopher Tielhard de Chardin. But even more recently out of this wing the popular movement known as 'liberation theology' has arisen. Liberation theology is the key to most of the revolutionary activity in Central America in the last decade.

What is liberation theology? It was first set forth by a Mexican priest, Gustavo Gutierrez, in papers in 1968 and a book, *A Theology of Liberation*, in 1971.[14] He concluded that the only answer to the inequity of Latin American economic, political, and social problems was Marxist-style armed overthrow of the oppressive dictatorships. Communism was dressed up with a veneer of superficial biblical arguments, such as the liberation of the Israelites from Egyptian oppression and Christ's quotation from Isaiah in the synagogue of Nazareth about 'liberating the captives'. It has spread among liberal Protestants, as well, but has its main impact upon Roman Catholics. This explains why priests and nuns have collaborated with the former Sandinista (Marxist) government of Nicaragua.

Conservatives against Ecumenism

Because the missionaries to Latin America have tended to be very conservative theologically, the churches have also tended to be the most conservative in the world. It has been estimated that as many as 95 percent of the Protestants in Latin America are conservative evangelicals. With the exception mentioned above, Pentecostals are evangelical, the 'faith missions' have stayed evangelical for the most part, and even in the old-line denominations a considerable number of the missionaries and pastors are solidly evangelical. The tendency has definitely been for more conservative missionaries to come to Latin America. Perhaps this is because the more liberally minded missionaries felt that Latin America did not really need missionaries. This easily explains the difficulty that the Ecumenical Movement has had in making much impact in Latin America. There are two flies in the ointment, however. The World Council of Churches has been able to recruit a few of the Pentecostal denominations, apparently because of doctrinal naivete. It has also been reported by George Peters that in his meetings with evangelical pastors in Central America he found that a significant number have unknowingly imbibed certain concepts of liberation theology.[15] In both cases it points up the lack of adequate theological training for many Latin American church leaders. This is one of the crying needs of this continent.

SEEDBED OF INNOVATION

Latin America was the scene of a number of very significant innovations in missionary methodology, which have already been described in chapter 11. Missionary radio was begun in Quito, Ecuador in 1931 by Clarence W. Jones. Latin America has been the scene of very significant missionary radio investment since then. W. Cameron Townsend became the father of modern scientific linguistic analysis among the Cakchiquel of Guatemala and founded Wycliffe Bible Translators in 1934. Evangelism-in-Depth was developed in Nicaragua in 1960 by Kenneth Strachan. Theological Education by Extension was developed in Guatemala in 1963 by Ralph Winter and James Emery. Thus missions in Latin America has had a worldwide impact upon missionary methodology.

THE UNFINISHED TASK

Johnstone suggests a number of challenges for outreach:[16]

Countries with few Protestants: Uruguay, Ecuador, and Colombia have below 4% Protestants.

Upper and middle classes. Most Evangelicals come from the lower classes.

The cities. There are tremendous needs in the slums ringing the affluent cities and among unwanted street children.

University students. Although InterVarsity (IFES) has well-established work in 12 countries, only a small minority on campus are Evangelicals.

Amerindian peoples. Despite the great progress among tribal peoples, there are a number of smaller tribes, numbering a total population of about a million, into which access has been prevented.

Immigrant communities. Chinese, Japanese, Muslims and Jews are often unreached. The largest unreached Jewish population is there.

1. Johnstone, 5th ed., pp. 46-49; 62-67. Statistics for the Caribbean area have been combined with Latin America. See also Kane, *Understanding Missions*, p. 224-37.

2. Kane, p. 225.

3. Latourette, *History of Christianity*, p. 943.

4. Ibid, p. 945.

5. Forster and Marston, *God's Strategy*, pp. 282-88.

6. Kane, *Understanding Missions*, p. 230.

7. W. R. Read, V. M. Monterroso, and H. A. Johnson, *Latin American Church Growth* (1969), p. 38.

8. Ibid, p. 47.

9. Johnstone, pp. 52-54, 62-67. Also under individual countries, en loc.

10. Kane, *Understanding Missions*, p. 233.

11. Wagner, *On the Crest of the Wave*, p. 23.

12. Wagner, *Look Out! The Pentecostals Are Coming,* republished as *Spiritual Power and Church Growth* (1986) in which he changes his first analysis.

13. Kane, *Concise History*, pp. 148-49.

14. Gustavo Gutierrez, *A Theology of Liberation* trans. Caridad Inda and John Eagleson (1973).

15. George W. Peters, class lecture, Trinity Evangelical Divinity School, July 14, 1981.

16. Johnstone, 5th ed., p. 67.

"Islam if the only one of the great non-Christian religions which gives a place to Christ in its book, and yet it is also the only one . . . which denies His deity, His atonement, and His supreme place as Lord of all in its sacred literature."

—Samuel M. Zwemer (1912)

THE MUSLIM WORLD: NEGLECTED CHALLENGE

In our survey of gospel penetration into the various fields of the world we have considered three continental areas: Asia, Africa, and Latin America. Why have we now begun to consider the domain of one of the world religions? The answer comes simply. Islam is the most widespread of the world religions and is found significantly on two continents and expanding into others. It is the largest of the world religions (other than Christianity) with over one billion adherents. It is unique among the non-Christian religions in that it not only claims to be the only true religion, but it has followed up that claim by a sense of world mission that the other religions lack. Thus the Muslim world is a unique challenge to the church of Jesus Christ that cannot be adequately treated in a merely geographical analysis, as helpful as that may be. All of the other religions are essentially limited to one continent, except for Animism. But pure Islam may be contrasted with Animism in the difficulty of penetration of the gospel (although 'folk Islam' is permeated with many animistic practices). So it deserves separate consideration. Before we can understand contemporary Islam, we must grasp a few facts of history.

FOURTEEN CENTURIES OF BLOODY CONFLICT AND EXPANSION

Two tides of Muslim conquest

We have already surveyed in chapter seven the two surges of Muslim conquest which established Islam from one end of Asia to the other, in North Africa, and in the southern parts of Europe. We have also noted the Crusades which were the 'Christian' reaction to that conquest and the fact that much of Islam's spread was by witness as well as by conquest. But this is not the whole story.

Internecine bloodshed among Muslims

Although Muhammad began his career by preaching the Surahs of the Qur'an, once he had achieved political power in Medina he began to use the power of the sword to promote his religion of Islam. The conquest of Mecca was only the beginning of bloody conquest. However, the bloodletting did not stop with pagans. The first four of the successors to Muhammad, the Caliphs, died by the sword, as did Ali's son, Hussain. This assassination marks the great dividing point between the Sunni and the Shi'ite Muslims. Since a Muslim who kills another Muslim is said to go straight to Hell, the strife between Muslims over the centuries is even more intriguing to the observer. It is reliably reported that the Khomeini regime in Iran executed at least eight thousand people, not counting street executions, when it took over. The recent war between Iran and Iraq cost a million or more lives—in many cases Shi'ite Muslim against Shi'ite. This has been the history of Islam through the centuries.

Independence, oil money, resurgence

With the spread of the western empires in the seventeenth through nineteenth centuries most Muslim peoples became subject to non-Muslim Europeans. With Islam's strong emphasis upon the integration of the religious with the political and social, this was a severe blow to Muslim growth. With the breakup of the western empires after World War II, most Muslim peoples gained independence. As they began to 'feel their oats', they got a larger and larger share of the profits from the oil being pumped from their lands. This all has led to a resurgence of Islam, which might not have been anticipated fifty years ago. Muslims are on the march, not just politically and militarily, but also religiously as they build mosques in non-Muslim lands. This is a fact of the contemporary scene with which we will have to come to terms. Muslim evangelism is the best way to deal with this new reality.

THE CHALLENGE OF ISLAM

Thus we see that Islam presents one of the greatest challenges to the Christian faith, certainly more serious than that of Communism, and possibly more than materialistic secularism. What is it that makes Islam such a challenge? Kane suggests six aspects of Islam's uniqueness:

1) It is the largest of the non-Christian religions.
2) It is the only non-Christian religion that makes any [consistent] claim to be universal.
3) It is the only non-Christian religion that has any sense of world mission.
4) It is the only great. . . religion that is younger than Christianity.

5) It is the only religion that has fought and conquered Christianity in certain large areas of the world.
6) Through the centuries it has proved to be by far the most resistant of all the non-Christian religions.[1]

The Christian witness to Muslims

North India. In modern times the first missionary who focused on reaching Muslims was **Henry Martyn**, an evangelical chaplain with the East India Company, who arrived in Calcutta in 1806. His great accomplishment in a ministry of only six years before his death was the translation of the New Testament into three key languages of the Muslims: Urdu (Hindustani), Persian, and Arabic. Although Martyn engaged in much dialogue (argument) with Muslim leaders, he was never very enthusiastic about argument but rather encouraged Muslims to read the Bible for themselves. **Karl Pfander** (1803-1865) was a German missionary working with the Anglican Church Missionary Society in north India who developed a very argumentative approach to Muslims in his book *The Balance of Truth*, which is so powerful that it is banned in many Muslim countries today.[2] **Thomas French** (1825-1891) was also a CMS missionary to north India, who although appointed Anglican Bishop of Lahore in 1877, continued to give priority to Muslim evangelism. Like Martyn he became increasingly disillusioned with mere argument, and sought to stress the spiritual dimensions of our relationship with Christ. The Scottish Presbyterians working among the Muslims stressed educational and medical work to gain entry into the Muslim heart. By the end of the nineteenth century the American Presbyterian work among Muslims in north India had become as large as the British and Scotch work. They adopted a church-oriented approach to Muslims, by seeking to invigorate the indigenous church to Muslim witness (even if they were not converts from Islam).

The Middle East. The other major area of early Muslim evangelism was in the middle-eastern countries: Turkey, Egypt, Syria-Lebanon, Arabia, and Persia (Iran). There was a significant difference in Muslim work in this area compared with that of the north of India. In India there was a mixed population of Muslims, Hindus, Sikhs, and lesser religious groups. In the Middle East the population was (and still is) predominantly Muslim with minorities of 'Christians' from the ancient Armenian, Coptic, and Syrian churches. The problem was whether to try to reach Muslims through these formalistic, dead churches, or whether to bypass them and go directly to the Muslims. The major thrust here also has been from the American Presbyterians, Reformed, and English Anglicans. We mentioned in chapter 10 the work of Edward Glenny and the North Africa Mission (1881), Ion Keith-Falconer (1885) and Samuel Zwemer (1888), pioneers to Arabia. We should also take note of William Gairdner (1873-

1928), who with his colleague Douglas Thornton carried on a very effective witness in Cairo, the intellectual center of Islam.[3]

Contemporary witness. The witness to Islam got a great boost with the surge of new missionaries after World War II. Many new ministries were initiated by IFMA and EFMA missionaries and the existing denominational missions were strengthened with new personnel. So just as the Islamic resurgence was beginning, God was raising up a new taskforce to penetrate the Muslim world.

In North Africa, just as the North Africa Mission (now Arab World Ministries) started to get major response to its correspondence-course ministry in 1964, the government heard of it and the mission was expelled from some North African countries. But moving the center to Marseilles, France made it possible to continue that very effective witness. Witness has continued under great pressure in most of these countries with the exception of Libya where there seems to be no existing witness to Muslims.

In the Middle East most missionaries must serve as 'tentmakers', entering for secular employment and carrying on a more subtle witness. In Turkey many workers connected with a number of organizations have seen the beginnings of indigenous churches. The arrest of many foreign and national Christians in 1988 has eventuated in acquittal and the possibility of gaining more government recognition. The prospect is positive.

In the Indian subcontinent in 1947, independence was feared because of the separation of Pakistan as an Islamic nation from secular India. The bloody aftermath of communal strife between Muslim, Sikh, and Hindu, has caused some Muslims to reappraise their religion. Pakistan has remained open to missionary evangelism and upon separation of the eastern half as Bangladesh, that nation became even more open. There have been some significant instances of gospel penetration of the Muslim community in both halves. In one isolated town in Pakistan, missionaries have seen a Muslim-convert church formed with hundreds of believers. After independence, not all Muslims went to Pakistan—they are still about 12 percent of the total population of India. Witness there suffers from the lack of Christians who especially focus on Muslim work.

Indonesia is the area of greatest gospel penetration in the Muslim world. Although nominally a Muslim country, only about half of the 79 percent professed Muslims can be called Quranic Muslims. The other half are more Animist than Muslim. When the Muslims slaughtered a half-million suspected Communists in 1965, out of the disillusionment and turmoil hundreds of thousands of both Communists and Muslims turned to Christianity. Although some made a Christian profession with ulterior motives at first, God has used this to bring many to Himself. There were revivals among the Christians (some churches going back to the earliest Dutch East India Company chaplains; see ch. 8) which broke through to win Muslims as well. Church growth continues very great in Indonesia. The government now recognizes Christianity among four religions, since 12.5 percent are professing Christians.[4]

WHERE ARE THE MUSLIMS?

COUNTRY	TOTAL POPUL. Million	MUS- LIM POPUL. Million	MUS LIM %	PROF. XIAN %	EVANG- ELICAL %	RATIO: EVANG. /100 MUSL.
INDONESIA	187.6	148.2	79.0	12.5	4.5	5.2
PAKISTAN	122.4	118.4	96.7	1.7	0.2	0.2
INDIA	897.4	107.7	12.0	3.9	1.0	8.3
BANGLAD.	113.9	99.1	87.0	0.4	0.1	0.1
IRAN	62.8	62.2	99.0	0.4	0.0	0.0
TURKEY	60.7	60.6	99.8	0.2	0.0	0.0
EGYPT	58.3	49.8	85.4	14.1	0.7	0.7
NIGERIA	95.1	38.0	40.0	40.9	15.0	15.9
CHINA	1178.	28.3	2.4	6.1	5.0	210
MOROCCO	28.0	27.9	99.8	0.2	0.0	0.0
ALGERIA	27.3	27.1	99.4	0.3	0.1	0.1
ETHIOPIA	56.7	19.8	35.0	51.0	13.0	37.0
SUDAN	27.4	19.2	70.0	14.4	3.1	4.4
IRAQ	19.2	18.3	95.4	3.0	0.0	0.0
AFGHAN.	17.4	17.2	99.0	0.0	0.0	0.0
S. ARABIA	17.5	16.3	93.4	3.2	0.3	0.3
UZBEKSTN	21.7	14.8	68.2	1.5	0.1	0.15
SYRIA	13.5	12.2	90.5	6.4	0.1	0.1
YEMEN	11.3	11.3	99.9	0.0	0.0	0.0
MALAYSIA	18.4	10.1	55.0	7.3	3.1	5.6
TANZANIA	27.8	9.7	35.0	36.6	9.7	28.0
SOMALIA	9.5	9.5	99.9	0.0	0.0	0.0
TUNISIA	8.6	8.5	99.5	0.2	0.0	0.0
NIGER	8.5	7.7	90.5	0.4	0.1	0.1
MALI	8.9	7.7	86.3	1.8	0.7	0.8
SENEGAL	7.9	7.2	90.8	5.1	0.1	0.1
KAZAKHST	17.2	6.9	40.0	11.2	0.7	1.7

In the Philippines the largest southern island of Mindanao is divided geographically between Roman Catholics and Muslims. Many churches have been planted among Catholics in some areas. Some missions are targeting the Maranao and Magindanao Muslims in unreached areas, and significant fruit is beginning to appear.

As you may recall, Africa is the scene of a struggle between Christianity and Islam. Not only are Animists turning to Christ more than to Islam, but in Nigeria, despite persecution, the strong ECWA church (of SIM) is seeing fruit in its witness to Muslims in the north, especially in the universities. Witness to Asian Muslims in Kenya and South Africa is beginning to bear fruit.

Why is the soil so hard?

There is no argument about the hardness of the soil in the Muslim world. Why is it so hard to get the seed of the word of God to germinate there? In the parable of the four soils, Christ spoke of the first kind which had been trodden underfoot and compacted and the birds coming to peck up the seed. This perfectly describes the Muslim world. Not only are there many factors which have compacted the soil, but also Satan's agents are especially busy in seeking to counteract the word of God before it can get a chance to germinate. What are the footsteps which compact and the birds which peck?

The only post-Christian religion. Islam alone among the major world religions is younger than Christianity. Islam alone among the major world religions reacted to a misunderstanding of Christian teachings. Islam alone borrowed heavily from Judaism and Christianity (including Apocryphal materials) and in the process changed some of the Biblical materials. For this reason it has been called by some a Christian heresy. Although this is an overstatement, there is an element of truth to it. It is close enough to the truth to inoculate Muslims against the truth.

No other religion so specifically poisons the minds of its adherents to Christianity. Muhammad was very offended with the doctrine of the deity of Christ and the Trinity. He explicitly taught that the greatest sin is that of *shirk*, which means to attribute partnership to God. Just like the Jewish leaders of old, his unitarian concept of the singleness of God left no room for Jesus of Nazareth to claim to be God incarnate. Thus Muslims are taught from childhood that attributing deity to any human being is a great sin. Muhammad understood the Trinity to include Mary and understood the sonship of Christ in sexual terms as relating to the virgin birth. This seemed offensive to Muhammad, and therefore he stressed that "Never has Allah begotten a son, nor is there any god besides Him" (Surah 23:91). Since Muslims understand Jesus to be a genuine prophet of God and sinless like all the prophets, they cannot accept the crucifixion of Christ. How could Allah allow his holy prophet Jesus to die on a cross? Thus Muslims are taught that someone else was crucified in place of Jesus. And the whole idea of salvation coming to us by grace based upon that crucifixion is also rejected. Salvation is by human merit.

Islam claims to be the ultimate and original religion and therefore supersedes all other religions. Although Muslims believe that there are four extant revelations of God: the *Taurat* (law of Moses), *Zabur* (Psalms of David), *Injil* (Gospel of Jesus), and the **Qur'an** (recitation to Muhammad), they believe that the Qur'an supersedes the others. To explain the differences between the Bible and the Qur'an, they claim that the Bible has been corrupted and changed by Jews and Christians. Thus they are 'brainwashed' against the Bible and its teachings.

Social and political factors. Islam claims to be the only complete and natural religion: it pervades all of life, the political and the social dimensions. Muslims have always used political pressure for their ends. Whether it be the more overt use of the sword to persuade heathen to convert or the more subtle pressure of making Christians and Jews second-class citizens in Muslim lands—both have been effective. Politics is an intrinsic part of Islam, so Muslims have always been aggressive in using political pressure to accomplish their goals. M. A. Jinnah's agitation to force the British to carve the Islamic republic of Pakistan out of undivided India is a classic example of this. Although Muslims are divided on many things, they have had great success in wielding political power to further the cause of Islam. In an Islamic country, that political power includes the sword of the government in many ways. Even where religious liberty is promised by the constitution (as in Turkey), harassment by Muslim officials can involve arrest and torture, as well as ignoring justice in the murder of a convert.

How can officials justify such things? The answer is found in the Devil's trump card: **the Law of Apostasy** found in Quranic Law. Although this is not written into the laws of most Muslim countries, it is a part of the Islamic faith. It is perfectly ethical for any Muslim to kill an apostate from Islam. This is explicit in the Qur'an: "Whoso shall apostatise from his religion, let him die for it, and he is an infidel" (Surah 2:214). Thus when a convert to Christ is mistreated or even murdered, the government officials look the other way. Even more outrageous is the **blasphemy law** recently passed in Pakistan, which makes it a capital offense for anyone to say anything derogatory about Muhammad or the Qur'an. Thus the Christian community is under incredible pressure not to witness.[a]

But even when more enlightened Muslims do not go to such extremes, there is the strong social pressure of Islam. Like the Pharisees of biblical times, Muslims practice their religion very publicly. Prayers are said very publicly on street corners and public places. The month of **Ramazan (Ramadan)** fast is also enforced by social pressure. In some

---

[a] During a visit to Pakistan in 1997 I visited a Christian village which had been torched by a mob of tens of thousands of Muslims a week earlier. This was the worst incident in Pakistan's 50-year history.

places it is impossible to buy any food or drink during the daylight hours of fasting. Although in some areas there are many who do not conform, in most parts of most Muslim countries the pressure for outward conformity is very great. The convert is quickly identifiable. Nevertheless, there is a long history of Muslims who, like Nicodemus, become secret believers. If they are really born-again, we believe that they eventually must surface.

Minimal moral demands. Islam is a very legalistic religion—it puts great religious demands upon its adherents. They must not eat pork or drink alcohol, they must go through their recited prayers, they must fast, etc. But when one examines the moral demands of Islam, one finds many loopholes in their ethical system. Because Allah is so remote and transcendent from man, Muslim ethics is not seen as a reflection of Allah's character (as Christian ethics should reflect God's character). It is common knowledge in Pakistan that the "three R's" are *rishvat* (bribery), *risooch* (influence), and *rishtadar* (relatives). Truth, honesty, and love are not valued qualities in Muslim society. It is axiomatic that when a Muslim swears on the name of Allah that something is true, one can feel quite sure that he is lying. Dishonesty in business is a way of life in Muslim countries. There are, of course, many exceptions, but the impact of Islam has not been very positive in these areas. The Law of Apostasy and the concept of *jihad* (holy war) have led to a cavalier attitude toward the shedding of human blood. Contemporary terrorism by Shi'ite 'fundamentalist' (extreme legalistic) groups is perfectly explainable in terms of the ethics of Islam. Although adultery is generally seen as sinful, the externalism of Muslim life does not necessarily promote sexual purity. Polygamy is tolerated (but limited to four wives), and lust is only publicly repressed by the purdah (veil) system.

The human bent to legalism and autosoterism. Man is innately religious and legalistic. This was true of the Pharisees of Christ's day; it is true of the Christendom of our day (the majority reverting to formalistic legalism); and it is overwhelmingly exemplified by the growth of Islam. Today we see a resurgence of the extreme legalistic forms of Islam. Man wants innately to earn his way to heaven; man wants to build up merit before God and other men. Islam perfectly satisfies this desire. It is a merit system and knows nothing of God's grace.

The nominalism and immorality of the 'Christian' West. Muslims have two major impressions of Christianity. They see the Western expatriates who come to their lands, most of whom are not born-again Christians, and also Western cinema, which hardly exemplifies Christian morality. They see the alcoholism, the sexual looseness, the sexually provocative dress, the degenerate music, and they react as Ayatollah Khomeini and his followers reacted. It certainly is no brief for Christianity.

Christians have not put proportional resources into Muslim evangelism. The law of agriculture is also a law of gospel propagation: "He who sows sparingly shall also reap sparingly; he who sows bountifully shall also reap bountifully" (2 Cor. 9:6). Muslim evangelism is difficult. Somehow we have been intimidated and have shrunk from the difficult. The writer observed that scores of missionaries in the Muslim country of Pakistan were involved in church development work while very few were devoted to Muslim evangelism. The Muslim peoples of the world were largely neglected until the 1970's. Ralph Winter's contribution of highlighting the Muslim world as one of the hidden frontiers of modern missions has made a significant difference. Some missions in Africa which had made a great impact among the Animists, have now begun turning to the Muslims at their doorstep.

A strategy for Muslim evangelism

Much is being written on strategy for reaching Muslims. There are a number of things which have been effective in different parts of the Muslim world, which need to be utilized wherever possible. Bible correspondence courses have proved their worth in several areas, provided that the students are followed up. Christian radio is part of the necessary saturation process in a world in which the transistor radio is ubiquitous. The growing number of Muslim refugees must receive due attention. Afghanistan was hitherto one of the most closed countries in the world. Today millions of Afghans have fled to Pakistan and on to other countries, where they are accessible and more open. National Christians must be challenged to witness to their Muslim compatriots, whether or not they themselves are converts from Islam. Christians should press for civil rights in Muslim countries. Through the United Nations, pressure should be brought to bear on Islamic countries to put religious freedom in their constitutions. At the appropriate time, Christians should pursue the full implementation of those rights in the courts of the land. Muslim students and immigrants here in the West should be won to Christ and sent back as evangelists. Lastly, we should say that contextualization issues are very important here. It is being done by some. Let's all get involved!

Perspectives enrichment: Chapters D-16 to 19

1. Kane, *Concise History,* p. 114.

2. C. G. Pfander, The *Balance of Truth,* trans. W. St. Clair Tisdall (1910).

3. Lyle L. Vander Werff, *Christian Mission to Muslims: the Record* (1977), pp. 30-201, passim; Zwemer, *Into All the World,* pp. 203-209.

4. Johnstone, *Operation World,* 5th ed., p. 292.

THE RELIGIOUS DIVISIONS OF EUROPE

Mixed Cath. Orthodox & Prot. Plural.
Mixed Orthodox & Prot. Pluralities
Mixed Cath. & Prot. Pluralities
Eastern Othodox Majority
Roman Catholic Majority
Protestant Majority
Muslim Majority

Percentages represent Evangelicals.

Finland 16.0%

Sweden 6.8%

Lutheran

Norway 9.8%

Estonia 7.5%

Denmark 4.8%

Latvia 5.6%

Netherlands 5.0%

Lithuania 0.3%

Russia 0.6%

REFORMED

U.K. Anglican 8.5%

Lutheran

Poland 0.2%

Belarus 1.0%

Ireland 0.9%

Germany 3.2%

Czech

Slovakia 1.4%

Ukraine 2.7%

Belgium 0.3%

Austria 0.5%

Hungary 4.9%

Moldova 1.5%

France 0.6%

Slovenia 0.2%

Croatia

Romania 4.9%

Switzerland 5.4%

Bosnia 0.0%

Yugoslavia 0.2%

Italy 1.0%

Albania 0.1%

Bulgaria 1.2%

Spain 0.8%

Macedonia 0.1%

Greece 0.1%

Turkey 0.0%

Portugal 1.0%

"... a deadening secular humanism has effectually become the dominating force in European society. This philosophy has corrupted every part of the culture—art, music, social values, morality and theology. The decline in churchgoing has been so disastrous that only about a fourth of Europe's population are regular worshippers in a church."   —Patrick Johnstone

EUROPE: RE-EVANGELIZING SECULAR 'CHRISTIANS'

Europe was the last major modern mission field to be recognized as needing missionaries. After all, the whole idea of sending missionaries was rediscovered in Europe. For centuries the bulk of the missionaries came from Europe. Why indeed should Europe need to receive missionaries? The answer points up the tremendous changes which have taken place in Europe in the last century—changes which have radically altered the spiritual situation in Europe today so as to make it a mission field again. The very complex changes can be boiled down to one word: secularism. In a nutshell, Europe has gone from being a 'Christian continent' to becoming a secularized continent in need of evangelization all over again.

Until a decade ago Europe was a doubly divided continent—politically and religiously. With the demise of the Iron Curtain the political divisions are fading. But the religious divisions continue. Before we can understand Europe's present situation, we must understand how it came to be that way. Let's go back and refresh our minds about the major facts of European history.

A RELIGIOUSLY DIVIDED CONTINENT

Eastern Orthodox/Roman Catholic

The evangelization and Christianization of most of Europe was essentially complete by the time of Charlemagne about A.D. 800. Within two centuries the 'Holy Roman Empire' and the Catholic (Universal) church had been split in two: the Western Church under the Bishops of Rome and the Eastern Church headquartered in Constantinople. The Greek and Slavic areas of eastern Europe were the domain of this 'Orthodox' church while western Europe was the domain of the western latinized church, which was evolving into what today is the Roman Catholic church.   The eastern church developed into today's Greek Orthodox Church, which is dominant in Greece, and the Russian Orthodox Church which has been dominant in Russia, Bulgaria, Romania, and Yugoslavia. Today there are about 125 million Orthodox adherents in Europe. Orthodoxy is formalistic like Roman Catholicism, including worship of Mary and the mass. There is a hierarchy of Patriarchs but no Pope. Theology is more mystical. Orthodoxy was unaffected by the Protestant Reformation.

Europe is still a nominally Roman Catholic continent, with about 264 million Roman Catholics out of the total population of 791 million (about one-third). After the split off of the Eastern Church in the eleventh century, the Roman Catholic church continued to evolve, as described in chapter 13, the Bishop of Rome claiming more and more political and religious authority. There were a few reformers before Luther, like John Hus of Bohemia, and John Wycliffe of England, who preached an evangelical gospel and won many to faith in Christ. But it was the Reformation which further divided Europe.

Roman Catholic/Protestant

The mainstream reformation. The Reformation started in Germany in 1517 with Luther's revolt against the apostasy of Roman Catholicism and expanded into many other countries under other reformers like John Calvin in France and Switzerland, Ulrich Zwingli in Switzerland, and John Knox in Scotland. Simply put, the Reformation swept northern Europe, but left southern Europe under the control of Rome. When all the dust had settled, the Lutherans were dominant in parts of Germany and all of Scandinavia (Norway, Sweden, Denmark, Finland, and some of the Baltic states). The reformed Calvinistic churches ended up being strongest in Switzerland and the Netherlands. They were strong in France until the end of the seventeenth century when persecution by the Catholics resulted in either the death or expulsion of most of the Protestant Huguenots. As a result France is one of the most unevangelized countries of Europe. John Knox's ministry resulted in a dominant Calvinistic Presbyterianism becoming the state church of Scotland. These became the main stream of the Reformation, but there were two other streams which are important to note.

A backdoor reformation. In England the infamous King Henry the VIII withdrew the Church of England from the control of Rome over an issue of remarriage. This opened the door for a gradual and partial reformation of the English church, especially under his daughter, Queen Elizabeth. Calvinists from the continent began to influence the doctrine of the English church so that it became somewhat Protestant but not wholly so. Right up to the present time, the Anglican church includes both an evangelical wing and a 'catholic' element, so much so that Anglicans see themselves as midway between Protestant and Catholic. There are today about 20 million Anglicans in Europe, mostly all in England. As we noted in previous chapters, the Anglicans have been very active in the modern missionary movement, having a large constituency in Africa and Asia. There is a strong evangelical element in the Church of England. Anglicans are called Episcopalians in the United States, but there are far fewer Evangelicals among them here.

The radical reformation. The other branch of the Reformation was the more radical branch, as seen in the Moravian Brethren, Anabaptists, and Mennonites, at first. To this was added the Pietistic movement within the Lutheran church and in England the nonconformist dissenters from the Church of England. At first the dissenters who left the Anglican church were mostly Congregationalists and Baptists, but by the eighteenth century the Wesleyan Methodist movement had also become separatist. The more radical Protestants were strongest in England and scattered among some central European countries. Because of persecution by the powerful state churches, many of these more radical Protestants emigrated to the New World (like the Pilgrim Fathers of New England). The dissenters did not believe that either the Anglican church or the other mainline Protestants had gone far enough in reforming the church of all unbiblical elements. The radical Protestants are nowhere near as numerous in Europe as they are in America, to the spiritual loss of Europe, we might emphasize. Today there are about 95 million Protestants in Europe, including the 20 million Anglicans mentioned above. However, only about 17 million of the Protestants could be considered evangelical. This raises an exceedingly important question. How did it come about that over 80 per cent of Europe's Protestants are not evangelical? Let us look into that question.

Protestant liberalism. Nineteenth century Germany was the seedbed of the destructive higher criticism of the Bible which was the foundation of modern Protestant liberalism (see chapters 10 and 11). We have already seen its impact upon missions. In understanding contemporary Europe it is important to understand the impact of liberalism upon the churches as well. When rationalism began to undermine the teachings of Scripture in the Lutheran State Church of Germany, there was no built-in mechanism to root it out. The government supported the church, theology was taught in the government-connected universities, and pastors and theology professors got paid, no matter what heresy they taught. In a state church in which the majority of the population (who are automatically church members) are not born- again Christians, it is virtually impossible to exercise any church discipline of false and unbelieving teachers. The result was that the unbelieving attacks upon the Bible in the religion departments of the universities went totally unchecked.

Since many British scholars went to Germany for theological education, the unbelief easily spread to England, where it also penetrated the churches very deeply. Only in America did it find some resistance and opposition by Evangelicals who tried (in many cases unsuccessfully) to exercise church discipline. The sweep of liberalism was overwhelming in Germany and on the continent. Although not as far-reaching in the United Kingdom, it still was devastating. God was depersonalized; Christ was humanized; man was deified; and the Bible was evolutionized, that is, made to fit the evolutionary mold of the liberal theologians. Let us see what the consequence of all of this was.

THE TRIUMPH OF SECULARISM

When the church becomes secular, we should not be too shocked if society also becomes secularized. When the great state churches of Europe became riddled with a secular, humanistic theology, it was only a matter of time before society followed suit in secularization. Since Christianity was emasculated of the supernatural element and became just one among many searches for God (if he exists at all), there was little point in continuing to profess Christianity at all. Europeans abandoned their churches in droves. Wayne Detzler has epitomized it well:

> Since 1960 the church in Europe has been plunged more deeply into the deep freeze of secularism, which had its beginning between 1870 and 1914 when the academic and labor world turned away from the church. From 1960, parish life in Protestant countries has quite dramatically lapsed into disuse and decay. By 1968 *Time* magazine could report concerning the continental churches: "In the traditional citadels of Christendom, grey Gothic cathedrals stand empty, mute witnesses to a rejected faith."[1]

Church attendance plummeted to only 2 to 4 percent of the people in some countries like Denmark, Sweden and Germany. As a result, church buildings have been closed by the thousands. Even the Baptist church building of William Carey's home church has become an Indian Hindu temple (in this case probably a change of neighborhood)! The consequence of this secularization upon the moral life of Europe has been appalling. Materialism, pornography, open drug use, suicide, and a political socialism in which the government replaces God—this is the fruit of humanistic theology. This has all been exacerbated by a flood of American and oriental cults and vast immigrations of non-Christians from Asia and the Near East.

Johnstone is not so negative: "A godless materialism has become the formative philosophy of the majority—particularly in Europe. To term Europe today as 'post-Christian' or as going through a process of 'de-Christianization' is a sad partial truth."[2] He sees some indications of renewal and turnaround, but the picture is still far from positive. The Catholic church has not escaped the trend. Nominally Catholic countries like France are as pagan and secular as can be found anywhere.

The roots of secularism

The state church compromise. It may be simplistic to blame the whole trend toward secularism on liberal theology. There are undoubtedly other factors as well. We have already highlighted the contribution of state churches to the theological decline. More can be said about its other ramifications. Johannes Warns, a Swiss Evangelical, has argued very cogently that when the state church christens all infants in a country, they think themselves to be Christians and that greatly hinders the evangelization of these 'Christians'.[3] The fact that the four largest 'Christian' groups in Europe all tend to hold to baptismal regeneration— that is, that we are born again in water baptism—also seriously contributes to the problem. Europe has been dominated by this devastating notion for centuries, which has caused millions to be "damned through the church."

Two great wars. Of great significance also has been the impact of two world wars and the failure of Christendom to stop Adolf Hitler and Benito Mussolini from their atrocities. Many church leaders, both Protestant and Catholic in Germany and Italy, supported these fascist leaders until it was too late. The holocaust was only the worst consequence of these regimes. Widespread disillusionment with such a powerless religion has had a serious impact. The physical impact of the wars should also be noted. Forty-five million people were killed in the second war; Europe was devastated; Christians and churches were uprooted. It left an indelible mark!

Communism. The postwar popularity of Communism also had its impact. Before the bankruptcy of Communism to accomplish even its own economic goals became so obvious, there was a time when a heady Marxist idealism was popular among the intellectuals of Europe. Strong atheistic and evolutionary propaganda turned many from religion. Indeed, the pseudo-scientific evolutionary propaganda coming from the scientific and educational establishment did great damage.

The Vatican Council. There is also a factor unique to the Catholic churches: Vatican II Council (1962-65). We have seen its very positive impact in making the Bible available to Catholics worldwide. In Europe, however, the negative factors of the council seem to predominate: the upsetting impact of all the changes in the 'church which doesn't change'. Young Catholics are disillusioned with the traditionalism of the Church. In Italy alone, "the long-powerful Roman Catholic Church has lost over nine million members in this generation. The decline in the number of priests and of influence has been dramatic."[4]

The ecumenical mirage. For half a century now European church leaders have been in the forefront of following an ecumenical mirage. They have been operating on the basis of one consuming ideal: that the external, organizational unification of Christendom would ensure success in accomplishing God's goals for the church. The present sad state of the churches in Europe is proof of the bankruptcy of that notion. They have swept away biblical doctrine and biblical evangelism to accomplish this goal. Although it is supposedly based upon Christ's words in John 17:21, "that they all may be one," these words have been taken out of context, misinterpreted, and allowed to be the only controlling factor in their agenda. The results speak for themselves!

THE CURRENT SITUATION

There are a number of positive developments which are most encouraging. **For the first time in history there is essential religious freedom in all of Europe.** Despite the continuing decline of the state-churches, Evangelicals are growing at a rate of 1.6% annually and are about 2.8 percent of the population over all. Evangelical seminaries and Bible schools are full, while liberal institutions are empty. The proportion of Evangelicals in old-line denominations is growing and the newer evangelical churches are growing and attracting young people. Noteworthy is evangelical growth in central Europe, especially Romania, Albania, and Bulgaria. Over 5000 Turkish Muslims have come to Christ in Bulgaria since 1990. Some immigrant groups are responsive: Antilleans, Caribbean peoples, Vietnamese, and Chinese. Gypsy people are turning to Christ in great numbers.[5]

Northern Europe

In general the lands of the Protestant Reformation are still the brightest part of the continent today. Norway and Finland are the most encouraging with 10 and 16 percent evangelical Christians respectively according to current statistics. We have noted that the part of Germany where the reformation was strongest was for many years behind the Iron Curtain—East Germany was one-third Lutheran. But now after reunification Protestants are 37 percent, with only 3.2 percent evangelical believers. The United Kingdom claims 8.6 percent evangelical believers, with England the lowest and Scotland the highest in church attendance.

Sweden and Denmark are reformation areas badly in need of revival, both with Lutheran State churches but with 6.8 and 4.8 percent Evangelicals, respectively. Sweden was the scene of great revivals a century ago, but today it is 'burned over' territory. We lived briefly in a town of nine thousand people in southern Sweden in the early '60s in which there were less than two dozen believers. The Netherlands formerly had a strong Reformed tradition, but only 5 percent today are Evangelicals.

Belgium shares more of the spiritual condition of its neighbor, France, with less than half of one percent believers. Ireland was untouched by the reformation with the exception of the northern counties, which are part of the United Kingdom. Over a million Scotch-Irish there are Protestant. But Ireland is counted as being only 0.9 percent Evangelical, and that is mostly in the environs of Dublin. Kane's picture is helpful, although dated:

> It is difficult for Americans to understand and appreciate the difference between the religious situation in Europe and that in the United States. In the whole of Europe there is only one [now many] Christian radio station, and that was erected and is maintained by an American mission, Trans World Radio. It is possible to buy time on Radio Luxembourg and Radio Monte Carlo; but prime time is almost impossible to secure and when available is extremely expensive. Even in England the local churches cannot buy time on the British Broadcasting Corporation network. The Bible, available in so many editions and versions in the United States, is a rare book in many countries of Europe. The Bible school movement of the United States and Canada, which has done so much for the cause of evangelical Christianity at home and overseas, is practically unknown in Europe. The few Bible schools that do exist are largely the result of American initiative in this postwar period. During the last two centuries Europe has produced no great evangelists such as Charles G. Finney, Dwight L. Moody, or Billy Graham. In fact, mass evangelism as we understand it is an American phenomenon and not particularly appreciated by most European church leaders.[6]

Southern Europe

For the first time in centuries southern Europe is hearing the gospel! The southern part of Europe has been solidly Roman Catholic since the Reformation. The Protestant Reformation made very little penetration into countries like Spain, Portugal, Austria, or Italy. Indeed, until recently there has not been the political liberty for the preaching of the gospel. As mentioned, the penetration of France was nullified by the severe persecution of the Huguenots in the seventeenth century, and only a small Reformed church remains. The Roman Catholic Inquisition in Spain set a pattern of repression of the gospel which carried through the death of Dictator Franco in 1975. Protestant churches were not allowed to have any sign of identification outside, and Protestants did not have basic civil rights such as the right to perform marriages, etc. Now the pressure has been lifted and the church is growing. There are 0.8 percent evangelical believers there now. Spanish minds have been poisoned against the gospel, but now with over 1100 missionaries, the word is being sown and the harvest is beginning to come.

While Portugal's situation has not been as extreme, it roughly parallels that of Spain. Now 1.0 percent profess evangelical faith. Although Italian disillusionment with the Vatican and its church is great, they have not turned to the gospel in great numbers, but have rather gone to Marxism, cults, or spiritism. The percentage of believers in Italy is just as low as Portugal: 1.0. Although Austria has over 5 percent Protestant (Lutheran and Reformed), most churches are dead and not giving witness to the Catholic majority. Indeed, they are hostile to evangelical missionaries. Evangelicals are estimated at a dismal 0.5 percent. Few Austrians have heard the gospel!

Greece is the only country in southern Europe dominated by the Greek Orthodox church, which being a state church still does not tolerate evangelical believers, who number only ten thousand (0.14%). The first countries evangelized by Paul are still in desperate need of the gospel. Only about 80 missionaries have succeeded in residing in Greece, and some of them have been imprisoned for "proselytization."

Eastern Europe

The Communist takeover of eastern Europe after World War II had a mixed impact upon the spread of the gospel in Europe. It meant that the Communist persecution of Christians had expanded from just the Soviet Union to all of the eastern European countries behind the Iron Curtain. In those countries which already had a strong evangelical witness, a purified and persecuted church has not only survived but grown. This is true in both Hungary and Romania, where there are now about 5 percent evangelical believers. But in those countries where there was a weak evangelical witness before the communist takeover, the repressive governments seriously hindered the spread of the gospel. Bulgaria and Poland are two countries where that was true, and the number of Evangelicals is now only about 1.2 and 0.2 percent respectively, and especially in Albania and former Yugoslavia where the percentage was 0.17, the lowest in Europe and among the lowest in the world! Persecution has actually helped to strengthen the churches in areas where there was a substantial church. In countries like Yugoslavia the church has never gotten a good foothold to start with. Officially there were no missionaries in eastern Europe, but some western missionaries had been able to stay and work in some countries on tourist visas.

East Germany was the only Protestant country behind the Iron Curtain, with over a third being Lutheran or members of one of the 'free' churches. Despite the greater freedom than in other Communist countries since 1978, the small number of Evangelicals has not been growing. This was the heartland of the Reformation.

Roman Catholic countries. There are seven eastern European countries with a Catholic majority. Among them Hungary has the largest Protestant minority (24%), but less than 5 percent are counted as Evangelicals. While the government did not openly persecute, the Communists did infiltrate and manipulate the churches. Revivals in past generations have brought some life and growth to the Reformed and Lutheran churches. Recently split Czechoslovakia's (Czech Republic and Slovakia) Protestant minority is only 5 percent, about 1.4 percent counted as Evangelicals. Czech Protestants have been persecuted for six centuries since John Hus was martyred in 1415. The United Brethren fled from there (Moravia) to missionary fame under Count Zinzendorf. The most powerful Catholic church in eastern Europe is in Poland (which has supplied a pope), with less than 0.5 percent Protestants, only half of whom are Evangelicals. Church growth is minimal, but there are some stirrings among Catholics, who are beginning to demand Bibles. Austria is joined by newly formed Lithuania, Croatia, and Slovenia as some of the most gospel-deprived Roman Catholic countries in the world.

Eastern Orthodox countries. Seven eastern European countries besides Russia are predominantly Orthodox: Bulgaria, Romania, and Yugoslavia are joined by newly formed Macedonia, Moldova, Belarus and Ukraine. Despite having had the most repressive of the former communist governments, Romania not only has the largest percentage of believers, but also the most encouraging church growth (if we include 'The Lord's Army,' an evangelical group within the Orthodox church). Bulgaria's small Protestant churches are mostly evangelical. Former Yugoslavia was a mix of Orthodox, Catholics, atheists, Muslims, and a minuscule 0.7 percent Protestants, less than 0.2 percent of whom are Evangelicals. Under the late dictator Marshal Tito's independent brand of Communism the country had some religious freedom. But Christians have taken little advantage of the opportunity, and church growth has been spasmodic. The largest number of clandestine missionaries in the eastern bloc was found there (about 25 in the 80's).

One eastern European country was at the same time heavily Muslim and fanatically Communist: Albania. It was one of the most closed countries in the world with virtually no gospel witness. But most of this has changed, as we shall see.

The Commonwealth of Independent States (CIS). The countries of the former Soviet Union were initially called the C.I.S., but we hear little about it now. Since the Bolshevik takeover of Russia in 1917, there had been a severe repression of religion in the Soviet Union, with 12 million Orthodox, Catholics, and Protestants martyred, especially under Stalin. The Russian Orthodox Church, the former state church of Russia, had suffered the closure of 88 percent of its churches and infiltration of its leadership by government agents (note: a member of the World Council of Churches). Nevertheless, it has survived with some 77 million members.   The 50 million Muslims, because of their stress on communal solidarity, have survived repression well.   The 11 million Catholics suffered severe repression.   The 1.1 percent Protestants, which probably includes about 2.5 million Evangelicals, have survived extreme persecution.   Some are in the government registered union of Baptist, Brethren, Pentecostal, and Mennonite churches, while others are unregistered Baptists and Pentecostals—the underground church, which grew even under persecution.

Rapid and radical changes. Now with the rapid sequence of incredible events triggered by former President Gorbachov's *Glasnost* policy, the whole situation has rapidly changed. With the demise of the Iron Curtain and the Soviet Union and the traumatic setback for communism, the religious and political scene is dramatically different. Eastern Orthodox, Roman Catholic, and Protestant churches and institutions are being reopened and people are turning from atheistic Marxism to religion by the millions.

The Muslims of the Caucasus and Central Asian republics are furiously building mosques and feeling a tremendous new political power. They are being courted by Saudi Arabia, Iran, Turkey, and Iraq, and are touting a Muslim federation in the area, which would have considerable political clout.

However, new religious tensions are also surfacing. Roman Catholics are trying to reclaim their churches in Ukraine and Belarus, which had been taken over by the Orthodox. Muslims and Armenian 'Christians' are at war in Azerbaijan and Armenia. The dissolution of Yugoslavia has erupted into a complex religious and ethnic war between Croatian Catholics, Serbian Orthodox, and Bosnian Muslims, which has its roots in the Muslim invasions of centuries ago.

MISSIONS TO EUROPE

There have long been a few missionaries to parts of Europe. The British Plymouth Brethren started work in Spain earlier in the century and have substantial assemblies there. There were only a few American missions which had worked in Europe before World War II, such as the Bible Christian Union, which began work in Germany in 1910, Spain in 1934, and France in 1938. For the most part American missionary work in Europe got its main impetus from the many Christian military personnel who saw the spiritual and physical devastation of Europe at the end of World War II. Robert Evans was one of them, who founded the Greater Europe Mission in 1949 out of postwar evangelistic campaigns there and the starting of the European Bible Institute in Paris. In 1963 he published, *Let Europe Hear*, which was a challenge to consider Europe as one of the neediest mission fields in the world.[7] Apparently many accepted his challenge, because the number of North American missions and missionaries have multiplied. In 1961 there were only about 400 missionaries to Europe. By 1972 the number had more than quadrupled to 1871, doubled again by 1985 to 3862, reached 5000 by 1988, and 9961 by 1993 and an additional 1073 to the Commonwealth of Independent States (CIS). France and Germany are the recipients of the largest number of Protestant missionaries with about 1300 each; and Spain third with over 1100. It should also be noted that there are over 15,000 European cross-cultural missionaries abroad, the largest numbers of which come from the United Kingdom, Germany, Sweden, Norway, and Finland.[8]

All of eastern Europe had only 440 missionaries in 1985, mostly from western Europe. Other than sending in missionaries, there were a number of other effective strategies for penetrating the Iron Curtain. One of the most effective has been missionary radio. Trans World Radio's transmitters in Monte Carlo have been most effective by broadcasting in eastern European languages in medium wave (standard AM band). Many other stations penetrate with short wave. Bible smuggling has been widely practiced by itinerant missionaries, tourists, and student summer missionaries. Thrilling stories have come out about the way that the Lord has incredibly brought together the smuggler and people searching for Bibles. A Dutch missionary called Brother Andrew has promoted and popularized (and defended the ethics of) Bible smuggling. Another strategy developed by a northeast India tribal Christian, Rochunga Pudiate, has been to mail New Testaments from India under a mutual trade agreement with that country.

Then under the *Glasnost* policy of former President Gorbachov of the Soviet Union, additional doors began to open. And now with the collapse of the Iron Curtain, the breakup of the Soviet Union, and the fall of Communist governments in Eastern Europe, there is a totally new and encouraging situation! There has been an astonishing openness to western missionaries and the proclamation of the gospel in most of these countries. Even in the most fanatic communist country of Albania there is an amazing openness to the West and to the gospel. Johnstone's summary is most helpful:

> **Training of leaders.** For so long forbidden, this is now being taken up with vigour. Numerous new seminaries, Bible schools and TEE programmes have sprung up across the region with many as cooperative efforts between indigenous churches and Western and Korean mission agencies. A 1993 survey revealed that by 1994 there will be up to 64 Protestant, 21 Orthodox, and seven Catholic institutions with most launched since 1989. There are approximately 2,000 Protestant students doing formal courses and a further 4,600 through TEE or BEE informal courses. . . . It is reckoned that by 1993, 105 million people had seen the Russian version of

the *Jesus* film.[9]

Now that God has so wonderfully discredited Communism and opened the door to eastern Europe and the CIS, how important that Christians wake up to the opportunities and take advantage of the situation, which could change again just as suddenly.

THE UNFINISHED TASK

To be realistic, evangelizing Europe is not just a mopping-up operation, since we are really just starting over to re-evangelize Europe. Johnstone gives the real picture:

> Great swathes of Europe are truly post-Christian with a small, 'irrelevant', committed Christian remnant, and need to be evangelized again—for example, North Germany, parts of Sweden, rural England and Wales and much of France. Many of these areas have not had much meaningful exposure to biblical Christianity for several generations.[10]

The neediest part is southern Europe, especially southeastern countries. Eleven countries have less than 0.2% Evangelicals. (See the Europe map at the beginning of the chapter.) There are major peoples with Christian tradition but very few Evangelicals: Lithuanians, Serbs, Montenegrin, Macedonian, Greek, and Basque ethnic groups. In addition, there are Muslim ethnic groups, which number 16.8 million: Bosnians, Albanians, Turks, and Kurds. And then there are the almost 300 unreached immigrant groups. Lastly, we should mention the young people of Europe, for whom Christianity seems irrelevant. They look instead to New Age "spirituality' and the occult. Our job is cut out for us. May we see the need and respond!

---

1. Wayne A. Detzler, *The Changing Church in Europe* (1979), p. 9.
2. Johnstone, *Operation World*, 4th ed., p. 81.
3. Johannes Warns, *Baptism*.
4. Johnstone, *Operation World*, 4th ed., p. 249.
5. Ibid, 5th ed., pp. 58-60.
6. Kane, *Concise History*, p. 154.
7. Robert P. Evans, *Let Europe Hear* (1963).
8. MARC, *Mission Handbook*, 14th ed., p. 584; also 17th ed.; Johnstone, *Operation World*, 4th ed., p. 35, passim and 5th ed., p. 647; Evans, *Let Europe Hear*, p. 505.
9. Johnstone, 5th ed., p. 53.
10. Ibid, p. 60.

PART V

HIS INSTRUMENTS:

THE FUNCTIONAL DIMENSION

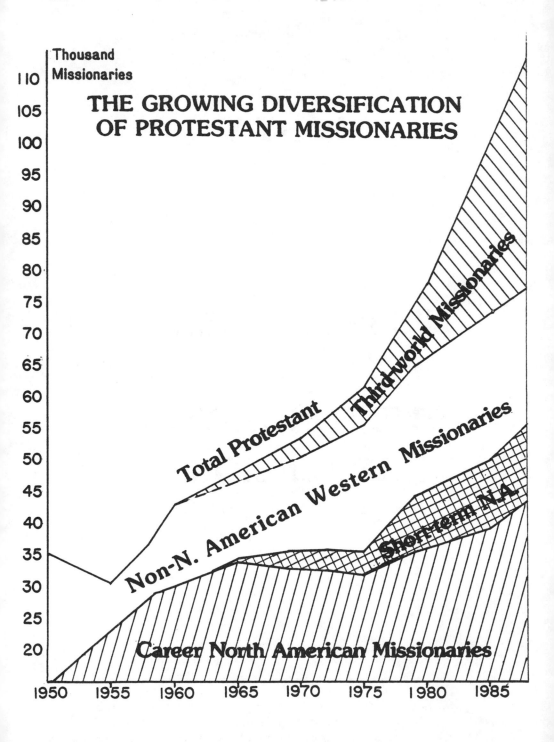

Thousand Missionaries

THE GROWING DIVERSIFICATION OF PROTESTANT MISSIONARIES

Total Protestant

Third-world Missionaries

Non-N. American Western Missionaries

Short-term N.A.

Career North American Missionaries

21

WHY IN THE WORLD DO WE NEED MISSION BOARDS?

THE BASIS OF MISSION BOARDS

Mission boards and missions are almost synonymous in the minds of most Christians. Mission boards were formed right at the beginning of the modern missionary movement and are the dominant force in missions today. It is only natural that most Christians would never question their existence. And yet there are a significant number of Christians who seriously question the validity of mission boards—some from a biblical point of view and others from the pragmatic. I myself was one of them and became an independent missionary for the first term on the field. What are their objections?

Some would suggest that although the organization of the local church is spelled out in the New Testament, there is no such thing as a mission board in the Bible. Believing in the sufficiency of Scripture, they feel that if it is not there, we should not have it. They view the Apostle Paul as an independent missionary and feel that mission boards are unscriptural. Others would point to the effectiveness of some independent missionaries and the ineffectiveness of some boards. They would also highlight the internal problems with which some boards have struggled. They might even refer pejoratively to a board as "something under which bugs hide."

The biblical basis of boards

Was the Apostle Paul really an independent missionary? It is true that the New Testament does not give us the organizational framework of Paul's ministry. However, it is very specific about who Paul's coworkers were. If asked to hazard a guess, most Christians might even venture to say that Paul had as many as a half-dozen coworkers. They would be astonished to find out that I have identified at least two dozen of Paul's fellow missionaries mentioned in the New Testament! This seems like the beginnings of a mission board, doesn't it? The Apostle Paul quickly took the leadership of this 'field-directed mission board'.

Who were they? We know that Barnabas and John Mark were his colleagues on the first journey, and most are aware that Silas, Timothy, and Luke joined Paul on the second journey. By the third journey we find reference to Erastus, Sopater, Aristarchus, Secundus, Gaius of Derbe, Gaius of Macedonia, Tychicus, and Trophimus accompanying Paul (Acts 19:22, 29; 20:4). Epaphras of Colossae, Epaphroditus of Philippi, Demas, Titus, Sosthenes, Artemas, Apollos, Zenas, and Jesus Justus are also mentioned in various places as associated with Paul in his missionary endeavors (2 Cor. 1:1; Phil. 2:25; Col. 4:11-12; Phlm 23; 2 Tim. 4:10-12, 20; Tit. 1:5; 3:12). Andronicus and Junias were relatives of Paul whom he calls 'apostles' (Rom. 16:7). The exact status of Crescens, Priscilla, Aquila, Apollos, Onesimus, Urbanus, and others might be questioned, but probably some of them should be considered as missionaries, not local church pastors or workers. This gives us a team of about two dozen workers. Paul directed his coworkers' comings and goings. He frequently left them to build up a church and then move on. Arthur Glasser points out: "This mobile team was very much on its own. It was economically self-sufficient, although not unwilling to receive funds from local congregations. It recruited, trained and on occasion disciplined its members."[1] Here we clearly have the function of a field-directed mission board without the organizational details.

Historical considerations

Ralph Winter has provided us with a stimulating perspective on the important place of monastic orders in the medieval church. He suggests that for the better part of a thousand years they were a major civilizing and missionary force in pagan Europe. We may be well aware that they preserved Biblical manuscripts, the literary heritage of past centuries, and learning and education in a society torn by barbarian incursions. But we may not be aware that they functioned as parachurch mission societies of a communal nature. Winter writes:

> For mission leaders the shattering of the "monks fled the world" stereotype is even more dramatically and decisively reinforced by the magnificent record of the Irish *peregrini*, who were Celtic monks who did more to reach out to convert Anglo-Saxons than did Augustine's mission, and who contributed more to the evangelization of Western Europe, even Central Europe, than any other force.[2]

Thus just as Paul's missionary team was not a part of local church structure, so the medieval monastic orders were not part of local church structure. In a real sense they were the medieval mission boards. After the reformation, the orders, including the newly formed Jesuits, kept the missionary thrust of the Roman Catholic Church alive, even when the Protestants had not yet awakened to their missionary responsibility. A number of writers have suggested that one reason for the slowness of Protestants to start implementing a missionary program was their lack of the organizational structure to do so: the parachurch orders.[3] We might also wonder whether Baron Justinian Von Welz in 1664 might have succeeded in planting the church in Dutch Guiana if he had had a mission board behind him with other workers to follow through after his death (see ch. 8).

Practical considerations

The fact is that God has greatly used many parachurch organizations in the last two centuries. In our day of specialization we have seen God raise up specialized ministries to meet needs that local churches simply could not meet. After the beginnings of modern mission boards in the 18th century, the trend was continued with the first Sunday School in the last century. Since most Sunday Schools came under the wing of local churches, few question their Scriptural basis today. However, since then a host of youth and campus ministries, radio and television, and home and foreign mission boards have been raised up to do what local churches were not doing nor could ever do.

How would it be possible for a local church to carry on an international radio ministry such as Trans World Radio or Far East Broadcasting Company? There is undoubtedly no local church that could staff, finance or administer such a world-wide ministry or even one such station. A local church would find it difficult or impossible to negotiate government permission to operate. The same sort of considerations would apply also to a specialized mission like Wycliffe Bible Translators. To insist that all this must be done by local churches or independent missionaries is to put a legalistic straitjacket upon God's work in its diversity.

The independent missionary

During my first term I did find some advantages to an independent missionary ministry. It does tend to avoid putting up too much 'organizational scaffolding' in seeking to plant indigenous churches. Historically mission boards have found it difficult to take down the scaffolding once the local church is planted. The independent missionary does not need to spend time and energy primarily in trying to relate to his fellow missionaries and can concentrate on relating to the nationals he seeks to reach.

There are serious disadvantages to the ministry of the independent missionary, however. Most seriously, his work lacks continuity when interrupted by furlough, illness, or departure from the field. The lack of proper supervision and accountability is also a serious drawback. Who back home is to know if the missionary is not doing his job, or is guilty of doctrinal or moral failure? For the pioneer missionary, lack of logistic support could be critical. Other difficulties of home representation, isolation, financial accountability, government representation, and provision of adequate financial resources to function effectively, are significant. One telling question that must be asked is, "What if all missionaries were independent missionaries?" There would probably be chaos!

THE FUNCTION OF MISSION BOARDS

What then is the function and purpose of a mission board? Quite a number of things are involved:

1. Mission organizations are most visible in recruiting, screening, and sending out missionaries. Most boards have a short-term candidate school which involves final details of training and orientation to the mission. The sending involves help with visas and travel arrangements.

2. Also obvious is the channeling of funds from donors to the field missionary and providing financial accountability to donors and to the I.R.S. This involves some complexity since the board has to be concerned about supervising expenditures for ministry funds, language study, medical, children's schooling, transportation, equipment and outfitting, field administration, home administration, provision for furlough, etc.

3. The mission must provide field orientation, supervision, leadership, and coordination for, and require accountability from, their field missionaries.

4. The mission facilitates the missionary's ministry with support infrastructure. This frequently includes housing, language-study help and supervision, help with representation to local governments, transportation, supplies, purchasing, etc.

5. The board administration acts as intermediary between the missionary and his supporters through continued local church ministries, correspondence, conferences, publications, and help with prayer/newsletters. This is so that the supporters might pray and give intelligently.

6. The board must provide planning, research, and coordination for the development of the ministries which the Lord has committed to them. This involves searching out unreached peoples and needy areas in which to start new work since the goal is "discipling all nations."

TYPES OF MISSION BOARDS

Denominational missions

We noted in the study of the history of missions that although the first mission boards were interdenominational, they soon became denominational boards. Thus most missionary activity in the first half of the

19th century was carried on by denominational missions. "Each denomination organized its own board of missions, supported and controlled by the denomination."[4]

Generally speaking, denominational missions get their support from the denominational budget and thus pay their missionaries a regular salary. They do not require their missionaries to 'raise their support'. This is not true of most Baptist missions, however, which function more like interdenominational missions in not having a denominational budget to draw from. Denominational missions are governed by a board of trustees which is usually appointed by the denominational leadership or elected by the delegates at the annual meetings of the denomination. There tends to be considerable home-base control, with many key decisions being made in headquarters. Most of the larger old-line denominations are now more liberal and ecumenical in nature and are members of the National Council of Churches, which dissolved its Division of Overseas Ministries a decade ago. The major exception to this would be the Southern Baptist Convention which was unaffiliated until recently when it joined the other evangelical denominational boards in the Evangelical Fellowship of Mission Agencies (EFMA).

Independent mission boards

Although they began in the last half of the last century, the interdenominational 'faith' missions became a major factor in the twentieth century. Although preceded by the Zenana and Medical Missionary Fellowship in 1852, the founding of the China Inland Mission (now OMF) in 1865 and its success in reaching inland China stimulated a succession of new interdenominational missions both in England and in America. More accurately we should call them transdenominational agencies since they draw individuals from diverse denominations and churches and do not relate directly to the denominations.

Ralph Winter has pointed out that although they have been called 'faith missions' because of Hudson Taylor's emphasis upon nonsolicitation of funds, they are more appropriately called 'frontier missions'. Their uniqueness was in pressing into the interior of the continents and countries they were working in. Thus terms like 'inland', 'interior', etc. were common in their original names.[5] Many such North American boards have banded together in the Interdenominational Foreign Mission Association (IFMA), founded in 1917.

Unlike denominational missions the governing boards of independent missions are either self-perpetuating or elected by the missionaries. A self-perpetuating board replaces its own members who do not continue (whether because of resignation, death, or completion of their term of office) by electing their own replacements. Some missions consider the missionaries not merely as employees, but as members who have a vote in the election of the governing board.

The great strength of the independent boards has proved to be the stress on 'personalized giving'. The statistics show very clearly that churches and individuals will give more liberally toward the ministry of a missionary they know personally, rather than the faceless budget of a denomination. Independent missions get their support from independent churches, churches in more loosely organized fellowship groups that do not have their own mission boards, denominational churches, and from individuals in all of these kinds of churches.

Independent boards handle the donations coming in toward their missionaries' support in essentially two different ways: the general-fund-pooling plan and the individual-support plan. The general-fund approach is a share-and-share-alike system under which support donations go into a general fund out of which the missionaries' allotments are drawn. If there should be a shortfall in income, the mission can either make up the shortage from contingency funds, if any, or remit allotments on a percentage basis. Thus one missionary's support deficiency is made up by another's surplus. On the other hand, under the individual-support plan each missionary gets only those donations which are designated for his support and perhaps a percentage of any undesignated funds coming into the mission. IRS regulations have tended to favor the general-fund approach.

Associations of mission boards

Most Protestant mission boards are members of one of the associational groups. The old-line denominations are members of the ecumenical **National Council of Churches** or the **Canadian Council of Churches.** The missionaries under these boards tend to be theologically liberal (not all, however), and the total number has been sharply declining in recent years due to the loss of missionary fervor in these groups. Most of the distinctively evangelical denominations belong to the **Evangelical Fellowship of Mission Agencies (EFMA).** The independent evangelical/fundamental missions generally belong to the **Interdenominational Foreign Mission Association (IFMA).** A number of more separatist fundamental missions belong to the **Fellowship of Missions (FOM).** In 1985 the **Association of International Mission Services (AIMS)** was founded for charismatic agencies. There are a number of exceptions to the above statements—missions which are unaffiliated with any association. These include Wycliffe Bible Translators, New Tribes Mission, the Churches of Christ, 'Plymouth Brethren', and many smaller groups. The number of missionaries serving under these unaffiliated missions has grown rather remarkably in recent decades.

Biprofessional missionaries (tentmakers)

There has been a growing number of missionaries who pursue a secular occupation to gain entrance into a 'closed country'. Thus they are not counted as 'professional missionaries', even though their intention is to be missionaries, as they are able, under the circumstances which prevail locally. This is the only way to get into some countries like mainland China, India, and the Muslim world. Frequently they teach English or some technical subject, which has the advantage of giving them close contact with the people. The main disadvantage is that they frequently have little time to learn the local language and must limit their witness to English. Because they also struggle with isolation, many mission boards try to maintain an unofficial link with them so as to help and encourage them in this difficult challenge. A variant of this is those Christians who work abroad because their company sent them, and who did not intend to go as missionaries. The experiences and profitability of these workers is as varied as the situations.

THE EXCITING STATISTICS

Some people think statistics are dull. However the latest statistics of missionary personnel are exciting. Although exact figures are hard to come by, the most important thing is to get a reasonably accurate picture of current trends. Two excellent sources with new editions in 1993 give us reasonably accurate figures. But we have no 1996 data worldwide.

PROTESTANT MISSIONARIES BY SOURCE AREAS[6]

Source Area	'74-75	'79-80	1985	1988
North American Career	32,023	35,861	39,309	43,648
N.A. Short-term total	5,764	17,633	27,933	31,519
N.A. Short-term factored	3,715	8,581	11,743	12,291
N.A. factored total	35,738	44,442	51,052	55,939
Europeans	#14,700	e15,350	#16,047	e16,300
Pacific/African Westerners	#5,300	e5,250	#5,210	e5,210
Two-thirds World	#5,840	@13,000	NR	@36,000
Composite Total Protestant	61,600	78,000		113,450

Note: Short-termers prorated on a person/year basis to adjust for those serving less than 1 year.   @ from Pate, *From Every People*, pp. 12, 22; # figures from Johnstone, 1st ed., p. 26; 4th ed. pp. 34-35; e indicates estimated figures;   NR no reliable figure available.

Total number of Protestant missionaries

The 1988 figure of about 113,450 Protestant missionaries worldwide is most encouraging. This compares with the 1979 figure of about 78,000 and for 1975, about 61,600. These composite figures include Pate's 1988 survey of two-thirds-world missionaries, which reveals an astonishing explosion from about 13,000 in 1980 to almost 36,000 in 1988![7]

N. American Missionaries of Major Agencies by Association[8]

Association/ Agency	1972 Career	1979 Career	1985 Career	1988 Career	1-3 yr	1996 Career	1-3 yr
National Council Churches	*5010	4817	4349	3873	NR	2040	921
Seventh-Day Adventist Ch.	*(1548)	996	1052	842	59	617	37
Mennonite Central Comm.	*(454)	431	527	504		195	186
United Methodist Church	1051	938	516	416	8	282	62
United Presby. Ch. (merger)	#(1005)	#(618)	445	436	32	414	421
Evang. Lutheran Ch. (merger)	340	#(477)	#(556)	485	25	303	35
Evangelical Fellow. Miss. Agen.	7074	8190	9101	10991	NR	†11871	3142
Southern Baptist Convention†	*2507	*2906	*3346	*3839	*200	†3513	654
Assemblies of God	967	1214	1237	1530	0	1640	192
C. & M. Alliance	803	809	874	1120	67	808	145
Nazarene Church	495	484	595	629	0	514	
Campus Crusade	114	500	574	619	44	685	373
Conservative Baptist Int.	530	534	560	568	116	471	103
Presby. Church in Amer.	-	-	263	384	98	384	128
The Navigators	NA	145	191	336	120	297	152
Evangelical Free Ch.	NA	204	209	306	61	254	60
Interdenom. Foreign M. Assoc.	6130	6575	6380	6897	NR	6411	610
TEAM (BCU merger)	992	#(1111)	#(1131)	#(1049)	70	801	53
SIM Int. (ICF+ AEM mergers)	818	#(658)	#(685)	#(591)	17	622	39
AIM Int.	514	511	515	564	76	477	83
Gospel Miss. Union	288	389	391	400	25	347	100
UFM Int.	260	312	338	371	5	342	33
Overseas Miss. Fellow.	NA	203	212	267	76	319	31
Greater Europe Miss.	NA	160	253	260	35	258	29
International Missions, Inc.	NA	132	159	192	0	270	12
HCJB World Radio Fellow.	NA	161	218	270	9	272	8
Send, Int. + (RBMU merger)	NA	#(302)	#(278)	#(293)	74	280	4
Pioneers		-	38	74	53	267	4
Fellowship of Missions	943	1251	1624	NR	NR	1500	38
Baptist Mid-Missions	511	608	636	636	NR	606	
Assoc. of Baptists for W.E.	351	502	462	618	16	629	36
Unaffiliated Agencies	14837	15450	18515	NR	NR	NR	NR
Wycliffe Bible Trans.	2200	?3181	3022	2619	316	2838	185
New Tribes Mission	701	1385	1438	1807	0	1605	80
Youth With A Mission	1009	887	1741	?	?	1086	1000
Christian Ch./C. of C.	1623	NR	?709	1717	NR	?	?
Baptist Bible Fellowship	379	630	620	734	NA	755	
Brethren Assemblies	538	554	554	617	NA	642	2
Baptist Inter. Missions	334	596	593	620	0	530	2
United Pentecostal Int.	NA	187	212	307	75	267	

Notes: #Combined figures   *Included retroactively   † SBC figures included in EFMA for first time in 1996

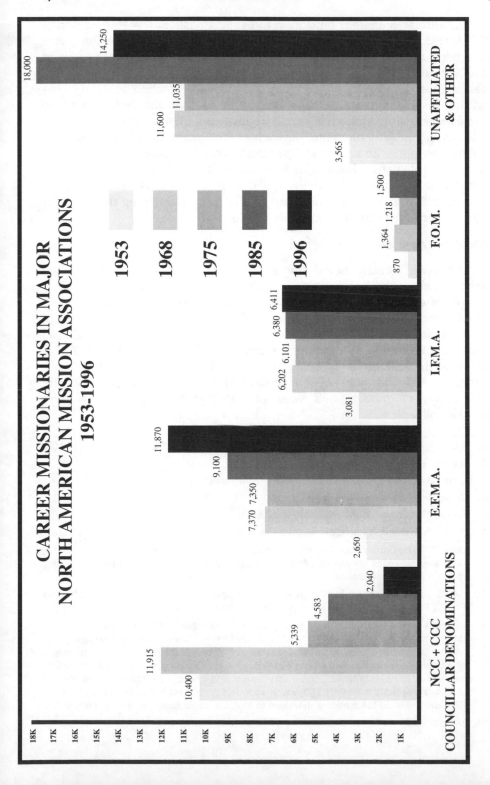

CAREER MISSIONARIES IN MAJOR
NORTH AMERICAN MISSION ASSOCIATIONS
1953-1996

Unfortunately there is tension in the 1992 statistics. The 15th edition of the MARC *Mission Handbook* (p. 59) would seem to indicate that there has been a decrease of over 10,000 North American missionaries since 1988, including over 7000 career missionaries. However, my personal research has not confirmed the magnitude of the decline as being anywhere near as great, perhaps only half of that number, mostly in nonevangelical agencies. It would seem from 1994 and 1996 statistics that evangelical/fundamental agencies are again growing modestly.[9] Johnstone in the 5th edition of *Operation World* indicates that there were 138,500 Protestant missionaries worldwide in 1993.[10] This would be a significant increase. Apparently any decrease in North American missionaries due to a heavy retirement rate is more than being made up for by the increase from the two-thirds world.

Mission association statistics

We have already noted the shift in missions personnel and the associations in the last decades. The most striking fact is that the NCCC figures of ecumenical missionaries have dropped drastically from a peak of over ten thousand in 1953 down to 2040 in 1996, which is a drop of over eighty percent. From the above table it is clear that the total number of Protestant missionaries has almost doubled since 1974-75. Most of the difference is being made up by Evangelicals from North America and the non-Western countries (two-thirds world). So the proportion of missionaries who are Evangelical continues to rise significantly.

1. Arthur F. Glasser, "The Apostle Paul and the Missionary Task," in *Perspectives*, p. 107.

2. Winter, "The Two Structures" in ibid, p. 182.

3. Kane, *Understanding*, p. 141; and Winter, "Structures," in ibid, p. 186.

4. Kane, *Understanding Missions*, p. 151.

5. Winter, "Structures" in *Perspectives*, p. 172.

6. MARC, *Handbook*, 11th; 12th, pp. 20-21; 13th ed., p. 562; 14th ed.; 15th ed.; 17th ed.

7. Larry D. Pate, *From Every People: a Handbook of Two-Thirds World Missions*, pp. 12, 22. I have integrated Johnstone's figures with the breakdown of North American statistics from the *Mission Handbook*.

8. MARC, *Mission Handbook*. 10-17th editions; compared with 1992 & 1996 reports from IFMA, EFMA, & YWAM. Only North Americans reported.

9. In 1993 I contacted four of the agencies which showed the greatest decrease. They did not confirm such a large decline (-1910 for YWAM alone). Then I tabulated the figures for the 60 largest agencies and found attrition of about 2600 North American career missionaries over this period (out of 32,900), which would be a loss of 7.8% (excluding anomalies or obvious typos). Three ecumenical and one other (with doubtful statistics) groups represented a loss of 1250, which accounts for almost half of the total. The 1997 IFMA and 1996 EFMA statistics did seem to indicate some resumed growth from 1992.

10. Johnstone, *Operation World*, 5th ed. (1993), p. 643.

"The harvest is plentiful; but the workers are few. Therefore, beseech the Lord of the harvest to send out workers into His harvest." ~Matthew 9:37-8

HOW IN THE WORLD DO WE GET MISSIONARIES?

THE NEW CHALLENGE OF RECRUITMENT

"God's method is a man." This oft-quoted statement highlights the obvious fact that the missionary is the key to missions. Without a continuing flow of new missionaries, God's worldwide program cannot grow to meet the growing challenge. Indeed, because of missionary attrition, recruitment is a continuing necessity. If we take into account dropouts, deaths, and retirement of career missionaries, the total attrition rate is about 4 to 10 percent per year.[1] In addition, the growing number of short-term missionaries needs to be replaced on a more urgent basis. Fortunately many short-termers stay on as career missionaries. Nevertheless, recruitment has become a high-priority concern of most mission boards!

A few may question the biblical validity of recruitment. But if God's method of missions means people, then God's method of recruiting missionaries involves the active involvement of people. In chapter 6 we dealt with the biblical basis for a 'missionary call' and concluded that God doesn't directly 'zap' prospective missionaries with a 'call', but that he uses human means in guiding individuals to personally respond to the Great Commission. Recruitment is not only biblically valid but absolutely necessary!

In 1971 Richard Bailey of International Missions, Inc. took a survey of students from thirty-four Bible and Christian liberal arts colleges, receiving nearly five thousand responses. Students responded to a question about the hang-ups which might keep them from becoming missionaries. The largest number (35%) checked the response, "I feel I am spiritually unprepared." The second biggest hang-up (32%) was, "I don't like the idea of going around to churches to raise my support." "I am afraid I might not be able to learn a foreign language" took third place with 20 percent, and fourth was "I feel that missions expect a lifetime commitment, and I don't know if that is God's will for me" (13%).[2] These and other hang-ups involve a lot of misconceptions and misinformation about missions which need to be dispelled. Some have called them missionary myths. Let us seek to clarify some of the fog surrounding these hang-ups by taking a closer look at the facts.

The myth of the super-spiritual missionary

Christians have tended to put the missionary on a pedestal because the missionary task seems so overwhelming to most of us. We read of the exploits of the great pioneer missionaries and think we could never qualify to become a missionary. We read the necessary qualifications of a missionary and think that we must become super-spiritual giants to ever make it. Somehow we see the great missionaries as plaster-of-Paris saints.

It is true that some of the great pioneers were highly spiritual people, and even today some missionaries are outstanding Christians. But let us face the fact that most missionaries are just ordinary Christians who have honestly faced the challenge of world evangelization by a personal commitment. Most missionaries would not think themselves particularly spiritual. The fact is that they struggle with the same problems of life with which other Christians struggle. Anybody involved in mission administration can testify that missionaries struggle with discouragement, personality, marital, and relationship problems, and all the other infirmities of the flesh that other Christians are subject to. Indeed, they sometimes struggle more because of the difficulties of living in another culture.

If the prospective missionary waits until he reaches that super-spiritual ideal, there will be few missionaries going out to meet the needs of a lost world! Indeed, the 'pre-field ministry' (formerly called deputation) of the missionary appointee can be a further opportunity for spiritual growth. And not only does the 'junior missionary' face the challenge of personal growth during the first years on the field, but missionaries like all Christians should see the whole of the Christian life as continued opportunity for growth and development.

Yes, we need more spiritual missionaries. But let us face the fact that all of us, even the most spiritual, are in process — in the process of growing to spiritual maturity. Let us take the missionary down off the pedestal, so that more dedicated Christians can join the ranks!

The hang-up of deputation

Does deputation ministry really mean going around begging for money? Nobody likes to be a beggar! It is demeaning to have to beg. These days many mission boards are referring to deputation as 'pre-field ministry', but that only changes the image, not the reality. What is the reality?

Many of the larger denominations have a unified denominational budget which makes 'raising one's support' unnecessary. This is also true of the Christian and Missionary Alliance. But most missionaries working under evangelical mission boards, whether denominational or interdenominational, have to 'raise their own support' before they can depart for the field. A number of missions stress nonsolicitation of funds after the example of Hudson Taylor in the founding of the China Inland Mission, so as to avoid 'begging'. The emphasis is upon asking God to touch his people to give toward the missionary's needs.

Perhaps a better perspective from which to view deputation is that of giving God's people an opportunity to get involved in worldwide missions by giving. But there are many other benefits of pre-field ministry. Not only does the appointee learn lessons of prayer and trusting God for supply, but there are other dimensions as well. The appointee has opportunity to 'sell' missions, sometimes in churches that have little missionary vision. Not only can the appointee encourage churches to be more missionary-minded, but also can recruit other missionaries. One classic example of this was the ministry of millionaire Bill Borden of Yale '09, who did not need support for himself, but recruited many other missionaries before he left for Egypt. The most important aspect of deputation is recruiting prayer supporters to stand behind the missionary while on the field. This is an essential for effective ministry.

The hang-up of learning another language

Many people have a very negative attitude toward learning a foreign language because of a bad experience with a Latin or French class in school. They did poorly and feel that they just can't learn a foreign language. But that probably is not true.

It is one thing to struggle with a dead language like Latin and quite another to experience the thrill of communicating in a living language spoken by thousands or even millions of people. Even if you had trouble with Spanish or German, that is not the whole picture. To be very frank, language learning in public schools may be poorly done based upon antiquated techniques. It is quite a different experience to be totally immersed in a language day in and day out. The direct method of language learning practiced by Berlitz and many missionary language schools makes language acquisition much more realizable and even enjoyable.

The hang-up of a lifetime commitment

Do mission boards expect a lifetime commitment to being a missionary? Yes and no! Does God expect a lifetime commitment? Yes and no! Let me explain. Mission boards prefer a commitment to career missionary service because the missionary should grow in effectiveness over the years. The first years on the field are principally spent in language study and learning the culture and the church situation. It is obvious that the most efficient expenditure of resources is effected with career commitment. However, boards also recognize the value of the short-termer. Increasingly it is also being recognized that the Bible does not speak of a lifetime missionary call (see chapter 6). The missionary who does not return to the field after some years of service is not necessarily out of the will of God.

But God does expect a lifetime commitment to do His will! This may mean a career change in midlife for a number of reasons. Obvious reasons would include health and family considerations. But there may be other less circumstantial considerations in a career change: a conviction of God's will, for example. And this should work both ways also. Increasingly we are seeing longtime pastors resign their churches to become missionaries. Retired people also are going out as missionaries.

We should not think of a commitment to the will of God as a bad thing. God is not some fiend who delights in making us do what we don't want to do. There is nothing as good and joyous as doing the will of God! We must live the Christian life one step at a time. However, there must be a basic commitment to God's plan for world evangelism, wherever He chooses to place us in that plan.

Bailey's survey detected another problem in this area. "Probably the second most significant finding in this poll is the fact that today's Christian college student is very much a part of the 'now generation' with its existential philosophy of 'who knows about tomorrow?' It is sad that in the above mentioned multiple choice question (about God's leading) 58 percent . . . "had to admit, 'I am just not sure what He wants me to do'." From various comments on the forms Bailey detected the attitude that "If I want to be a true disciple, I must follow Christ without an obvious plan or program."[3] Careful study of the New Testament will show that this was not the apostles' concept of discipleship and the will of God. Paul most certainly made long range plans, even though God sometimes changed his plans. We see this on a number of occasions in the book of Acts (15:36; 19:21; 20:3, 16) and in his epistles (2 Cor. 1:15-24; Rom. 15:22-28). Effective ministry involves forethought and planning, and the Christian worker must not fall into an existen-tialist's way of doing things. So we conclude that we must balance commitment to long-term plans with flexibility and openness to change.

Fear of failure

Bailey's survey revealed that most students feel that they are either spiritually unprepared or might fail to raise support or else fail to learn the language. In a nutshell, the main obstacle is fear of failure of some kind. Some might fear they could not adjust to another culture. It is all the fear of the unknown and yet fear of a job that is known to be tough!

These fears are real. Some do fail! We all fail in some measure and succeed in some measure. But the missionary failure seems so much more traumatic and complete. The missionary comes home, sometimes from halfway around the world. People ask the reason. The failure may seem more absolute than if one had stayed home. We may fail in Christian ministry here at home, but obviously we have a better chance of success here in our own culture.

The first thing to consider is that we are all in the process of becoming what God wants us to be. None of us have arrived. Even Paul could say in Philippians 3:12-14 that he had not yet attained, but that he was pressing on toward God's goal for him. Even if right now we are not yet ready to become missionaries we must press on, get the preparation we need, and trust God to equip us to do what He wants to do through us. It may be that after education, there is ministry experience here at home. That will help to equip and mature us. So it is irrelevant if we are unprepared now and afraid of failure. Wait for God's time—but wait expectantly!

Another thing to consider is that **it is far better to try and have failed, than not to have tried at all!** Think what would have happened if William Carey had yielded to fears, doubts, and the opposition. He had overwhelming obstacles, and yet he pressed on and succeeded at long last. But the whole modern missionary movement might not have gotten started or at least would have been delayed if he had yielded to his fears. Millions would have remained in heathen lostness, who now have had a chance to hear and be saved.

Pastor Erwin Lutzer has written a book entitled, *Failure—the Back Door to Success.* God can even use our failures. Think of John Mark who failed the Apostle Paul! Not only did Paul later write that he is "profitable," but Mark became the author of the Gospel of Mark. This is the essence of faith — to launch out and put ourselves at risk. As the old proverb goes, "Nothing ventured; nothing gained."

Lack of direction

This is the day of the 'uncommitted generation'. Young people (and many not so young) struggle to find direction in their lives. In chapter six we suggested that one reason may be that we have false expectations as to what kind of guidance we can expect from God. Another reason may be a lack of commitment on our part. We may take the Lord for granted and be too passive in our relationship with Him. It all goes back to a willingness on our part to do the will of God, honestly coming to terms with the Great Commission and relating our gifts and abilities to the needs of a lost world. We can't go wrong in obeying our Lord's commands to "look on the fields" (John 4:35), and to "pray the Lord of the harvest to send out reapers to His harvest field" (Mt. 9:38).

It is impossible to steer a car that is not moving. It is impossible to steer a Christian who is not moving. The key is to get moving in obedience to the revealed word of God, and we will not lack for guidance. He commands us to be His witnesses. Simple obedience will open up fantastic vistas of direction and guidance. Try it!

Loss of personal freedom

Western civilization is on a freedom binge! In the United States we have experienced over two hundred years of political freedom (at least for the majority). Our culture is in danger of disintegration because of the worship of freedom without any recognition of responsibility. The pendulum has swung very far in regard to sexual freedom. Now people are finding out that irresponsible sexual activity without the responsibility of marriage is destroying not only the family but the whole fabric of society. Venereal disease has long been a hint of the evil consequences of abuse of sexual freedom, but now the fear of AIDS has forced even many homosexuals to avoid promiscuity.

Let's face it, our culture affects our thinking as Christians. With the spiritual freedom of redemption comes responsibility. The Bible is clear about the Christian's responsibility to submit to authority: children to their parents, subjects to rulers, church members to their spiritual leaders. Most of all we must submit to the authority of God. That is the path of real joy and blessing!

The fact is that the average evangelical missionary today gives up precious little of his personal freedom in serving the Lord abroad. "As for the individual within a mission, it is fair to say that the missionary on the field has at least as much, maybe more, personal freedom than the pastor at home."[4] I would go beyond Kane's statement and say that the average missionary probably has too much freedom from authoritarian control. The fact is that mission board administrators are not in-terested in making life difficult for the missionary. Their job is to facilitate life and ministry for the missionary. Senior missionaries may fre-quently be very open to new ideas and prove to be amazingly flexible, when it comes down to it. But the guidelines and parameters are spel-led out in the bylaws and the manuals of each mission. If a prospective missionary does his homework and agrees with those principles, he shouldn't feel his personal liberties being seriously infringed upon.

HOW IN THE WORLD CAN I GET PREPARED?

There are a number of stages in the process of becoming a missionary. First there must be a willingness to become a missionary. Secondly, the individual comes to the conviction that it is indeed the will of God. The third step is deciding on a mission board and actually making application to that board. We have dealt with a few hang-ups which keep Christians from the second and third steps. But not all who reach the second go on to the third. And not all who apply actually become missionaries. What are the roadblocks that Satan uses to keep potential missionaries from actually getting there?

Avoiding Satan's sidetracks (sidetraps)

Love and marriage. The Bible makes clear that marriage is a good thing. It is certainly far better than today's promiscuous singles. However, a good thing can sometimes become a hindrance to something better. Many prospective missionaries get sidetracked by marrying someone who is not sympathetic with missions or personally willing to become a missionary. Sometimes the other person has a spiritual problem that causes the blockage. Sometimes it is just God's leading in another direction. I had a seminary classmate whose fiancee was headed toward missions. However, he was just as definite about pastoral ministry. It took wisdom and courage for her to break the engagement, but marriage probably would have sidetracked her from missionary service.

Better to miss marriage than to miss the will of God. Christ spoke of those who become eunuchs for the kingdom of God's sake (Matt. 19:12). The apostle Paul advocated the single state in order to give undistracted devotion to the Lord (1 Cor. 7:7, 25-28). This is an option that many today do not seriously consider. But the principle and the opportunity are still valid today.

For married prospective missionaries, the issue of children becomes important. It is difficult with a large family to raise support, get established in another culture, and learn a new language. Mission boards used to have fairly rigid restrictions in this regard: they would not look at applicants with more than two or three children. Today most boards are more flexible. However, the difficulties have not gone away. Couples should pray about postponing children until language study is completed. I am convinced that this is appropriate since the Bible leaves marital birth control as a matter of Christian liberty.

Parental opposition. We would expect that the prospective missionary with non-Christian parents would have a problem in this regard. The tragedy is that there are many with Christian parents who also face parental opposition. How can the sincere Christian balance his responsibility to his parents to his responsibility to the Lord?

Christ said a lot about giving Him higher priority in our lives than even our parents. For example, in Matthew 10:37 He said, "He who loves father or mother more than Me is not worthy of Me, and he who loves son or daughter more than Me is not worthy of Me." On the other hand, Christians are to honor father and mothers just as Jews were to do under the Ten Commandments. So we recognize a tension between the two. However, where there is a conflict, the Christian is to put Christ first.

Some missionaries have not only experienced initial opposition, but

also upon going out to the field have been plagued by 'false alarm' letters, telegrams, and phone calls from parents feigning illness to get the
son or daughter to return. The Christian's duty is clear. Christ must
come first!

Accumulation of debt. Traditionally, mission boards have not accepted a candidate who has any significant debt outstanding, since a
missionary allotment is not adequate to pay off debt. However, with the
high cost of education these days, many graduate from Bible college or
seminary with horrendous debt. What is the solution?

As much as possible the prospective missionary should try to work his
way through college and try to get scholarship aid, rather than to depend
too heavily on student loans. Churches need to do more to aid prospective missionaries to get their education. In some cases mission boards
today are trying to be more creative in working with the candidate to
solve the problem. Usually, however, the graduate must work to pay off
most of the debt before it is possible to move toward going to the field.
Better to try avoiding the debt in the first place.

Getting the right preparation

Educational preparation. It is of highest importance to get the right
preparation for the job. Unfortunately there are a number of misconceptions that Christian collegians have which need to be corrected to
avoid inadequate or wrong training for missions.

One widespread myth is that one only needs a one-year concentrated
Bible course to become a missionary: thirty-two semester hours of Bible
and doctrine. This myth arises from the fact that some mission boards
will accept specialized missionaries, such as medical personnel, teachers, technicians, etc., if they have taken the one-year Bible program.
Somehow the myth has spread that this is adequate for all missionaries.
Nothing could be farther from the truth!

I was exposed to an even more extreme point of view from a guest
speaker in seminary who claimed that missionaries only need a six-week
course in soul winning. But why after all do we need more than that,
especially if one goes to a primitive tribal people? Such a perspective
arises out of an incredible ignorance of the nature of missionary work.
One can indeed become a soul winner here at home among nominal
Christians of one's own culture through a brief training course. However,
most missionaries are not working among nominal Christians and face a
gap between themselves and the people they are trying to reach that
needs to be understood. In addition, missionaries do more than personal
soul winning.

1) The **language gap** demands extensive study to bridge. Frequently
the student's lack of grammatical background is a hindrance to progress.
Hence, English and linguistic courses are important. Frequently the

missionary gets involved in language reduction and translation work, and even adult literacy programs. All take specialized training.

2) The **cultural gap** requires some knowledge of anthropology and sociology to avoid offending the people and to understand their ways. Today we understand as never before the pitfalls of cross-cultural communication and the importance of courses in this area.

3) The **religious gap** is undoubtedly the greatest. The Animist, Hindu, Buddhist, or Shintoist has a world view that is so radically different from the Christian one that understanding of "where they are coming from" is vital to effective witness. The mind of the Muslim or Jew has been so conditioned against Christianity that here too special preparation is needed (see chapter 12).

4) The missionary cannot stop with winning people to Christ. He must go on **to plant a church and disciple the believers**. If the missionary is not well taught in Bible, theology and principles and practices of missions, he will make serious blunders in laying the foundation which can greatly hinder further progress. Most missionaries get involved in biblical teaching at some level. Do they themselves have sound teaching to pass on to the nationals?

How much education is necessary? The tendency of denominational missions is to require some seminary training. Most of the interdenominational missions have not required as rigorous academic preparation, usually accepting a good Bible institute or college program. A good missions curriculum from a Bible college ought to be adequate preparation for the first term of service. However, every missionary should take every opportunity to upgrade his education, and furlough is that ideal opportunity. Some colleges and seminaries have a one-year master's program in missions that is tailored for this.

Another myth in the area of education for missions was exposed by Bailey's survey which identified a problem

> due to the warped picture of missionary opportunity. . . . First, 68% of the students believe they cannot 'obtain a visa for most countries without some special training to offer'. . . According to the information we have been able to gather so far from many mission boards, . . .there are at least 60 countries with a combined population of 1,163,000,000 where U.S. citizens can enter and work as 'missionaries' without any secular training at all! There are only 15 countries with a combined population of 115 million where secular training has any effect on the obtaining of visas![5]

Although this study is not up to date, it probably represents reasonably fairly the present state of affairs. Currently there are thirteen countries which are closed to overt missionaries and do not have a viable indigenous church, which could be called "creative-access countries." There are 19 other such countries which do have a viable church. In the past decade about 35 countries have opened to missionary activity to some extent.[6] Thus the vast majority of countries in the world are wide open to missionary access.

The point is that unless you are intending to be a tentmaker in a creative-access country, biblical training should have a higher priority than secular training. Where there are secular requirements, they should be gotten after the completion of the biblical foundations.

Physical preparation. "What in the world is this mission coming to?" I thought as I met that summer's crop of missionary candidates. "After all he's a cripple!" As he rose from the ground, I realized that he could barely walk without arm crutches.

Does a missionary have to be a perfect physical specimen? Back in the pioneer days it was very important. But in our day, perfect physical wholeness is not a prerequisite. Some mission-field situations are not at all primitive, like Europe, Japan, and many of the cities of the third world. With modern transportation, handicaps which once were considered serious are not too important. One of my missionary colleagues in Pakistan had a glass eye. His hobby was birdwatching with a monocular. I'm sure he must have chuckled many times at the Urdu proverb we learned in the language course, *undhon mein, kana rajah hai.* "Among blind men, a one-eyed man is king." His handicap wasn't even known to most people, slight as it was. But what about the crippled young candidate? He was the innocent victim of a stray bullet. But his love for Christ overcame and he completed a useful term on the field.

Oh, yes, some physical limitations can disqualify a potential missionary. Especially something that which could later become a disabling and serious hindrance to effective service. That's why mission boards require rigorous physical exams. But they don't rule out the less than perfect physical specimen these days, but take into account the nature of the limitation.

Curiously one of the most serious physical obstacles today is obesity. In our affluent overfed society, we see a growing problem of overweight. Yet there is the counterbalance of the 'fitness craze'. For the prospective missionary the latter is the better option. Some mission boards take significant overweight quite seriously. Not only is it hard for an obese person to raise support, but it can be quite limiting in many field situations. But lest we be accused of being 'fat-bashers' let us state that this is not an absolute. There is a lot a prospective missionary can do to get into good physical condition. A myriad of books have been written about this so I needn't elaborate.

What about age? It used to seem like the mission boards were in a conspiracy with the 'now generation' in rejecting anybody over thirty as 'over the hill'. Missionary candidates had to be young to endure the rigors, learn the language, and have a full lifetime ahead for service. Here also things have changed radically. It doesn't take six months to sail out to India as it did when Carey went. We have found out that older people only marginally lose their language-learning ability. And the rigors of the 'field' are not generally as great. With the lack-of- direction problem mentioned above, more and more prospective missionaries are not applying until after thirty. If they have good solid experience behind them, this is a real plus. Thus most mission boards have totally scrapped the age limitation.

Spiritual preparation. We have tried to demolish the myth of the super-spiritual missionary. But let us make it abundantly clear that we do need spiritually-minded missionaries to withstand the pressures of missionary service. It should go without saying that we need born-again missionaries. I remember the wives of two ecumenical missionaries we knew who got saved on the field! But obviously being genuine believers is only the starting point for missionary service.

Here is an area where much can be done to get prepared. And most of the preparation doesn't come from formal training. This is a personal matter. It starts with establishing regular devotional habits, a quiet time. Certainly the word of God and prayer are basic. A superficial knowledge of the Bible will not do. Frequently the missionary does not have the resources of people and books to turn to in getting the answers needed. He must have a 'handle on' the word of God for himself.

One key qualification of missionaries who have made an impact is self-discipline. It takes discipline to maintain an effective devotional life. It takes discipline to develop regular Bible study habits. That discipline carries over into other areas of life: the proper use of time and money, etc. The word discipline comes from the same root as 'disciple.' Ultimately the key issue is discipleship. Six times in the Gospels we find the Lord's emphasis on this imperative for all believers, but especially for prospective missionaries: "If anyone wishes to come after Me, let him deny himself, and take up his cross daily, and follow Me" (Lk. 9:23). This could not be referring to salvation since it a daily matter. He is talking about the necessity of self-denial and put-ting self to death in the life of the true believer. This is basic to preparation for missionary service. Much of missionary failure goes back to this issue.

Ministry experience. Many Bible college and seminary graduates do not have the ministry experience necessary for missionary service. It is unthinkable to try to be a cross-cultural missionary without experience in many phases of God's work here in our own culture. Certainly much of this can and should be gained in one's home church. Various forms of internship training are absolutely vital for this. There are also organizations like Missionary Internship, Inc., which have programs geared to the local church. Many mission boards also have training programs for their candidates and/or appointees. It has been my privilege to work with the unique Summer Training and Outreach Program of International Missions, Inc. It is designed to give the prospective missionary experience and training in reaching Muslims, Hindus, or Chinese right here at home (Brooklyn, NY). Short-term missionary programs also help to fulfill this need.

Attitudinal preparation. The success or failure of a new missionary not only depends upon spiritual preparation, but also upon the attitude or mind-set with which he enters into the work. This is why mission boards have candidate schools and on-field orientation. The attitude of the 'junior missionary' is so important.

Some come with a know-it-all attitude. They have had all the latest courses in missionary anthropology, linguistics, and missiology, and they are going to straighten out those benighted senior missionaries who didn't have such good training and who haven't kept on the cutting edge of missionary theory. But let us remember that it is just that — theory. The senior missionary may have a lot of good practical experience which frequently counts for more.

On the other hand, I do remember that in my missionary ministry there really were a number of 'old school' missionaries who did seem to be living in the nineteenth century. There were a few who did more harm than good because their attitudes toward the nationals were not right. We are now living in a day when increasingly the nationals are running their own show, and we are invited guests of the national church. So how can the 'young Turks' effect change? It may not be easy, but new missionaries have to earn the right to be heard. That may take some patience and a lot of prayer, but it will be worth it. But the key is the attitude of the individual (Phil. 2:5-11).

---

1. Johnstone, *Operation World*, 4th ed., p. 63
2. Richard Bailey, "Missions—Christian Collegians' Concepts," *Eastern Challenge* 7, no. 3:3.
3. Ibid.
4. Kane, *Understanding Missions*, p. 55.
5. Bailey, *loc. cit.*
6. Johnstone, 5th ed., p. 31.

"... how I did not shrink from declaring to you anything that was profitable, and teaching you publicly and from house to house, solemnly testifying to both Jews and Greeks of repentance toward God and faith in our Lord Jesus Christ.

–Acts 20:20-21

WHAT IN THE WORLD DO MISSIONARIES DO?

It would be naive to think that the nature of missionary work is self-evident. When we read missionary biographies we find that missionaries have gotten involved in a vast spectrum of activities: evangelism, church planting, education, medicine, exploration, community development, and many other good things. And the right question is not only what do missionaries do, but also what ought missionaries to do? How does the missionary choose from among the wealth of possible and profitable activities? Cook lists their diversity:

> For example, missionaries often have been explorers. David Livingstone was only one of many. They have tried to avoid getting entangled in political affairs. Yet in primitive areas like the Pacific islands they couldn't avoid it. Kings and chieftains asked them to be their advisors. Sometimes, like Christian Friedrich Schwartz in India, they were asked to carry out delicate diplomatic missions when no one else could be trusted. It was a missionary, Guido Verbeck, who helped to write the constitution of modern Japan.
>
> From William Carey and Robert Morrison to the present day, missionaries have served in large numbers as linguists, grammarians and translators. Until fairly recent years cultural anthropology could almost be called a missionary science. Not only missionary schools but a number of great universities owe their origin to missionary initiative. Healing, from the roadside dispensary to the city hospital, has played an important part in missionary work. It was missionaries who called attention to the woeful plight of the lepers and who still carry much of the burden of their care.[1]

The missionary must set priorities to make sure that all that activity actually accomplishes what God wants accomplished. In addition, there is considerable controversy as to just what evangelism is and how other missionary activity relates to evangelism. This especially comes from ecumenical and other non-evangelical leaders. Even among Evangelicals there is considerable diversity of definitions of evangelism. Thus it is imperative that we go back to the word of God to understand just what our priorities should be.

THE BIBLICAL PRIORITY OF EVANGELISM

One cannot read the New Testament with an open mind without concluding that evangelism must be the number-one priority of the missionary. "Evangelism is at the heart of the missionary movement. Missionary work that doesn't include evangelism isn't missionary work at all."[2] This is clear from the Great Commission; it is clear from the example of the apostles; and it is clear from the New Testament epistles. The word 'evangelize' comes from the same root as the word 'gospel' and has to do with the good news of Christ. We have already noted the use of the word *mathēteuō* (to make disciples) in Matthew 28:18. David Hesselgrave has pointed out that there are actually about fifteen different words used in the New Testament to describe the task of missions and evangelism.[3] Although some (like McGavran) have understood it to refer to the making of converts, and others (like the Navigators) have stressed the development of the spiritual life of the new convert, it is more probable that Christ was encompassing both ideas in the one word. We are responsible both to win people to Christ and to encourage their spiritual growth. Christ's reference to baptizing and teaching the disciples not only confirms this but also implies the planting of local churches to accomplish these things. The example of the apostles in Acts confirms our responsibility to plant churches.

From this it is obvious that missionaries of a more liberal stamp who are satisfied with 'presence evangelism' fall far short of the mark. Even Evangelicals like J. I. Packer, who would limit our responsibility to 'proclamation evangelism', are not going far enough. Only 'persua-sion evangelism' fulfills the intent of the many words used in Acts to describe apostolic activity. In Acts 17:2-3 for example, we see that Paul "reasoned with them from the Scriptures, explaining and giving evidence that the Christ had to suffer and rise again from the dead." Many other examples could be given.

A serious problem in modern missions is the drift away from the priority of evangelism, especially in mission institutions like schools and hospitals. In most cases it represents an unintentional drift. In some cases it is the consequence of liberal theology, which minimizes the place of evangelism. I will never forget the response of a liberal missionary in Pakistan to the proposal to have a dorm Bible study in a mission college: "We couldn't allow that — it would be forcing Christianity down the Muslim students' throats!"

Some evangelical Christians, on the other hand, feel that evangelism is only one among many activities of the missionary, but not primary. They are very concerned about the 'whole man' and social action as an important part of evangelism. They will say that a starving man cannot listen to our gospel. (Although historically the poor have always been the most responsive to the gospel.) They would stress the 'cultural mandate' of Genesis 1:28; 2:15 as being of equal validity with the gospel mandate of the Great Commission. George Peters responds with characteristic directness:

> Neither do I find anywhere in the New Testament that the church of Jesus Christ as a church is charged with the mission of special cultural contributions, though every member as a member of mankind has a contribution to make.
>
> . . . .
>
> Today we are pathetically confused, believing that social action is to replace the feeble prophetic voice of the church.
>
> . . . .
>
> I do not find anywhere in the Bible that the first mandate comes under the biblical category of missions.[4]

We must remember that Paul was very concerned that the gospel and evangelism have priority. He wrote the Corinthian Christians: "For I determined to know nothing among you except Jesus Christ, and Him crucified" (1 Cor. 2:2). He wrote the Romans that the reason that he was unashamed of the gospel was that it is the power of God unto sal-vation to everyone who believes (Rom. 1:16). The same could hardly be said for the 'social gospel' or even the 'social implications of the gospel'. After all, the consequences of success or failure to fulfill the two mandates are radically different. If we win someone to Christ they will re-ceive eternal salvation but may suffer poverty, etc. If we concentrate on social issues, we may make the circumstances of life better for people here on earth, only for them to end up in Hell in eternity. I remember speaking to the Principal of a large mission high school in Pakistan (with over a thousand Muslim students), about a new government pro-hibition against Muslim students taking Bible classes. I was shocked at his unconcern over the loss of the primary purpose of this institution. This is far too common in institutional missions today. How important it is to keep biblical priorities constantly before us in God's work!

There are many kinds of evangelism possible on the mission field. Personal evangelism can be done anywhere and is exemplified in the ministry of Christ and the apostles. This is basic to all other forms of evangelism and frequently the most effective. It is also basic to church growth that new converts should be encouraged to become personal witnesses of their faith.

In many countries street evangelism of various kinds is a very important part of the thrust. Whether it be full-fledged street preaching, door-to-door work, or literature distribution which may draw small groups to hear the gospel, the example of Scripture is again very clear. The shame is that frequently the cults are in the forefront of using the biblical methods, even though their message is corrupted. Acts 20:20 gives what I refer to as **Paul's 20/20 vision for evangelism:** "how I did not shrink from declaring to you anything that was profitable, and teaching you publicly and from house to house, solemnly testifying to both Jews and Greeks of repentance toward God and faith in our Lord Jesus Christ." Itinerant evangelism has been popular in the centuries of missions evangelism. It received an impetus with the advent of the sound-truck. It has declined recently because of weakness in actually planting churches. More recently the trend has been to continue an evangelistic thrust in one location for a number of months until the nucleus of a church is formed.

Although church evangelism was not an important factor in the early church, unsaved people did come into the meetings (1 Cor. 14:24-25) and were saved. Even though the primary purpose of the pulpit is to teach believers, the gospel should be regularly made clear in every local church. Although special services for evangelism in the local church have declined here in the West, it is still feasible in most third-world countries (and still is here). Local church evangelism has the advantage that the converts can immediately get tied into that local church. That is not always true with large cooperative crusades. Follow-up of converts is always a problem with mass evangelistic crusades. The counseling process is critical to the spiritual success of the meetings (if we are not just to have numbers to refer to) since it is my experience that most people who respond to a public invitation have not yet understood the gospel and come to saving faith. They need to be led to Christ in the inquiry room.

There are many other types of evangelism possible today. Radio evangelism has come into its own as one of the most fruitful of methods. It is especially necessary for penetration into closed countries and out-of-the way places. For example, most converts in Eastern Europe today first heard the gospel on the radio, even though they were won by local Christians. Various types of literature evangelism are important in a world which is growing increasingly literate. Whether it be distribution of Gospel portions, handing out tracts, literature stalls at fairs, newspaper evangelism, Bible correspondence courses—the use of the printed page is basic to most missionary evangelism today. Modern technology has provided us with additional options: gospel recordings and cassettes, which will be played over and over again; audio-visuals which communicate through two senses, telephone evangelism, etc.

Increasingly, modern missionaries have returned to that which was a clear-cut goal of the early missionaries—church-planting. With the proliferation of service ministries after the Second World War, there was a tendency to get away from church-planting objectives. However, more recently the emphasis has returned to the importance of church planting. It has been noted that one of the best ways of seeing church growth is the planting of new churches. Thus evangelism which does not directly contribute to church planting and growth is being evaluated more critically at the present time. It should also be noted that increasingly the main burden of evangelism has been taken over by the national church. It is where the national church either does not have the resources or the vision that the western missionary must still fill the gap. Where the national church lacks the burden, the missionary must seek to stir up an evangelistic/missionary concern among them. "It is imperative that the churches of the Third World assume responsibility for the evangelization of their own people. Other things being equal it is better for a person to hear the gospel **for the very first time** from the lips of one of his own people."[5]

ON-FIELD PREPARATION

What do new missionaries do? The first step is to complete one's preparation for ministry. Although some ministry may be possible in English shortly after arrival, most mission boards stress a time of orientation and language study. The new missionary will need some orientation to the culture of the people. Some missions have a well organized orientation program; others have only the informal input of the senior missionaries. Over the years missionaries have learned from sad experience that learning the vernacular of the people is absolutely essential for effective ministry. Use of a second language greatly hampers spiritual communication. Use of interpreters also proves to be an exercise in frustration. Rarely is it wise to start language study at home unless a qualified native speaker is available to teach.   Better to wait for the total immersion experience on the field. Usually the first year is devoted primarily to language study, depending upon the difficulty of the language and the aptitude of the student. If the missionary is in language reduction and translation work (in an unwritten language), then the first term and more will be devoted to language study. If there is a well-structured language course, frequently it will include cultural material as well. This contributes immeasurably to the new missionary's well-rounded orientation.

EDUCATIONAL MINISTRIES

One of the first and certainly one of the most widespread forms of ministry supplemental to evangelism in the modern missionary movement has been educational work. In the beginning it came in two forms. Where there was a tribal, preliterate society, the missionary had to reduce the language to writing, translate the Scripture and other materials, and then teach the people how to read. Thus adult literacy assumed an important part of the pioneer missionary's ministry. Shortly following upon that was often elementary education since there was rarely any other provision made for that. Generation after generation the need to expand the system was constant, and in many countries missions found themselves starting colleges and universities. In literate and more advanced civilizations, the immediate need was the training of national leadership for the churches. Thus biblical education was the primary form in those situations.

The motives for getting into education were numerous. As noted above, the necessity to effectively communicate the word of God demanded adult literacy work at minimum. As the educational program expanded to the elementary level the purpose was to enable Christians to take leadership roles. Very early the question arose of accepting non-Christian students into the schools in an effort to win them to Christ. Many schools did so. The result was that in many countries great numbers of non-Christians are graduates of mission schools. Many of them made some sort of a profession of Christianity. The majority did not make a profession of Christ, but many have a favorable attitude towards missionaries and Christianity. But in some far too common cases the non-Christians picked up the worst of the western educational system and did not really hear the gospel, either because priorities were lost by a school that was evangelical but not evangelistic, or else by a school that was liberal. Some of the graduates of such mission schools turned to Communism because of its idealistic solution to the social problems of emerging nations. After raising the problem that national churches have in supporting the educational institutions financially, Harold Lindsell has pointed up the problem:

> In the second place, many of the great educational institutions have long since lost their relevancy to missionary work. They have become secularized to a degree and extent that is amazing. From their doors have come graduates who instead of having been reached effectively for Christ have become arch opponents of the Christian faith and have leveled their sights for the destruction of missionary work. And they were trained in the very schools created to produce Christians. It is true that there is a normal hazard in educating those who may not become Christian, but when the institutions turn out a significant number of graduates who become leaders of movements opposed to Christianity, the natural question arises whether educational missions should not be destroyed entirely or at least that such institutions be made to operate within boundaries which will insure no repetition of this unfortunate result in the years ahead.[6]

Add to that the serious danger that schools may be seized by hostile governments (and some have been!), and it becomes clear that a general educational program in missions must come under penetrating scrutiny. The major denominational missions have invested heavily in education, the 'faith' missions much less so. When the Pakistan government decreed some years ago that Muslim students in mission schools must be taught Islam by Muslim teachers, only one mission school refused to do so. The TEAM school in Abbottabad closed its doors to Muslims rather than do so.

The most defensible form of educational missions has been biblical and theological educational programs. They usually started with lower-level Bible schools and as the educational level of the community was raised, the level of the biblical education was also raised. Seminaries in many countries ultimately were able to look for college graduates, just as here in the West, although with a small student body in most cases. Short-term Bible schools also proved effective in training leadership for the churches.

The major recent innovation in theological education was mentioned in chapter eleven: **Theological Education by Extension.** The main feature of **TEE** is that it is in-service training which does not pull the student away from his work or ministry as resident schools do. In a nutshell, the teacher goes to the student since the student cannot come to the teacher. Programmed study materials are the key to successful TEE courses, since most of the time the student has to study on his own. Periodically the teacher meets with a class at a convenient field location to discuss what they have studied and help them with problems. But it is essentially a guided program of self-study. TEE has not only spread widely over the continent of its origin (Latin America) but it has been widely implemented in Africa and Asia as well. Ralph Winter has argued that since it is a superior form of education, it should be used more in western countries. Because of the massive investment in residential campuses for our educational institutions, TEE has not been widely used here.

MEDICAL MINISTRIES

There is no question that healing was an essential part of the ministry of the Lord Jesus and the apostles. Christ's ministry on earth was full of miracles of compassion, most of them healings. Among the forty miracles in the book of Acts a majority were healings. There seems to have been an immediate cessation of the gift of healing after the apostolic period (Heb. 2:4), and it does not seem to have played a significant part of the early missionary expansion in the Roman empire and without. But with the rise of modern medicine missionaries saw an opportunity to restore works of compassion to the missionary kitbag. Although these were not primarily supernatural healings, they nevertheless manifested the compassionate nature of the Christian faith and were mostly accompanied with fervent prayer. There were many incidents of confrontation with witch doctors in animistic societies with God intervening to heal a dying person to give greater credibility to the gospel. (The term 'power encounter' has been coined by missiologists to describe such situations.)

The rationale of medical missions

What are missionaries seeking to accomplish through medical ministry? Since the missionary cannot heal in the same sense as Christ and the apostles did, as an obvious direct manifestation of God's power, what is the justification for medical missions?[7] Herbert Kane has suggested a number of reasons which justify medical missions. We will consider his points:

"1. To alleviate human suffering." Medical ministry has an intrinsic value, not just as a means to an end. The world is full of disease and physical suffering. Americans spend over 10% of their income for medical care. Most two-thirds world peoples not only don't have money for medical care, but they also have little access to medical help. There is a pressing need, and the missionary frequently can do a lot to help meet that need. Even untrained and semiskilled missionaries have frequently been greatly used to alleviate human suffering.

On the other hand, because of the overwhelming medical needs on most mission fields, there is always the danger of the missionary getting sidetracked from his primary concern: evangelism and church planting. Here is where it is important to prioritize.

"2. To combat ignorance and superstition.. . . In many instances the sufferings of the people stem from ignorance as much as from poverty. They are totally unaware of the basic factors that contribute to sickness and disease: the existence of germs, the presence of parasites, contaminated food, impure water, etc." Thus medical missionaries share their medical knowledge with the nationals in the hope of dispelling the ignorance. They train nationals in medicine and employ them in clinics, dispensaries, and hospitals.

"3. To dispel prejudice and create good will." Right from the beginning of modern missions, medical help has opened doors for the gospel and contributed to a positive attitude on the part of the people. In some cases it has saved the missionaries' lives. One missionary friend in Pakistan was about to be stoned by irate Muslims during his street preaching. However, a community leader intervened with these words, "Stop, you all know what his wife (a doctor) does for our women. Anyone who harms him will have to answer to me!" Indeed, in Muslim lands medical missions is an important part of the overall ministry, even to just being able to maintain a Christian presence.

"4. To promote public health." Missionary medical personnel have been at the forefront of public health programs. The trend today is toward preventive medicine since in many ways smaller resources can accomplish a lot more. It may not have the same dramatic effect, but national leaders frequently appreciate its great value and welcome such workers, even when they bring the gospel. Vaccine distribution and public health instruction can be invaluable. The old proverb is right: "An ounce of prevention is worth a pound of cure." Poor sanitation is the cause of amoebic dysentery, which is endemic in most third-world countries. Yet millenniums ago God gave Israel many preventive medical instructions for the multitude to maintain public health while camping in the wilderness. "And the LORD will remove from you all sickness; and He will not put on you any of the harmful diseases of Egypt which you have known" (Deut. 7:15). Among the many simple preventive measures God gave Israel was the command to bury their excrement (Deut. 23:13). How tragic that there are billions of people in the world today who don't know enough to do that and get a multitude of diseases as a result.

"5. To demonstrate the love of God." One striking factor in non-Christian lands has been the total unconcern of the adherents of the major world religions for the physical suffering of their people. Part of it can be attributed to the fatalism of their religions and part to ignorance. But it is also significant that these religions know little or nothing about the love of God. Muslims believe that love is merely a human emotion and unworthy of God. It shows in their attitude and behavior. They did not start hospitals and dispensaries for compassionate purposes until shamed by the Christian missionaries.

That love for Christ shows in the quality of the medical care they get from the Christian community. I vividly remember the impact of a missionary nurse friend who ran a clinic in the foothills of the Himalayas. Women who would walk miles past professional doctors' offices to get to her clinic would explain, "She may not be a doctor, but she has healing in her hands." She showed love and never failed to give the gospel to every patient who came to her. Such incidents could be told from all over the world.

"6. To point the patient to Christ."[8] There has been considerable discussion as to whether it is ethical to use medicine as a means to get people to listen to the gospel. Obviously their eternal salvation far outweighs the importance of their physical healing. While I do not subscribe to 'the end justifies the means' type of ethic, we should note that the means is not an evil means. The issue really is: does a good end justify the use of evil or questionable means? Here we have a good means to a good end, and those who raise the objection are guilty of very fuzzy, even muddled thinking. Kane also points out that we do not coerce the patient to accept Christ; patients who come to Christian medi-

cal facilities usually know that they will be exposed to the gospel there; and we increasingly recognize the importance of 'holistic' medicine to be most effective (treating the emotional, mental, and spiritual needs as well as the physical).[9]

The danger of medical work

It is tragic that sometimes missionary medicine fails to present the gospel of Christ for the eternal salvation of the patient. I was a patient in a mission hospital for forty days once and never heard any attempt by the staff to present the gospel, other than the singing of Christmas carols on Christmas eve. Yes, medical ministries can become an end in themselves, but how vital to get our spiritual priorities straight in fulfilling the command of the Lord Jesus to be witnesses.

LITERATURE MINISTRIES

The missionary pioneers almost all gave immediate attention to literature work. The highest priority in literature missions is obviously Bible translation, publication, and distribution work. It apparently was not so obvious to the missionary (legendary, we hope!) who translated *Roberts' Rules of Order* before the Bible. With the availability of training in scientific linguistics and the better knowledge of the original languages on the part of the translators, we can be confident that the current translations are far superior to those done by previous generations of missionary translators.   Now we also have the continuing task of retranslation of older Bibles since language continually changes.

The second stage of missionary literature work is usually the production of adult literacy materials, since most of the new translations are into unwritten languages for which adult literacy teaching is a prime necessity. Then the missionary can move on to the production of a diversity of Christian literature, including tracts and literature for believers. The production of Bible-study tools usually takes high priority, since it is especially important that budding pastors and church leaders have some helps available. With the massive amount of Christian literature available in English, it is hard to realize that most third-world Christian workers do not even have a three-foot shelf of Christian books. Many would settle for a three-inch stack of books and pamphlets!

During the early years of gospel penetration the tendency was for missionaries to produce more literature to evangelize non-Christians rather than materials to build up the Christians. This may help to explain the spiritual weakness of some third-world churches.   More recently there has been a growing awareness of the necessity of good Christian-life materials, as well.   Many countries have one or more Christian publishers.   For example, Pakistan has long had the Punjab Religious Book Society with its wealth of older apologetic literature for Muslims. After the second world war the Christian Publishing House (MIK) was formed to meet the need of books and periodicals for the Christian community, especially of a more evangelical tone.

There is an endless list of kinds of literature needed in missions: Bibles and portions, literacy materials, Bible study tools, devotional books, Bible study guides, Sunday School lesson materials, gospel tracts, Bible correspondence courses, TEE study materials, flannel-graph, hymn-books, commentaries, etc. Most Bibles are published by the United Bible Societies, but increasingly evangelical/fundamental missionaries are dissatisfied with its ecumenical leadership and are forming their own Bible societies. Frequently one mission cannot cope with the diversity of literature needs in a language area so that many missions participate in a cooperative evangelical publishing and distribution effort (such as ELFI, the Evangelical Literature Fellowship of India). Internationally there are a number of service organizations to strengthen and support such national literature efforts, of which the best known is **Evangelical Literature Overseas (ELO)**. Some American publishers also have foreign language branches for the major world languages (such as David C. Cook Publishers).

Although much of Christian literature is still translated material, increasingly national writers are being tapped to produce truly indigenous materials. After the writing of the material, printing may be somewhat different than in English. Some language scripts are not conducive to letter press and must be hand written by calligraphy for printing by photo offset. The first missionaries brought their own presses and in some countries in the last generation local presses would not do Christian literature. Today increasingly the missionary can get his work done and must learn how to 'buy print' in the local marketplace. The greatest bottleneck in Christian literature remains the distribution phase. Especially in poorer nations, people do not have money for literature and the tendency is to subsidize it. Since that tends to limit new literature production, more aggressive promotion is a better solution. Christian bookstore, reading room, and bookmobile ministries are being expanded to get the literature out. But the colporteur, even though not as common as previously, has been revived by organizations like Operation Mobilization with tremendous impact. They have been famous for their literature ships going from port to port. Too often it is the missionary himself who has to be the greatest promoter of literature. We need to infect nationals with a like burden for literature.

COMMUNITY DEVELOPMENT

Community development work is the least prevalent type of involvement, but as circumstances change it is becoming a more major factor in missionary work. Allusion has been made to Robert Moffat's attempt to make Kuruman a model mission station in regard to agriculture and development work. Legions of missionaries have given considerable effort to helping the nationals to develop more effective agriculture, some becoming outstanding agronomists in the process. Community development work seeks to deal with hunger, poverty, floods, isolation, and famine. It involves well drilling, irrigation, road-building, agriculture, flood control, cottage industries, technology, and many other projects. Some of the evangelical organizations which specialize are **World Vision Int., Compassion Int., Food for the Hungry, Farms, Inc., MAP Int.,** and many relief organizations. The ongoing famine crisis in the Sahel of Africa has expanded Christian concern to meet these needs. Many missions have a modicum of development programs and most have chosen to do it on their own or in cooperation with other missions. Some, however, are working in cooperation with governments in projects beyond their own capability. Sometimes missionaries have served as "community organizers." They give rural people a voice to help protect them against exploitation by land-grabbers, profiteers, or government bureaucrats.

While meeting a very real need, development projects always have the serious danger of diverting missionary resources from their primary purpose – evangelism. Indeed, so frequently has evangelism gotten lost or repressed in these projects that serious consideration must constantly be given to maintaining it.

Perspectives enrichment: Chapters D-4, 22, 23

---

1.   Harold R. Cook, *Missionary Life and Work* (1959), pp. 197-98.

2.   J. Herbert Kane, *Life and Work on the Mission Field* (1980), p. 241.

3.   David J. Hesselgrave, *Communicating Christ Cross-Culturally*, p. 20.

4.   George W. Peters, *A Biblical Theology of Missions*, pp. 169-170.

5.   Kane, *Understanding Missions*, p. 305.

6.   Harold Lindsell, *Missionary Principles and Practices* (1955), p. 211.

7.   Although the Pentecostal/Charismatic movements today claim to evidence a restoration of the apostolic gift of healing, it is incontrovertible that 'healers' today do not do what Christ and the apostles did: they healed everyone who came to them in need (Matt. 8:16; Acts 10:38).

8.   Kane, *Life and Work*, pp. 285-87.

9.   Ibid, p. 293.

"At Antioch, in the church . . . the Holy Spirit said, 'Set apart for me Barnabas and Saul for the work to which I have called them.'"

~Acts 13:1-2

WHAT IN THE WORLD CAN MY HOME CHURCH DO?

Although we have argued for the place of the parachurch mission board as a biblical and necessary instrumentality, the local church still retains a major priority in the work of God. This is true also in regard to missions. The missionary and the mission board can hardly function without the backing of the local church at home. Indeed most mission boards consider themselves as arms of the local church. Sometimes the attachment of the arms to the body is not what it should be. Here the local church has to take the initiative to fulfill its responsibility. How can a home church missions program function most effectively?

IMMEDIATE GOALS AND ULTIMATE OBJECTIVES

In any undertaking it is always wise to spell out goals and objectives. Let us distinguish the near-term goals from the long-term objectives. First let us look at some ultimate objectives:

1. To stimulate prayer for missions
2. To raise up financial support for missions
3. To recruit, train, and send out potential missionaries
4. To help missionaries both personally and in their ministries (before departure, on the field, on furlough)
5. To help mission boards (giving time and talent)
6. To help the national churches and workers
7. **To encourage all members to become world Christians**

Some more immediate goals should be identified:
1. To involve all members in the missions program
2. To provide accurate and up-to-date information about missions
3. To educate in the biblical basis and all phases of missions
4. To challenge all regarding missionary service
5. To create interest and concern for missions

THE BIBLICAL MODEL: ANTIOCH[1]

The first missionary-sending church was not Jerusalem but Antioch of Syria. Although we don't know anything about its financial support of Paul and Barnabas, we do know enough about this remarkable church to state that it provides a model for sending churches today. What were its characteristics? The answer is in Acts 11:19-26; 13:1-3.

A leadership free to evangelize cross-culturally (11:19-20)

It seems clear that the 'kosher' Jewish leadership of the Judean churches were unable to bridge the cultural gap to reach Gentiles for Christ. From Acts 11:19-20 it is clear that the unnamed founders of the church in Antioch, who had come from Cyprus and Cyrene, were the first to follow through on Peter's winning the Gentile Cornelius to Christ. They were not 'hung-up' on their Jewishness and perceived that God's plan had now moved away from national Israel to a witness to the diversity of Gentile peoples. As the church grew more Gentile, their concern for Gentile relatives and others grew. This was the root of the sending out of the first missionaries, Paul and Barnabas.

Mobilizing all believers in witness (11:20-1)

Apparently the Antioch church was not founded by apostles but rather by the witness of ordinary, unnamed Christians who moved to Antioch. This is the pattern of the apostolic and post-apostolic church; it grew by the witness of 'laymen'. Every Christian is to be a witness. This is what is meant by the priesthood of all believers.

Expanding the ministry of the word of God (11:22-26)

We don't know who the first leaders were. The Jerusalem church sent Barnabas down to make sure that this diverse church stayed straight. Despite great blessing on his ministry, Barnabas needed help. After all, he had a unique church situation on his hands. This was the very first integrated, mixed church. Indeed, what was the church to be? Barnabas apparently felt that a gifted teacher named Saul of Tarsus could help answer these questions, and thus brought him into the ministry there. Saul's teaching on the nature of the church was so clear (see Eph. 3) that even non-Christians perceived that this was not just a Jewish sect, and had to give them a new name, 'Christian' (11:26).

This expansion of gifted leadership did not stop there. After Barnabas and Saul returned from the famine-relief trip to Jerusalem, we find that the leadership had expanded to five men (13:1)! The Antioch church could spare two of them for missionary service. Thus the expanding leadership of spiritually gifted men provided an overflow for missions. This is the way it should be for churches today.

A cosmopolitan, multi-ethnic church (13:1)

The secret of the missionary vision of the Antioch church was the fact that its members were ethnically diverse. For example, two of its five leaders were Gentiles. Simeon called Niger was probably black. Lucius of Cyrene would be a white Gentile. Although the other three were presumably Jews, Saul and Barnabas were non-Palestinians, familiar with Gentile culture. This gave a solid basis for a missionary concern. This is the ideal for missionary-minded churches today!

Giving its best for world evangelization (13:2)

The Antioch church sent out the best men they had for the demanding task of Gentile evangelism. Missions today is such a demanding ministry that the church must sacrifice its best resources for the task, both personnel and support. But many Christians have the "used-tea-bag" mindset — missions gets the leftovers.

Centered in prayer for world outreach (13:2-3)

It was out of prayerful worship that the leaders understood the calling of the Holy Spirit for missions. Isaiah had said that God's temple should be "a house of prayer for all nations" (56:7). The Lord Jesus commanded his apostles to "beseech the Lord of the harvest to send out workers into His harvest" (Matt. 9:38). Missions is rooted in prayer.

Pentecost arose out of the upper-room prayer meeting, which was the beginning of cross-cultural witness. The apostles put prayer first (Acts 6:4). Saul of Tarsus was praying when Ananias came in and gave him God's commission to the Gentiles (9:11). Paul later exhorted us to pray for all mankind, since Christ died for all (1 Tim. 2:1-4). David Brainerd and William Carey were first of all men of prayer. It was the Haystack Prayer Meeting which started foreign missions from the USA. Neesima has said, "The early church advanced on its knees."

How many missionaries can give signal testimony to God's intervention on their behalf in direct answer to prayer of supporters back home! We are engaged in spiritual warfare, and prayer is a vital weapon in it (Eph. 6:18). A missions-minded church today must be a praying church. We must pray for workers; for God's provision, for the effectiveness of the missionary, for unsaved contacts, and the national Christians and churches. Yet how many churches are self-centered in their prayer life; how seldom is missions at the heart of prayer in the average evangelical church, let alone, non-evangelical?

THE CRUCIAL ROLE OF PASTORS AND PULPIT

Harold Cook wrote extensively on a church missionary program and highlighted the importance of church leaders being sold on missions:

The life of any missionary program in a local church depends largely upon the leadership. Someone has to have the interest, the vision, the initiative to inaugurate a program, plus the persistence to carry it through. Normally the pastor should be that leader. People usually look to him for leadership, and in this matter they expect him to be much better informed than the members. Besides, he must cooperate if missions is to be a church concern and not just a fringe activity of a small group within the church.[2]

Unfortunately not all pastors are sold on the centrality of missions and enthusiastic in advocating it. Perhaps some have never faced the biblical basis of missions already expounded in earlier chapters. Possibly others have reacted emotionally to high-pressured appeals to missionary service. Since they did not respond to that appeal, there may be some needless guilt which blocks wholehearted enthusiasm. In some cases, there is a serious failure in their training to deal with the issues. But probably most pastoral lethargy can be accounted for by a natural tendency to give attention to that which is most immediate—the tyranny of the urgent. The mission fields are far removed from sight and sound, and their advocates must compete with oversaturated media (i.e., lots of junk mail?). Perhaps also some financially struggling churches see missions as in competition with their own local-church budget. Cook rightly reminds us that "the church itself will get a great blessing from taking an active part in the work."[3]

If there is silence on missions from the pulpit it will be difficult to stimulate missions interest in the pew. This does not just mean bringing in missionary speakers, but especially concerns how pastors themselves communicate. Do they ever preach on the Bible basis of missions? Do they frequently or ever use missions illustrations in their sermons? Do they read missionary prayer letters from the pulpit? Do they include prayer for missions in their pastoral prayers? Do they ever refer to tribal peoples, Hindus, Muslims, etc. as those who must be won to Christ? Do they ever contrast biblical truth with Islamic theology or Hindu pantheism, etc.? There are many possibilities here.

How can pastors prepare themselves to be able to respond to all the above questions positively? They **must** include significant books on missions in their reading programs. In this jet age it would be helpful for pastors to visit foreign fields to be able to grasp global realities firsthand. When they bring in missions speakers, they can take careful notes of what is presented. They can also from time-to-time attend missions conferences in other churches, Bible colleges, and seminaries to try to keep up-to-date in the rapidly changing field of missions.

Pastors should hardly need to be reminded to use missions speakers and audio visuals. And yet the competition for pulpit time may make that reminder necessary. The recently returned furloughing missionary is probably in the most demand. But mission administrators, missions professors, and missionary appointees should also be used. Appointees should not be automatically shunted to the least significant time slots. While not all can minister well on a Lord's Day morning service, some appointees should be given the best opportunities. My experience in doing this has not been disappointing.

MISSIONS CONFERENCES

Special missions conferences are an essential of a local church missions thrust. Note that the word conference is plural. It need not be limited to one a year. Certainly an annual conference is the minimum. Note also that a contemporary conference is not a 'missionary', but a 'missions' conference. Our concern should not be just for the American missionary. Two-thirds-world churches and missions are an important dimension today.

An annual missions conference should be the climax of the church's missions program. Since the beginning of this century it has become the focus of many congregations' use of the Faith-Promise Plan. The Faith-Promise Plan is a means by which every member is challenged to "decide prayerfully how much each will trust God to let him give weekly for a year to share the gospel outside his own community."[4] God has greatly used it in thousands of churches for the multiplication of financial support for missions. It has also proved to be a great blessing to the life of those churches. It has proved over and over that sacrificial giving to missions does not hurt the local-church budget. Full details can be found in Norm Lewis's book quoted above.

Some churches today are dropping the traditional full-week conference in favor of weekend conferences because of poor attendance midweek. I believe this is a mistake since it is hard to build momentum in just a weekend or two. Some of the better-attended conferences start on the weekend and carry on through Tuesday or Wednesday. Alternatively Wednesday through Sunday works well.

The music in a conference is very important and should be missionary in nature. It is surprising how frequently church musicians do not bother to prepare music that is distinctly missionary. The use of panel discussions in the program is also highly recommended. It takes a knowledgeable moderator, but hopefully a pastor can be that person. This gives excellent opportunity for that interaction which is so important to effective communication.

It should also be said that the congregation will get a strong impression of the degree of priority given to missions by the effort expended or not expended on the conference. Are wall mottoes, national flags, curio displays, and decorations essential to the conference? Possibly not! However, it does communicate to those in attendance how important missions is viewed by the church leadership as indicated by attention to these details. Don't minimize their importance!

MISSIONS EDUCATION AND INFORMATION

A number of channels of education and missions information should be emphasized: (1) a current missionary map showing missionaries' locations, (2) a missions bulletin board featuring current prayer letters, (3) missions books in the church library and reading program; (4) mission magazines and literature made available to the congregation through literature racks and tables, (5) a brief summary of the ministry of a 'missionary of the week' in the church bulletin, (6) an insert in the church paper summarizing the ministries of all the supported missionaries, and (7) use of missionary prayer letters in all services of the church, especially prayer meeting.

A major resource of information and education is the ACMC (Advancing Churches in Missions Commitment) founded in 1974. It is an association of local churches to provide helps for the local church in strengthening its missions program. They help with setting up a missions policy, an effective committee, missions curriculum, conference planning, etc. They also hold national and regional conferences supportive of these goals.[5]

MISSIONS SUPPORT

Local churches are and should be the foundation of prayer and financial support for missionaries, even though a significant amount comes from individuals directly. Both denominational and interdenominational missions have struggled with the problem arising from a missionary having thirty or more supporting churches, some of which are "nickel and diming it." Recently consortiums of ten or less churches are being formed to eliminate this problem. The missionary's home church takes on a substantial portion of the support (typically 30%) and others make up the balance. A major purpose is to shorten the length of pre-field ministry for the missionary.

---

1. Tapes of my sermon on the *Model Missionary-Sending Church* are available from the publisher.

2. Cook, *Introduction*, p. 222. Note detailed discussion in chapters 23-27.

3. Ibid, p. 223.

4. Norm Lewis, *Faith Promise for World Witness* (Lincoln, Nebr.: Back to the Bible, 1974), p. 20.

5. ACMC, PO Box ACMC, Wheaton, IL 60189-8000, or call 800-798-ACMC.

"After these things I looked and behold, a great multitude, which no one could count, from every nation and all tribes and peoples and tongues, standing before the throne and before the Lamb, clothed in white robes. . ." —Revelation 7:9

WHERE IN THE WORLD
DO WE GO FROM HERE?

The Lord Jesus promised that in reference to the fulfilling of the Great Commission He would be with us until the end of the age. Missions is in our future until the Lord Jesus comes back. However, missions will undergo significant changes from what we have been experiencing in the past. The job is not yet done. But to finish that job we will have to adapt to the changed and changing conditions in the world. The message has not changed in twenty centuries. The priorities have not changed; evangelism is still number one. But the world into which we go keeps changing and at an accelerating rate at that.

THE UNFINISHED TASK

We are moving into a new era of missions. William Carey was the 'prophet' of the first era of modern missions. Hudson Taylor was the 'prophet' of the second era according to Ralph Winter. He suggests that W. Cameron Townsend was the 'prophet' of the third era, in which we find ourselves. Townsend trumpeted the needs of the thousands of tribes without the Bible in their mother tongue. Winter was too modest to name himself as a 'prophet' of the third era, but that is probably the reality. He had proclaimed the 'hidden frontiers' represented by a mass of over two billion people who are not now being effectively reached for Christ: the Muslims, Hindus, Chinese etc. Thousands of young people have responded to his proclamation with the result that there is new interest in mainland China, Muslim, and Hindu work.

Most of all, Ralph Winter has reminded us that the task is not nearly finished. The myth of the completed task is one of the most dangerous myths of all because it lulls us into complacency. We can rejoice over the fantastic progress made in the last two centuries since William Carey, as we highlighted in our introduction. But we must remember that we have just scratched the surface.

World population has reached the six billion mark. Today there are over three hundred million evangelical Christians in the world. That is still only less than six percent of world population. Over a quarter of those evangelical Christians are here in North America. So although the church of Jesus Christ is increasingly becoming non-Western, most of the two-thirds-world peoples are not now effectively being reached for Christ. When Ralph Winter first set out the concept of the 'hidden frontiers' at the Lausanne Congress in 1974, the number he used was somewhat over two billion. With the population explosion that number is fast approaching three billion: those among the 'hidden peoples'.

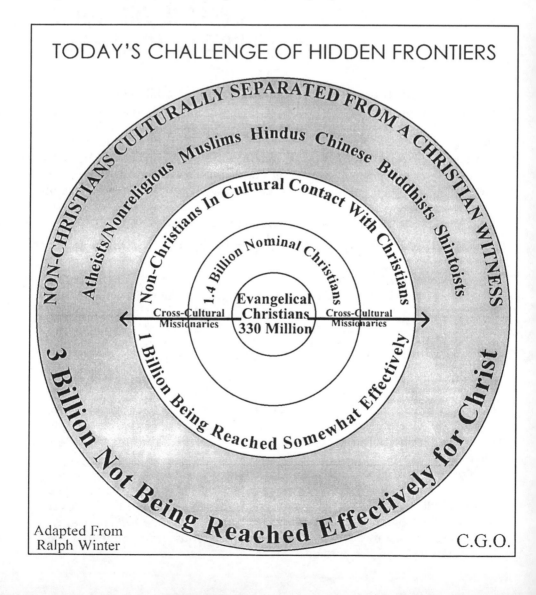

TODAY'S CHALLENGE OF HIDDEN FRONTIERS

NON-CHRISTIANS CULTURALLY SEPARATED FROM A CHRISTIAN WITNESS

Atheists/Nonreligious Muslims Hindus Chinese Buddhists Shintoists

Non-Christians In Cultural Contact With Christians

1.4 Billion Nominal Christians

Evangelical Christians 330 Million

Cross-Cultural Missionaries   Cross-Cultural Missionaries

1 Billion Being Reached Somewhat Effectively

3 Billion Not Being Reached Effectively for Christ

Adapted From Ralph Winter

C.G.O.

Hidden peoples. For some decades now a number of missiologists have been working to identify the 'hidden peoples'. Hundreds of previously unidentified tribal or linguistic groups have now been targeted. But the concept needs to be continuously expanded. Japanese Shinto-Buddhists should be included as a massive group of upward of a hundred million who are not being effectively reached. Theravada Buddhists in Southeast Asia are another group that is not being adequately penetrated with the gospel.

The billion nonreligious, secularists, and communists also need to be targeted. When we see the triumph of secularism in Europe and the great cities of the world we realize that this is another 'hidden frontier'. Some of them are in relatively 'closed countries'. With the increasing success of tentmaker missionaries in penetrating them, we must call them "creative-access countries." The military defeat of the West in Southeast Asia should not obscure the spiritual need of the people there: Vietnam, Cambodia, and Laos. Americans tend to want to forget Vietnam! But we can never forget the millions there who need to hear the gospel. As we saw in our study of Europe, the needs in Eastern Europe are quite diverse. Countries like former Yugoslavia and Albania are among the neediest in the whole world. Missiologists will need to continue to strategize and to target unreached people groups.

The 'closed countries' are part of the 'hidden peoples'. I remember hearing a native-born Chinese evangelist (of all people!) speak in Bible college chapel in the mid '70s, saying that God was finished with Red China. Fortunately the events of recent years have not only proved him to be wrong, but dead wrong. We must never become pessimistic about the so-called 'closed countries'. Today tentmaking missionaries are penetrating Muslim countries as never before. There are other areas we must pray to creatively penetrate. Remember the Lord Jesus is the One who "has the key of David, who opens and no one will shut" (Rev. 3:7). He is the One who sets before us an open door. With 35 countries opening up to the gospel resulting from the demise of the Iron Curtain among other factors, we have great cause for encouragement to press into these opening doors.

The 10/40 window. At Lausanne II conference, Luis Bush proposed the concept of the 10/40 window. This is the area of Africa and Asia between 10 and 40 degrees north latitude. He suggests that it is the neediest part of the world in many different ways: spiritually, economically, health-wise, educationally, etc. It includes most of the Muslim world, India, China, and most of southeast Asia. This is a helpful, simple way to view the world, and it has been picked up by many missions leaders and spokesmen as a valuable concept for strategizing. The problem with any simplification, however, is that it may not fit all the facts and may be somewhat misleading. The 10/40 window does not include the very spiritually needy areas of southern Europe (and for that matter, northern Europe), the CIS republics, Mongolia, and the northern part of mainland China. While it is true that Europe is not as deprived in other ways, it certainly is so spiritually. This would also leave out the heavily Muslim areas of Malaysia, Indonesia, and the southern Philippines and omits many unreached tribes of Africa as well. So as helpful as it is, it can be improved upon. Perhaps we should focus on a 5/50 window instead. This would include these other very needy areas just mentioned.

People-group focus. Far more valuable in getting the big picture is the concept of focusing on people groups, rather than the political national entities, or their geographical locations. Currently missiologists are especially keen on the value of this perspective. The recent fifth edition of *Operation World* gives great attention to this perspective as a basis for missionary strategy. We believe it is a biblical concept, evidenced in the Great Commission itself. In reference to Matthew 28:19 and Luke 24:47, Dayton and Fraser point out that the term *ethnē* is used of both Jew and Gentiles and has the sense of a 'people.'

> The Great Commission's goal is not simply to organize Christian communities within the political units currently recognized as nation-states. It aims at all peoples and people groups which exist in various states of natural cohesion because of shared language and life. However we classify them (as tribe, caste, class, clan, language-group, status group, etc.) all peoples and people groups are to be given the gospel.[1]

At this point then the next step is to define an unreached people group. Perhaps the best available definition is: "A people group within which there is no indigenous community of believing Christians able to evangelize this group."[2] Patrick Johnstone distills the results of 20 years of Christian researchers' conclusions into the following figures: There are about 12,000 ethno-linguistic people groups in the world, of which 4000 are least evangelized or "unreached peoples." This gives us a better perception of the dimensions of the unfinished task.

HOW CAN WE MEET THE NEED?

We are must use creative means to meet the changing needs of a lost world. Nineteenth-century missions and its approaches are long since gone. Even twentieth-century approaches are not going to be ade-quate. A number of serious problems and challenges to the missionary movement have been developing in recent decades which will undoubtedly continue to be problems in the years to come. Let us look at them.

Continuing problems in world missions

Political Chaos. We can be sure that political chaos will increasingly be part of the scene. With the growth of nationalism as a major factor after the Second World War, centrifugal political forces reversed the centripetal force of colonialism. The legacy of this is increasing political chaos. As this is being written, the media reported two coups d'etat in one day. Ted Ward's analysis is penetrating:

> Two related realities confront us. The key reality is nationalism. It is a sort of nuclear explosion (rather, a series of explosions) breaking the back of political colonialism. The fallout is surprisingly lethal. The other reality is totalitarian government. The self-fulfilling prophecies of the colonial powers that most of their colonies would be unable to govern themselves are coming true. The fallout of nationalism has engendered 'benign' dictatorship, which in turn has its own evil consequences in cycles of anarchy and totalitarianism. The prospects for participatory democracy seem dark indeed. There are notable exceptions—India, Kenya, Egypt, Israel, Mexico, Jamaica, to name several—but the larger reality is that the trend, though ostensibly to the left, is actually toward anarchy as the prelude to absolute dictatorship.[3]

In addition to the broader political problems of the context into which missionaries go, there is the more immediate problem of international terrorism. From time to time in different parts of the world missionaries have been kidnapped by various political groups for a variety of reasons —Marxists, Muslims, etc. In most cases the missionaries have ultimately been released, but it is an ongoing problem as to how to deal with it.

Resurgence of non-Christian religions. A major factor in the last half of the twentieth century has been the resurgence of the non- Christian religions, when it was expected that they would decline. Shintoism in Japan has not only recovered from the trauma of the war and American occupation, it has surged, especially in its sects. Hindu sects have invaded the West. Islam with its oil money is on the move. Muslims have targeted Europe for missionary activity, and especially England as the bridgehead to Europe. Not only have millions of Muslims migrated to Europe for work, but they are having some success in converting people from a secularized society.

Indigenous theologies. We have already highlighted the impact of Liberation Theology in Latin America and its spread to Africa where it is emerging as 'Black Theology', which is very similar. As long as there are oppressed peoples, there will be a market for these revolutionary theologies among professing Christians. Additionally African theologies are surfacing which seek to blend Christianity with the indigenous animistic religions. It is also having a significant impact. In Asia we are also seeing those same syncretistic tendencies—to blend Christianity with indigenous religious ideas. The impact of modernistic liberal theologies has long since penetrated many theological seminaries in Asia and opens the door for such compromise, which is so harmonious with the Asian mindset.

A liberal ecumenical movement. David Hesselgrave sees some signs of convergence between Evangelicals and Ecumenists: the Evangelicals are becoming more ecumenical, and the Ecumenists are becoming more evangelical. He also points up the growing gap, which we have noted, between the shrinking number of ecumenical missionaries and the substantial growth of evangelical/fundamental missionaries.[4] Even though the number of ecumenical missionaries is declining, the ecumenical movement is still very powerful, especially in Asia and Europe. This is because a significant number of nationals have been infected with ecumenism and the liberal and neo-orthodox theologies predominant in that movement. It is nationals in these areas who are developing the indigenous theologies which are so destructive of genuine biblical faith. And this movement still maintains an aggressive organizational outreach, even though it has an uncertain missionary outreach. It would like to dominate Christendom.[5]

There are two factors which bode well for the distinctively evangelical cause in the 'Two-thirds World'. The first is the resurgence of fundamentalist missions.   The second is that few of the rapidly expanding two-thirds-world missions are from ecumenical churches.

One recent cause for concern, however, was a 1994 announcement of plans by some outstanding evangelical leaders to form a consortium with Roman Catholic and ecumenical leaders to address some current concerns. This all seems part of a broadening pattern developing among evangelical leaders to water down the definitions of a Christian and of the gospel to include all of Christendom. This is exacerbated by the denial by professedly evangelical theologians, like Clark Pinnock, of the lostness of the heathen. We have already dealt with the serious consequences of such foggy theology in the first and fifth chapters. This all seems to be part of the de-emphasis upon doctrine and theology in this experience-oriented day.

Pentecostal/charismatic movements. The last generation has seen a striking growth in the Pentecostal denominations, especially in Latin America, but also throughout the world. Charismatic practices have penetrated Roman Catholic, Eastern Orthodox and Protestant churches around the world. Pentecostals have especially used the media very effectively in recent years. Although the Bakker and Swaggart scandals have tarnished these movements, it is undoubtedly a temporary setback. Mainstream evangelical/fundamental missions and missionaries cannot ignore these movements. Certainly we must learn from their successes and their excesses. We must not determine what is true from that which succeeds. The Bible is still the standard of truth, and these movements must be tested in the light of Scripture. Biblical revelation, not contemporary experience, must be the basis of what we believe. But how will we relate to these movements? This will continue to be a crucial question as we move into the twenty-first century, if the Lord Jesus does not come first.

One very disturbing fact reported in the current edition of *Operation World* is that although there are about ten million active Catholic Charismatics, there are also an estimated 60 million post-Charismatic Catholics. These are Catholics who have dropped out of the charismatic movement. Whether they now have been inoculated against the true gospel or are more open to it, is the question. There are also reported to be from five to 20 million evangelical Catholics worldwide.[6]

Strategic trends

The prospective missionary has far more options open to him today than ever before, and the options are likely to increase in the years to come. Today there are about 2,500 Protestant mission agencies and the number is rapidly expanding. It is not just the number that is escalating, but also the diversity of types and functions.[7] In addition, the options of career versus short-term and of professional versus biprofessional (tentmaker) ministries present themselves.

Short-term missionaries. The developing trend toward short terms will undoubtedly continue. Missionary leaders can be heartened to note that it does not seem to have undermined the basic core of career missionaries necessary to carry on the work. Also encouraging has been the large percentage of short termers who return as career missionaries. But missionary leaders will have to work out creative ways to gain maximum effectiveness from short termers. Field missionaries will need help and guidance in the use of short termers. Indeed, mission boards will have to encourage a positive attitude toward the short-term missionary for maximum utilization.

A changing missionary role. Since World War II the role of the missionary has been in a process of change. This will surely continue. As national churches awaken to their responsibility for evangelism, and even for missions, the missionary will assume more of a support role. Training of national leadership is and will continue to be the highest priority. This will require better trained and educated missionaries. Missionaries will have to be increasingly sensitive to their relationship with national leaders. This is no longer an option (if it ever was), but a prime necessity. Its imperative is further heightened by the current explosion of cross-cultural missionaries from the two-thirds world (see below). The missionary cannot be satisfied to have a merely 'official' relationship with the nationals. It must be a deeply spiritual relationship, for which the Apostle Paul's relationship with the churches he founded is a model. This will increasingly have to be emphasized in missionary orientation.

Biprofessional 'tentmaking' missionaries. As Christians we have been slow to learn that "the word of God is not bound." In my younger years of ministry I used to wonder why I never heard of missionaries to Turkey. The reason was simple: there were none! But a score of years ago a number of missions and individuals found creative ways to reside in Turkey as 'tentmakers', or biprofessional missionaries. Over the years hundreds of Turks have come to Christ and churches are being planted in a number of cities. Other Muslim and Marxist 'creative-access countries' are being penetrated as missions become more innovative. Some become English teachers (TESL), teachers in English medium schools, tourist agents, journalists, business professionals, etc

With the growing emphasis upon penetration of 'closed countries', the number of biprofessional missionaries will necessarily increase. Mission boards are seeking to work out unofficial relationships with such missionaries. It is difficult for them to succeed if they are totally on their own. As much as possible, mission boards will need to provide encouragement, fellowship, and support of various kinds. Help in training, orientation, and other areas will have to be discreetly developed. The potential is great and needs to be tapped more aggressively.

Another related area, which is more difficult to develop, is seen in the Christian who is sent abroad by his employer without any intention of becoming a 'tentmaker'. Hundreds of thousands of Americans work abroad, and some of them are Christians. Creative ways need to be developed to utilize their potential for witness in needy areas.

Two-thirds-world missionaries. The most encouraging development of recent decades has been the emergence of a significant number of two-thirds-world missionaries. From about 3,000 in 1972 the number had grown to about 13,000 by 1980. Pate's thorough recent study indicates that the number has exploded to about 36,000 by 1988, working in 2,425 people groups in 118 countries.[8] This is undoubtedly the wave of the future and long overdue. Certainly the demise of colonialism greatly contributed to this development. As long as the colonial mindset dominated the two-thirds-world, there was little likelihood of nationals becoming missionaries. Indeed, the western missionaries contributed to the situation by failing to challenge third-world churches in regard to their missionary responsibility. But now this is all changing rapidly. Not only are we seeing the development of home missions, but also significant foreign missionary enterprise on the part of the third-world churches. Obviously, western missionaries must continue to support this trend.

New patterns of missionary support. With the increased costs of supporting missionaries in some parts of the world, it will be imperative to develop new patterns of missionary support. Here is where mission boards will need to educate local churches and their pastors of the contemporary realities. The question arises as to the best use of our resources if pre-field ministry becomes too prolonged. The missionary's home church will have to recognize a prime responsibility to take on a large block of support and to help aggressively in assisting the missionary appointee in pre-field ministry. We have already alluded to the growing interest in support consortiums of churches.

A strategy for the next century

Missions strategy is not new. But the emphasis upon strategizing has been accelerating in recent years and will undoubtedly continue into the future. With organizations like Missions Advanced Research and Communication Center (MARC), U.S. Center for World Mission, the Billy Graham Center at Wheaton College, and the A.D. 2000 Movement, and consultations such as the Lausanne I (1974) and II (Manila, 1989) and the 1989 Singapore Consultation, etc. the trend is clear. Localized conferences on world-evangelism strategy are proliferating. With a growing number of major seminaries offering doctorates in missiology, there will be a rapid growth in research and writing to utilize our resources more effectively to get the job done. Add to that the expansion of church growth and contextualization discussion and it becomes clear that there are many fruitful avenues for innovation in the way our cross-cultural witness is carried on. We will try to touch briefly on some of the most salient topics.

Contextualization. Contextualization is a term coined in ecumenical circles in the early '70s and increasingly being discussed and utilized in evangelical circles as well. The main point as Evangelicals understand it is to communicate God's eternal message and plant His church untainted by our own culture into the diverse cultures of the world. First we have to recognize that the message came into two different cultures (Hebrew and Greco-Roman) and we must first distinguish what is merely cultural and what is eternal. Then as we communicate it to people of a different culture, we must be careful not to impose our own cultural understandings. Then it must be communicated in a way which is understandable to people in their own culture. Most importantly it involves the message of the gospel and this is the process of cross-cultural communication. There has also been a growing recognition that our theological approach has been essentially western, and we do need to examine other theological structures for each culture. Educational method is also colored by culture. Also significant is the effect of culture on church structure. Modes of worship need to be contextualized for each culture.

The nonresidential missionary. One very innovative recent strategy is the concept of the 'nonresidential missionary', which term was coined in 1986 by a team of researchers working with the Southern Baptist Foreign Mission Board. Apparently it had been developing under various names and emphases by different people all over the world at that time. It is another very creative way to evangelize those 'limited-access countries.' David Garrison gives a definition and description:

> A nonresidential missionary is a full-time, professional career foreign missionary who is matched up with a single unevan-gelized population segment for purposes of concentrating on priorities of initial evangelization and eliminating gaps and inadvertent duplica-tions with other agencies. . . . From this nonresidential base, he or she networks with all other concerned Christians (denominations, agencies, and individuals), both local and non-local, to do the following:
> 1. Research and survey the situation of that single population seg-ment, becoming expert in the subject for purposes of evangeli-zation and ministry;
> 2. Become fluent in that population's main language;
> 3. Draw up and help to see implemented a wide range of evange-lizing ministry options directed towards that population by per-sistently advocating the evangelization of the population before the world's host of Christian resources;[9]

Hitherto there have been itinerant missionaries and Bible smugglers who were nonresidential, but this goes a step a step farther in its emphasis upon networking and coordinating. "Rather than trying to make all of the primary contacts himself, the nonresidential missionary relies on hun-dreds of other individuals and agencies." In effect he is the catalyst in God's using many people in different locations and nationalities to reach a target people group. The examples Garrison gives show the exciting possibilities.

A.D. 2000 Movement. Arising out of the Global Consultation on World Evangelism by AD 2000 and Beyond in Singapore in 1989 is a continuing organization and movement being spearheaded by national Christian leaders from a number of countries. The main emphasis is on strategy to complete the task of world evangelism by the end of the century. Since even the secular world is taking note of the new millennium ap-proaching as significant, we Christians should set measurable goals for reaching every people group in a meaningful way by then. Many mission organizations have been setting goals for 2000 and the movement seeks to coordinate, research, focus, and cooperate in pressing toward those goals.

There is a question of the relationship of the year 2000 with the return of the Lord Jesus, but by including the words "and beyond," the initiators are not making that connection. The main point is to set goals and actively seek to reach them.

Partnering. We have already noted the amazing growth of not only the numbers of two-thirds-world missionaries, but also of leadership and initiative coming from them. What can western mission boards do to make the most of this trend? A generation ago, Fife and Glasser gave some practical suggestions for nullifying the impact of racism in missions. They not only suggested "enlarging the contribution of the American non-Caucasian," but also "utilizing international teams" and "providing partnership status in mission boards."[10] These suggestions are even more relevant today. Increasingly, mission boards are recruiting American non-Caucasians and including foreign nationals in the missionary taskforce. With the continuing problem of racism in the world and the accusation that Evangelicals have not been adequately concerned to deal with it, it is imperative that we aggressively do so. The Apostle Paul's missionary band was ethnically very diverse. This is a strong testimony to the unity of the body of Christ and the oneness of the Holy Spirit.

The pressing strategic question, however, is how western missionaries are to relate to the two-thirds-world missionaries. It would be foolish to just "let them do their own thing" for a number of other reasons. Obviously we want to avoid duplication and tension. Then there is the inexperience of third-world churches in missions — westerners have been at it for three centuries now and can share what we have learned. Korean missionaries are already a major factor in the former Soviet Union and other areas, and Latin Americans are targeting the Muslim world. In 1987 the First Iberoamerican Missionary Congress (COMIBAM) was held in Sao Paulo, Brazil. Then in 1993, 1200 people gathered in Orlando under the banner, North American Hispanic Missions Cooperation (COMHINA). For further information on the possibilities of partnering see, Kraakevik and Welliver, *Partners in the Gospel.*[11]

A vital question has arisen in connection with non-western missionaries and patterns of financial support. Since the Second World War there has been an emphasis upon indigenous principles of missionary funding. This means that national workers should not be supported by foreign money. More recently, however, there has been a trend in the opposite direction. Some mission organizations have been specializing in channeling money to national evangelists and missionaries. At an IFMA/ EFMA conference some years ago Chris Marantika, an Indonesian theologian, proposed a method of subsidizing and training national missionaries with western funds. A challenging book by a south Indian evangelist, K. P. Yohannan, has been used of God to shake up affluent American Christians as to their responsibility to help national evangelists in poor countries.[12] This type of scenario will undoubtedly become more common in countries like India, where it is extremely difficult to get missionary visas. However, care must be taken not to undermine indigenous churches with the corrupting influence of western money.

Our time may be short

We do not know how much time we have before the return of the Lord Jesus Christ. We do not know how long we have for world evangelization. We must not fall into that common rationalization that the time is so short that nothing more can be done. We cannot set dates, as so many have wrongly done in the past. Christ was very explicit: "But of that day and hour no one knows, not even the angels of heaven, nor the Son, but the Father alone" (Matt. 24:36). But in any case the Lord made it clear that He would be with us to the end of the age in this task of world evangelization (Matt. 28:20). May we be found faithful until He comes!

Perspectives enrichment: Chapters D-25, 26, 28

1. Edward R. Dayton and David A. Fraser, *Planning Strategies for World Evangelization,* rev. ed. (1990), pp. 86-7.

2. Ibid, p.72.

3. Ted Ward, "The Future of Missions: Hangovers, Fallout, and Hope" in *New Horizons in World Mission,* ed. David J. Hesselgrave (1979), p. 25.

4. David J. Hesselgrave, *Today's Choices for Tomorrow's Mission* (1988), pp. 101-10.

5. Fife and Glasser, Missions in Crisis (1961), pp. 128-35.

6. Johnstone, 5th ed., p. 24.

7. Hesselgrave, *Today's Choices,* pp. 27-46.

8. Pate, *From Every People,* pp. 12, 22.

9. V. David Garrison, *The Nonresidential Missionary: A new strategy and the people it serves* (MARC/New Hope, 1990), p. 13.

10. Fife and Glasser, *Crisis* pp. 155-61.

11. James H. Kraakevik and Dotsey Welliver, *Partners in the Gospel* (1991?).

12. K. P. Yohannan, *The Coming Revolution in World Missions: God's Third Wave* (1986).

GLOSSARY OF TERMS

Church Growth Movement: A trend initiated in 1955 by Donald A. McGavran in his many writings and teaching at Fuller School of World Mission, which emphasizes strategies by which people movements to Christ can be initiated and encouraged. Use of statistics, research, anthropological, and sociological factors are studied.

Contextualization: A strategy which takes into account the various cultures into which God's eternal message comes and is communicated to people of diverse cultures. Beginning in ecumenical circles in the early '70s, it is increasingly becoming a part of evangelical strategy, not only in cross-cultural communication of biblical truth, but also in biblical interpretation and adapting the forms of church life to the receptor culture.

Cultural Mandate: An understanding of Gen. 1:26-28 as implying a responsibility of Christians to society and the environment. It is in contrast with the evangelistic mandate of the Great Commission, and held by some to be of equal or greater importance.

Culture Shock: The emotional impact upon the individual who moves into a new and strange culture. At first there is usually curiosity, but frequently this is followed by a repulsion and aversion to the cultural differences.

Ecumenism: The Ecumenical Movement which arose out of the worldwide missionary conferences in the beginning of the century, eventuating in the World Council of Churches and a strong movement toward church union or the merging of deno-

minations. It seeks a strong organizational unification of all Christendom.

Ethnolinguistic People: "A distinct homogeneous ethnic or racial group, speaking its own language." There is a strong cultural unity within the group, even if living in different political countries.

Frontier Missionary: A cross-cultural missionary, working among an unreached people group, not having any indigenous church.

Hidden Peoples: A term coined by Ralph Winter to describe some of the major blocks of unreached peoples in the world, who were being bypassed by missions because of our superficial mindset. They are not necessarily geographically isolated or hidden, but were hidden to our perception. This would include most Muslims, upper-caste Hindus, nonreligious, and many others.

Inclusivism: The view that unevangelized peoples can be saved through the cross of Christ without explicit faith in Jesus Christ.

Identification: The attitude of the missionary in which he seeks to identify with the nationals in their culture and life situation as much as possible without compromising the message. This involves distancing oneself from a colonialistic mindset and attitudes of cultural superiority, narrowing the economic gap by a simple lifestyle, and an empathy with the culture and aspirations of the target people.

Indigenous Church Principles: A church planting strategy formulated by Rufus Anderson and Henry Venn, implemented by John Nevius in Korea in the 19th century, and popularized by Roland Allen in the early 20th, which stressed that missionaries should try from the very beginning to plant churches which are self-supporting financially, self-governing, and self-propagating. Thus the missionary should be free to move on to plant other churches. This is based upon the model the Apostle Paul provided.

Liberation Theology: A movement started among Latin American Catholics in the early '70s but spreading to Protestants and to other continents, advocating liberation from oppressive political and economic circumstances "on the basis of sociological and often Marxist presuppositions," frequently advocating armed overthrow of oppressive structures.

Marginal Groups: Cultic groups of a semi-Christian or quasi-Christian nature, which accept part of the biblical message, but frequently hold to additional revelation which is given equal or nearly equal authority with the Bible.

Parachurch Organization: Organizations which work alongside the local church to carry on Christian ministries, ideally supportive of the local church. In some cases they were formed to do what local churches have failed to do, but in other cases they do what local churches cannot do. Denominational organizations of autonomous churches are really also parachurch in nature.

People Group: "A significantly large grouping of individuals who perceive themselves to have a common affinity for one another because of their shared language, religion, ethnicity, residence, occupation, class or caste, situation, etc. or combination of these." (Garrison) It is generally used of the largest grouping within which the gospel can spread without encountering significant cultural or sociological barriers.

People Movement: A term coined by McGavran in the beginnings of the Church Growth Movement, to describe what had been called in India "mass movements." The gospel spreads along lines of natural relationship in such a way that a significant number of related people turn to Christ either simultaneously or in a short timeframe. Since in many cultures decisions are made jointly in a group, this is their cultural way of turning to Christ.

Syncretism: The tendency to merge diverse religious beliefs and practices into one composite system. The most striking example is the Sikh religion, a merger of Hindu and Muslim beliefs and practices into one. Bahai and some African Independent churches are syncretistic. Oriental multireligious systems operate syncretistically. There is some syncretism in Roman Catholicism, and each of the major religions.

Tentmaker: A term used for nonprofessional missionaries in reference to the fact that the Apostle Paul worked at tentmaking when his funds ran out. Actually the tentmaking missionary is a biprofessional person. The main purpose is usually to gain access to those countries closed to overt missionaries.

Universalism: The teaching that all people will ultimately be saved, whether they believe in Christ or not. It is taught in liberalism under the concept of the universal fatherhood of God. Sometimes it takes the form of 'second chance' thinking, or of 'implicit faith.'

"The election of God will be a fatal laby-
rinth for anyone who does not follow the
clear road of faith. Thus, so that we
may be confident of remission of sins,
so that our consciences may rest in full
confidence of eternal life, so that we
may boldly call God our Father, under no
circumstances must we begin by asking
what God decreed concerning us before
the world began."   -John Calvin

It has been my privilege to teach both missions and theology for over
three decades. A major benefit has been the cross-pollenization between
the disciplines. My master's degree was a major in theology and the doc-
torate in missiology. This paper will seek to give some of the fruit of this
integration. In teaching theology I wrestled with the lack of inductive
methodology in much theological enterprise and the missiological problems raised by such deductive theology. In writing the historical section
of this present work in the late '80s, I realized the deadening impact of
such deductive theology upon the missionary enterprise. Indeed, the
great scandal of Protestantism was the "Great Protestant Omission," the
two centuries in which Protestants did virtually nothing about world
evangelization, with another century of inaction in the English speaking
world. We must face the theological roots of that inaction.

Since the early '80s I have been working on an inductive, exegetical
soteriology and have concluded that a 'middle way' or mediate theology
of salvation is more viable biblically, historically, and missiologically. It
should go without saying that the biblical basis is the sole foundation for
any soteriology; the historical and missiological is only confirmatory. The
biblical exegesis is the subject of a whole volume I trust to publish shortly, and space does not allow more than a summary.

WHAT IS A MEDIATE SOTERIOLOGY?

Many Christians are unaware that there is a whole spectrum of soteriological viewpoints intermediate between Calvinism and Arminianism.
Indeed, many theologians do not admit that there are any other alterna-
tives. However, long ago B. B. Warfield pointed up at least six distinct
soteriological viewpoints among evangelical Protestants. He listed two
types of Calvinists, the Amyraldian general redemption view, the Lutheran, the Wesleyan "evangelical" Arminian view, and the Remonstrant

Arminian view.¹ There has come to be a polarization of viewpoints today among evangelical Christians, which does not foster honest inquiry into what the Bible really teaches. It is widely recognized that Arminius never really became an Arminian, and that Calvin's views are not well represented by contemporary developed Calvinism. In almost every point in which I have checked out Calvin's views, I find him ambivalent where Calvinists are dogmatic, or else in disagreement with his followers. First I will sketch out the historical background.

The historical theological background. As we survey the first four centuries from Pentecost to Augustine (d. 430) we find little reference to predestination, election, or irresistible grace. Indeed, Reformed theologian Paul K. Jewett states, "As has often been observed, the first true predestinarian was Augustine."² For four hundred years the church fathers struggled with the fatalism of Gnosticism and Manicheeism and were careful to defend human free agency or free will. Augustine, in opposing Pelagius's emphasis upon human ability in salvation, sought to emphasize the gracious nature of salvation, and in the last years of his life began to write about absolute, unconditional predestination and irresistible grace. Until that time the church had consistently held to general redemption—that Christ died for the sins of the whole world.³ For a century the church struggled to resolve the conflict between Augustine's and Pelagius's views, and in 529 the Synod of Orange (Arausio) came to a semi-Augustinian conclusion. It maintained the emphasis upon grace and God's initiative in salvation without reference to unconditional election or irresistible grace. Although the evolving Roman Catholic church lapsed into a semi-Pelagianism, officially the semi-Augustinian view was the standard until the reformation.⁴

It was Martin Luther, the Augustinian monk, who upon his conversion saw the predestinarianism of Augustine as a way to reverse the semi-Pelagianism of the Roman Church. Zwingli in Zurich and later Calvin in Geneva followed his lead, and Calvin's *Institutes* set a standard for much of Protestant theology until now. However, I have been able to trace at least seven reactions to this view which began immediately.

In 1524 a group of seven of Zwingli's associates broke from him in advocating a more radical reformation of the church, thus beginning the Anabaptist movement, which swept Europe and still has strong representation in North America. They held to a more mediate view of salvation truth.

Luther's protege, Philip Melanchthon, began very early to moderate Luther's double predestinarian views. He wrote most of the early Lutheran doctrinal standards, and although he sought to avoid conflict with Luther in his lifetime, his views influenced Lutheranism to a more moderate view.

Zwingli's successors, Henry Bullinger and Theodor Bibliander, are also recognized as moderating Zwingli's extreme predestinarian views. Schaff called Bibliander the father of biblical exegesis in Switzerland and a forerunner of Arminianism.[5]

As the reformation spread to the British Isles, many church leaders took a mediate view. Archbishop James Ussher held to general redemption and was looking for a "middle way." The great Puritan evangelist, Richard Baxter brought Bishop John Davenant and Dr. John Preston to this view.

In Amsterdam James Arminius was an outstanding Calvinistic pastor and professor, who began to moderate the rigid predestinarian view he had held. Tragically, after debating the subject in 1609, he took sick and died. Some of his followers, known as Remonstrants, pressed his view farther and were excommunicated from the Reformed churches, thus beginning the Arminian movement, later popularized by the Wesleys.

Shortly after this, John Cameron of Glasgow began an extended ministry in France, where there were substantial Reformed churches. He taught in the theological Academy of Saumur for only three years, but his disciples and successors adopted his view of general redemption, that is, that Christ died for the sins of all mankind. His student, Moyse Amyraut, was an outstanding Calvin scholar and became the head of the Academy (Seminary). When he published an exposition of the doctrine of election harmonious with general redemption, the hyperCalvinists in Geneva and the low countries attacked him so severely that he and a colleague were tried for heresy in a national synod at Alencon in 1637. They were vindicated, but asked to moderate the statement of their views somewhat. The persecution of the Huguenot Protestants in France forced the loss of that theological Academy, however, and the advocates of general redemption were scattered. Because of the notoriety of the trial, Amyraut's name was given to the general redemption view—Amyraldian soteriology.[6]

Contemporaneously, Johannes Cocceius was developing a more inductive, biblical approach to theology which came to be known as Covenant Theology. Being influenced by Melanchthon, he saw in the covenant theme a "way to blunt the sharp and highly debated views on predestination current in his day."[7] Unfortunately Herman Witsius undermined Cocceius's intention by developing the idea of a Covenant of Redemption in eternity past, which in effect reverted Covenant Theology back to a deterministic mode of thought.

There were other significant evangelical movements after the reformation which did not buy into Augustinian determinism. We have already referred to the Moravian movement in Central Europe and the Pietistic movement among Lutherans which were important to the restoration of global evangelization to Protestantism.

Mediate theologians of the 20th century. Samuel Fisk documented hundreds of reputable scholars in the last centuries who held mediate views, but none of them wrote a systematic theology until Lewis Sperry Chafer and Henry C. Thiessen in this century Among theological writers, only Buswell and Warfield seemed aware of the historical background, and Strong made only a passing reference to Amyraut.[8] Current theologies, Bible encyclopedias, and commentaries are notable for their silence about any mediate views in church history.

My proposal for an inductive mediate soteriology. I would follow Calvin in starting the system with faith and depart from Calvinism's omission of faith from its five points.[9] My starting point is that many of the NT words for Christ's saving death refer to a potentially universal dimension for the whole world of unregenerate sinners.[10] I would see Christ and the apostles demanding repentant faith from the sinner as a necessary condition for salvation.[11] I see God's work as mediate or indirect in influencing the circumstances of people coming to saving faith in Christ. I would stress the importance of the convicting work of the Spirit as the key as to how dead sinners can come to faith.[12] It is crystal clear that the Spirit works mediately in bringing people to faith through the proclamation of the word of God, not directly or immediately.[13] However, it is important to distinguish the process by which sinners come to repentant faith from the new birth itself, which is totally the direct and immediate work of the Holy Spirit. The biblical order is that repentant faith must precede the new birth as a necessary condition, not the reverse as many hold deductively. I would affirm that faith is an essential of every part of the *ordo salutis* (plan of salvation) which the Apostle Paul sets out in Romans 8:29-30 since the theme of Romans is a righteousness of God revealed "by faith from first to last" (1:17 NIV). Therefore, predestination is conditioned on foreknowledge of faith.[14] And hopefully we would all agree that calling and justification are by faith alone. Early in my Christian life I concluded that the Bible consistently affirms the eternal security of the truly born-again believer in Christ. My paper summarizing this position is available and is the basis of the inductive soteriology I am writing.[15]

The missiological historical background

The principal background for this discussion is the "Great Protestant Omission," that is, the fact that Protestants did little or nothing about obeying the Greatest Commission for two centuries after the Protestant Reformation, three centuries in the English-speaking world. In chapter 8 I have already chronicled the paucity of missionary activity during those centuries and even the downright hostility toward missions by Protestant leaders and have sought to analyze the reasons behind it. Among the many reasons which can be given, the theological ones are most provocative. Although it is common to blame the second generation reformers, it seems clear that even the first generation did not have any clear missionary understanding, despite the strong contemporary Roman Catholic missionary outthrust. Harry Boer faults all of the reformers but Bucer in this regard.[16]

Thus it was at the fringes of the Reformation that the modern missionary movement began. It was Verceslaus Budovetz coming from the "fringe" Unitas Fratrum church of John Hus, who first tried to evangelize the Muslims (1577-81). It was non-conformist pastor John Eliot who first evangelized the Algonquins of Massachusetts. It was the "fringe" Quakers who sent out three missionaries to China in 1661, never to be heard from again. It was the "fringe" pietistic Lutheran movement which was behind the Danish-Halle Mission of 1705. It was the "fringe" Moravian movement which invested the most effort in missions in the remainder of the 18th century. It was Anglicans who were possibly influenced by Roman Catholic missionary endeavor who founded the SPG and the SPCK around 1700. It was "fringe" non-conformist Baptists who started the missionary movement in the English-speaking world in 1792. On the whole most American Protestants have been part of what has been called the radical reformation, and the American outthrust got its momentum from that radical non-mainstream contingent.

One of the great enigmas of missionary history is the incredible lack of action and implementation despite the significant missionary interest in England and the British colonies all through the 18th century, as Herbert Kane has delineated (see the quotation on p. 126-7). The theological root of the problem is confirmed by an investigation of the theological currents among British Baptists in the time of William Carey. Carey did not come to his missionary convictions in a vacuum. Samuel Fisk has documented these currents from a host of historical sources. He quotes Underwood as to the influence of rigid predestinarian views upon the early Particular Baptists:

> Such a theology had a paralysing effect upon the preacher. The notion that for multitudes of men no salvation was either intended or provided in Christ, devitalized evangelistic preaching and effort, depriving men of any feeling of responsibility for extending the Kingdom of God. As early as 1611 Thomas Helwys had put his finger exactly on the spot when he wrote of Calvinism that it "makes some despair utterly as thinking there is no grace for them and that God hath decreed their destruction. And it makes others desperately careless, holding that if God have decreed they shall be saved then they shall be saved, and if God have decreed they shall be damned they shall be damned." . . . But early in the eighteenth century a change came over them [the Particular Baptists]. They preached according to what Ivimey calls the "non-invitation scheme" and contented themselves with expounding doctrine. If

Christ died not for all but only for the elect, it was useless to invite all to repent and believe in Him. . . . He [one of their leading preachers, John Skepp] made no attempt to awaken the consciences of the unconverted lest he should despoil God of the sole glory of their conversion.[17]

This was the theological background of William Carey among the Particular (as contrasted to the General) Baptists. The influence of Andrew Fuller upon Carey needs to be seen. At age 16, Fuller joined a hyper-Calvinistic Baptist church of antinomian tendencies. Fuller was a leader among Particular Baptists from about 1780 to 1815. "It was to Andrew Fuller, more than to any other individual, that the restoration of the Particular Baptist body to its original evangelical position was due." Fuller greatly influenced the theology of Carey toward a more Amyraldian viewpoint and thus was a vital link in the formation of the Baptist mission society in 1792.[18] The well-known story of the elder John Rylands' put-down of Carey when he advocated evangelizing the heathen in the Baptist ministers' association clearly illustrates the predestinarian hostility to missions that Carey had come out of and confronted. And the title and text of his *Enquiry* shows very clearly the opposition to the use of human means among the Particular Baptists. "We must not be contented with praying, without *exerting ourselves in the use of means* for the obtaining of those things we pray for. Were *the children of light but as wise in their generation as the children of this world* they would stretch every nerve to gain so glorious a prize, nor ever imagine that it was to be obtained in any other way."[19]

How did Fuller and then Carey come to a more Amyraldian point of view? Amyraut's works on universal grace had not been (and still have not been) translated into English. Of course, English theologians of the time could read his Latin works. A number of his English contemporaries espoused Amyraldian views, the most famous of whom was Richard Baxter, the great Puritan preacher. Baxter listed many other English preachers who held Amyraldian views, including E. Polhill, Ed. Calamy, Ed. Williams, and George Payne. John Davenant (1579-1641) held views similar to those of Amyraut, but we don't know whether there was a connection or not.[20] I have not had opportunity yet to research the linkage between Baxter and his colleagues and Fuller a century later, but the connection seems clear.[21] And it is quite clear that mediate views were common in England in the seventeenth century and influenced Fuller and Carey in the eighteenth. Indeed, Lindsay clearly states that, Carey "broke down the barrier which 17th cent. divines had reared against the possibility of the salvation of the heathen, by their statement that those to whom the external call is not addressed cannot be held to be recipients of the benefits of the saving work of Christ."[22]

On the other side of the Atlantic American missionary activity was beginning to stir among the Congregationalists as a consequence of the Haystack Prayer Meeting. The striking thing about that significant event was the strong conviction after prayer that "we can do it if we will," which was the basis of their resolve to become the first American foreign missionaries. They saw the place of human responsibility in God's plan. But years later when Judson and his colleagues became Baptists in Serampore, they decided to send Luther Rice back to America to contact the Baptist churches to start a missionary society. "Largely through his efforts, they formed the General Missionary Convention of the Baptist Denomination in the United States. There was stout resistance to the project. Some objected on theological grounds, the old hyper-Calvinism maintaining that such efforts were blasphemous, since God would save those whom he chose, and the others could not be saved in any event."[23] Luther Rice influenced John M. Peck to take leadership in Baptist outreach in the expanding nation and around the world. He too found strong opposition, especially from the Primitive Baptists, to the idea of any use of means in the work of God, whether at home or abroad. Dan O. Shelton, appreciated Peck and tells of his struggles:

> He met pastors who strongly opposed missions. They were obstinate and did not recognize individual responsibility. In consequence of their views they were prayerless, objected to the use of means in the conversion of men, and denied the necessity of sending the Gospel to the destitute. At one meeting they passed a resolution debarring from a seat any one who was a member of a missionary society. One of their number was asked to state clearly his objection to missionaries. His reply was: "We don't care anything about them missionaries that's gone amongst them heathens 'way off yonder. But what do they come among us for? We don't want them here in Illinois."[24]

This was the deadening situation among the Baptists. I have not researched the situation among the Presbyterian, Reformed, or Lutherans in this regard. I suspect that the record will show that it was a lot worse.

The missiological implications of soteriology

In wrestling with some soteriological problems, I found that the realities of having been a missionary in a predominantly Muslim country raised some serious soteriological questions. A crucial soteriological question is whether God gives faith immediately as Augustinians hold, or whether He gives faith mediately (if at all)? In my 1982 ETS paper I gave fourteen reasons why I believe that God does not give faith immediately and directly to sinners, that is, He does not strike them with faith like a lightning bolt. Most of the reasons are derived from the Gospels and Acts. Two of them arise from the realities of the lost world.

Why are some classes of people harder to win than others? One does not have to be an expert to realize that Muslims have been and continue to be a gospel-resistant people. Not far behind we find the caste Hindu and the Theravada Buddhist of southeast Asia. Why are they so hard to reach? Missiologists have come up with many answers. In chapter 19 on the Muslim world, for example, I have summarized six of the most obvious reasons why Muslims are so hard to reach. All of these factors are human factors or else demonic factors. If the Holy Spirit immediately and directly produces faith in the hearts of the elect then how do we explain these obvious human factors? Cannot the Holy Spirit overcome these human obstacles just as easily as the factors keeping nominal Christians and Animists from faith in Christ? There should be no difference in the difficulty of winning diverse kinds of people to Christ.

The Apostle Paul recognizes human, cultural factors as obstacles in discipling people. In Titus 1:12-13 Paul writes, "One of themselves, a prophet of their own, said, 'Cretans are always liars, evil beasts, lazy gluttons.' This testimony is true. For this cause reprove them severely that they may be sound in the faith. . ." Is Paul evidencing racial prejudice here? No, he is just recognizing what missiologists have recognized—that some cultures present special problems. Most missionaries to Muslims have similarly struggled with discipling Muslim converts. Even after conversion there is overhang from the Islamic background which seriously impedes spiritual growth. Amyraldian soteriology has no problem with this; those who believe in irresistible grace surely do have a serious problem.

Why does God give the gift of repentance/faith to so many Americans, and to so few Saudis, Libyans, Afghans, Turks, Mongolians, Tibetans, and North Africans? If one starts with the doctrine of unconditional election, then it would seem that God loves Americans more than He loves these other kinds of people, and that God is a discriminator between peoples. However, God had to use a vision to get the Apostle Peter straightened out in this regard: "'I most certainly understand now that God is not one to show partiality, but in every nation the man who fears Him and does what is right is welcome to Him'" (Acts 10:34-35). But if no human means or conditions are involved in an individual coming to faith and in eternity past God has decided his eternal destiny apart from any foreseen human factor, then God does indeed discriminate! As a missionary in Pakistan I never met or heard of a Muslim who was zapped with faith like a bolt of lightning; all converts come to faith by human agency.

The implications of biblical anthropology

When we move into the area of biblical anthropology, we also find some problem areas in relating our theology to our missiology. A number come to mind.

Are the heathen too depraved to be saved? Historically this was one area of rationalization on the part of the hyper-Calvinists. They argued that the heathen were too depraved to be saved. This was one of the arguments that Johann Ursinius used against missions. This argument was developed from the biblical doctrine of the total depravity of mankind. However, a little reflection uncovers a non-sequitur here. The biblical teaching is that all mankind is totally depraved, not just the heathen peoples. Europeans in his day were also totally depraved according to Scripture. Thus we have here a kind of prejudice springing from pride. Indeed, a distorted doctrine of election does tend to foster pride in one sense, even if we may cry loudly, "It is all of God's sovereign grace!" It should be noted that Ursinius misinterpreted Matthew 7:6 as referring to the heathen and failed to note Peter's interpretation and application of this to false teachers in the church (2 Pet. 2:22).[25] Granted that this was a non-sequitur, but the abuse was to some extent based upon a distorted doctrine.

Does total depravity mean that men are spiritual corpses and that we are powerless to bring them to Christ? Scholastic Calvinism has built much of its soteriology upon the anthropological analogy of spiritual death. As the analogy is frequently drawn, since man is spiritually dead, he is like a corpse in a funeral parlor. One can shout the message to him with all of one's might but he cannot respond. There are at least four problems with that analogy.

The first is that the book of Genesis does not portray mankind as losing the image of God in the Garden of Eden, because Genesis 9:6 relates the capital punishment provision for murder to the image of God in man. Thus it is usually held that the image of God was marred in the fall but not lost totally. Thus the corpse analogy is inappropriate and misleading.

Secondly, the Lord Jesus did speak about unsaved dead hearing the gospel in John 5:25: "Truly, truly, I say to you, an hour is coming and now is, when the dead shall hear the voice of the Son of God; and those who hear shall live." Christ does not say that the regenerate shall hear; he says that the **dead** shall hear.

Thirdly, Christ foretold that when the Spirit was to come on the day of Pentecost, He would convict the spiritually dead, unregenerate world of sin, righteousness, and judgment (John 16:8-11). Virtually no attention has been paid by commentators and theologians to the fulfillment of this prophecy in Acts 2:37-38, when after Peter's Pentecost sermon, "Now when they heard this, they were pierced to the heart and said to Peter and the rest of the apostles, 'Brethren, what shall we do?' And Peter said to them, 'Repent, . . . for the forgiveness of your sins; and you shall receive the gift of the Holy Spirit.'" It is the convicting ministry of the Spirit working mediately through the proclaimed word of God which breaks through man's depravity. But that convicting work is always accomplished through means, even though the new birth itself is a direct, immediate work of the Spirit upon the human heart.

Fourthly, the Lord Jesus commanded us to disciple all nations. He didn't just tell us to proclaim the message; we are to **make disciples.** Calvinists have generally said that it is the Spirit's work to make disciples; we cannot do it. However, Christ commanded us to do it. Likewise, the Lord commanded Paul at his conversion to go to the Gentiles, "to open their eyes so that they may turn from darkness to light and from the dominion of Satan to God. . ." (Acts 26:18). So Paul was not to powerlessly and passively wait for the Spirit to zap sinners with saving faith!

The ministry implications of soteriology

How do unconditional election and irresistible grace affect missionary activity? I have observed a number of specific effects of strong predestinarian doctrine.

Effect on methodology. Buswell, a Calvinist, explained an abuse of the doctrine of election:

> From the basis of the words, "as many as were ordained to eternal life," some have argued that in that particular mission of Paul and Barnabas, every individual in that city who was among the elect of God was saved at that particular time. This thought has been carried to the length of a doctrine of "burnt over ground." I have heard it argued that missions to Europe are futile, because Europe has been evangelized.[26]

Logically it could also be argued that missionaries need only preach once in a given place and need never return because then all the elect will certainly believe the first time. Indeed, some missionaries have followed this practice on this basis. Such illogic is not worthy of refutation.

It provides a cop-out for failure. Some years ago a student of mine expressed the opinion that if we fail to obey God in proclaiming the gospel as commanded, that God has a plan "B" and will send somebody else. I pointed out to him that in the book of Jonah, when Jonah failed to go the first time, God's plan "B" involved Jonah, not somebody else. There is not the slightest Scriptural indication of such a principle. Indeed, the history of missions indicates that over the centuries nobody went!

Logically, it undermines motivation. Someone has well said, "The heart cannot revel in that which the mind rejects." Augustinians have usually resorted to paradox, antinomy, and the secret counsels of God to explain their doctrine rationally. History confirms that the logical inconsistency between such theology and aggressive missionary outreach does indeed bleed through.

CONCLUSIONS

I would thus suggest that there is a strong biblical basis for a mediate theology of salvation, which is confirmed by the church historical background, and that there continues to be logically a very beneficial impact of mediate views upon the cause and progress of world missions.

1. Benjamin B. Warfield, *The Plan of Salvation*, (1935), p.33.

2. Paul K. Jewett, *Election and Predestination* (1985), p. 5.

3. Roger T. Forster and V. Paul Marston, *God's Strategy in Human History* (1973), pp. 243-277; Norman F. Douty, *The Death of Christ* (1978), pp. 136-8.

4. Philip Schaff, *History of the Christian Church*, 8 vols. (1910), III, pp. 866-9; J. L. Neve, *A History of Christian Thought*, 2 vols. (1946), I, 151.

5. Schaff, VIII, pp. 210-11.

6. Brian G. Armstrong, *Calvinism and the Amyraut Heresy: Protestant Scholasticism and Humanism in Seventeenth-Century France* (1969). This is the only adequate and sympathetic source in English.

7. Charles C. Ryrie, *Dispensationalism Today*, pp. 185-7.

8. Warfield, p. 31; James Oliver Buswell, Jr., *A Systematic Theology of the Christian Religion*, II: 134-35, 142.

9. John Calvin quoted by Armstrong, p. 163.

10. John F. Walvoord, *Jesus Christ, Our Lord* , pp. 163-90; Robert P. Lightner, *The Death Christ Died*, pp. 73-91.

11. Roy L. Aldrich, "The Gift of God," *Bibliotheca Sacra*, 122:487.

12. Lewis Sperry Chafer, *Systematic Theology* 8 vols., VI, pp. 88-99; Buswell, II, p. 163.

13. John F. Walvoord, *The Holy Spirit*, p. 111.

14. Henry C. Thiessen, *Lectures in Systematic Theology (1949)*, pp. 156-57.

15. C. Gordon Olson, "Beyond Calvinism and Arminianism: Toward an Amyraldian Soteriology," a paper delivered at the ETS annual meeting, Toronto, December 29, 1981.

16. Harry R. Boer, *Pentecost and Missions*, p. 18.

17. A. C. Underwood, *A History of the English Baptists*, pp. 134-35, as quoted by Samuel Fisk, *Calvinistic Paths Retraced* , pp. 143-44.

18. Albert Henry Newman, *A Manual of Church History*, vol. II, pp. 687-689. Samuel Fisk gives extensive documentation of the shift in Fuller's soteriology and in turn the shift in the viewpoint of the Particular Baptists. See pp. 145-150.

19. William Carey, *An Enquiry into the Obligation of Christians to Use Means for the Conversion of the Heathens* as excerpted in Winter and Hawthorne, Perspectives, p. 234.

20. Roger Nicole, "Amyraldianism" in *The Encyclopedia of Christianity* (1964), vol. I, p. 193.

21. James Strong, "Amyraut" in John McClintock's Encyclopedia (1867-81) reprinted by Baker Book House in 1968, I, p. 209.

22. Thomas M. Lindsay, "Amyraldism," in *Hastings Encyclopedia*, I, p. 405.

23. Brooks Hays and J. E. Steely, *The Baptist Way of Life*, p. 23, quoted by Fisk, p. 171.

24. Dan O. Shelton, *Heroes of the Cross in America*, p. 109, as quoted by Fisk, p. 172.

25. Gustav Warneck, *Outline of a History of Protestant Missions*, p. 38.

26. Buswell, II, p. 152.

INDEX

SELECTED BIBLIOGRAPHY

Books

Alexander, John, ed. *Believing and Obeying Jesus Christ: The Urbana 79 Compendium.* InterVarsity, 1980.

Allen, Roland. *Missionary Methods: St. Paul's or Ours?* Grand Rapids: Eerdmans, 1962.

_____. *The Spontaneous Expansion of the Church.* GR: Eerdmans, 1962.

American Tract Society. *Ecumenical Missionary Conference: New York, 1900.* 2 vols. NY: ATS, 1900.

Anderson, Sir Norman. *Christianity and Comparative Religion.* Downers Grove: InterVarsity, 1971.

_____, ed. *The World's Religions.* 2nd ed. Grand Rapids: Eerdmans, 1951.

_____. *The World's Religions.* 4th ed., completely rev.. GR: Eerdmans, 1975.

Armstrong, Brian G. *Calvinism and the Amyraut Heresy.* Madison: U. of Wisc. Press, 1969.

Bacon, Daniel W. *Who, Me? a Missionary?* Singapore: Overseas Miss. Fellowship, 1985.

_____. *From Faith to Faith: The Influence of Hudson Taylor on the Faith Missions Movement.* Singapore: Overseas Missionary Fellowship, 1984.

Barrett, David B. *World Christian Encyclopedia.* New York: Oxford, 1982.

Bavinck, J. H. *An Introduction to the Science of Missions.* Nutley, N.J.: Presby. and Ref., 1960.

Beaver, R. Pierce. *The Missionary Between the Times.* Garden City: Doubleday, 1968.

Beyerhaus, Peter. *Shaken Foundations: Theological Foundations for Mission.* GRapids: Zondervan, 1972.

Boer, Harry R. *Pentecost and Missions.* Grand Rapids: Eerdmans, 1961.

Bonino, Jose Miguez. *Doing Theology in a Revolutionary Situation.* Phila.: Fortress, 1975.

Bradley, David G. *A Guide to the World's Religions.* Englewood Cliffs: Prentice-Hall, 1963.

Broadbent, E. H. *The Pilgrim Church.* London: Pickering and Inglis, 1931.

Broomhall, A. J. *Hudson Taylor and China's Open Century.* Kent, UK: Hodder and Stoughton, 1981.

Bryant, David. *In the Gap: What It Means To Be a World Christian.* Madison, Wis.: Inter-Varsity, 1981.

Cable, Mildred, and French, Francesca. *Ambassadors For Christ.* London: Paternoster, 1946.

Chambers, Oswald. *So Send I You.* London: Simpkin Marshall, 1961

Chapman, Colin. *Christianity on Trial.* Wheaton: Tyndale House, 1975.

Coggins, Wade T. *So That's What Missions Is All About.* Chicago: Moody, 1975.

Coggins, Wade T., and Frizen, E. J., Jr., eds. *Evangelical Missions Tomorrow.* Pasa.: Wm Carey Lib., 1977.

Collins, Marjorie A. *Who Cares About the Missionary?* Chicago: Moody, 1974.

Cook, Harold R. *An Introduction to Christian Missions.* Chicago: Moody, 1954.

_____. *Missionary Life and Work.* Chicago: Moody, 1959.

_____. *Highlights of Christian Missions.* Chicago: Moody, 1967.

Costas, Orlando E. *The Church and Its Mission: A Shattering Critique from the Third World.* Wheaton: Tyndale House, 1974.

Covell, Ralph R. *The Liberating Gospel in China: Christian Faith among Minority Peoples.* GR: Baker, 1995.

Cowan, George M. *The Word that Kindles.* Chappaqua, N.Y.: Christian Herald, 1979.

Craig, William Lane. *The Only Wise God: The Compatibility of Foreknowledge & Freedom.* Baker, 1987.

Crim, Keith, ed. *Abingdon Dictionary of Living Religions.* Nashville: Abingdon, 1981.

Crockett, William V. and Sigountos, James G. *Through No Fault of Their Own?* GR: Baker, 1991.

Culver, Robert Duncan. *A Greater Commission: A Theology for World Missions.* Chicago: Moody, 1984.

Davis, Walter Bruce. *William Carey: Father of Modern Missions.* Chicago: Moody, 1963.

Dayton, Edward R., and Fraser, David A. *Planning Strategies for World Evangelization.* GR: Eerdmans, 1980.

Detzler, Wayne A. *The Changing Church in Europe.* Grand Rapids: Zondervan, 1979.

Dixon, Larry. *The Other Side of the Good News.* Wheaton: Victor, 1992.

Douglas, J. D., ed. *Let the Earth Hear His Voice: International Congress on World Evangelization,* Lausanne, Switzerland. Minneapolis: World Wide Publications, 1975.

Douty, Norman F. *The Death of Christ.* Irving, TX: Williams & Watrous, 1978.

Dowsett, Dick. *'God, That's Not Fair!'* Kent, U.K.: OMF Books, 1982.

DuBose, Francis M., ed. *Classics of Christian Missions.* Nashville: Broadman, 1979.

Duncan, Homer. *The Divine Intent.* Lubbock: Missionary Crusader, 1971.

Dyrness, William A. *Let the Earth Rejoice: A Biblical Theology of Holistic Mission.* Westchester, Ill.: Crossway Books, 1983.

Dussel, Enrique. *A History of the Church in Latin America.* Trans. & Rev. Alan Neely. GR: Eerdmans, 1981.

Eddy, Sherwood. *Pathfinders of the World Missionary Crusade.* New York: Abingdon-Cokesbury, 1945.

Edman, V. Raymond. *The Light in Dark Ages.* Wheaton: Van Kampen, 1949.

Eerdmans' Handbook to the World's Religions. Grand Rapids: Eerdmans, 1982.

Engel, James F. *Contemporary Christian Communications: Its Theology and Practice.* Nash.: Nelson, 1979.

Engstrom, Ted W. *What in the World is God Doing?* Waco: Word, 1978.

Erickson, Millard. *How Shall They Be Saved?* GR: Baker, 1996.

Evans, Robert P. *Let Europe Hear.* Chicago: Moody, 1963.

Fakre, Gabriel, Nash, Ronald H., & Sanders, John. *What About Those Who Have Never Heard? Three Views on the Destiny of the Unevangelized.* Downers Grove: InterVarsity, 1995.

Falk, Peter. *The Growth of the Church in Africa.* Grand Rapids: Zondervan, 1979.

Fenton, Horace L, Jr. *Myths about Missions.* Downers Grove: InterVarsity, 1973.

Fernando, Ajith. *Crucial Questions about Hell.* Wheaton: Crossway, 1991.

Fife, Eric S., and Glasser, Arthur F. *Missions in Crisis.* Chicago: Inter-Varsity, 1961.

Finley, Allen, and Lutz, Lorry. *The Family Tie.* Nashville: Thomas Nelson, 1983.

Fisk, Samuel. *Divine Sovereignty and Human Freedom.* Neptune, NJ: Loizeaux, 1973.

_____. *Calvinistic Paths Retraced.* Murfreesboro, TN: Biblical Evangelism, 1985.

Forster, Roger T., and Marston, V. Paul. *God's Strategy in Human History.* Minn.: Bethany House, 1973.

Friesen, Garry. *Decision Making and the Will of God.* Portland, Ore.: Multnomah, 1980.

Frizen, Edwin, & Coggins, Wade T., eds. *Christ and Caesar in Christian Missions.* Pasa.:Wm. Carey, 1979.

Fuller, W. Harold. *Mission-Church Dynamics.* Pasadena: Wm. Carey Library, 1980.

Glasser, Arthur F., and McGavran, Donald A. *Contemporary Theologies of Mission.* GR: Baker, 1983.

Glover, Robert Hall. *The Bible Basis of Missions.* Los Angeles: Bible House of Los Angeles, 1946.

_____. *The Progress of World-Wide Missions.* Rev. & enl. by J. Herbert Kane. NY: Harper, 1960.

Goldsmith, Martin. *Don't Just Stand There!* Downers Grove, Ill.: Inter-Varsity, 1976.

Godbey, J. E. and A. H. *Light in Darkness: Missions & Missionary Heroes.* St. Louis: Imperial, 1892.

Green, Michael. *Evangelism in the Early Church.* Grand Rapids: Eerdmans, 1970.

Griffiths, Michael. *Changing Asia.* Downers Grove: InterVarsity, 1977.

_____. *The Church and World Mission.* Grand Rapids: Zondervan, 1980.

_____. *What on Earth Are You Doing?* Grand Rapids: Baker, 1984.

Gunther, Peter F., ed. *The Fields at Home.* Chicago: Moody Press, 1963.

Gutierrez, Gustavo. *A Theology of Liberation.* Trans.: Caridad Inda & John Eagleston. Maryk.: Orbis, 1973.

Hahn, Ferdinand. *Mission in the New Testament.* Translated by Frank Clarke. Naperville, Ill.: Allenson, 1965.

Harr, Wilber C., ed. *Frontiers of the Christian World Mission.* New York: Harper, 1962.

Hay, Alex Rattray. *The New Testament Order for Church and Missionary.* Audubon, N.J.: NTMU, 1947.

Hesselgrave, David J. *Communicating Christ Cross-Culturally.* GRapids: Zondervan, 1978.

_____. *Dynamic Religious Movements.* Grand Rapids: Baker, 1978.

_____. *Planting Churches Cross-Culturally.* Grand Rapids: Baker, 1980.

_____, ed. *Theology and Mission.* Grand Rapids: Baker, 1978

_____, ed. *New Horizons in World Mission.* Grand Rapids: Baker, 1979.

_____, & Edward Rommen. *Contextualization: Meanings, Methods, & Models.* GR: Baker, 1989.

Hiebert, Paul G. *Anthropological Insights for Missionaries.* Grand Rapids: Baker, 1985.

Hislop, Alexander. *The Two Babylons.* New York: Loizeaux., 1916.

Hocking, William Ernest. *Re-thinking Missions: Laymen's Inquiry After One Hundred Years.* NY: Harper, 1932.

Hodges, Melvin. *Growing Young Churches.* Chicago: Moody, 1970.

_____. *The Indigenous Church and the Missionary.* Pasadena: Wm. Carey Library, 1978.

Hoke, Donald, ed. *The Church in Asia.* Chicago: Moody, 1975.

Howard, David M. *Student Power in World Missions.* Downers Grove: InterVarsity, 1979.

Hulbert, Terry C. *World Missions Today.* Wheaton: ETTA, 1979.

Hull, J. Mervin. *Judson the Pioneer.* Philadelphia: American Baptist Publ. Soc., 1913.

Isichei, Elizabeth. *A History of Christianity in Africa: From Antiquity to Present.* GR: Eerdmans, 1995.

Johnston, Arthur P. *World Evangelism and the Word of God.* Minneapolis: Bethany Fellowship, 1974.

_____. *The Battle for World Evangelism.* Wheaton: Tyndale, 1978.

_____. "The Ecumenical Movement." Course notes at TEDS, Deerfield, Ill., July 1980.

Johnstone, Patrick. *Operation World,* 5th ed., Grand Rapids: Zondervan, 1993.

Kane, J. Herbert. *A Global View of Christian Missions.* Grand Rapids: Baker, 1971
_____. *Winds of Change in the Christian Mission.* Chicago: Moody, 1973.
_____. *Understanding Christian Missions.* 1st and 2nd eds. GR: Baker, 1974, 1982.
_____. *Christian Missions in Biblical Perspective.* Grand Rapids: Baker, 1976.
_____. *A Concise History of the Christian World Mission.* GR: Baker, 1978.
_____. *Life and Work on the Mission Field.* Grand Rapids: Baker, 1980.
_____. *The Christian World Mission: Today and Tomorrow.* GR: Baker, 1981.
_____. *Wanted: World Christians.* Grand Rapids: Baker, 1986.
Kauffman, Paul E. *China, the Emerging Challenge: A Christian Perspective.* GR: Baker, 1982.
Kinsler, F. Ross. *The Extension Movement in Theological Education.* Pasadena: Wm. Carey Library, 1978.
Kraemer, Hendrik. *The Christian Message in a Non-Christian World.* New York: Inter. Miss. Council, 1938.
Lageer, Eileen. *New Life for All.* Chicago: Moody, 1970.
Latin America Mission. *Evangelism in Depth.* Chicago: Moody, 1961.
Latourette, Kenneth Scott. *A History of Christianity.* New York: Harper and Row, 1953.
Lewis, John. *Religions of the World Made Simple.* Rev. ed. Garden City: Doubleday, 1968.
Lewis, Norm. *Faith Promise for World Witness.* Lincoln, Nebr.: Back to the Bible, 1974.
Lightner, Robert P. *The Death Christ Died.* Des Plaines, IL: Regular Baptist, 1967.
Lindsell, Harold. *Missionary Principles and Practice.* Westwood: Revell, 1955.
_____. *An Evangelical Theology of Missions.* GR: Zondervan, 1970.
Lyall, Leslie. *Missionary Opportunity Today: A Brief World Survey.* Chic.: InterVarsity, 1963.
_____. *God Reigns in China.* London: Hodder and Stoughton, 1985.
Malaska, Hilkka. *The Challenge for Evangelical Missions to Europe.* S. Pasadena: Wm. Carey Lib., 1970.
MARC, *Christian Collegians and Foreign Missions.* Monrovia, Calif.: MARC, 1968.
_____. *Mission Handbook.* 10th, 11th, 12th, 13th, 14th, 15th, 17th (sic). MARC, 1973,76,79,86,89,93,96.
Matthews, Reginald L. Missionary Administration in the Local Church. Des Plaines, Ill.: Reg. Baptist, 1970.
McBrien, Richard P. *Catholicism.* Study ed. Minneapolis: Winston, 1981.
McDowell, Josh, and Stewart, Don. *Understanding Non-Christian Religions.* San Bern.: Here's Life, 1982.
Mc.Dowell, Josh. *Evidence That Demands a Verdict.* San Bernardino: Campus Crusade for Christ, 1972.
McGavran, Donald Anderson. *The Bridges of God.* New York: Friendship, 1955.
_____. *Understanding Church Growth.* Grand Rapids: Eerdmans, 1970, 1980.
_____, ed. *Eye of the Storm: The Great Debate in Mission.* Waco: Word, 1972.
McQuilkin, Robertson. *The Great Omission: A Biblical Basis for World Evangelism.* GR: Baker, 1984.
Miller, Basil. *J. Hudson Taylor: For God and China.* Grand Rapids: Zondervan, 1948.
Moffett, Samuel Hugh. *A History of Christianity in Asia.* Maryknoll: Orbis, 1998.
Montgomery, James. *Journal of Voyages and Travels by Daniel Tyerman and George Bennet for the London Missionary Society.* 3 vols. Boston: Crocker and Brewster, 1832.
Morgan, Helen. *Who'd Be a Missionary?* Ft. Washington: Christiann Literature Crusade, 1972.
Neill, Stephen. *A History of Christian Missions.* Middlesex, Eng.: Penguin, 1964.
Nevius, John L. *Planting and Development of Missionary Churches.* Phila.: Presby. and Reformed, 1958.
Newman, Albert Henry. *A Manual of Church History.* 2 vols. Philadelphia: American Baptist Publ., 1902.
Nicholls, Bruce J., ed. *The Unique Christ in our Pluralist World.* GR: Baker, 1994.
Noss, John B. *Man's Religions.* 5th ed. New York: Macmillan, 1974.
Nunez, Emilio A. & Taylor, William D. *Crisis in Latin America: An Evangelical Perspective.* Moody, 1989.
Orchard, G. H. *A Concise History of Baptists.* Lexington, Ky: Ashland Ave. Bapt. Church, 1956.
Parrinder, Geoffrey, ed. *World Religions: From Ancient History to the Present.* NY: Facts on File, 1983.
Parvin, A. Earl. *Missions USA.* Chicago: Moody Press, 1985.
_____. *Missions In North America.* Beckley, WV: Assoc. of North American Missions, 1997.
Paton, William. *Jesus Christ and World Religions.* Edinburgh: Edinburgh House, 1916.
Pearson, Dick. *Missionary Education Helps for the Local Church.* Palo Alto: Overseas Crusades, 1966.
Pentecost, Edward C. *Reading the Unreached.* Pasadena: Wm. Carey Library, 1974.
_____. *Issues in Missiology: An Introduction.* Grand Rapids: Baker, 1982.
Peters, George W. *Saturation Evangelism.* Grand Rapids: Zondervan, 1970.
_____. *A Biblical Theology of Missions.* Chicago: Moody, 1972.
Pfander, C. G. *The Balance of Truth.* Translated by W. St. Clair Tisdall. London: Rel. Tract Society, 1910.

Pierson, Arthur T. *The Crisis of Missions.* New York: Robert Carter, 1886.

_____, *Evangelize to the Finish.*

Read, William R.; Monterroso, Victor M.; and Johnson, Harmon A. *Latin American Church Growth.* Grand Rapids: Eerdmans, 1969.

Richard, Ramesh P. *The Population of Heaven.* Chicago: Moody, 1994.

Richardson, Don. *Eternity in their Hearts.* Ventura, Calif.: Regal, 1981.

Ridenour, Fritz, ed. *So What's the Difference?.* Glendale: Regal, 1967.

Rommen, Edward, and Netland, Harold, eds. *Christianity and the Religions: A Biblical Theology of World Religions.* (EMS Series #2) Pasadena: Wm. Carey, 1995.

Sanders, J. Oswald. *How Lost Are the Heathen?* Chicago: Moody, 1972.

Sauer, Erich. *The Dawn of World Redemption.* London: Paternoster, 1951.

Schreck, Harley, and Barrett, David. eds. *Unreached Peoples: Clarifying the Task.* MARC, 1987.

Shepard, Walter D. *Sent by the Sovereign.* Nutley: Presbyterian & Reformed, 1968.

Sibley, Inez Knibb. *The Baptists of Jamaica: 1793 to 1965.* Kingston: The Jamaica Baptist Union, 1965.

Sookhdeo, Patrick, ed. *New Frontiers in Mission* GR: Baker, 1987.

Sudan Interior Mission. *Missions Idea Notebook: Promoting Missions in the Local Church.* SIM, 1967.

Stock, Frederick and Stock, Margaret. *People Movements in the Punjab.* Pasadena: Wm Carey Lib., 1975.

Tallman, J. Ray. *No Higher Calling: An Introduction to the Mission of the Church.* Chicago: Moody, 1985.

Taylor, William D. ed. *Too Valuable to Lose: Exploring Causes & Cures of Attrition.* Wm. Carey, 1997.

Thiessen, Henry C. *Lectures in Systematic Theology.* Grand Rapids: Eerdmans, 1949 (orig. ed.).

Tucker, Ruth A. *From Jerusalem to Irian Jaya.* Grand Rapids: Zondervan, 1983.

Tuggy, A. Leonard, and Toliver, Ralph. *Seeing the Church in the Philippines.* Manila: OMF, 1972.

Twedt, Linda, and Myers, Bill. *Let's Communicate Missions.* Lincoln: Back to the Bible, 1975.

Van Rheenen, Gailyn. *Missions: Biblical Foundations & Contemporary Strategies.* GR: Zondervan, 1996.

Verkuyl, Johannes. *Contemporary Missiology: An Introduction.* GRapids: Eerdmans, 1978.

Vos, Howard, ed. *Religions in a Changing World.* Chicago: Moody, 1959.

Vos, Johannes G. *A Christian Introduction to Religions of the World.* GR: Baker, 1965.

Verwer, George. *Literature Evangelism: A Manual.* Kansas City: Walterick, 1963.

Wagner, C. Peter. *Frontiers in Missionary Strategy.* Chicago: Moody, 1971.

_____. *On the Crest of the Wave: Becoming a World Christian.* Glendale: Regal, 1983.

_____. *Spiritual Power and Church Growth.* Altamonte Springs, Fla.: Strang Communications, 1986.

Walker, Arthur L., Jr. ed. *Educating for Christian Missions.* Nashville: Broadman, 1981.

Warfield, Benjamin B. *The Plan of Salvation.* GR: Eerdmans, 1935.

Warneck, Gustav. *Outline of a History of Protestant Missions.* Trans. by George Robson. NY: Revell, 1901.

Warns, Johannes. *Baptism: Original Christian Baptism.* Trans. by G. H. Lang. London: Paternoster, 1957.

Weber, James M. *Let's Quit Kidding Ourselves about Missions.* Winona Lake, Ind.: Don Wardell, 1979.

Weiss, G. Christian. *The Heart of Missionary Theology.* Lincoln: Back to the Bible, 1976.

White, Jerry. *The Church and the Parachurch: An Uneasy Marriage.* Portland: Mult., 1978.

Winter, Ralph D. *The Twenty-Five Unbelievable Years.* Pasadena, Calif.: William Carey Library, 1970.

_____. & Hawthorne, Steven C., eds. *Perspectives on the World Christian Movement.* rev. ed, 1992

Wolff, Richard. *The Final Destiny of the Heathen.* Ridgefield Park, N.J.: IFMA, 1961.

Woodward, David Brainerd. *God, Men, & Missions.* Glendale, Calif.: Gospel Light, 1964.

Yohannan, K. P. *The Coming Revolution in World Missions.* Altamonte Springs, Fla.: Creation House, 1986.

Zwemer, Samuel M. *Thinking Missions With Christ.* Grand Rapids: Zondervan, 1934.

_____. *"Into All the World"; The Great Commission.* Grand Rapids: Zondervan, 1943.

Periodical Articles and Miscellaneous

Bailey, Richard D. "Missions—Christian Collegians' Concepts." Eastern Challenge 7 (July 1971):3-4.

Chaney, Charles. "The Missionary Dynamic in the Theology of John Calvin." The Reformed Review 17 (March 1964): 24-38.

Coates, Thomas. "Were the Reformers Mission-Minded?" Concordia Theological Monthly 40 (October 1969): 600-611.

Robertson, Irvine. "World Religions—Study Graph. Chicago: Moody, 1966.

Zwemer, Samuel M. "Calvinism and the Missionary Enterprise." Theology Today 7 (July 1950): 206-216.